D0102779

TWENTY AGAINST THE UNDERWORLD

TWENTY AGAINST
THE UNDERWORLD

by Thomas E. Dewey

Edited by RODNEY CAMPBELL

Doubleday & Company, Inc., Garden City, New York
1974

COPYRIGHT © 1974 BY DOUBLEDAY & COMPANY, INC.
ALL RIGHTS RESERVED
PRINTED IN THE UNITED STATES OF AMERICA
FIRST EDITION

Library of Congress Cataloging in Publication Data

Dewey, Thomas Edmund, 1902–1971.
    Twenty against the underworld.

      1. Dewey, Thomas Edmund, 1902–1971. I. Title.
E748.D48A37   973.91′092′4 [B]
ISBN 0-385-01904-1
Library of Congress Catalog Card Number 74-3546

CONTENTS

FOREWORD

"Never Go Home When It Rains"

"I remember the first day it rained. I unhitched the cultivator and went back to the farm. Earl Putnam asked me, 'Why?' I said: 'I thought we didn't work when it rained.' He replied: 'We do.' So I went back to the field and went on cultivating, and I never went home again when it rained."

That, of course, was one of my father's great qualities—he "never went home when it rained." The determination that what was right should never fail of accomplishment through lack of total effort was part of the blend of attitudes and abilities which so rarely come together to make greatness; and which blend he had in full measure.

In many ways this first volume is particularly appropriate for 1974 America, because it is a book of hope and of confidence. Here is a series of highly visible and dramatic achievements which helped in the process of bringing the country up from the cynicism, despair, and self-doubts that crime, corruption, and economic disaster had so thoroughly instilled. Today we suffer from many of the same problems and fears, so this testimony to the occurrence of purge and renewal should indeed be a welcome event.

Of course this volume illuminates only one portion of the multi-faceted career of one of the most remarkable men of our era. By taking the form it has, this type of treatment cannot provide, except for the reminiscences of others, much of a window on the warmth and compassion my father had, as well as the many other attitudes and reflective qualities that were often masked by an exterior that came across as more forbidding than intended. The further volume of these memoirs will help, but the real appreciation of the whole man in all his depth and versatility must, as always, await the time-consuming biographer.

One of the remarkable things that will strike you as you read this book is the shower of names of bright young men who, touched by the wand and trained under the rod of Thomas E. Dewey, went on to achieve eminence in their own right. The Cabinet, state and national administrations, the New York Bar and, in great numbers, the federal and New York State judiciary were and still are adorned by the generation of public servants known as "Dewey men."

The extent of this may possibly be the most important part of the whole story, as the breadth of my father's impact on his generation comes to be realized. Especially to be noted, in this day when the quality is less fashionable, is the degree to which loyalty was given and received. Steeped in certain clear common principles, and tied together by mutual trust and devotion, these many men of such varied backgrounds became and remained "Dewey men," proud of it to their later years and now, in many cases, their graves. Groups of survivors still gather at periodic dinners and luncheons to reminisce about "the old days," each other, and, above all, about "the boss." No matter what other impressions or conclusions you develop, you will have to marvel at the effect of the man on the men who worked with and for him.

What Mr. Campbell's skillful weaving together of my father's various writings has accomplished so well is some sense of the public man, his tenacity, his fearlessness, and his high sense of duty both to the state and to his own exacting standards. The influence of Thomas E. Dewey on his times, not yet fully understood, will come to be appreciated with the publication of this and the future volume. It is my own belief that every nation, state, or city, particularly in time of trouble, has historically required a standard-bearer or a lodestar. Upon reading these pages, I hope you will agree with me that Thomas E. Dewey and his times shared a mutual destiny.

THOMAS E. DEWEY, JR.

New York, New York
1974

METHOD

Governor Dewey began to prepare his memoirs fourteen years before his death in 1971. He ordered the gathering together of public papers and private reminiscences of the racket-busting days of the 1930s.

Through the 1950s his papers were compiled, organized, and sent to the Rush Rhees Library at the University of Rochester. For the private reminiscences, he commissioned Dr. Harlan B. Phillips to conduct major research and oral history interviews with himself and with many of his associates in the racket investigations and trials. Those included Charles D. Breitel, Stanley H. Fuld, Sol Gelb, William B. Herlands, Paul Lockwood, Manuel B. Robbins, and Harris Steinberg.

Toward the end of the 1960s Governor Dewey dictated a narrative of his early years, some 70,000 words long, parts of which he edited, and parts of which he put aside, hoping, as he told his associates, "to take some time off sometime and finish it." At this time, in addition to the oral history interviews, contributions were written for the work by other Dewey associates, including Frank S. Hogan, Aaron Benenson,

Murray I. Gurfein, Victor J. Herwitz, and Harold Keller. Additional research for the project was conducted by Tania Melich.

At the time of his death the Dewey memoirs material was centered in three places: (1) the public papers at the University of Rochester; (2) the private reminiscences, held in the offices of the Dewey, Ballantine, Bushby, Palmer & Wood law firm; and (3) the trial transcripts, the verbatim records of Dewey's trials, including eight volumes on the Lucky Luciano trial alone, held at Dewey, Ballantine, Bushby, Palmer & Wood.

The University of Rochester, moreover, maintained a press clipping file of Governor Dewey's racket-busting years, replete with Dewey interviews and quotations, and remarks and comments from his contemporaries. The work of crime and court reporters was also filed at the Rush Rhees Library.

Numerous biographers and magazine writers interviewed Governor Dewey and researched these years, and their work was also filed at the University of Rochester. Most notable of these was Rupert Hughes's *Attorney for the People* (Grosset and Dunlap, 1944) which was produced with the help of material and co-operation from Governor Dewey, his office, and his associates. Other important works on the period included Stanley Walker, *An American of This Century;* Burton B. Turkus and Sid Feder, *Murder, Inc.;* Feder and Joesten, *The Luciano Story; The Valachi Papers;* and *Ninety Times Guilty,* by Hickman Powell, an editorial assistant to Governor Dewey.

Presiding over this very large and diverse input was Miss Lilian G. Rosse, Governor Dewey's personal secretary since 1934, and a member of the rackets investigation staff. From her own knowledge of the personalities, events, background, and relative importances of these years, she was able to retain this mass of information in the perspective of what was very important and what was less so.

In 1972, Gene Farmer, a senior editor of *Life* magazine, died not long after he had been assigned to bring this material into a single focus for the first volume of the memoirs.

In 1973, Thomas E. Dewey, Jr., and R. Burdell Bixby, co-executor of the Dewey estate, decided to produce the memoirs on a rapid schedule. Ken McCormick, editor-in-chief emeritus of Doubleday & Company, Inc., commissioned Rodney Campbell to edit the memoirs. Campbell, formerly an associate editor of *Time* magazine, and an editorial assistant to Governor Rockefeller and President Nixon, was given access to Dewey material at the University of Rochester, and at Dewey, Ballantine, Bushby, Palmer & Wood. Ben C. Bowman and Robert H. Volz of the Rush Rhees Library co-ordinated the editorial work at Rochester.

Bixby meanwhile obtained the independent judgment of other Dewey associates on the phases and points of the early years that ought to be stressed. These men included Arthur H. Schwartz, Francis E. Rivers, and Lawrence E. Walsh.

Campbell, working with Miss Rosse, threaded together the most significant Dewey material into a draft of more than 200,000 words. The method chosen was to concentrate on the most important facets of Governor Dewey's career—as identified by his associates—in depth, while moving more rapidly through the chronological narratives. This made possible a major use of trial transcripts, addresses on points of law, and reproduction of campaign speeches, while on several occasions the best of Governor Dewey's various descriptions of major incidents could be coalesced into the single account. The oral history contributions of his associates were used extensively. Campbell wrote connective and transitional passages, which were embodied into the story, and edited the text into publishable form.

In 1974, Ken McCormick and a group of former Dewey associates —Bixby, Schwartz, and Gurfein—"top-edited" this first volume of the memoirs. Thomas E. Dewey, Jr., also edited the manuscript and wrote the personal foreword. The material in the University of Rochester covers Governor Dewey's later career in even greater detail and the second volume will soon appear. This has all been made possible because Lilian G. Rosse preserved the story of these tempestuous years, kept faith with her late chief and also with her own sense of the history of America.

TWENTY AGAINST THE UNDERWORLD

INTRODUCTION

Among the many reflections expressed in connection with the unexpected death on Tuesday, March 16, 1971, of former Governor Thomas E. Dewey, aged sixty-eight, none was more personal than that of Frank S. Hogan, who "broke in" as a young prosecutor under Dewey and then succeeded him as District Attorney of New York County in 1942, a position he held until February 1, 1974. Hogan's remarks, which follow, were delivered as part of the proceedings in Part XXX of Supreme Court before Mr. Justice Myles J. Lane:

WITH YOUR HONOR'S KIND PERMISSION, I should like to express a few thoughts on the passing of a great and good man. We in the District Attorney's office were shocked and saddened, yesterday, when word came that Thomas E. Dewey had died. He was our teacher and dear friend. Thirty years after he left this building, he remains a living presence in our office, one whose precept and example we aspire to emulate in the administration of criminal justice.

I first met this remarkable man in 1935. Your honor will recall that, in 1935, a proposed investigation of organized crime in the county of New York held with dramatic force the attention of the entire country.

Discerning editors recognized the unique quality of the investigation and appreciated also the enormous difficulties in the way of success. Wrote one: "The task is comparable to that of charting the Gulf Stream and analyzing its effect on an immense territory. The material with which this must be done is extremely elusive, and deeply hidden."

Everyone agreed that the mobs, which had become increasingly arrogant during the Prohibition era, constituted a national problem and disgrace. Opinions differed as to the extent of their activities. Enough was known, however, to convince the most skeptical that the country was faced with a menace of such proportions that its removal would require the persistent application of rare courage and great ability in the administration of a major undertaking.

Except for a few wayward souls, everybody agreed that the man for the job was Thomas Edmund Dewey. Mindful of his splendid record as United States Attorney in the Southern District of New York, the grand jurors, the press, civic groups, bar associations, and many prominent citizens lined up solidly behind him. He was appointed.

All of this made fascinating reading. I was one of hundreds of young lawyers who made application for positions on his staff. I sent the usual letter and, after a few preliminary bouts with chief assistants, I met the newly appointed Special Prosecutor.

Now, I have been examined by prospective employers since I was thirteen. But this meeting proved to be something else again. In less than an hour he raked me fore and aft with questions, held me up to the light, put me under a microscope, and turned me inside out. He rooted out facts deeply buried in my subconscious mind and put together an inventory of my physical, mental, and spiritual condition and its possible development. Not only did he put it together, he never forgot it. To the day when I last saw him, three or four weeks ago, he could tell—after ten minutes' conversation—whether I had a new thought or discharged an old debt.

In that same interview he stated the problem confronting him. he did it with a thoroughness, a clarity, and a vigor unmatched in my experience. He also told me what he proposed to do about it. Few persons have a plan. Most of us have a fuzzy awareness of where we are heading, and some wobbly notions of what to do next, but no blueprint of action. When the Governor outlined a plan, he not only made sense; he also made converts. On this occasion he aroused my enthusiasm, galvanized my energies, and kindled my soul.

Well, I was hired. The years passed by. It was a privilege and a rich educational experience to work in close association with the Governor. His genius for organization, his great talents, his matchless courage were a constant source of inspiration to all who shared his tasks. No person who has not worked with him can fully appreciate how completely he won the admiration and the affection of his associates.

In Emerson's phrase, he knew the depth, the draught of water of every one of his men. In addition, he had an insatiable curiosity about them, and there was nothing he would not do to help them. One could take any problem to him, however personal, and he would not rest until he had helped to find a solution. Generous and loyal to an unbelievable degree, there was no effort too great for him when friendship called. Many of my associates remember a particular kindness, a generous act, aid extended when the going was rough. To my own knowledge, the list is long, very long indeed.

In discussing moral courage, Napoleon once said, "I have rarely met with the two o'clock in the morning kind. I mean, unprepared courage, which is necessary on an unexpected occasion; and which, in spite of the most unforeseen events, leaves full freedom of judgment and decision."

The Governor had that type of moral courage in rare degree. He had a mind entirely free of panic. Firm in heart and in purpose, his comprehension of a problem, the directness of his attack upon it, and the unity of his action inspired confidence and insured accomplishment.

I shall not forget a Sunday afternoon during the second trial of James J. Hines, a political leader. A few of us were hurriedly summoned to the office. We found Mr. Dewey, then the District Attorney, absorbed in the composition of a letter. As we entered his room he looked up and said, "Glad you came. There's plenty to do. I have just had word that George Weinberg has shot and killed himself." I reached for a chair. The other assistants needed support also. Weinberg was our most important witness next to J. Richard "Dixie" Davis, a racket attorney who was giving testimony for the People. Our case!

But Mr. Dewey brought us to with a snap, gave us precise and detailed instructions as to what we were to do, and then calmly returned to his letter—a letter to the House of Representatives Judiciary Committee in Washington, which resulted in the removal, prosecution, and conviction of Martin T. Manton, presiding judge of the Circuit Court of Appeals.

Those who were closest to him feel that, in large measure, the Governor's successes can be characterized as and truly are dividends to courage.

It is not my purpose, nor is it within my power, to catalogue the achievements of Governor Dewey. Many of us, and millions more, are witnesses, whose memories need not be refreshed, with regard to his exceptional record as the greatest District Attorney of our time, as an outstanding Governor of the state of New York, and as the national leader of his political party. In 1944, and again in 1948, I thought that he would be a great President of the United States. I shall always so believe.

I have touched on a few of the Governor's qualities of mind and heart. Those qualities have been priceless public assets for over thirty-five years. They have also been personal possessions, cherished in the memory of those of us who were so fortunate as to think of him as and call him Chief. Personally, and I know I speak for Mr. Alfred Scotti, the Chief Assistant District Attorney and other senior associates, I and they would value no compliment higher than to be thought worthy of his approval and good opinion.

We mourn the loss of our leader and our friend, and we ask, your honor, that, when the court suspends this day, the record show the adjournment was in deference and tribute to the memory of Thomas E. Dewey.

Sol Gelb, an Assistant District Attorney and trial associate of Special Prosecutor Dewey in the conviction and sentencing of Charles "Lucky" Luciano, the Mafia leader, to thirty to fifty years' imprison-ment in the epochal trial of the 1930s, reminisced before Dewey's death:

You know, it's funny, but I worked for Dewey a few months and I said to Hogan: "This man's got to run for Governor, because he's bound to succeed here." Dewey impressed me tremendously as a doer. I had no doubt he would succeed. I knew and felt that he would become a national figure. He couldn't help that. He had great ability to inspire you with that confidence. He didn't inspire you with a lot of rhetoric. He conveyed that he's got some real ability, knows how to use it, and knows how to give directions. I said, "You know, this is the smartest man I've ever met."

At first I didn't know anything about whether he had wisdom, or whether he was a deep thinker, but he impressed me as a man who spoke his thoughts very precisely, very crisply, and didn't slop all over himself speaking. He impressed me as a man with a very orderly mind, and a quick thinker. Whatever thought the business at hand required, he had. I later learned that what distinguished Dewey generally was that he had complete control of his mental energies. There was never mental panic. That's a marvelous control of the mentality because he can just close it and start it going at his will. Now, I can't do that. Very few people can do it.

He's a hell of a decent man, a man of good instincts. He has a strong sense of loyalty. He's a good man. Another thing, he doesn't hem you in, and he gave his men great latitude. All he wanted was trust, and you felt pretty good working for Dewey. He always spoke of his men as first-class men. He didn't demean them, berate them, lower them. I think that's a good quality.

Dewey made it very clear above everything else that he was interested in breaking the hold on the community of big-time mobsters. He told me once, "We are not to waste our time on the small fry. It's important people in the underworld who will be the objects of the investigation."

In 1935 the mobs had a tremendous hold on the legitimate business life of the community. As a matter of fact you could feel it. It was almost as if you could touch it, because the fear in those who were the victims of the mobs was so strong that the very notion of getting people to be witnesses in any criminal cases involving mobsters was considered extravagant, a wild one.

As a matter of fact people were predicting that nothing would come of this investigation. Before I was hired I ran into Judge Martin Manton on the street. He knew me from appearances in his court, the Circuit Court of Appeals, and Manton asked me what I was doing, and how I was doing, and I told him, "I want to get into public office. I've made some effort to get with Tom Dewey, who is starting his rackets investigation." Manton said to me, "Oh, that's a waste of time." I replied, "Why do you say that?" He said, "It won't amount to anything. In six months it will be dead." I commented, "There's a real need for it." He said, "Oh, this is a lot of publicity hunting. These things are never genuine, and, what's more, it's overplayed."

Well, I left him, still wanting to work for Tom Dewey, but there was a general feeling that the investigation couldn't succeed because the hold of the mobs on the community was so strong that you could never break it.

But Dewey's principal aim was nothing less than to go after the big-timers, men like Lucky Luciano, Dutch Schultz, Lepke, and Gurrah. Each man had a sphere or empire of control, but all of them deferred to Lucky Luciano. It was whispered about on pretty good authority that Luciano was the boss. This didn't mean that Lepke took orders from him, but Lepke deferred to him. He recognized that Luciano was boss.

All of these gangsters in the 1930s had certain areas of control. For example, the Italian mobs always handled narcotics. Let's say that Luciano's man, Tom Pennochio, who was in charge of narcotics, was supposed to be the boss of narcotics. That didn't mean that an arrangement couldn't be made whereby some of Lepke's boys couldn't also handle narcotics, but all of it was pursuant to arrangement. These big-shot leaders used to meet together. Dewey knew all that.

Now—how to get at them. One group of assistants and investigators was put to work on the restaurant racket. It was known to anybody with some intelligence, some savvy, that restaurant owners were being shaken down and that Dutch Schultz was behind it. So restaurants were a natural area of investigation. It was known that Lepke and Gurrah had made God knows how much money in the garment industry. Because of their connection with the union, they could shake manufacturers down about putting union pressure on them. That was a natural area, and so some assistants were investigating the garment industry.

When I first started I was investigating window cleaning. Now, why window cleaning? Our information was that Lepke was involved in the window-cleaning business. He was making money improperly through illegal means by having a hold on the people in that business.

Now that doesn't mean that, if I started to work on window cleaning, worked for a few weeks, and it was not productive, that I was going to stick on window cleaning. The investigation was just probing. It was a probing tactic. Maybe it would yield results and maybe it wouldn't. But it didn't necessarily follow that I was stuck with window cleaners because when we raided the various houses of prostitution and picked up scores of prostitutes, madams, pimps, and the bookers of women, the people who "booked" the women into the houses, then I was taken out of the window cleaners' case and put in charge of the prostitution racket with a view to trying to get the big shots. The question always was, Who is in charge of the racket? Who is the top man?

Dewey's idea was to hit at the big shots in any way that was possible. When we went to work on prostitutes we weren't interested in prostitutes. Dewey said, "You're never going to eliminate prostitution, and I'm satisfied you won't wipe out prostitution, but by investigating it, we may find the weakness in the line which will lead to the big shot."

Dewey's plan was to start finding people against whom you could obtain some evidence and then offer them the choice of co-operating with the investigation. The only way you can make a person a witness, particularly a person engaged in a crime, is to have the goods on them. If you do, you have leverage, and then you begin to use that leverage and work on them to go your way. That was the aim of Dewey. But it was a backbreaking job because the fear the witnesses displayed was so great. Witnesses would have done anything to avoid testifying against Luciano.

So—there were prostitutes, madams, bookers, and we gradually found the evidence that led to a so-called combine operating above the bookers. Little Davie Betillo, a Luciano man, had come from Chicago where he had been Al Capone's bodyguard. He was a killer and he was in charge of the combine. We finally obtained evidence on which we obtained an indictment against Luciano, and during that whole process Dewey was right in the middle of it. He knew what he was doing, knew the objective, discussed the details, helped guide me and several others who were working under me toward our destination.

The Luciano case knocked off the head man in the underworld—*the* head man. Luciano had never gotten any publicity to speak of before. After he was convicted the newspapers began to write about his position in the underworld and, frankly, for the first time I realized how big he was. But Dewey had always appreciated the fact that this was the kind of racket investigation that would be successful—a plodding, arduous working from the bottom right up to the very top.

You need a lot of patience for that. Also hard work, and accurate orientation, where you're going, and what you're leading to.

Dewey had another very big investigation going into the "numbers" racket, and the inside information was that Dutch Schultz was the big-time mobster who controlled that form of gambling. So Dewey's aim was to get Dutch Schultz. The first thing he did was to work toward getting an indictment on income tax evasion—this had worked against Capone in Chicago, and Dewey himself had won a major conviction when he sent a racketeer named Irving Wexler—called Waxey Gordon—to prison for ten years on tax charges. But while we were working on Dutch Schultz, Schultz was killed in a gangland murder. There was no point in pursuing his income tax any further.

But Dewey also knew that you couldn't operate a big numbers racket combination the way Schultz had done without political protection, and the big man in politics was James J. Hines, *the* leader of Tammany Hall and the most powerful Democratic politician in New York State.

Dewey's objective was to get Hines. Why Hines? Because Dewey knew that Hines didn't protect the numbers racketeers from the cop on the beat or from the cop assigned to a division who would make a casual arrest of somebody who was collecting betting slips. Hines would give big-time protection. The District Attorney of those days wouldn't bother the racketeers. There wouldn't be any big raids. There wouldn't be any police headquarters activity against the numbers racket "banks," so they could operate without risk. In other words, the racket was safe—and so it was, until Tom Dewey came along.

Dewey also had very strong feelings about alliances between crime and politics, from the moral point of view. He had very strong feelings about a democratic nation that tolerated that kind of thing. In fact, Dewey had very strong feelings.

I considered him an excellent lawyer. He could argue very cogently, very forcefully. And there is something else you must bear in mind. Dewey was a very young man. In 1936, at the Luciano trial, he was only thirty-four years old.

I remember some fellow, who was a knowing fellow in New York, saying to me when we indicated who the defendants in the Luciano case would be, saying to me, "Jesus, you've got the real thing there." From the standpoint of just that one Luciano case, in fact, the rackets investigation was aimed to weaken the power of the underworld, remove the fear, and break their grip—and it did. That doesn't mean that, in the years that followed, there weren't people in power who had illegal activities going on. But the conditions as they were in the 1930s never returned to New York.

The whole country—I say "the whole" and maybe there were a few spots that weren't, but wherever you had urban civilization you had the same thing in miniature, maybe not so big, and law enforcement authorities, whether it was in Detroit, or Kansas City, or Minneapolis, had the same problem.

What Tom Dewey did was to spark other communities to follow suit. I remember being impressed by the fact that, in various parts of the country, cleanups began. There were determined efforts everywhere in America to accomplish what Tom Dewey was trying to do and, in part, accomplishing.

Is that a valid point?

Dartmouth College, attempting to set these early Dewey years in the perspective of United States history, awarded Dewey an honorary degree on June 18, 1939, with this citation:

DEVOTED IN SPIRIT TO THE REBIRTH OF IDEALS IN THE ADMINISTRATION OF JUSTICE, IN HARDLY MORE THAN A DECADE YOU HAVE MADE YOURSELF INFLUENTIAL IN TURNING THE TIDE OF PUBLIC CYNICISM, AND REVIVING THE ANCIENT CONCEPT OF JUSTICE AS A FLAMING SWORD.

Part I | TRIAL LAWYER

Boyhood in Owosso: "The Lure, the Drama, Persist to This Day"

On July 30, 1935, not long after my appointment as Special Prosecutor, I made this radio address to the people of New York over stations WABC, WOR, and WMCA:

This is the first and, I hope, the last time I shall make a public address during the course of the criminal investigation which yesterday commenced with the selection and charge of a grand jury by Mr. Justice McCook. In general, it is my belief that a talking prosecutor is not a working prosecutor, and that a promising prosecutor rarely performs. I think it is proper, however, that I should state at this time the purposes and aims of the investigation.

Your businesses, your safety, and your daily lives are affected by criminal conditions in this city. I believe you are entitled to know how this investigation will affect you, and what part you, as citizens, are expected to take in it. Governor Lehman has permitted me to say that the views I am about to express are also the views held by him in ordering this investigation.

In his order convening the extraordinary term of the Supreme Court, Governor Lehman defined the scope of this investigation to include: first, any and all acts of racketeering and vice; second, any and all acts of organized crime and vice; third, any connection between such acts and any law enforcement officials in the county of New York.

This has, from time to time, been miscalled a "vice" investigation. If this were merely an attempt to suppress ordinary prostitution, gambling, and lottery games, I think I am safe in saying the Governor would not have ordered it, and I know I would not have undertaken it. The ordinary prostitution, lottery, and gambling cases are routine in character, and the present facilities for handling them should be quite adequate.

This investigation will deal with vice only where it exists in an organized form. We are concerned with those predatory vultures who traffic on a wholesale scale in the bodies of women and mere girls for profit. We are concerned with professional criminals who run large, crooked gambling places, and lotteries, at the expense of the public.

Petty gambling and bets of ten or twenty cents in the policy or so-called "numbers game" are not involved in this investigation. We are concerned, however, with gambling or numbers games operated on a large scale by criminals, for the profit of the criminal underworld. Any criminal operation which pours money into the coffers of organized crime is a continuing menace to the safety of the community.

Modern racketeering may be defined as the business of successful intimidation for the purpose of regularly extorting money. It is conducted by organized gangs of low-grade outlaws who lack either the courage or the intelligence to earn an honest living. They succeed only so long as they can prey upon the fear and weakness of disorganized or timid victims. They fail, and run to cover, when business and the public, awakened to their own strength, stand up and fight.

There is today scarcely a business in New York which does not somehow pay its tribute to the underworld—a tribute levied by force and collected by fear. There is certainly not a family in the city of New York which does not pay its share of tribute to the underworld every day it lives, and with every meal it eats. This huge, unofficial sales tax is collected from the ultimate consumer in the price he pays for everything he buys.

Every barrel of flour consumed in New York City pays its toll to racketeers, which goes right into the price of every loaf of bread. Every chicken shipped into the city of New York pays its tribute to the poultry racket, out of the pockets of the public. There are few vegetable or fish markets in the city of New York where merchants are not forced by sluggings, destruction of goods, threats, and stink bombs to pay heavy toll.

Most racketeers operate in disguise. The first step in organizing a racket is to make it look like a legitimate business. Rackets differ mainly in the different false faces they wear. The object is always the same.

The racket is found in its crudest form in the many vegetable, fish, and other food markets. There the racketeer frequently calls himself a "watchman." For regular pay from the businessmen in the market, he agrees to protect them from himself. Sometimes the businessman gets stubborn and won't pay, and sometimes he finds he simply can't pay both his employees and the racketeers. It is always a case of pay up or take the consequences.

They follow swiftly. Truck tires are slashed in the night. Fresh vegetables and fish are soaked with gasoline, or stolen. Customers are intimidated, employees are beaten up, plate-glass windows are broken, and often whole stores are completely destroyed.

The businessman quite quickly starts paying if he can, or closes his business if he cannot pay. Tragically enough, many businessmen have reached the cynical conclusion that rackets cannot be broken up. They keep their own counsel and fight their losing battle.

I do not agree with that philosophy.

In some industries in New York, organized crime has actually been invited by certain groups of businessmen to "organize," as they call it, in the industry. Some merchants find they cannot make as much profit as they would like. They decide to "organize" the industry to raise prices, at the expense of the public. Legitimate trade associations cannot and will not serve their purpose. These businessmen promptly discover, however, that the underworld is always ready to serve any master for a price.

The result has been the organization in many industries in this city of pretended trade associations which are in fact nothing but cloaks for racketeers. Sometimes the greedy businessman starts the association. Sometimes the racketeers start it for their own purposes and force it on the industry. The result is always the same. The businessman and the public pay, and the racketeers take the profits.

Here is racketeering in its most effective disguise and its most modern form. The association is set up as a corporation with a constitution, bylaws, and full legal window dressing. A few members of the industry are bribed or intimidated into becoming officers, as front men for the racketeers. It is announced that the association will save the industry from trade abuses and gather information for legitimate trade purposes. On the side, it is hinted that the association will protect members from labor union troubles.

Businessmen are first politely urged to join. If a businessman has his own suspicions and does not join promptly, more powerful methods are brought to bear. His windows are broken and his employees are assaulted. Stink bombs ruin his goods and drive away his customers. If he surrenders and joins the association, as he almost always does, he starts out by paying heavy dues, and from then on he pays and pays.

The criminal underworld plays no favorites. It preys on the public, industry, and labor alike. Organized labor has been one of its most recent and most tragic victims. Many originally honest and sound labor unions have been infected with the virus of organized crime. Today, certain corrupted leaders operate as extortionists both upon industry and upon the members of their own unions. Just as surely as public office is a public trust, so labor leadership is a labor trust.

I wish to speak frankly about the labor union situation of today. No intelligent man, whether he be employer or employee, can fail to support enthusiastically the cause of organized labor. Neither business nor labor can prosper unless business is fair to organized labor, and labor, by collective bargaining, can enforce its demands for decent living conditions and a fair wage. It would indeed be a calamity if a few gangs of thugs, masquerading as labor union delegates, should discredit the cause of organized labor in this country.

The public must not be allowed to believe that organized labor is represented by those few unions in which union delegates have become criminals, or criminals have been made into union delegates. Unless they are purged, labor unions which have been thus taken over by criminals will, just as certainly as night follows day, wreck the cause of organized labor in this country and set back its progress many years. The officers of these unions are all too frequently the willing tools of professional criminals who direct their activities and keep them in office by means of force and fear.

The president of one labor union in New York County was murdered last fall in the presence of twenty-two witnesses, consisting of employers and members of his own union. The terrorism in that union was such that, when the witnesses were examined, all twenty-two of them claimed that they did not see the murderer and could not identify him. All of the witnesses claimed they were under one small table which, in fact, was big enough to cover only two people at the most. The murderer has not been brought to justice, a new leader has been elected, and the union carries on.

William Green, president of the American Federation of Labor, recently said, "We are against racketeering within our organization. I will co-operate with any effort to eliminate racketeering in unions under our jurisdiction no matter where it strikes." I wholeheartedly accept Mr. Green's statement and will rely upon his co-operation.

I have said that I do not agree with the philosophy that businessmen must continue to suffer the depredations of thugs. I certainly cannot agree with the philosophy so frequently heard, that the cause of organized labor must continue to suffer betrayal by a few corrupt leaders in a handful of unions. I am convinced that it is possible to rid both business and labor of racketeers.

I want to say to labor union members who have been betrayed: You can save yourselves. I consider it one of the most important parts of the investigation I am undertaking to help you save yourselves. If you will come to my offices in the Woolworth Building, you will be seen by a responsible member of my staff. He will welcome your help. He will respect your confidence. He will protect you. You will not read your testimony in the newspapers, nor will the heads of your union learn you have been to the office.

To the wholesale food merchants, the restaurant owners, the racketeer trade association victims and the other businessmen of New York, I want to say this: In my opinion, you can be freed from organized racketeering in this city. There is not the slightest excuse for any honest businessman paying tribute to any racketeer. Those of you who have knowledge of criminal conditions owe it to yourselves and to the people of this city to give this investigation your co-operation. It is not only your privilege but your duty to bring that information to my office.

The people of this city are entitled to the co-operation of every citizen who has evidence of racketeering or other organized crime. I do not ask that co-operation in my own name. I ask it in the name of the Governor of this state, who brought about this investigation, and in the name of the people of this city who, in the long run, pay every penny of the cost of racketeering in the price of the goods they buy.

There will be twenty Deputy Assistant District Attorneys in my office in the Woolworth Building who are at your service. Any man who brings testimony to my office can be certain that his name, his testimony, and his person will receive absolute protection. In no criminal prosecution with which I or any of my assistants have ever been connected has any witness been touched either before or after trial. A prosecutor's strongest weapon is complete secrecy and the protection of his witnesses. I will use that weapon to the fullest measure.

There has been loose talk of politics in connection with this investigation. I should like to deal with that subject and dispose of it. The immediate origin of this investigation was a grand jury of unselfish and public-spirited citizens who represented all shades of political opinion and views. The newspapers, representing a wide variety of political views, have given their unanimous support. The investigation was ordered by the Governor of the state of New York, who happens to be a Democrat. I happen to be a Republican. I was appointed by a Democratic District Attorney and have received the magnificent support of Mayor LaGuardia, who was elected on a Fusion ticket, and of Police Commissioner Valentine, who, so far as I know, has no politics at all.

A Board of Estimate and a Board of Aldermen consisting of Democrats, Republicans, and Fusionists have unanimously passed the appropriation. I am choosing my staff from among Republicans, Democrats, Fusionists, and men of no political party. They are being chosen without regard to party, and they owe no allegiance to any political party or any political leader. There will be no politics in this investigation as long as I conduct it.

I do not expect immediate results in this investigation. The Capone case in Chicago took three years of day and night work by several Assistant United States Attorneys and a dozen agents of the Intelligence Unit of the Treasury Department of the United States. The same is true of the Dutch Schultz case, the Waxey Gordon case, and many others here in New York.

I do not expect this investigation to take anything like three years, but I do know the job cannot be done in a few months. Most racketeering depends on petty acts of intimidation which, repeated many hundreds of times, build up the racket to huge proportions. It is not at all likely that we will produce, within a few months, important jury trials of major indictments. We may, however, procure evidence within a few months which will warrant our starting criminal prosecutions.

Every shakedown, every threat, every stink bomb throwing, is a state crime. We will prosecute every crime which is part of an organized racket, where we can get evidence. However minor the crime may be, we will prosecute it if it is a part of organized crime. If it is a misdemeanor, we will try it in a magistrate's court, or in the Court of Special Sessions before three judges. We will prosecute any crime in the book from conspiracy and malicious mischief to assault in the first degree, from extortion to perjury, from income tax violations all the way to murder. The object of this investigation is to rid this city of racketeers. Only by vigilant, continuous prosecution of every overt act, of whatever type, can this be done. We will prosecute the cases we get in the appropriate court, whether the individual case itself be large or small.

This investigation is totally different in character from the legislative investigation so successfully conducted by Judge Seabury. That investigation was conducted by the legislature for the purpose of investigating, and exposing, corruption in public office. Its object was to develop facts and to expose them publicly. Its object was not the prosecution of crime. Judge Seabury neither had the power nor was it the purpose of his investigation to prosecute crime.

The present investigation is conducted for the sole purpose of prosecuting crime to conviction. It must develop facts and keep them secret for presentation to a grand jury where secrecy is not only required by law, but is absolutely essential to successful prosecution. When criminal cases have been developed, they must be prepared for trial and then tried publicly before a court and jury.

Crime cannot be investigated under a spotlight. Publicity does not stamp out crime. It is my sincere hope that the work we are doing will vanish from the newspapers until it produces criminal cases to be tried in court. You will doubtless hear rumors as to what, and whom, we are investigating. I ask you to ignore them. I will neither confirm nor deny rumors.

The surest way to destroy the effectiveness of criminal prosecution is to advertise in advance the names of those you intend to prosecute. Sensational raids and arrests without months of quiet and painstaking preparation in advance result in nothing but acquittals in court. This only encourages the already overconfident underworld. When we have developed cases we will present them in court. Until then, we will work hard and quietly.

I am confident that with your help we can stamp out racketeering in New York. We can make this city too dangerous for organized crime.

To what extent this investigation succeeds, and how promptly it succeeds, is largely in your hands. Your co-operation is essential. Your confidence will be respected. Your help will be kept secret and your persons protected.

If you have evidence of organized crime, of whatever kind, and however large or small, bring it to us. The rest is our job. We will do our best.

Twelve years before, when I came to New York at the age of twenty-one to finish law at Columbia University, I could scarcely have dreamed that I would ever be appointed to investigate and prosecute several of the worst criminals in our nation's history. However, I did bring with me an inborn conviction that the Tammany Hall political machine was the epitome of corruption and oppression and that the Republican Party was the only worthy instrument of government. There was also a latent, incurable impulse to cure the wrongs of the body politic that emerged later. As it turned out, these developed into a combination of driving forces which gradually took command of my life.

As near as I can tell, this was the fault of my grandfather, George Martin Dewey. My parents, uncles, and aunts were comparatively peaceable citizens. They were teachers, editors, or merchants. Only Grandfather Dewey was a crusader, a political reformer, a pamphleteer, a thorn in the flesh of all he believed to be wrong.

Grandfather Dewey was born in Lebanon, New Hampshire, in 1832. His father and his grandfather and great-grandfather had lived there ever since his family moved from England. His first American ancestors had settled there on their arrival from England in the 1630s.* These men had fought the Indians, the British in the Revolu-

* The first Thomas Dewey took this Freeman's Oath in Dorchester, Massachusetts, on May 14, 1634:

"I, Thomas Dewey, being by God's Providence an inhabitant and freeman within the jurisdiction of this Commonwealth—do here swear by the great and

tionary War and the British again in the War of 1812. When the wars were over they all went home and stayed there equably for the rest of their lives.

It was different with George Martin Dewey, who was born restless and stayed that way. He left home at the age of fourteen to go to nearby Lowell, Massachusetts, where he was graduated from high school at sixteen. He entered Harvard College that fall and, before he graduated, he signed up with an astronomical expedition to the upper reaches of the Amazon.

Nothing more about the expedition was reported except that my grandfather survived it and returned home eighteen months later to settle down as a schoolteacher in Lowell. Soon he was off again, this time westward, and he settled in Niles, Michigan. There he taught school for one year and was appointed deputy superintendent of public instruction at the state capital in Lansing. It was a high-sounding title for a twenty-two-year-old, but one might suspect that he was the entire staff of the superintendent. Michigan was still largely a wilderness and had been admitted to the Union only a few years before. It was a time when almost anybody who could read or write would be accepted as a teacher, and state standards and supervision were far in the future.

After two years of this he went back to Niles to become the editor of the weekly newspaper, the Niles *Enquirer*. The nation was seething over the issue of the extension of slavery to new territories, and my grandfather was in the forefront of the agitation. He was a delegate to the first Republican "Convention Under the Oaks" at

---

dreadful name of the ever living God, that I will be true and faithful to the same, and will accordingly yield assistance and support thereunto, with my person and estate, as in equity I am bound; and will also truly endeavor to maintain and preserve all the liberties and privileges thereof . . . that I will not plot or pratice any evil against it, not consent to any that shall do so, but will truly discover and reveal the same to lawful authority. . . .

"I will give my vote and suffrage as I shall judge in mine own conscience may best conduce and tend to the public weal of the body without respect to persons or favor of any man."

The Deweys were said to have been descended from Huguenot refugees who had left France for England in the sixteenth century. Their name had been "Douai." In England, it became "Duee," then Dewey.

Among Thomas Dewey's American descendants was the famous Admiral George Dewey, one of Farragut's executive officers in the nineteenth-century American Civil War and victor of the Battle of Manila Bay against Spain in 1898. Admiral Dewey was, in fact, third cousin to Grandfather George Martin Dewey.

Jackson, Michigan, and to the Republican National Convention at which Abraham Lincoln was nominated for President.

Some years afterward, having sold the Niles paper and bought the Hastings, Michigan, *Banner,* my grandfather wrote of this period:

"Franklin Pierce was President of the United States, Jefferson Davis Secretary of War and the Hall of Congress filled with Southern Traitors and Northern Dog Faces led by Douglas of Illinois, who had just secured the repeal of the Missouri Compromise and the practical nationalism [sic] of the barbarous institution of Negro slavery. The Press of this country, and especially in our State, was in the hands of aiders and abettors of these treason-loving demagogues, and, that the friends of personal liberty and political honesty might have a hearing, it became necessary to start papers devoted to the advocacy of Free Soil, Free Speech and Free Men."

My grandfather was never unsure of his views nor was he given to understatement. When the battle to end slavery was finally won, he plunged with equal dedication into other Republican causes, including the maintenance of the protective tariff. He regarded the tariff as the essential protection of the fledgling industries of developing America, and the only possible protection of the jobs of American workmen. Yellowing copies of newspapers of the day describe him, still in his thirties, as a towering, bearded man, passionately filling speaking engagements in addition to operating his newspaper and serving as a state senator. When, in 1880, he sold the Hastings *Banner* and bought the Owosso, Michigan, *Times,* the old owner wrote:

"Besides Mr. Dewey's many years of editorial experience, he brings with him what so few country editors have—capital—hence the business passes into hands where it will surely grow and prosper."

In his first issue my grandfather wrote: "Under our management, the *Times* will be an outspoken Republican paper, and we shall, to the best of our ability, advance the prosperity of the Party, and labor for the success of the bedrock principles on which the superstructure rests, knowing no faction, recognizing no 'bosses' to the detriment of the public interest, and the triumph of that policy which has made glorious the history of the Republican Party."

In the same issue my grandfather asked a rhetorical question: "How can I afford to circulate 800 copies a week and only get paid for 500? Failing to get a satisfactory answer to that conundrum, the editor of the Cadillac *News* has come down to hard pan, cash in advance, just as all publishers should do, and as we shall do January 1st."

A small item in the Owosso *Times* the following week illustrated the point:

"As we were going to press last week, the agent for the company that produced 'Bankers Daughters' at Opera Hall last evening called on us to advertise for him. The space required was four inches; we charged him $2 and he went away mad. Now, we should have been glad of his work, but when an advertisement is not worth for a single insertion 50 cents an inch, we prefer others should do the work."

Grandfather obviously had an eye for business and it was only a year later that he proudly announced the acquisition of a large new modern press and the trebling of circulation. He had successfully established the newspaper, which was edited successively by him, then by my uncle Edmund, then by my father, and by me for the summer of 1922 when I was at the University of Michigan.

Before he left Niles my grandfather had found a wife, Miss Emma Bingham, whom he had married in 1857. She was a twenty-year-old schoolteacher and the daughter of the only lawyer I have found among my ancestors. This was Judge Lemuel Bingham of Niles, a native of Connecticut.

Republican campaign commitments grew in importance in my grandfather's life. The Owosso *Times* reported on October 13, 1882, that the editor was off to New Hampshire to make a series of political speeches. During the next election, he was off to New England again, and afterward the Lansing *Republican* said that "George M. Dewey during the campaign just closed made 82 speeches and travelled 15,000 miles." Of one of his speeches, the Ontario, New York, *Times* reported: "The speaker held his audience with the closest attention for nearly three hours, receiving frequent and hearty applause."

It is hard to conceive of any political speech lasting three hours, but in those days people traveled for miles on foot or on horseback for political meetings. The visiting orator was announced long in advance in the local press and on broadsides posted on barns and buildings throughout the countryside. •

My grandfather was also an advocate of Prohibition, which came along quite early in Michigan. Owosso was always a leader in the dry vote. As a friend said about him: "He was a strong opposer of the

American saloon. He believed in the suppression by law of the saloon."

A prophetic piece appeared in the Owosso *Times* in 1891, reporting that editor Dewey had been "asked by Chairman Brookfield of the New York Republican State Committee to assist in the campaign against Tammany Hallism in the Empire State."

By 1892 my grandfather's influence was national, and he campaigned hard for William McKinley who, for the time, was thought by many to be a dangerous liberal. Grandfather traveled with McKinley for part of the campaign, and his job was to make "the longer" speech so that the presidential candidate could save his voice and climax the meeting with a short crowd-rouser. But this was my grandfather's last campaign. His health failed gradually until his death in 1897. At the memorial services in Owosso, the Rev. George H. Wilson said about him:

"To such a man, the world of thought is a battlefield. . . . He does not speak to please; he does not tarry to adorn with rhetoric; he does not look for stories to enliven, far less to amuse; he does not seek to provoke laughter, but slaughter.

"Life is too serious in its great efforts to stop and laugh. . . . The very voice of the man will gather to itself a quality . . . alive with the agony of intensity."

My grandfather Dewey left a widow and five grown children: Edmund Otis, for whom I was given my middle name because he was my mother's favorite, Emma Grace, Henry Bingham, George M. Dewey, Jr., my father, and the young daughter Hannah. He was also survived by his sister, Mrs. J. P. Williams of Council Bluffs, Iowa, and two brothers, Otis G. Dewey of Ayer, Massachusetts, and Edmund F. Dewey of Twin Bridges, Montana.

I inherited more than my political persuasions from my grandfather. He was a vast enthusiast for causes but he had no great taste for public office. He stayed only eighteen months as deputy superintendent of education in Michigan and he could stand only a few terms as alderman in Hastings and one term as a state senator. After the election of 1896 he declined the offer of an appointment from President McKinley to be minister to Turkey. Contrary to all appearances, and probably nobody will believe it, I always shared his reluctance to hold public office, and left every office I ever held voluntarily.

My grandfather also left me a feeling for his hobbies. He loved cows and he always had a small herd not far from his home. The task of bringing the cows in from pasture and milking them night and morning fell successively to each of the boys in turn, ending up with my father as the youngest. In later years my uncle Edmund kept his own half dozen purebred Jerseys in a barn behind his big house on Oliver Street, the best residential street in Owosso. He cleaned the stable, milked and fed the cows, and cared for the calves every morning before going to his office and every night after returning from his office for all the years I can remember. He took two or more of his Jerseys to the state fair every year and always came home with a ribbon or two.

I always had the same weakness. I too liked cows, but not as a hobby so much, and Holstein, not Jerseys. Our own farm on Quaker Hill at Pawling, New York, was basically my home for thirty years and it might well have been that my herd of 200 Holstein dairy cattle provided more rest and diversion for me than any other activity. Our accountants' reports showed our farm every year to be decently in the black, and so much for the cynical comments about city men who own farms and write off the losses on their income taxes. Most of the credit went to my neighbor-partner, Arnulf Miller, a wonderfully good farmer who supervised the day-to-day work on the farm in addition to supervising his own. We made the decisions jointly and were partners in dividing the profits. But this is anticipating events.

My uncle Edmund was the one I knew best. Our houses were only two blocks apart on Oliver Street in Owosso, and he and my father were very close. They shared the family interest in public affairs as a matter of duty and tradition, even though their approach was different. Uncle Edmund, as I remembered him, was quiet, plump, with a twinkle in his eye, not at all given to polemics. He was not a public man, but he did become the Republican county chairman of our local Shiawassee County, and he later became postmaster of the town. He was succeeded by my father as county chairman and subsequently as publisher of the Owosso *Times*.

My uncle Henry went to Tacoma, Washington, after his graduation from the University of Michigan. He taught in the public schools there, became superintendent of schools at Tacoma, and was twice elected state superintendent of education for Washington on the Republican ticket. Thirty years afterward, when I was campaigning through the state of Washington, literally hundreds of middle-aged people would come up to me to show me their graduation certificates signed by my uncle.

Uncle Henry's career as an educator ended in 1912, the year of the Taft-Roosevelt split. He accepted the Republican nomination for congressman at large and, though he ran 50,000 votes ahead of his ticket, he was defeated. But this was probably just as well. Uncle Henry was a reserved, gentle man, primarily a scholar. The hurly-burly of politics was a strain for him, and he decided to join the Western division of the Houghton Mifflin Company in charge of schoolbooks. Not long after that he moved to the head office in Boston, and there produced schoolbooks for Houghton Mifflin for the rest of his happy and useful life.

Of my grandfather's two daughters, Hannah married a young scientist, Dr. Howard S. Reed, who became professor of biology at the University of California at Riverside. The other daughter, Grace, never married. Aside from my grandfather, who died five years before I was born, it was Aunt Grace who had the greatest influence on my own life of any relative except my parents. I knew Aunt Grace well all my life until she died at the age of ninety-four.

She was a tall, stately, maiden lady, a bit forbidding but at the same time charming, with an air of elegance and authority. Upon her graduation from Wellesley College she had taught at Harcourt Place Seminary at Granville, Ohio, and conducted tours for girl students in Europe. In her middle thirties she decided to become an accountant. This accomplished, she became in due course an examiner of corporate income tax returns in the Internal Revenue Service of the Treasury Department. When she reached the age of seventy, they gave her a two-year extension beyond the mandatory retirement. At the age of seventy-two, she undertook the preparation of income tax returns for a number of friends. She did this until her eyes got so bad she could not do it any more.

When I was about to go off to the University of Michigan, in the fall of 1919, Aunt Grace was visiting us in Owosso. She asked me what I was going to do and I said I had not decided. In those days it was somewhat shocking for a young man of seventeen not to have a course set for himself, and she expressed that point of view clearly. I told her I might decide to come home and run the Owosso *Times*. She expressed serious doubts. I also confessed to Aunt Grace that I had given some thought to a career as an opera singer and she expressed even more serious doubts about the idea of my becoming a "professional entertainer." I was to be a lawyer, she said, and as far as she was concerned, that settled it.

It was to be quite a tortuous trail to Aunt Grace's "decision" but I was intensely grateful to her.

My father, George Martin Dewey, Jr., was born at Hastings, Michigan, in 1870. He was the youngest boy, a six-footer, straight, handsome, somewhat more outgoing than his brothers, and all he ever really wanted to do was to go to West Point. In the examinations held for congressional appointments in 1889, he came out No. 1 out of thirteen and he entered the United States Military Academy. It was his greatest disappointment in life when, two years later, he fell while jumping in the gymnasium and broke a small bone in his spine. That was the end of his military career, although he gradually recovered his health completely.

After a spell on the Owosso *Times*, my father followed his brother Henry to Tacoma, Washington, where he worked for a year as a reporter on the Tacoma *Ledger*. Then he came home to work on the *Times* and also, for two years, in the office of the state auditor-general in Lansing. For many years he was also county supervisor of Shiawassee County.

Essentially, my father was the lifelong editor of the Owosso *Times*. He tended to write easily, and I think he wrote most of the *Times* in longhand. He also ran the plant, a good job-printing plant, and there was a steady but not large income. My father used to take in something like $1,500 a year when I was in high school in the 1910s. I remember this well because, at that time, I was making ten cents an hour on the Owosso *Times* as a printer's devil.

Not long after his return from Tacoma my father met his future wife, Miss Annie Thomas, at a dance. She had been a little girl in Owosso, seven years younger than he, and of course he had never noticed her before. But now she was grown up, beautiful, outgoing and, incidentally, a superb dancer. She was an excellent skater and before long they were doing all their dancing and skating together that winter.

The week of January 27, 1899, was momentous for our family. On that day my father and mother were married at the home of her parents, Mr. and Mrs. Alfred T. Thomas, in Owosso, and they left for their honeymoon. Three days later they returned home because the health of her grandfather, George Thomas, was failing rapidly. Two days later he died at the age of eighty-seven.

In that same week my uncle Edmund learned that he was to be appointed postmaster—and also that he would nonetheless be able to continue in his private enterprise work of publishing the *Times,* a dispensation granted to few office holders. It was possible that the Administration in Washington thought it well to allow Republican postmasters to continue publishing Republican newspapers.

My maternal great-grandfather George Thomas made such a remarkable impact on his family and community that he was always a part of our lives. His was an amazing story. Born in London, England, on March 25, 1824, he was bundled away to the stern discipline of a British public school before he was twelve. Among my mother's papers I found a letter he wrote to his mother at the age of twelve. The letter was dated May 28, 1824:

> My Dear Mother:
> I received your letter duly, and was much pleased to find that you were coming down in a short time. I shall feel unmingled pleasure in seeing you. I have no excuse to make for not writing you oftener. I am really ashamed of my conduct, and shall endeavor, for the future, to express my disapprobation of such behavior by a more frequent and regular correspondence.
> However, to let you know that I have not been altogether idle, I shall give you an account of what I have done this half-year. I have learned 100 Spelling, 42 Grammar, 42 Geography lessons and 20 Speeches, 180 verses in the Bible and 20 collects. I have also corrected 65 exercises, written 70 copies and worked about 300 sums; I have made out 42 pages of Merchants' Accounts, besides many other things occasionally, such as Reading, Catechism and Dictation.
> I have enjoyed unremitted health lately.
> I hope Mr. Cobbett will be able to give a very favourable account of my behaviour this half year. I have only to add that

it is my sincere wish that you, and also all my Dear Friends, may enjoy every possible blessing. Our friends here unite with me in kindest love to you all.

I remain, My Dear Mother,

Your dutiful and affectionate Son,

George Thomas

P.S. Mr. and Mrs. Cobbett present their most respectful compliments.

When young George Thomas was in his middle twenties, his family moved to London, Ontario, where they founded a bank. I did not recall the name of it, but I had a vivid recollection of visiting my mother's maiden cousin Nellie Emery, whose father had presided over the bank. She lived in a large gray stone house at 95 Ridout Street South with a back yard equipped with sandbox, slides, and all the trappings I needed to make the visit a success.

It was in London, Ontario, that my great-grandfather married his first wife, Emily Corrigan, whose family had come there from Dublin, where her father had been a professor at Dublin College. Not long after that the young couple moved to Connecticut, then to Detroit, and after that to Owosso, in 1869. At the time of my great-grandfather's death in 1899 it was reported that "his parents were both of time-honored lineage dating back to William the Conqueror; he was, as became his ancestry, a fine, courteous Christian gentleman, ever a friend of the poor and needy. He was prominently identified with the Church as Vestryman and Senior Warden for more than 60 years, being a member of Old St. Paul's, London, England; one of the first promoters of St. Paul's Cathedral, London, Canada, and also of Christ Church, Chatham; St. Paul's and St. John's, Detroit, and for the past 30 years in Christ Church, Owosso."

The obituary further reported: "In the business part of [Owosso] he was the earliest to venture large amounts of money in modern city-like business places, and thereby show his faith in the future of the City and at the same time helping to make it what he believed it would become. . . . [He] effected changes in West Owosso and built the fine Thomas block at the corner of Main and Washington Streets."

I knew about this Thomas block in great detail because his son, my maternal grandfather Alfred T. Thomas, inherited it. My mother was to inherit her share, and she bought out the balance. The shares descended to me at the time of her death in 1954.

Great-grandfather Thomas' personal life had a tragic side. His first wife Emily was killed when a railroad train struck the carriage in which she was riding. His second wife also died early and then, pursuant to a not uncommon custom of those times, he next married his first wife's sister Esther, the third Corrigan sister. The extraordinary aspect of all this is that he married two of the seven Corrigan daughters and his son and my grandfather married the youngest, Augusta Margaret.

My mother's father, Alfred Thomas, remained vividly in my memory. He was born on Christmas Day, 1850, in Chatham, Connecticut, moving with his parents in March 1869 to Detroit and to Owosso, where he lived for the rest of his life. After his marriage to Augusta Corrigan he struck out on his own, building his own general store on Main Street. Here was a wondrous place for a small boy in a small town—and here my first boyhood memories took shape, filled with the good things of life.

Here was the great round American cheese sitting on the counter, with slabs to be cut in whatever thickness the customer wanted. The great head cheese was next to it, and I always thought it a very poor substitute for good cheese. Even in those days there were canned goods and, of course, all the staples of life in the grocery department. The store was almost in the geographical center of the city and it had all kinds of overalls and work clothes for the factory workers who came in from the West Side and business clothing for the male residents of all parts of the city.

The cellar of the store extended out under the sidewalk and, to me, it was a mystic place. Eggs were stored there in waterglass for the periods of the year when fresh eggs were not coming in from the country. Since the store did not handle meats or many fresh products, the regular meats were stored in the cold room for family use. The fat goose was always hanging there at Christmastime.

My grandfather Thomas' pride and joy was the garden back of the store. It was an oasis of beauty, hidden entirely from Main Street by a row of additional stores he had built. It was crisscrossed by cinder paths and kept in a state of perfection by my grandfather. Whenever he was tired or troubled he went out and worked in the garden, tend-ing a profusion of all the flowers that would grow in Michigan, as well as strawberries, gooseberries, and many vegetables.

There were times when my grandfather was troubled greatly. Of the three major factories in Owosso, two were sharply affected by business cycles. The most stable was the Owosso Casket Factory, naturally enough. Then there was the somewhat larger factory that made screen doors in winter and snow shovels in summer. The largest was the Woodward Furniture Company, which waxed and waned in production in accordance with the demand for its products.

Probably all the factories together employed fewer than a thousand men, but it seemed to me that a good share of the men bought their staples at my grandfather's store, and he knew them all. When times were hard, none of them was ever turned away, whether he could pay or not. Wages were small, averaging probably less than three dollars a day, and few had any savings. It was not until 1914 that Henry Ford startled the world by his sensational announcement that he would pay factory workers five dollars a day. But my grandfather Thomas trusted these men he had known all his life and the relationship was close and personal. There were few who failed to pay their accounts when they were finally able to do so, but when the period of unemployment lasted unusually long, it was a strain and worry to this fine, gentle merchant.

We usually had Sunday dinner in my grandfather Thomas' home, my mother, my father, my mother's younger brother Peter, and I being the regulars. It was an affectionate, closely knit family, and these were happy Sunday afternoons. It is perhaps not surprising that the sharpest recollection of the only small boy there involved popcorn. After dinner, when the cook had cleared away the kitchen and we had all had a visit, Grandfather Thomas would go to the kitchen for the great, shining bread pail in which the homemade bread was kneaded. Then he would pop a mountain of popcorn, fill the bread pail, mix it with a lavish supply of melted butter, and make the afternoon complete.

I was born on March 24, 1902, in the second floor above Grandfather Thomas' store, where my mother could rest under the watchful care of her parents. I lived my early years in a comfortable Victorian home on Oliver Street. I was the only child.

There were shiny—well, tan would be the nearest color—banisters and stairs running to the second floor immediately on the right as we entered the hall, a nice, comfortable, old-fashioned hall with a coat closet and telephone. A chair and telephone stand were there, as was a radiator. On the left there was a parlor, which was, I suppose, maybe sixteen by sixteen feet. Next to the parlor with the old-fashioned doors that drew across on rollers when they were closed (though they almost never were) was the sitting room, which was about the same size.

Then, for a great many years, and I did not know just when it was built, there was a sunroom on the side which was accessible both from the sitting room and from the parlor. The parlor did not have particularly comfortable chairs in it, as was the nature of furniture in those days, and was very rarely used except when there were a whole lot of people around.

There was a dining room which was straight ahead as we walked through the hall. It was perhaps eleven or twelve feet wide by sixteen or eighteen feet long, with a big, old-fashioned, beautiful buffet at one end and an old-fashioned but quite charming delicate buffet at the other end. Beyond the dining room was the kitchen, and to the left of the kitchen and behind the living room was the bedroom that my mother and father used. Behind that room was the bath.

Upstairs was my bedroom on the right, and there were two other bedrooms on the left. Behind my bedroom was a bedroom always used by a maid. Then there was a little room in front of the bath, which was across the hall from the maid's door, and this room was always used as a storage room and there was a cot in it. When I was a small boy and the house was full, I moved in and slept on the cot a few times. It was hot in the middle of summer.

How many memories, and how long ago. Our home was always comfortable and it was a lovely atmosphere. I could not remember ever hearing my mother and father have an argument.

There were lots of family books, four bookcases in the house. There were very few current books, but all of the classics, Thackeray, Shakespeare, and the like. I remember specifically Cooper's *Leather-stocking Tales*. I also read Shakespeare one summer—just about everything he wrote.

My father read the *Congressional Record,* and he took great interest in it and read it quite faithfully. Sometimes he would quote from it, partly for the oratory and partly for the facts that can some-

times be gleaned from the *Record*. It seemed like a long chore but
the *Record* was not so long in those days. The sessions of Congress
were shorter and there was a limit to the business they had to transact,
and Congress moved with much greater speed through what there
was. In fact, they sat about three months, and this was all they
needed. In recent years Congress has spent most of its time holding
hearings that really had nothing to do with legislation.

Our normal family routine was that my father would leave the
house at a quarter to seven to walk to the office and would get there
at seven o'clock. He would walk home for lunch at twelve, and walk
home again at five or five-thirty, and we would have supper at six.
I think lunch was called dinner in those days. Then my mother and
father would sit around the living room reading the paper or talking
and sometimes friends would come in. On Saturday night they usually
played penny-ante poker with the Ellises and whoever else happened
to drop by. My father would occasionally play cards at the Elks Club
of an afternoon. I did not remember his going there evenings but he
must have, because he was active in the Elks and he became the
Exalted Ruler at one time.

With me, my father was patient and probably far too indulgent. If
there was work to be done, he insisted that it be good work and, as a
result of his lifetime in newspaper work, he had a strong sense for the
precise use of both the written and the spoken word. He was easy to
be with and I always felt close to him.

My mother adored her husband and kept a happy and comfortable
home. She did very little cooking but she was an excellent trainer of
cooks and she had the financial mind of the family. For me, she was
everything.

Nearly every boy in Owosso had a lawn to mow and other chores.
I also had to weed the garden, take care of the furnace, run errands,
and in the winter shovel snow off the long sidewalk. A daily chore was
to walk the two blocks to my uncle Edmund's home and bring back
a can of rich, warm, unpasteurized Jersey milk.

In addition I kept chickens. I cannot remember whether I started
this with parental encouragement or on my own. Anyway, it was a
mistake. My parents paid me for the eggs and chickens we used, and
I sold some to the neighbors, but I came to despise chickens and all
that was connected with them. If my mother or a neighbor wanted a
chicken, naturally the chicken had to be beheaded and plucked.

Naturally, too, there was nobody but me to do it. I was repelled by the problem of holding a fluttering chicken correctly, and chopping its head off. Plucking and cleaning the chicken were equally repulsive.

Then came the end. There were always some chicks coming along and once they all got lice. I had to pick up each chick and rub oil in it. In the process, I got chicken lice all over my arms, and I remembered for years the crawling sensation. I finally got deloused, but the impression of lice on the arms remained for days. This completely cured me of chickens and I managed to get rid of them for good, soon afterward.

Like most of the other boys in Owosso, I did my share of odd jobs. I worked as a printer's devil at the Owosso *Times* some of the time after grade school and on an occasional Saturday. My father paid me ten cents an hour, and I learned to set type by hand and to hand-feed a printing press. In order to have the imprint of the type perfectly even, there was always a need to cure irregularities in the bed of the press. After taking an initial impression, the fine art was to take a thin piece of paper and draw lines showing the areas where the imprint needed to be heavier. Then, cutting out the balance, putting the cut-out on the bed of the press, in due course, by trial and error, an even impression was produced all over the page.

A major adventure was the building of a tree house. The first one was a modest effort. Two friends and I managed to find the necessary boards and nails and we built a platform in the lower branches of a tree in our side yard. Our skill was not quite up to building sides for it, so we settled for borrowing some burlap bags and tacking them onto uprights we erected at the corners. We had a hideaway. Naturally our mothers viewed this whole business with a good deal of concern, and we were continually showered with warnings and precautions. These were well justified because a summer storm soon blew the whole tree house down. This was a serious blow. It hurt our pride and, moreover, our retreat from civilization had been destroyed. After many conferences we decided it was too late to start a new one that summer but that we would build a good one the next year.

The following spring we enlisted the help of more boys, and we moved the venture several blocks from home to an orchard at the Welch place, where we could build a sturdy, lasting house which would be a real refuge. This time it was a success. We found a good-sized tree and enough lumber to build a strong platform. Then we erected four corner posts and enclosed the house in strong and work-manlike fashion. Once done, it lasted all summer. The only trouble was that, having finished the job, we rarely bothered to go up into the tree house afterward.

My next effort at carpentry came a few years later when we were spending a vacation at a lake in Upper Michigan. There were no sail-boats on the lake, and I had an abiding passion to learn about sailing. The other boys had scant interest in the project, so I undertook it alone. The first step was to find a rowboat whose owner would let me erect a mast on it. This accomplished, it was no problem to find a pole that would serve as a mast and, before long, it was put up in the rowboat and held fast with stays. Then I needed a boom. Another, shorter pole served the purpose.

The sail was a more complicated problem, but a bedsheet finally offered the solution. It could be folded over and made into a passable three-corner sail. This accomplished, with an oar used as the rudder, our boat finally went to sea in a light breeze and it was one of the great thrills of my boyhood. Finally one or two of the others risked their lives going out with me and the summer was a success.

After that I spent a number of happy sailing trips in genuine sail-boats owned by others, but I never had my own again until many years afterward. During succeeding summers on the shores of Long Island I had a series of sloops, and I finally ended up with a 40-foot ketch which gave us a particularly happy summer. Then for four years in Tuxedo Park, New York, racing sailboats occupied almost all of our weekends with what was, in many respects, the most delightful of all sports.

Of course the winter brought a variety of delights. There were hills all around for sledding, and it seemed that we had frequent and deep snows in central Michigan. Near town there was Hopkins Lake which froze over early and stayed frozen all winter. When we could get it cleared of snow, people of all ages came out, often whole families together as in our case, bringing hot chocolate and sandwiches for a whole day of skating on the lake.

A favorite memory of Grandfather Thomas' store was Otto, the de-liveryman. It made no difference whether the rain was coming down in torrents, groceries had to be delivered. It made no difference whether the snow was two feet deep and still coming down, the horse could be hitched to the sleigh and deliveries could be made.

However much of a nuisance I must have been, Otto would always let me climb up on the front seat with him and make the rounds. Finally I learned how to hitch up and drive the horse, and got so I could be of help to Otto in making some of the deliveries.

I also remembered George Valentine, who lived in our house for many years. My mother always had a roomer, and that paid for the maid. Mr. Valentine was an extremely fine person, a bachelor, who lived there most of my youth, and he showed me how to make kites and helped me fly them. I had no gift for that sort of thing.

As the only child, however, it sometimes seemed there was so much to do in Owosso that it was never possible to be idle. There were no swimming pools in those days, but on the other side of town there was a railroad trestle which crossed the Shiawassee River at an elevation of approximately twelve feet. That was upstream of the city and above the waste of the city, which went into the river as it passed through. At the trestle the water flowed clean and deep, and that was where we all learned to dive and swim. We played cowboys and Indians, and one-o'-cat, and soon it was the Boy Scouts, tennis, and football.

Then there was Hallowe'en with all its exciting challenges. Trick or treat never reached Owosso, at least during my youth. Hallowe'en was the time to scout the places where there were still outhouses out back, and long before the day we had them all located. It was the one night of the year when the young roamed the town, writing in soap on the windows of householders and storekeepers and turning over every outhouse we had the time and energy to reach. Nobody seemed to protest too much about this outburst. It happened only once a year and there was no juvenile delinquency in Owosso.

The circus was a great annual event and it came to Owosso, as I recall it, many times. We always used to have free tickets which the circus advance agent gave to the newspaper editors in the community, in exchange for good space in which to announce the fact that the circus was coming. This was the old-time practice, so we always had tickets. I used to get up early in the morning to go out and watch them unloading, bringing the elephants off, one by one, along with the cages of lions and other wild animals, the many horses, and the steam calliope.

You've never seen a circus parade through a small town? They would parade some—probably all—of the elephants, some giraffes, a cage or two of lions and tigers, and they would have some clown cavorting along the side, and one float with clowns on it. The parade was several blocks long.

The circus itself was almost anticlimax, but the lure, the drama, persist to this day. The whole town turned out for it. I did not see how anybody could be jaded with circuses and not come.

The Fourth of July was the only event that rivaled the circus. There were no laws against fireworks in those days and everything went, firecrackers, torpedoes, even lighted snakes which wiggled across the sidewalk as they burned up. Usually there was a great celebration at the county fairgrounds with a wonderful display of fireworks following the patriotic speeches. The Fourth of July was not scorned in those days. It was an opportunity to see and hear the leading speakers of public life, as well as to enjoy fireworks and see all the friends and neighbors.

The one terrible event of my boyhood in Owosso was the tornado, on November 11, 1911. It stopped the clock in my grandfather Thomas' store at eleven minutes after eleven o'clock on the eleventh day of the eleventh month in the eleventh year of the century.

To me, at the age of nine, the tornado was highly personal. It missed our own neighborhood, so our first knowledge of it came when my grandfather and grandmother Thomas staggered into our house in the middle of the night. She had been badly hurt. A brick had fallen on her, and would have hit her squarely in the temple, but she always slept with one arm over her head, and the brick hit her arm instead of her face. Their bedroom was on the southwest corner of the building, in the back, and that whole corner, the roof and the side walls, had been blown right off by the tornado.

Then, of course, the water had poured in torrents through the whole store, and I had no idea at that age whether they had insurance against that sort of damage. But they finally gathered themselves together, got out of the wreckage, walked the mile to our house, and came in. This upset the whole family terribly.

The tornado was a terrifying event. It did great damage in Owosso. Nobody had ever seen anything like the tornado before and there were dire forebodings.

Not two years afterward, on February 14, 1913, my grandfather Thomas died. His obituary read: "Rarely ever has a community been more shocked than Wednesday morning when the news passed quickly over the city that Albert T. Thomas had passed away very suddenly. . . . Few men in the City commanded the confidence of the community to as large a degree as did the deceased, his word was never questioned, his motives never impugned, and in his quiet way he built up a trade that was loyal to him at all times."

We had no warning that my grandfather Thomas, my great friend, was ill. The loss left a void in my life and for the first time I sensed what it meant to lose an admired and beloved relative.

My grandmother lived eight years longer. She died at sixty-nine.

The University Spreads Over
Michigan Like a Great Oak Tree

My mother in later years played a good game of golf, an excellent game of bridge, a skillful hand at the stock market, and she used to love out-of-town shopping trips to New York. Sometimes when a saleswoman acted confused about being asked to send a package to Owosso, it amused Mother to explain very rapidly: "Why, don't you know Owosso? It's in Shiawassee County on the Shiawassee River."

Owosso lies in the eastern Midwest, about halfway between Detroit and Chicago, halfway between the manufacturing center of Flint and the state capital at Lansing. It rests in a gently rolling plain, a rich agricultural landscape. Its population, some 8,000 when I was born in 1902, has since more than doubled.

Owosso was a lovely, balanced, well-planned small city with wide streets lined, in the residential sections, by beautiful rows of maple trees. There was comparatively little industry, and when the automobile came along it became accessible to all the people of an extensive farming region.

As we grew into our teens the boys in Owosso worked very hard indeed, even those who were fairly well off, like the Storers. That family had a very nice clothing store in town and the boys worked in the store just as I worked in the print shop.

When I was eleven I took a considerable step forward and managed to obtain the agency for distributing the Curtis Publishing Company magazines in Owosso. This all began when somebody else had the agency and I started out as one of his salesmen. When the *Saturday Evening Post* arrived in town, I think on a Thursday, I would go down and get mine. I developed some customers. I remembered trying to sell a *Ladies' Home Journal* subscription to the president of the furniture factory once. He was exceedingly pleasant but he kept on saying no. I could not understand why he kept on saying no when he was so pleasant about it. When the *Country Gentleman* came to town I would pick that up and sell it too.

This had been going on for two years when the agent gave it up, and I got the agency at the age of eleven. I thought things could be expanded, and I soon had ten or twelve boys working for me selling Curtis magazines throughout Owosso. In fact I was able to pay my first year's expenses at the University of Michigan with the $800 I saved on this job. For a while I had the agency for the Detroit *News* as well.

The first time I left Owosso on my own I went to Chicago to testify at a hearing involving the Curtis Publishing Company's contracts with local agents. The government was suing them for violation of the anti-trust laws and the company picked a number of agents around the country to testify. I was one of those picked. I remember a great problem was how I could go without being marked absent from school. My mother was very proud of an extraordinary record she had made. In twelve years I was never once late or absent from school. But the problem was solved when the teacher suggested that the class elect me as a delegate to go and "observe" the Chicago hearings.

One Christmas vacation I worked in the sugar factory. The first job I had there was washing windows, until I fell off a ladder and sprained my ankle, after which I was put in the stockroom. The factory operated during an intensive period while the sugar beets were plentiful. When the beets were used up the factory was closed down. It was not a full year's operation. I remembered that in Owosso, in the center of important sugar beet territory, anybody who was not for protecting the sugar beet industry with sensible tariffs would have been ridden out of town on a rail. This was a cardinal principle of Republican policy in those days. In fact the Democrats talked about free trade, but when they got in in 1913 they did not seem to do very much about it. Since then we have had the most curious reversal—it is Republicans who believe in world trade and Democrats in the restriction of imports, at least in philosophical direction.

From the age of eleven I knew it was a principle that I was to earn my own spending money and I never had to ask for any.

My mother had this sense about investing. Her sister and brothers had all been away when the three stores on Main Street were left to the four of them jointly. My mother bought out the others at an appraised value and over many years the stores increased in value substantially. She managed them herself to the extent of finding a new tenant if one moved out, collecting the rent, talking about fixing the roof, negotiating who was going to pay for putting in a new front or repairing a leaky wall—all these things she handled in part even while my father was alive. I am sure he did some things, but it was no chore for my mother to take on their full management when he died in 1927 because she had really been in charge all along.

Then, too, she had always invested funds in securities. She had income from the stores, surplus over their living expenses, and she invested this in common stocks. The sum involved was not large, probably $7,000 or $8,000, but she was interested and had the good sense to invest and not just put it in the savings bank. Once, before the Depression, she got on a sucker list of some boilerplate people who used to operate out of New York and sell gold mining stocks. She bought some, and they kept going up and up, and they kept calling and telling her to buy more. And she sold before the stock disappeared.

My mother came from a family of entrepreneurs and my father from a family of intellectuals. They had totally different gifts.

Politics, thanks to my father, was as natural a part of our home as eating and sleeping. It seemed there was always an impending visit for a meal or longer from the Republican candidate for governor or senator, and Congressman Fordney was a regular. So was Chase Osborn, one of the fine Michigan governors, a pioneer leader among conservationists and a close friend of the family. To me he was "Uncle Chase" and in later years we carried on a lively correspondence. Our visitors never seemed to object to the presence of a boy in the room, and I spent many days and evenings listening to the great men talk about such faraway subjects as legislation in the Congress and foreign affairs.

Our own county affairs were not much discussed. County affairs were always sort of in hand. I do not believe that my father, in his races for the county Board of Supervisors, was ever once defeated. I think Mr. Seegmuller, who lived a block away, ran against him once or twice, which caused a slight strain in good neighborly relations, and my family never held Mr. Seegmuller in high regard, probably for that reason. He was the chairman of the Democratic Party in Shiawassee County.

Music, the theater, painting, and the arts were not generally a conspicuous part of life in Owosso. Neither of my parents was especially musical, but my mother was determined that I should learn to play the piano. So from the age of seven until I was fourteen I walked all the way across town once a week to take lessons from an aging German piano teacher. I practiced an hour a day, not always willingly, but such skill as I acquired later turned out to be pleasant and useful.

It was in my uncle Edmund Dewey's home that I first heard an early Victrola, the revolutionary invention which brought sound recordings to Owosso and the rest of the world. It was a marvelous experience, and I still recall the thrill of the quartet from *Rigoletto,* the sextet from *Lucia,* and of the great voices of our time, Caruso, Melba, Schumann-Heink and, ultimately, Chaliapin. While my uncle was not particularly musical, his wife, Aunt May, was, and she and her companion put up with my desire to hear their records over and over.

My cousin Harriet was the only child of the Edmund Deweys and we were raised almost as brother and sister, although she was three years older than I. It was at their home that we had Sunday night suppers, Victrola music, games, and singing around the piano. Harriet continuously put up with her bumptious younger cousin with unique and endearing tolerance and charity.

Occasionally the miscalled "Broadway cast" of a play would come to the Opera House, and finally motion pictures arrived in Owosso. These were not exactly a cultural influence, and my most vivid recollection is of the serials. Each showing would end with the heroine in a dreadful plight, and we had to hold our breath for a whole week until she was saved in the next installment.

I have warm remembrances of Chautauqua. I went to practically all performances of this grand American institution, in the afternoons and evenings, and we sought cultural distractions as our people had down the years of our history. My uncle and father were sponsors of the Chautauqua in Owosso. Sponsors had to get together and agree to put up, raise, or see to it that the Chautauqua received a certain number of subscriptions so that we could bring in the talents from the outside. They were always on the sponsoring committee, and usually there was a business meeting after one of the Chautauqua sessions. I remember my father speaking at two or three of them on a point of debate about the finances, speaking with intensity and great vigor.

It was wonderful. We had lots of music, some humorists, some orators. Chautauqua was a fine institution and I was sorry to see it fade out.

Of course, television later brought a good part of the old-time Chautauqua into our homes. Once, many years afterward, I happened to walk into a room and find my oldest son Tom looking at television and thoroughly enjoying an old-time vaudeville show. There was Jerry Mahoney, a superb, imaginative, clever, attractive act, followed by a man with two trained bears, followed by a juggler who was exceedingly good. Then the ventriloquist came on again. It was a half-hour show and certainly the old-fashioned entertainers never produced in thirty minutes anything as fast-moving or sophisticated as this was.

All those years in Owosso we went to church every Sunday morning—to the Episcopal church. My mother's father and mother used to walk all the way from the store up to Washington Street and then up Washington Street to the church twice every Sunday, fifty-two weeks of the year. They never took a vacation that I can remember, although I think they did go and visit relatives two or three times. Our branch of the family went to church just on Sunday mornings.

When I was confirmed in the Episcopal church, probably at thirteen or fourteen, my father also was confirmed. He became a vestryman and was one for the rest of his life. He took up the collection and I began to sing in the choir. I sang from before I was in high school until my voice changed. Then I sang as a bass.

My mother was a devout Episcopalian. My father never discussed religion much, and I would not say there were many religious discussions in our family. It was one of those things we took for granted, not a subject of controversy or analysis. It was assumed, as it was assumed sometimes that all good people were Republicans. It was a matter of learning what was in the Bible, which one takes on faith, and that was the total of it.

Washington, of course, was awfully remote from Owosso, and Europe was even more so. To my father and to many others, I think that the coming of the First World War was a bolt from the blue, something of a betrayal by a Democratic President who had just been re-elected on the grounds that he had kept us out of war. International affairs just did not penetrate in those days and were disposed of with fairly simple clichés. There was no radio, and if newspaper coverage of foreign affairs then was no better than it was even after the Second World War, it would have astonished me if there had been any comprehension of the world outside.

In retrospect, it was amazing that the American people could reach as many sound decisions on foreign affairs as they did in the twentieth century in view of the inadequacy of real information. But in the 1910s anything foreign was as remote as Mars, and Europe was a place you took a trip to if you had enough money, and that was a precarious venture then.

So 1918 was a distant war. The draft was felt, as was rationing. We went without sugar on our oatmeal, voluntarily as I remember. Fuel shortages did not impinge because we did not own a car. George Valentine, our roomer, owned a car. I think it was an old Studebaker. I was too young to go to war, sixteen years old, in the summer of 1918.

When the call came for boys to enlist in the Boy Volunteers, to work on the farms, I joined up. It was a national program, and a good one. The Boy Volunteers was set up to solicit student help in running the farms because there was a shortage of manpower. In due course I was assigned to help a farmer named Earl Putnam, in Ovid, Michigan, not far from home. My family took me there in George Valentine's car and my war effort began.

I must admit it was quite a shock—up at four in the morning, which I had never done in my life. We cleaned the stable, milked the cows, and fed the horses and hogs. Then we went in to breakfast. Earl Putnam read a chapter of the Bible to his wife and me after breakfast, which consisted of an enormous four or five eggs apiece, ham, toast or bread, and coffee. After the Bible was read, we went out and I hitched up the horses.

On my first day out, I rode a roller which was about eight feet long, two feet in diameter, made of steel and extremely rough, but it was a way to flatten the ground to prepare it for seeding. I wrote a postcard to my family:

Dear Folks: Its 8:00 P.M. and am thru chores. He has 3 cows, 4 horses and 18 pigs—large and small. Rode a roller this P.M. and the woman who went to the M.D. for a corn cure after riding 500 miles in a Henry had nothing on me now. Tomorrow I do it all day. . . . Lots to eat and pretty good but not like home, however. Tried to milk a bossy tonight and got milk. (Thats all I can say.) Can hitch and unhitch a team of horses. Putnam drilled beans in the ground. I rolled and have to roll it all over again Fri. and some more too. Bed has plenty blankets. You win on the napkins but they have tablecloth. His wife is quite nice and kind all right. Will write again next week. Great stuff—this farming. T.E.D.

After the Friday rolling, I wrote again to my family:

Dear Folks: Time same—Fri P.M. Last night I found out how hard one bed could be. My mattress is straw and immediately on sitting on the bed we find out how hard the slats are. The springs might just as well be in Hong Kong. Slept well, however, as long as they sleep out here. Rode the roller all day today, that is, all the time I was not in the air directly above it. Farm machinery sometimes has a seat which is iron. I found out today that iron is the hardest metal on earth. I am sitting down very carefully this P.M. I also renewed my acquaintance with Old Sol. My hands are a glorious red, and the wind and heat decorated my mug some, too. I didn't know so many rocks could collect on one plot of ground. I did 16 acres today. Out here I am Mr. Dewey, Ovid R.F.D.No 1.

Next I learned to ride the cultivator and cultivate the corn. You had to guide the horse and take care that you stayed on the right path. That had to be precise. You had to get the horse in the right path and the cultivator in the right path or else they would dig up the corn which had been planted. In that case, you had better go home quick. I remember the first day it rained. I unhitched the cultivator and went back to the farm. Earl Putnam asked me: "Why "

I said: "I thought we didn't work when it rained."

He replied: "We do."

So I went back to the field and went on cultivating, and I never went home again when it rained.

We went through the harvesting when the combine came around, and we harvested the oats on our farm. Oats and barley can itch almost more than anything else. It was a general farm, with cash crops —wheat, corn, and oats—in addition to the livestock, and there were also chickens, which were the prerogative of Mrs. Putnam and her daughter who, as I recall, was deaf.

Earl Putnam and I were the only males on the place in the summer of 1918. His son was away and it was a big job. I got thirty dollars a month for it, and I got to go home on Saturday night and stay through Sunday and back to the farm Sunday night. It was not what you might call an idyllic summer. It was full of exhausting work, but I liked it, and learned a lot, and I suppose this was where I got my love of farming and dairy cattle first hand.

On Saturdays before going home for the weekend, I would take the weekly bath in the kitchen, in an iron tub filled with water we had pumped by hand and heated on the stove. I was to visit the Putnams many, many times over the years, because they became my lifelong friends, and they were among the finest people I ever met. And I was glad to see they finally got hot water, bathtub, and full bathroom facilities inside the house. And they did not read the Bible any more at breakfast.

Toward the end of that wartime summer I wrote another postcard to my family:

> Dear Folks: Went last night to hear an Australian Artillery officer who is just out of a British hospital. He has been wounded nine times and his right arm is gone. He is on his way home.

And as family, friends, and acquaintances increasingly were called to service, the war was coming closer to home. After the American Army got into heavy fighting in the summer and early fall, the casualties began to be reported and it was close indeed. I remember some gruesome stories about our casualties and the way the reporting was handled so atrociously. I remember one in particular about somebody who lived a block or two from us in Owosso. A reporter called a woman, told her that her son was dead, and asked her if she had any comment. He had gotten the news before she did and this was the first she knew. Everybody in town was very unhappy about that.

But on November 11, 1918, the eleventh day of the eleventh month, World War I ended.

From the fall of 1915 until the summer of 1919, along with most of my friends, I attended high school in our combined Central School in Owosso. It was the high school for the whole city. I stood eighth in my class, an achievement which was not particularly distinguished. Wilbur Dyer was ahead of me together with six girls. Margaret Reineke was No. 1. She was the brightest person in our class throughout the whole four years.

On the high school faculty, Hazel Goodrich, in English, I remember well. She was a lovely, sharp, redheaded, very attractive girl, no more than five or at the most ten years older than the students. She married C. C. Tuck, who became the principal in my senior year.

Then there was Leon J. Carr in manual training. He was there all the time I was in high school and, as I had no gifts in that field, I found manual training difficult. Somehow I managed to do the necessary things, such as carving out a platter, which has been in my house for all the years I can remember after that. I think it was in my senior year, perhaps junior, that I made a porch swing which was hung out on our front porch. It stayed there until it collapsed when three of us sat in it during either the 1940 or 1944 presidential campaign. It was one of those rigid, frame, wooden porch swings which hang from the roof by two chains.

Louise Worden, in music, was a very nice, very attractive girl. There was an earlier music teacher I disliked so intensely I never opened my mouth while she was there. But Louise Worden was wonderful.

I remember the superintendent of schools, M. W. Longman, and O. H. Voelker was the principal who became superintendent after Longman resigned. Longman was a tall, serious man without too much personality. Voelker was a more impressive, vital person. The new principal, C. C. Tuck, whom I have already mentioned, was a great big stooping bulldog of a man, strong and, I think, able.

Montie McFarlane was the football coach. I played left tackle. For the rest of my life I have been able to show where a tooth got knocked out playing football, as I have had a peg ever since I was sixteen years old. I stood five feet eight inches, and it was a bit hazardous to be a left tackle. But I did enjoy the game.

Debating I enjoyed, and Miss Goodrich showed great wisdom in requiring debaters to stand before the audience with notes, not with memorized and canned speeches. The graduation yearbook ribbed me: "First in the Council Hall to steer the State/And ever foremost in a tongue debate." At any rate, I enjoyed it.

I remember with pleasure the junior and senior plays, the minstrel shows of 1918 and 1919, the cadet corps, and the sleigh rides out to Clayton Cook's house. His father was a farmer and a prominent one later on, active in the state and national Grange. Clayton Cook took over the farm and he married Margaret Reineke. I did not enjoy editing the yearbook *Spic*. This was an awful chore. I remember the great problems of getting copy in and keeping that stray and ill-assorted group of people at work to produce a good magazine. I had a bad time with that. It came out all right but it was a lot of hard work, a lot of pulling and hauling. I also played the E-flat bass horn in the band. I think the instrument belonged to the school and I never had it at home.

In June 1919 I graduated. The speaker was the Rev. Ernest B. Allen, of Oak Park, Illinois, and his title was "Service, the Goal of Life." He devoted himself to a discussion about low salaries for teachers, illiteracy among immigrants, the northward trek of Negroes, and he endorsed the League of Nations. Everything changes, but it's always the same.

This last year in high school was the prelude to one of the most exciting trips I would ever take in my life. My grandmother Thomas lived with us after her husband died, and we were devoted to one another. With her rich, cultured Irish accent and her wonderful sense of humor, she was a joy to be with. Moreover, she spoiled me rotten and I loved her company. She had promised to take me to California as a graduation present, to visit two of her other children, my aunt Emily Warren and my uncle George I. Thomas. Unhappily, we lost her in the early spring, after a sudden, massive heart attack. This was a deep tragedy, and I gave no more thought to the trip to California. After all, we had planned it together, and without her it would not be fun any more. But my parents decided that I should get to know the California branch of the family, and they sent me anyway, and on my own.

This was sheer romance, in the summer of 1919, traveling nearly five thousand miles alone. Following the train trip to Chicago and the traditional layover, I got on the train for Los Angeles. It was a three-day trip, long and hot and wearing, but it was blessedly interrupted. Since there were no dining cars, we stopped three times a day for half an hour, for breakfast, lunch, and dinner, at the Harvey houses along the route.

The Great Plains seemed endless, the deserts equally endless, and the mountains of California were a glorious relief. At Los Angeles my aunt Emily Thomas Warren and her husband met me at the train, and there followed a month of joy in the San Bernardino Mountains with them and their three children Tom, Eleanor, and Florence. This was my first meeting with these three cousins I have cherished ever since. Tom was to develop a thriving business in Los Angeles and, perhaps because we were almost the same age and had similar interests, I felt very close to him. Incidentally, of all Alfred Thomas' grandchildren, he and I were the only males.

The Warrens took me in as a member of the family. I had never been in mountains before, and I had never spent days and nights outdoors hunting and sleeping by streams. Nothing had prepared me for drawing lines in the hope of preventing rattlesnakes from coming in and sleeping close in, which they did because the nights were chilly.

It was a wonderful world, and there were a lot of people around. We went hiking, caught our trout, cooked our meals, did some shooting, and the Warrens had an aged Hupmobile. It was just one of those glowing experiences.

Then I visited Riverside, California, which was hotter than the hinge of Hades. My father's sister Hannah lived there with her husband, Dr. Howard S. Reed. The University of California's experiment station was there, and he was the resident biologist and professor of biology. He was experimenting with mice at the time and was also running experiments designed to prevent the freezing of oranges during winter cold spells. He was a quiet, thoughtful character, and I enjoyed his company very much even though Riverside was the hottest place I had ever visited. It was over a hundred degrees in the shade on a good many days, and this was a new and unwelcome experience.

From Riverside we went off for a week at La Jolla, on the northern outskirts of San Diego. It was then a modest summer resort with small cottages which college professors could afford. I swam in the ocean, saw sting rays and all the phenomena along the Pacific coast, and went mackerel fishing off a long dock. While the mackerel were running, we could pull them in on occasion, one on each of three hooks on the same line. My uncle Howard used to salt the mackerel down for the winter.

I had never seen an ocean before.

Going to the University of Michigan in the late summer of 1919 seemed like just one of those things, like going on from second year to third year in high school. It was the state university. One or two boys in Owosso had gone to Eastern schools. I remember the son of the leading lawyer, Pulver, went to Princeton, but that was regarded as a little strange and effete. Michigan was the normal thing to do for those of us who were going to college, except those who were going to become farmers, and they went to the State Agricultural College, later known as Michigan State University.

In those days Michigan played Michigan State as a warm-up game, and it was just a question of how many of their men they could give a chance to play, and whether they would beat Michigan State by fifty or seventy-five points. Now, of course, Michigan State wipes the earth with our University of Michigan.

My uncle Henry and aunt Hannah were graduates of the university. My cousin Harriet was there ahead of me. I think she quit after about two years. She had a good deal of trouble with her eyes. She had worn glasses ever since she was a girl, and her eyes got extremely tired. Academic work was not her particular strength anyway. She was just a terrific mother and wife.

Then, of course, I had friends from Owosso High School who were there the year before. Everybody in Michigan knew all sorts of people who had been to the university ahead of him, from boys a year ahead in high school to the family doctor, to the neighbor across the street. The University of Michigan spread over Michigan like a great oak tree.

I had visited the campus before. The costs did not intrude on me much. The curriculum in the School of Literature, at least, was pretty much an extension in the beginning of high school French, English, history, and mathematics. It did not seem like a very hard life. So the result was that I took on too much, as I was to do all my life. I had already entered the School of Music for weekly voice lessons and daily practice. This led naturally to my joining the Glee Club. The Michigan *Daily* seemed like a continuation of work with which I was familiar from the Owosso *Times,* and I became a reporter, covering the Law School and writing some reviews of concerts.

It was natural, in this context, that I should be pledged to the national musical fraternity, Phi Mu Alpha (Sinfonia), which at Ann Arbor was a general house at that time. I had done some singing around and because of the usual way people will say something nice to anybody who even tries to sing—well, it seemed to be a good idea, so I enrolled in the voice department with William Wheeler. He immediately took me into the Methodist church choir at Ann Arbor and, curiously enough, his lessons were seven dollars and fifty cents each, and the Methodist choir paid me that precise fee.

Bill Wheeler was a tenor. His wife Bess was a soprano. Doris Howe was the contralto. That was our quartet. Doris was a student in the School of Music. She had a beautiful, low contralto voice and she was a statuesque woman in every respect with no temperament whatsoever that I knew of. Some twenty years afterward I had a letter from her indicating that she was assistant superintendent of a ladies' home, or something like that.

In fact I got a good deal of encouragement from people, to the point where I began to consider singing as a possible career. You know, the glamorous chance to be an opera or concert singer is attractive to anybody who has any flair for it. But, looking back, I feel that people probably should not have encouraged me because my range was not quite big enough. It was just barely two octaves. I was neither a bass nor a baritone. I was a *basso cantante.* I did not really have any great gifts as a musician. I was a fairly good singer of songs.

To judge from the notices I got after singing in student concerts, I guess I had a gift as a performer, which is perhaps not unrelated to being a trial lawyer. Moreover, I liked to sing. The musicianship was another matter.

It was enough, I suppose, that I could keep time and pitch and read music. I had studied piano for seven years, so I had a certain amount of the musical discipline, but I never took any musical theory, or orchestral work, or composition. In any event, I worked for at least an hour a day in a studio at the School of Music in addition to my music lesson. I had Wheeler all the way through the University of Michigan, all four years.

Bill was a very husky fellow, a robust five foot eleven maybe, a little on the fat side, a genuine tenor and not a robust tenor. He had a rather thin, lyric tenor voice, and he was the sort of fellow who sang beautifully. Bill had good musicianship, but I do not think anybody ever had a thrill go up his spine as a result of Bill's singing, and that really is essential to greatness. Therefore, Bill did the right thing to come out and teach at the University of Michigan, and he was a good teacher as well as a very good friend for many years. Bill and Bess Wheeler entertained at their house and it was always a joy to go out there for a visit with them and a musical evening.

Voice work is a problem of learning how to place your voice and make the right kind of sounds, give the sounds the right kind of float—also how to modulate the voice so it can give colorations and meanings, a variety of tone textures, as well as learning the languages. I sang in French, Italian, German, and a little Russian. I sang the Jewish holiday services in Yiddish, and that was no problem. It was close enough to German. I just had to go over it once and it would be all right.

Without using any pressure, Bill and Bess Wheeler both encouraged me to pursue a career as a singer. They both thought better of concert work than opera, but made no great point of it. Flattering reviews of the occasional concert in which I was involved gave a further push in this direction and in my senior year I was invited to sing a concert on Station WWJ, a pioneer radio station in Detroit, with its own studio symphony. Perhaps my greatest thrill as a singer came during the rehearsal, when the hardened musicians of the orchestra applauded in their own fashion, with the violinists tapping their bows on the music stands. This was heady wine for a twenty-year-old amateur.

The annual tour of the Glee Club gave us all a welcome respite and a chance to visit a variety of cities under pleasant circumstances. The Michigan Opera took an even wider tour. It was wholly written by students each year, and its obvious inadequacies were to some extent compensated for by the enthusiasm of the all-male cast and a first-class professional director.

I remember taking part in one opera—*Top o' the Mornin'*. The role I had was that of a pretender to an Irish throne. There were four

Irishmen in the opera of whom I was one—four Irish principals. Years later I heard one of the songs from that opera sung in something the Flint Club in Michigan did, a kind of review of my life. It was nice to hear that song again. I do not think I was in another opera but I was in altogether too much at the University of Michigan.

Toward the spring of 1923, I was entered as a contestant in the state-wide State of Michigan Singing Contest and I won it. Then I traveled to Asheville, North Carolina, for the national contest of the forty-eight state winners, in which I came out third. I had a delightful three days in Asheville and got back to Ann Arbor just in time to attend my graduation from the School of Literature. I sang the solo from *The Pilgrim's Song* before my class, and my parents, in the Hill Auditorium.

The University of Michigan was my first time out in the wide world. I had had the summer in California but these were the first years living in a college, in a so-called academic atmosphere. Certainly no fraternity house is a very academic atmosphere but it seemed like it at the time.

Sinfonia had several athletes and very high academic standing and a number of people who were musicians. In the five or ten years before I was there, they had very fine standing on the campus. They were not as good after I joined them, although I do not know why. As a freshman, I took the hazing. I did not like it very much but I took it. The initiation involved what was called Hell Week, one long night of stunts in which they put you through all kinds of paces, but they were not impossible. I did not remember having much interest in it. It was a little juvenile, the whole business.

As sophomores, we saw to it that the freshmen behaved and did extra chores. I took part as a sophomore in the freshman-sophomore games. We kidnaped Harry Kipke, who was the biggest football player on the campus, up and coming. We held him out in a house in the country overnight so that he would not be in the games against us.

Bull sessions were a substantial feature of life at the fraternity house, but one of the evils of the fraternity house was that we lived fairly limited lives. Our social life was largely confined to our own house, and there it tended to some extent to seek the lowest level. In the conversations around the house, the interest was not very often in literature, philosophy, art, history, or world affairs. Even World

War I, just over, was remote now, and we were going to have the world safe for democracy.

The three o'clock sessions in the fraternity house, when they did occur, were likely to be bull sessions or poker, and they were likely to be on a Friday or Saturday night. By Sunday night everybody had gotten a little scared about the condition of his homework, and the place was rather quiet.

At the university, I think I had about a B average. I forget whether it was a B plus or B minus, but it would not have been lower on the average than B.

I took a course in *Hamlet* which I enjoyed enormously. A young instructor from Harvard, who had unlimited enthusiasm for Shakespeare, taught *Hamlet* with great gusto, and this was contagious. I took a year or two of French, which I always liked. Languages were comparatively easy for me. I took accounting, which was a little dreary. I always liked playing with figures, but accounting and figures were not always the same.

The course that stood out the most in my three years in the School of Literature was a course in fine arts, which was the most dramatic and colorful lecture series I ever attended. The instructor was a man named "Fine Artie" Cross. I think he left later on for personal reasons. I took the course because it was what we used to call a "pipe" in those days, roughly meaning a cinch, but it turned into the most interesting course I took. Cross could really encourage students with little understanding or background to get really interested in Praxiteles. He could make the life of Leonardo da Vinci and the variety of his achievements a matter of living interest.

I studied comparative religion for one year. I loved it, and I have sort of followed it ever since. The more I got into it, the more my interest grew. For example, there was a fellow named Robert Borden Reams, who was in our consular service for many years. When I was in Calcutta in the 1950s, he was our consul general there. He and his wife met us at the airport, gave us a dinner that evening, and took us around. He was very generous with his time. And the more time we spent with him, the more impressive he became. Calcutta was generally regarded as one of the most difficult posts in the world, but he was perfectly willing to serve another three years there because he was studying the Hindu religion. He was totally absorbed by it, and totally dismayed because, the more he studied it, the less he found in it, and the more dismaying he found it as an alleged religion.

Reams was fascinating on the subject and on the way the Indians were rewriting their history. The Black Hole of Calcutta was being reversed, even. The Indian government was rewriting the whole history of India, making it the reverse of the way the British wrote it— the same as the Russians had done with their story in recent years.

We studied the Moslem religion, but I do not recall ever learning that, to Mohammed, Jesus was a saint, which made it a little more curious that so many holy wars were fought between the Moslems and the Christians.

Nothing was taught about the Mormon religion, however, which I had always found extremely interesting. I thought the Mormons had probably the highest set of standards of any religion that I was familiar with, and they were certainly fine people. I did not know any finer people than Mormons. By and large they were really religious—even the so-called "Jack Mormon." He was a "Jack Mormon" because he did not observe some of the requirements of the religion. He would drink coffee, or tea, or Coca-Cola, or a cocktail, or whiskey, all of which were technically forbidden. I did not believe it was any longer required of the true Mormon that he bathed with his underwear on for fear of exposing his body.

The insistent advice of my aunt Grace that I become a lawyer was not forgotten and so, without a firm decision on the subject, I included in my academic work the courses required for admission to the University of Michigan Law School at the end of my third year in the School of Literature. That would make it possible for me to be graduated with a B.A. degree at the end of the fourth year, with one year of law completed.

As a reporter for the Michigan *Daily,* I had been covering the Law School and had met Dean Bates. He raised the point that his roommate at the university had been my uncle Henry. But I never took a course from Dean Bates when I was in the School of Law because he taught constitutional law, and I was too young to take that.

The Law School was graduate school and here I really did my homework, and I enjoyed it. I was still doing too much on the outside, but it was quite a different atmosphere. For example, the Law School pursued the case method wholly. This was the system used by the Harvard Business School. This method certainly made me think in terms of acute application of the law to factual situations, and this is the only real preparation for the law there is.

The law professors I had were pretty good, particularly some of the younger ones. A couple of the older ones were bored, I thought. Grismore in contracts was excellent. I never found the study of property particularly interesting. The rules of real property were dull, almost scrivener's work. It was this vast, dreary business of checking over every technical defect, just metes and bounds, the whole history of the title, which was not exciting legal work. I did a fair amount of it, but it was never anything but dull after I learned how.

Also, common law pleading was pretty much out of date to some extent even then, and it was more of an intellectual exercise, not particularly fun.

But criminal law and procedure—that had a little more sparkle. There was quite a difference in it. I thought I would be interested in becoming a trial lawyer. There were many rules in the conduct of criminal law, many things that you could do and could not do, and these we learned. It was sort of like learning to read or write—and from there on you became a criminal lawyer or you did not. You learned how to lay the foundation but not yet how to build the cathedral.

All these four years at the University of Michigan, I had been studying voice at the school with Bill Wheeler, and all four years I had been singing bass in the quartet at the Methodist church. It had been a long time, and now there was a sudden opportunity.

Before coming to Ann Arbor, Bill Wheeler had been a student of one of the master voice teachers of his time, Percy Rector Stephens of New York. The Stephens studio had produced distinguished singing artists, including Reinald Werrenrath and Paul Althouse of the Metropolitan Opera, Jeanette Vreeland, and others. Wheeler thought Stephens was the finest of all teachers, and in the summer of 1923, Stephens was planning to go to Chicago to give a master class. This meant that former Stephens students, singing or teaching voice in other parts of the country, were to come to Chicago for what might be called refresher courses. The Wheelers urged me to go there for the summer.

This offered real adventure for me. My parents were agreeable, though I suspected their attitude toward my musical aspiration really was "Let Tom get it out of his system."

At the same time, my mother's cousin, Leonard Reid, was a member of the Chicago law firm, Litzinger, Healy and Reid. My parents thought it would be a good idea if I could divide my time between studying voice at the Stephens studio and working in Leonard Reid's law office. Nobody expected me to be of much use in law since I had only finished my first year at the Law School but at least it would keep me out of mischief.

When I arrived at the Stephens studio in Chicago the first news I heard was that there was to be a contest for a scholarship. I entered it on the spot and soon found myself the happy possessor of a complete scholarship for the summer season.

It was many years later that I learned that a beautiful young lady who was also studying voice at the Stephens studio was one of the judges for the scholarship. Her name was Frances Hutt, and it turned out that this was a fateful meeting.

I also enjoyed my time with Litzinger, Healy and Reid. Leonard Reid was my favorite collateral relative on all counts. He was a delightful, charming, able man with a great sense of humor, great capacity to enjoy a good time, and a good lawyer in a general practice. He was also in politics. He was a district leader on the South Side of Chicago, and a part of the Dineen faction. This was regarded as an upper-crust group, so to speak, standing for good government. Senator Charles S. Dineen was its spokesman.

As for the other partners, Litzinger was a fellow who had come up the hard way. He always wanted to be mayor of Chicago—why, I never could see, but he did. Healy did not have any outside activities. He was just a first-class lawyer.

There were probably fifteen lawyers in the office. I just did whatever there was to do, looked up points of law a few times, served papers, went over and answered court calenders, and generally did what a non-lawyer law student does in a law office. I was getting a worm's eye view.

In fact I was an alien in the beginning. When I left I knew my way around at least and knew some of the things law clerks did.

And I never liked Chicago. Chicago was—and into the 1960s still was—a gangster town with the lowest set of moral standards I ever saw in my life.

Just before leaving Ann Arbor for these multiple adventures in music and the law, I had for some reason taken on a new, non-paying job. As president of the Ann Arbor chapter of my fraternity, I had attended the national convention in my senior year and come away as national historian and editor of the national magazine, the *Sinfonian*. I had expected to stay at the University of Michigan for another two years.

By the end of this summer of 1923, however, I received more encouragement about my singing, and I had the glamorous idea of following the Stephens studio back to New York City. New York also included not only the Stephens studio but Frances Hutt, and there was also the Columbia University Law School there. Who was to suggest that Columbia Law School was not just as good as the University of Michigan Law School?

My parents rather thought that if I did want to go east for my final two years of law they would prefer Harvard, but once again they were indulgent. By September, I was entered in the Columbia Law School and on my way to New York.

Upon arrival in the city which I was to make my home, I signed in at the Stephens studio and was engaged as the bass soloist in St. Matthew's and St. Timothy's Episcopal Church, with two rehearsals a week. I was told I would get fifteen dollars per Sunday, which was the precise price of my weekly voice lessons with Percy Rector Stephens.

As I had ruminated upon my graduation at Owosso, the more things changed, the more they stayed the same. But this time everything would be totally new.

At McNamara and Seymour

Between 1923 and 1925 my new life in New York was exhilarating. I was living in a furnished room on West 122nd Street, no longer in an undergraduate fraternity house, and that accounted for some of the difference. The intellectual atmosphere of Columbia was markedly different, also, from that of Ann Arbor. The discipline, the curiosity of the Columbia Law School were not always compatible with the artistic dedication of the Stephens Studio. It was a little like living in two worlds at once. The law and music. I had never been so happy in my life.

Before long Percy Rector Stephens suggested that I begin working with a coach. It was Stephens' business to teach voice. It was a coach's business to develop style and the artistic use of the singing language. My diction was respectable in English, French, and Italian, but the time had come to polish both diction and interpretation. The leading coach of the day was Charles Baker, and I started going to him weekly. Baker opened up still further avenues of refinement and skill, making a singing career ever more attractive to me.

As the spring of 1924 came to a close Stephens and Baker decided that I was ready for a full-scale studio concert. Programs were printed, a selected audience was invited, and my parents came in from Owosso for the event. I developed a deep chest cold just two days before the concert. We thought I would be well enough to go through with it when the time came, and anyway it was too late to send out cancellations. The cold grew into a mild laryngitis, however, and I approached the concert with deep apprehension.

The first group I sang went passably well, but the laryngitis was getting worse. The second group started off passably, but then came *Der Doppelgänger*. This is a magnificent German Lied, dramatic, long, and taxing. I lasted halfway through and my voice gave out. The concert was over. Despite all the nice things people said, it was clearly a disaster.

Although I recovered from the laryngitis in a few days and resumed normal practice, lessons, and coaching lessons, the doubts that had always been in the back of my mind began to grow. Whether or not I had the artistic skill and equipment to reach the top as a singer, it seemed a perilous existence. Of course, all life was a gamble, but to engage in a profession which depended so completely on the fine tuning and perfect condition of a pair of vocal cords seemed increasingly precarious.

By then, too, I had come to know a number of much older singers. Some of them had been the finest artists of their day, but in their middle fifties the human voice was simply not what it used to be. Even the appearances of the immortal Chaliapin were sometimes preceded by the announcement that, although he had throat trouble, he intended to persevere. Looked at in this light, the prospect of my scrounging around for pupils when I could no longer sing well was unattractive. By contrast, in business, in the professions and other arts men would be beginning to reach full capacity at the very time a singer would be approaching the end of his career.

Moreover, as singing seemed to become less and less attractive, the law was taking hold. The intellectual challenge grew as my knowledge and understanding increased. There was great teaching at Columbia, and this stimulated my imagination and my desire to go deeper and deeper into the law and to grow with the law. By summer I had decided that I wanted to be a lawyer and nothing else. The glamor of a singing career had faded completely.

The next fall, voice and coaching lessons were things of the past and so was my church soloist job. Also my tour as editor of the national fraternity magazine, the *Sinfonian,* was over. I could now devote myself entirely to the Law School. I probably should have done this sooner, but at least I got all the other things out of my system. So the law began to take on its full flavor of fascination and reward. And while the faculty members in earlier years had been first class I had never, for example, encountered anyone like Herman Oliphant. He made anti-trust laws and trade regulation at Columbia the most exciting intellectual adventure I had ever known. Soon the love of the law caught fire.

In addition I was able to spend more time with some of the new friends I had made at Columbia Law School. Bill Douglas, who became an associate justice of the United States Supreme Court, Carroll Shanks, who became president of the Prudential Life Insurance Company, Al McCormick, who was to become a partner in the Cravath law firm and special assistant to the Secretary of War and later to the Secretary of State in World War II—all of these men were brilliant scholars and tremendously engaging companions.

Our group also included Bob Scholl and Ogden Marsh, both of whom had distinguished successes later in life. We were close friends, and the three of us started a minor rebellion at the Law School. There were moot courts at Columbia, as at other law schools, where students took theoretical cases and argued them. After the process of eliminations, the winners argued the case before a court over which well-known lawyers or judges were invited to preside. Bob Scholl, Ogden Marsh, and I thought there ought to be a new moot court, so we organized the Judge Burdick Moot Court in our senior year, and we had a lot of fun and stimulation from it.

My only outside interest in the senior year was Frances Hutt, whom I began courting in earnest. We were both busy, but we took time out to go to the opera occasionally, and to concerts oftener. We also shared a great affection for the theater, and there was never quite enough time for everything. Aside from personal beauty and intellectual charm, she possessed the most beautiful mezzo-soprano voice I had ever heard. The attraction was totally irresistible. Before long, however, she had launched her own singing career.

Meanwhile, at Christmastime of the last year in Law School, the third-year students were following the customary pattern of looking for a job. It never occurred to me to go back to Owosso or anywhere else, or to look any place but New York City. It was not the vogue

then for law students to seek places in government, as it has since become, and it would not have occurred to me to seek this kind of place
anyway.

In my family, government had always been politics, and politics
was the science of government. It was a fairly simplistic approach,
generally shared by most of us. Government employees were employees only, and they did what they were told. Elected officers made
policy and the important thing in government was policy. That was
made by those who had the time or inclination to go out and run for
office, and this was not uppermost in the minds of many Columbia
Law School seniors in 1925.

As far as I was concerned, New York was also the capital of music, literature, and the arts, as well as business, science, and the law.
So I took the inevitable trips to Wall Street and I called at the offices
of the leading law firms of the city. They were not half as large as
they were to become in mid-century, but with fifty or sixty lawyers
apiece they were impressive enough to a young lad from Michigan.
I did not know a soul in any firm or in any business in New York but
the reputation of the Columbia Law School opened the doors.

My tour of the downtown law offices was enlightening, to say the
least. Some were cordial and helpful, some had already hired all they
wanted from among the young men who had connections in New
York. The hiring partner of one of them was particularly distant and
advised me, "You know, of course, that for the first two years a young
lawyer is nothing but a pair of legs to us." However true that might
have been, it did not seem necessary to rub it in. I did not like him
and I did not learn to like his firm in years to come.

After receiving three offers—interestingly, all of them for precisely
thirty-five dollars per week—I took a month to think it over. And I was
happy indeed to accept the invitation from Larkin, Rathbone and
Perry to start work for them in the following September.

Meanwhile I had developed a great desire to see Europe, so
three of us set off together as soon as I had completed taking the New
York State Bar examinations. My companions were Ward Jenks, an
old friend from Owosso, and Marland Gale, a classmate at Columbia
Law. The ship landed at Plymouth, England, and on the following
day we met a young man from Tasmania who was studying architecture at Cambridge University. He was spending his summer work-

ing at a shipyard as part of his course. The next day we all set off in a battered old Ford on a leisurely trip through rural England, winding up with a day at Oxford and up to London. Our new-found Tasmanian friend went back to work in Plymouth, and none of us ever saw him again, to our great regret.

After a few days in London we sold the Ford and took the channel boat to Le Havre. It was a rough trip I hoped never to repeat. Thence to Paris, where we did all the things that young American tourists would do. We bicycled out into the countryside and saw the World War I battlefields, went to the Louvre, spent a day on the Left Bank, visited the cathedrals and night clubs, and just made it back to Le Havre in time to catch our boat. The rest of the summer I spent in Owosso.

It was on this trip to Europe, incidentally, that Ward Jenks and I decided on a race to see who could grow the first mustache. I have kept mine ever since.

Practicing law in Wall Street turned out from the outset to be as demanding as its reputation. Research must be total—no cases missed; analysis must be total, with all the best arguments marshaled; papers must be perfect. Preparation for litigation must also be total and exhaustive. There was no legal training in the world comparable to the standards and discipline of a great law firm. Over the years I had many hundreds of lawyers working for me, and my conviction grew ever stronger that there was no substitute equal in training and discipline for a future at the bar.

It was not all interesting, even in Wall Street. There were papers to be served, and that sometimes fell to the lot of the youngest lawyers. There was always law to be looked up and there were the court calendars to be answered. There were also railroad mortgage releases to be prepared, and drafts of court pleadings. It was varied, however, and it gave me legal insight and discipline.

At Larkin, Rathbone and Perry there was a large bullpen in the old-fashioned tradition with seven desks. The three desks farthest away from the windows were occupied by Robert Lewis, who later became a partner but died in his forties, Robert A. Allen, who became a vice-president of the Guaranty Trust Company, and me. Another inmate was Parker "Noisy" Newhall, so named because he dictated so loudly. He used to pace up and down the bullpen dictating at the top of his voice. He later became a senior partner and died not long ago.

Then there was Sewell T. Tyng. Here was a most extraordinary man. He was the son of a wealthy and cultured family, a brilliant scholar and broad-gauged lawyer and the finest of men. He had served as an officer in World War I, in the Battle of the Marne, and while practicing law he had written a definitive book, *The Battle of the Marne*. He gave an annual lecture on the battle at West Point for many years.

Tyng became a partner and, for reasons of his own, abandoned the practice of law for other cultural activities. But in 1935, when I became Special Prosecutor of the rackets investigation, I helped persuade Tyng to return to the Bar. In fact he enlisted with me as an ordinary assistant at $4,000 a year. Tyng was one of the ablest and most popular of all our men, and he eventually became the Assistant District Attorney in charge of General Sessions. There he rendered fine service to the community until his health failed some years later.

Sewell Tyng introduced me to New York politics. He had no personal political background or interests. It was just a matter of good citizenship with him. I had not been practicing law for thirty days before he discovered that I had some interest in politics. His home was in the old Tenth Assembly District where he was a volunteer captain. Marland Gale and I were sharing an apartment, which was also in the old Tenth. Sewell promptly introduced me and I became an assistant district captain in an election district bordering his.

The following year I became captain of the two-block district between Tenth and Eleventh streets, extending one block east and one block west of Fifth Avenue. I called on all of the voters in my district in each of the years 1925, 1926, and 1927. I called on every single voter I could find in. If I did not find them the first time, I went back the second time. If I could not persuade the voter to go along with the whole Republican ticket, then, in accordance with the custom of all local people, I sought to get a vote for the state Assembly candidate for the district.

Of course these labors occurred normally only during the six weeks before elections, and they were illuminating. They were also disillusioning, because it turned out that very few other district captains were taking their responsibilities very seriously. Most of them did appear on Primary Day and Election Day and that was about all. We were supposed to get people out to vote in the primaries and to get them registered.

On Election Day we were expected to be in the polling places before six o'clock in the morning to make sure that the voting machines opened with zeroes across their boards. Incredibly, we even had to see to it that the Tammany captains had not marked up fifty or seventy-five votes for their candidates before the first voter arrived. During the day, with such help as was available, we tried to prevent non-registered voters and plain floaters from casting illegal votes, and at the same time we tried to get our own voters to the polls.

It was not easy, to say the least, because in those days fraud was a way of life in New York. In many districts, too, gangsters were present to create chaos at one time or another during Election Day, so that a large number of phony votes could be recorded while nobody was looking. It became clearer and clearer to me that Tammany Hall was all that my grandfather Dewey and the rest of the family always thought it was, only worse, and more sophisticated.

My roommate and former classmate Marland Gale recalled some off-duty moments:

"Tom and I lived for about a year on Christopher Street in the Village, and then we moved to a place in Chelsea, which was much nicer, on Twenty-second Street between Eighth and Ninth avenues. We had the whole ground floor in a remodeled brownstone. An aunt of mine knew the people who had lived there and she had attended the wedding of the daughter there, and the daughter had attended her wedding, and she gave us for that place a vase which she had received from the daughter who lived there. That's New York for you.

"In any event, we had a grand piano, and I mean a concert grand piano, and for two years we had a concert almost all the time. We had tenors there, baritones, and often one soprano, Miss Hutt. She played very nicely and she had a lovely voice, and it was one of the great pleasures to have her sing occasionally, accompanying herself. In fact, people gravitated from all around to sing.

"Tom, however, was very strong in his convictions about singing. One time there was some tenor singing, and Tom burst out of the shower, which was near the salon where the piano was located, and he said, 'For God's sake, put some guts into it.' That was just what this tenor needed."

Suddenly what seemed like the promised land opened up for me in a small law firm at 120 Broadway. Stuart McNamara, the head of it, was a handsome blond man of middle age with a broad career behind him. He had spent several years practicing in Washington and in his youth he had served as an Assistant Attorney General handling among other matters a prosecution of the old New York *World* for libeling President Theodore Roosevelt. While McNamara had done a good deal of litigation, he was the head of the firm, with wide duties, and he needed a young man with some experience. He decided I was it.

The next few years in this firm brought me lawsuits to handle, and a bit of everything else. It consisted of corporate and real estate work for a hotel chain which also included Sherry's and the Savarin restaurants, the financing of the new Waldorf-Astoria Hotel, working on the listing of the stock of the Equitable Office Building on the New York Stock Exchange as well as some bank, estate, and tax practice.

I liked working in this small office and I was very happy there.

Usually in the beginning a young lawyer does work that he alone can do. He goes to the library and reads the cases that are relevant to the subject. Then he lines them up and tries to distinguish them, establish what the law is, and find the cases that are most relevant. If he is trying to establish a point of view, of course, he looks for analogies in other cases that are similar and follows them down to see whether they have been overruled, or changed, and that is fairly lonely work. But it is also intellectually and deeply stimulating, in my opinion. I found that I greatly enjoyed just working alone on briefs and studying cases. Later there would be hours of conferences and discussions on the relevance of cases and that sort of thing, but you do not feel that it is lonesome. Basically, the young lawyer operates alone. He is a scholar, a professional man.

Then of course when you come to questions of policy you have conferences. When you come to the drafting of instruments, somebody will write the first draft, and then his senior will go over it, but usually the organization of any matter in a law office is perpendicular, not horizontal. There is the partner in charge, then perhaps a junior partner, a senior associate, and a junior associate. That would be the normal organization.

But there was more consultation at McNamara and Seymour because at each stage of a matter you would come to questions of judgment. And of course the joy of a small place such as this was that McNamara was freely available to all the people in the office. He had periods of great pressure, and I would either be working with him or somebody else would, but when I first went there it was Stuart McNamara's office. A year later he made it McNamara and Seymour so as to call it a firm. There was Raymond B. Seymour, and also a junior partner named Henry Wheeler. Then there was me, and a younger man named Ballard. That was the office.

When McNamara got into periods of undue stress he would retain outside counsel to carry the extra load, to write the brief or do research. He kept his overhead to a minimum that way, usually by employing old friends, contemporaries, who had their own single-practitioner offices.

Actually, during this period, it occurred to me that you know more law when you graduate from law school, and less about how to use it, than you will ever know again in your professional life. You have simply taken an apprentice course and, while you have the tools, you have not the slightest idea how to handle them. You are usually filled with a lot of theoretical concepts which are wide of the mark when it comes to practice.

How the law fits into the stream of life is a long distance away. The rest of your life you are at the opposite end. You have a set of facts, and the question becomes how to accomplish the desired result legally, how to take the set of facts you have, or the desired corporate reorganization if you like, or the lawsuit, and how to appraise it against the law. Until then you have done it theoretically, but basically you have been learning how to think legally, not how to deal with people and practical problems.

Lawbooks have been there a long time, and they are going to be there a lot longer.

And certainly you do have all kinds of human problems in the practice of the law. In a corporate reorganization, you will run into temperamental people who will make great difficulties about things that are really of no consequence. You will have one individual who occupies a position, maybe nothing but a nuisance position, but the problem of how to handle his objection, or his special interest, can be the most serious problem of all.

This requires great imagination and inventiveness both in the law and in handling people. It also requires diligence—hours and hours, days and nights.

In 1928, a presidential election year, I served as a Special Assistant Attorney General helping supervise the polls at the 110th Street schoolhouse in Harlem. Before the polls opened there was an obvious infestation of hoodlums, one or two young men to each of the six polling places in the large ground-floor area of the schoolhouse. Some had guns in evidence in their pockets. Some had guns bulging from holsters under their coats.

The word soon got around the district that the Dutch Schultz mob had taken over. When a group of obviously unregistered voters would come in, the hoodlums raised such a hullabaloo that everybody was intimidated. All we could do was try to check on these voters and hold them for fraud. But the police turned their backs. It was worth their jobs to try to keep order.

Every policeman that day appeared to know this was politics, that Tammany Hall was in charge, and that if they attempted to enforce the law they would be sent to pound a beat in the far recesses of Staten Island many miles from their homes.

Some of my friends on poll duty had worse luck even than the honest policeman. Carl Newton, who became a senior partner of Donovan, Leisure, Newton and Irvine, was kicked down a flight of iron steps at one of the polling places. Other friends of mine were beaten up and thrown off their posts. Obviously this system was evil and it was the duty of every good citizen to do something about it.

Shocked by this spectacle, we tried hard but could make no impression. Tammany was riding very high in 1928. And few people remember that, in 1929, Congressman Fiorello LaGuardia ran for mayor of New York against Jimmy Walker and was snowed under. It was a period of prosperity and not very many people cared about decent government. The populace was cynical. Moreover, a good many thought there was nothing anybody could do about Tammany Hall anyway. It was always unwise and sometimes unsafe to fight City Hall.

Political power in 1928 was in fact used ruthlessly against anybody who owned a house or a business, and who opposed the city government. Political favors were granted lavishly to those who cooperated. There were many fine citizens and some newspapers brave enough to fight but the tide was overwhelmingly against them.

The grip of this Democratic Party organization on the mass of the people, and on a very great share of the businessmen, always mystified me. It seemed absolutely impossible to me that anyone could support such a foul government. It took a good many years for me to understand that merchants, from street peddlers to large businesses, had to co-operate or face reprisals. To the masses of the poor and the immigrants, Tammany Hall was the only indigenous friend they had, with its Thanksgiving turkeys, free buckets of coal for cold-water flats, Christmas handouts, and its control of the courts whenever somebody wanted to be gotten out of trouble. In due course I learned to understand this but never to like it.

Despite the increasing demands of legal practice, it seemed to me natural in this context to become active in the Young Republican Club. It was a first-class group of young men, dedicated to better government through the Republican Party. The club had recently been revived after some years of somnolence, and before long we were up to 1,000 members. Committees did special research on matters of city, state, and national politics, and the pronouncements of the committees as well as the votes of the club at formal meetings were controversial and newsworthy. We believed we were a useful influence.

This group of Young Republicans, mostly young Wall Street lawyers, kept fighting in the good cause. In addition to Carl Newton, who had been injured in 1928, we had Ed Lumbard, later chief of the Criminal Division of the United States Attorney's office, long a distinguished practicing lawyer and later Chief Judge of the United States Court of Appeals; David Peck, whom I later as Governor had the privilege of appointing to the Supreme Court of the state and who became a superb presiding justice of the Appellate Division; Archie O. Dawson, who became a federal judge; Paul Williams, later a Supreme Court justice and after that United States Attorney; Herbert Brownell, later manager of my two campaigns for President and of the 1952 campaign of General Eisenhower, and after that Attorney General of the United States; Charles Garside, later a colonel in the Army in World War II, a judge, and still later president of the Blue Cross; Frank Rivers, whom I had the privilege of appointing as judge of the City Court of the city of New York, the first black in America to hold such a high office; and William C. Hecht, for much of his career the only Republican Supreme Court justice in the District of Manhattan and the Bronx and one of the finest judges the state ever produced.

There were many others in this remarkable group of men, able,
high-minded, unselfish. We worked together, spent our social evenings
together, and later they, together with many others of our original
group, formed the basic strength of my various political campaigns.

Through the 1930s, 1940s, 1950s, and 1960s we dined together
periodically during the winters, settling the affairs of the world, as
always.

It was not impossible to have a public career as a Republican in
a city which was three to one Democratic, but it certainly took a
unique degree of dedication. But these men were not in politics out of
any desire for public office. Herbert Brownell was an interesting example of this. Soon after I was elected Governor of New York in
1942 there was a vacancy in the state Supreme Court and I offered it
to Brownell. He was happy in his law practice and he declined. The
next year Alex Rose, the chairman of the Liberal Party, tried to induce him to undertake a lawsuit, which he decided not to take on.
Rose told him that if he would undertake it he would guarantee that
Brownell would be sent to the state Supreme Court before too long.
Brownell told Rose he had already declined the Supreme Court, and
Rose said: "That is absolutely impossible. I can't believe it." As a postscript, the only appointive public office Brownell ever accepted was
that of Attorney General of the United States under Eisenhower from
which, after five years of service, he voluntarily retired to his first love,
the practice of the law.

For the record, the first political speechmaking I ever did was in
the campaign of 1929, for Fritz Coudert for District Attorney. It was a
hopeless campaign during which I spoke from the backs of trucks. Nobody had any sound equipment and we were lucky to get the trucks.

Meanwhile my mind was turning toward trial work. No one in a
responsible office was likely to try many cases until he had had substantial experience as an assistant to a senior at the trial bar. The issues
were too significant to be entrusted to the neophytes. One case did
come my way, defending a suit to dispossess a black porter from his
apartment. The man thought he had a defense and wanted the case
tried, so it was assigned to me as one of those things lawyers do without compensation. I threw everything I had into this dispossess case,
but unhappily my client had no defense at all and the judge quite
promptly ordered him dispossessed. There were other matters to be

tried, such as technical violations of city ordinances by corporate clients, but the number and quality of the cases that came my way was small.

Another small legal matter came my way. I wrote this letter to the Paramount Cleaning and Dyeing Corporation in New York City:

Gentlemen:

My client, Miss Frances Hutt, has requested me to write you in reference to a certain dress left by her with your agent, Economy Hand Laundry, 200 Ninth Avenue, New York City.

You are undoubtedly familiar with the facts. Miss Hutt left the dress at Economy Hand Laundry with instructions to have it cleaned, in case the work could be done without removing or in any way affecting the plaited collar or cuffs. Upon the return of the dress, the plait had been removed from the collar and cuffs, and an ordinary plait put in, both the collar and cuffs had been badly frayed, a cigarette hole had been burned in the front of the collar, and large stains appeared on each cuff. In addition, a belt which was an inseparable part of the dress, and was entirely sewed in, had been torn out, and has now been lost by you.

The dress was purchased, I believe, for $68, and can be replaced in New York only for that price. The collar, which is more than six inches wide, and runs down the front of the dress to the waist, had a special and very unusual plait, which could be put in only at the time the dress was made, and by machine. This special plaiting constituted a large part of the value of the dress, and has been entirely ruined. The cigarette hole completes the work.

The belt was an integral part of the dress, and only the most gross negligence could have been responsible for its removal. It cannot be replaced, and no possible excuse can be given for removing it. Its loss, of course, completes the work of making the dress entirely useless.

If you desire to inspect the dress, I shall be happy to show it to you in exactly the condition in which it was received. If you desire to ascertain the retail price of the dress, I believe I can give you the name of the shop where the dresses are sold in New York, and I understand, also, that one such dress is still in stock at that shop, so that you may compare the dresses to make sure that they are identical.

Miss Hutt expects to be reimbursed for the ruin of her dress. The value of it will be practically its replacement cost, inasmuch as it is approximately two months old, and had been worn very little.

I should be happy to extend any courtesy to you, or give you any information you desire to have, and I request that you give me an answer not later than Monday, July 25 [four days from the date of the letter]. If I do not receive a satisfactory reply from you by that time, I will be forced to commence action.

Yours very truly
s/Thomas E. Dewey

On June 16, 1928, Frances Hutt and I were married in the chapel of St. Thomas' Church in New York City with three friends in attendance. Marland Gale was best man. The historian Rupert Hughes later wrote about Mrs. Dewey:

On February 7, 1903, Frances Hutt first appeared in the Texas town of Sherman. When she was eleven, her parents moved to Sapulpa, Oklahoma, where they still live. Her father is Orla Thomas Hutt, a railroad man. She has one brother, Dr. Harold Davis Hutt, now living in Holly, Michigan.

Frances Hutt has all the traditional graciousness and charm of a Southern woman. Behind her exquisite mask her soul glows with quiet amusement and deep feeling. Her heart is a hearth of warm devotion. . . . Yet she exacts all the joy there is in life, takes it with bravery, spices it with a quick wit, and has, as Dewey says, "plenty of horse sense."

She went to the public schools in Sherman and in Sapulpa. She led her class and was valedictorian of her junior high school class when she was fifteen; and valedictorian again of her senior high school class at eighteen. She was an ardent player of tennis and loved to swim, studied the piano and toiled in the art of a singer. At seventeen, she won a prize in the Voice Division of the State Fine Arts Contests at Norman, Oklahoma.

Percy Rector Stephens heard her sing and was impressed. . . . But Miss Hutt had to live and work her way up to the opportunities and the responsibilities of her warm and brilliant mezzo-soprano.

She was just twenty-one when she secured a straight singing role in a road company of George White's annual musical institution called the *George White Scandals*. . . . She was featured under her stage name, Eileen Hoyt.

At the end of a six month season, she returned to New York. She sang in two of John Murray Anderson's productions, after which she supported herself again with church choir and concert engagements, studying voice further with Enrico Rosati. . . .

There is a legend that when at last the cautious Dewey made a formal proposal for her hand, he put it in writing. . . . Both principals deny the story flatly.

After the great crash in October 1929 a singular event occurred at McNamara and Seymour. A lady named Mrs. Nanny Glover Kaufman sued one of our clients, the Empire Trust Company. She had owned preferred stock in a company which had offered to exchange it for common stock. The stock market was booming, and the common stock was going nowhere but up. As a result, she took her securities to the Empire Trust Company and signed her request for the exchange.

When the stock market collapsed in October 1929 the price of the common stock she had exchanged for her preferred collapsed with it. Her lush profit was wiped out. So she sued the bank, claiming that she never did ask to exchange that preferred stock for common after all.

For McNamara and Seymour, I made the necessary investigation, handled a variety of motions and two appeals to the Appellate Division, and prepared the case for trial. Suddenly Mrs. Kaufman decided she had been much further damaged, and she doubled the size of her claim. This was getting serious. I went in to McNamara and said that this case was important enough to our client, and I questioned whether a twenty-eight-year-old lawyer who had never tried a jury case should be entrusted with the trial. I wanted to try it, but I thought perhaps the Empire Trust Company might not think well of the idea, particularly if I lost. McNamara agreed, and asked me if I had a recommendation.

It so happened that I had been playing squash two or three nights a week with a young Assistant United States Attorney named

Thomas T. Cooke. He had repeatedly mentioned one trial lawyer at the New York Bar, George Z. Medalie. Cooke noted that Medalie had represented defendants in three bankruptcy fraud cases Cooke had prosecuted, and Medalie had won all three of them. Now this would not normally endear the defense lawyer to the prosecutor he had defeated. But Cooke said that he not only liked and respected Medalie but considered him the finest trial lawyer at the New York Bar. He said Medalie never permitted any witness to commit perjury and generally adhered to the highest standards of the British barrister. Tom Cooke had unlimited admiration for his integrity as well as for his skill. Incidentally, said Tom, Medalie was not only a fine trial lawyer but a good appellate court lawyer, and those two qualities were not always found in the same individual.

So I recommended to McNamara that we hire George Medalie, and he agreed. I called Medalie on the telephone, and after I told him my purpose he invited me to come up and discuss the case with him so he could determine its merits. I went up at ten o'clock in the morning. We worked all morning, through lunch, all afternoon, through dinner, and until midnight. Medalie took the Nanny Glover Kaufman case.

In the first week of January he tried it, brilliantly, but unhappily before a judge who would not read the papers. The jury brought in a verdict for the plaintiff, Mrs. Kaufman. Long afterward, this verdict was affirmed by the Appellate Division. Not until the case got to the highest court of the state, the Court of Appeals, would the judges read the papers! At this altitude, the case was reversed and the complaint dismissed.

This Nanny Glover Kaufman case was a turning point in my life. On the last day of the trial Medalie received a telephone call from Washington while he was in court. The Attorney General of the United States was on the telephone, inviting him to become the United States Attorney for the Southern District of New York. This was, by all traditional standards, the most important prosecuting office in America. One Attorney General of the United States had accepted appointment to that office after he had served a term as Attorney General. The office had a tradition of integrity and competence, having been headed by distinguished leaders of the bar, including Henry L. Stimson and Emory R. Buckner. Medalie accepted.

After summing up to the jury, Medalie had gone home with a bad case of influenza and a temperature of 103. Soon after that he called me on the telephone from home. He said he felt that the United States Attorney's office had not recently been living up to its traditions, and he wanted to bring an infusion of able young lawyers to the staff to replace those he regarded as political hacks. He asked me to search around among my friends in the Young Republican Club and in the downtown law offices. He wanted young men whose future was before them, who would bring the highest standards to the administration of justice. I undertook the chore, and when he had recovered he interviewed the men I proposed, and many others.

The day he took the oath of office, on March 1, he sent for me and offered me a place on the staff. Attractive as it was, I knew I would ultimately decline it, so I did so promptly. A week passed and he sent for me again. This time he asked me if I would like to become chief of the Criminal Division of the office. It was the choice assignment, widely sought and very tempting. It was a flattering offer, and I went back and talked to McNamara. After extensive consideration we concluded that I was doing well where I was and the financial sacrifice would be too great. By this time I was making $8,500 in a Depression year.

The next week Medalie sent for me again. This time he invited me to become Chief Assistant United States Attorney. This, at the age of twenty-eight, seemed overwhelming, and I said I would like to talk with McNamara. As a result McNamara invited Medalie and me to lunch the next day and, after we talked it all over, McNamara concluded that I should accept the offer. The very idea of taking charge, under Medalie, of an office of sixty lawyers, most of whom were older than I, at a time when I was young and inexperienced in criminal matters, seemed to me to be unrealistic and irresistible.

Frances and I talked it over at length and she agreed that, whatever security, opportunity, and income I was foregoing, it was an opportunity for public service and a chance to progress at the Bar which could not be declined. She was also reassuring about my prospects as a trial lawyer. She insisted I was born one.

The final problem was to get political clearance. This was not imperative, but it made things easier. The trouble was that the county organization already had a candidate in the person of the incumbent, a pleasant, honest, ineffectual, much older man. Moreover I had by no means worked in the vineyard of party politics long enough to warrant

such an exalted position. I had recently become chairman of the
Board of Governors of our Young Republican Club, but this was no
recommendation to the regular Republican organization we had been
attempting to shake up.

Finally Medalie sent word to Sam Koenig, the county chairman,
that I was going to call on him to seek his blessing. Medalie added
that I was going to be appointed anyway but he hoped I would be approved. That solved the problem.

Chief Assistant
United States Attorney

By the year 1931 the bubble of world-wide speculation had burst. The euphoria of the boom of the 1920s was gone; unemployment was widespread and cynical acceptance of municipal corruption was turning to anger. The Tammany District Attorney of New York County was doing nothing, and the first charges brought against the Mayor of New York, Jimmy Walker, had been dismissed by the Governor.

Prohibition was no longer a joke. It was becoming an outrage as public demand for liquor made it possible for common hoodlums to become rich, smuggling, corrupting, murdering barons of crime. The names of Al Capone, Waxey Gordon, Dutch Schultz, and Legs Diamond were already household words. Lucky Luciano was still in the shadows. We were seeing massive, organized, orchestrated crime for the first time in America, and the public was fed to the teeth.

Then three apparently unrelated events involving three disparate personalities occurred. Samuel Seabury, a descendant of Episcopal bishops, former judge of the Court of Appeals, a towering, reserved, lofty soul of civic virtue, began getting to the reality of matters in the city as counsel to a legislative investigating committee.

George Zerdin Medalie, born on the Lower East Side, of Russian immigrant stock, son of a rabbi, a scholarly, brilliant barrister, became United States Attorney for the Southern District of New York.

Scarface Al Capone, the violent, degraded spawn of Prohibition, the undisputed master of organized crime in Chicago and an undisputed mass murderer, was convicted of—of all things—failure to pay his income taxes and sentenced to ten years in prison. This spectacular conviction resulted from a long investigation, personally ordered by President Hoover and conducted by special agents of the Intelligence Unit of the Internal Revenue Service. Promptly after this conviction, the Special Staff was reassigned to New York to start work on the lush underworld of the East, where Dutch Schultz and Waxey Gordon held sway.

We had little time to lose in the new United States Attorney's office. Of course organized crime could not occupy the attention of more than a fraction of our office. We were Uncle Sam's lawyers and we had the largest such district office in the country. Our Criminal Division handled the ordinary run of narcotics cases, stealing from the mails, the long mail fraud cases against stock market swindlers, violations of the immigration laws, bankruptcy frauds, and infringements of countless other federal statutes. The Civil Division dealt actively with matters for the Departments of State, Treasury, Defense, the Post Office, Interior, Agriculture, Commerce, and Labor. At that time there was also the Prohibition Division, with its unpopular but unavoidable duties in the then present context of the law.

George Medalie was sworn in as United States Attorney on February 12, 1931. It was characteristic of him that he sought a private ceremony, but the officiating judge decreed that it should be public. Medalie then had no statement to make to the press, beyond the comment that he intended to conduct his office in a lawyerlike manner, letting actions take the place of words.

Medalie was a quiet man, quiet socially, quiet in the courtroom, with a gentle and sometimes lusty sense of humor. Educated in New York public schools, he was graduated Phi Beta Kappa from City College of New York and three years later, with honors, from Columbia Law School. He had worked his way through college and law school. Medalie in fact met his wife while they were both attending City College and they were both studying Greek. She taught Greek thereafter, and Medalie was a Greek scholar. All their lives they wrote notes to one another in Greek. They were both fine scholars.

Medalie became an assistant on the famous staff of District Attorney Charles S. Whitman, where he acquired five years of trial experience. After that he returned to private practice and he also, as Special Prosecutor for the state, handled a large number of election fraud cases with success. A Republican, Medalie was appointed by Governor Alfred E. Smith, a Democrat, to conduct removal proceedings against Florence Knapp, a Republican Secretary of State. By 1931 he was one of the two or three leading criminal lawyers in the city. He really tried only a few criminal cases, but civil lawsuits rarely made news, and the occasional criminal case did.

Medalie had an irresistible warmth and a unique capacity for friendship in depth. I never met anyone who did not like and respect him. I never knew a man of finer integrity and generosity of spirit. Serving as his Chief Assistant in these early years was, in all ways, the most enriching experience of my professional life, and in many ways it was the happiest.

The Chief Assistant, as I soon found, had a variety of duties, not the least of which was to manage the entire civil service staff. It quickly became apparent that one of the principal clerks in the office was a drunk. Very few people came in on time. The stenographic room even had a frequent, noisy hair-pull. My first job was to send some people on their way and to bring order and discipline to the staff.

Handling administrative matters with Washington, reading incoming mail and signing outgoing mail were also part of my duties, and it seemed to me that a man could make a career out of sitting at that desk. After about a month of it I borrowed Barent Ten Eyck from the United States Attorney's staff to take over most of these administrative duties, which he did well.

Ten Eyck was a graduate of Columbia Law School in the class of 1925, one of my classmates and a personal friend of many years. He came from an old Dutch family in New York, went to Princeton and then to Columbia Law School. "Barrie," as he was known, was a tall, slender, good-looking chap, prematurely bald, with a good sense of humor and terrific accomplishment. He was able to teach himself foreign languages, played the piano well, and had been active in the Princeton Triangle shows. During the next several years he was to become one of my principal assistants.

Murray I. Gurfein was another very important member of the staff. Murray was a graduate of Columbia College in 1926 and Harvard Law School in 1930, and he came from a very fine family in New York. His father was a notable importer of diamonds. Murray had a brilliant scholastic record and he showed interest at once in the labor situation and in questions relating to civil liberties. He was extremely useful in piloting our ways through these rather uncharted fields. He had a wide acquaintance with people in these areas, and they had a good deal of confidence in Murray. He was also an excellent trial lawyer, and he had been law secretary to federal Judge Julian Mack. He was a short, stocky man with dark brown hair and a mustache. I could not say enough about his legal skill and ability, as well as his integrity and intelligence.

William B. Herlands, for some time an associate of Medalie, was a very astute, careful, precise, methodical lawyer, a rather stocky fellow who had made a brilliant scholastic record at the City College of New York. Incidentally, he made an athletic record there, too, and for several summers he was an athletic director at Grossinger's, the well-known Catskill Mountains resort. In 1928 he had graduated from Columbia Law School at the top of his class.

If I remember correctly, Herlands, Gurfein, and Ten Eyck all sported Phi Beta Kappa keys. In fact, in later years, there were so many Phi Beta Kappa keys dangling from the watch chains of our staff that one of the General Sessions judges remarked that defense lawyers thought they should be classed as "dangerous weapons."

Jacob J. Rosenblum, known as "Jack," was another important man in these early United States Attorney's office days. He graduated from New York University Law School in 1923 and was, as such, one of the oldest men in our group. Jack had been raised on Orchard Street, on the East Side, where his father managed a paint store. Upon graduation he got a job in Medalie's downtown office, starting as the usual law clerk, serving subpoenas and the rest of it. Jack became a thoroughly grounded and competent trial lawyer who knew every trick in the book. He was as sharp as a tack, a man of medium size, very dark hair, sparkling eyes, and a sort of rough and ready manner.

In a very few weeks our whole staff was almost completed, with an infusion of young and able people, mostly recruited from downtown law offices. The whole office vibrated, I thought, with enthusiasm tempered by a large amount of inexperience.

United States Attorney Medalie was now ready to announce policy. Many of his views were refreshingly novel in an office of a public prosecutor. No assistant would be permitted to conduct any outside law practice. No photographs were ever to be allowed of an assistant together with a defendant: this was considered to be cheap publicity degrading to a public official. No public announcements about investigations and forthcoming investigations were to be permitted, except to the extent necessary to the court procedure, relative to the handing up of an indictment, for example, or upon an arraignment.

There was to be no "leaking" of information and we were not to give away or reveal our evidence or telegraph our punches.

Above all, there was to be no trial by newspaper.

In fact, Medalie said, there was to be no discussion of the work of the office outside the office at all. He said walls had ears, and so had elevators.

The bail bondsmen who haunted the corridors of the ancient Federal Court House were conduits of information from the office to the underworld, Medalie said. As long as they were around, information about pending cases was bound to leak out. Worse than that, the presence of potential witnesses in our office would become known to the wrong people, and this was a hazard to the witnesses. So Medalie ordered that the bail bondsmen were to be cleared out of the building and kept out.

Medalie made a final point: our office was not going to sit there, as in the past, and wait for cases to be brought in on a platter. Medalie said: "We are not sludges or political hacks, like the state prosecuting offices. We have the benefit of the Federal Bureau of Investigation, the Intelligence Service of the Treasury, the Post Office inspectors, the Secret Service, the Narcotics Squad, and all the other federal agencies. Many of them are superb. However, there are limits to what they can do alone, while together we can do a great job."

Typically, Medalie arranged for his young staff to practice their skills in mock trials held within the office. Typically, he served as the judge.

Herlands recalled: "Medalie was one of the best-read men I ever met. He would spend hours discussing the latest law school theories, the latest literature. He was fond of referring to Wigmore's book, *A Panorama of the World's Legal Systems,* and he would drift off into Talmudic law, into canon law, into Roman law. He also had a fantastic command of the precise word, what the French call *le mot juste,* and that too is something that was handed on to all the Dewey and Medalie men, the recognition that the right word, the right phrase, is a matter of great importance in trial work. So was the colorful phrase, what Walter Pater used to call 'wild flowers of expression.'

"Both Medalie and Dewey had a phrase—well, each had a separate phrase. Dewey would say, 'What's the dirt in the situation?' Translated, that meant, 'What is the atmospheric fact about the situation which, regardless of detail, niceties of distinctions, and legalisms, conveys a legal picture which could be understood by anybody?' Medalie would say, 'How do you put a ruby nose on it?' A ruby nose meant that certain feature which stood out, and which created the physiognomy of a witness, a transaction, or a case.

"Medalie would find juggling coins convenient on occasion when he wanted a little time to think of an answer. Dewey picked up the habit. With Medalie, one or two of the coins would fall out of his hands, roll on the floor, and break the conversation for a few minutes. While he was looking for the coin, the tenseness would be broken, it would furnish a breathing spell.

"Medalie also quoted Huxley: 'The smallest fact is a window through which the infinite may be seen.' "

In our first month the Seabury investigation exploded with a scandal about the extraordinary wealth of a New York City vice squad policeman, James J. "Jimmie" Quinlivan. Between 1927 and 1929 he was charged with depositing more than $80,000 in graft taken from speakeasies and brothels. In 1931 this was a fortune.

Needless to say, exposure and charges were not proof of anything, and long hard labor would be necessary to identify the sources of this money, the reasons it had been paid, the ownership of the involved bank accounts, and the elements of the crime. And, needless to say, the Tammany District Attorney did nothing. But this time United States Attorney Medalie ascertained that Quinlivan had probably paid no income taxes on his take, and Medalie determined to seek out the proof needed for a federal income tax evasion indictment.

Then Medalie assigned the Quinlivan case to me. It was still my first month in office. I was appalled to find myself cutting my teeth on a case of such widespread public notoriety. Usually new assistants had a few simple narcotics or stealing-from-the-mail cases to cut their teeth on. But Medalie did not think that kind of breaking in would be appropriate for his new Chief Assistant. In any event he said his theory was to drop young men in deep water and let them swim out. With opportunity came responsibility, he said, and that applied to all of us, including me.

The Quinlivan case was fascinating. It presented a historical microcosm of life in New York City in the 1920s, seamy and widespread, and without benefit of hindsight and afterjudgments, I will present it as it happened in court. After months of preparation and investigation the trial opened—my first—with newspapers and the radio seemingly hanging on every word. I presented my star witness against Quinlivan, a onetime taxi driver named Harry Levey, thirty-five years old, three times convicted of petty larceny, a man who had never earned an honest living since his eighteen months' service in the Army in World War I.

Q. When did you first meet the defendant [Quinlivan]?

A. The latter part of 1915.

Q. When?

A. Around December of 1915.

Q. And where did you meet him?

A. I was an usher in the Harlem Opera House, 125th Street and Seventh Avenue.

Q. Did you have conversation with him at that time?

A. I did.

Q. And what was that conversation?

A. He asked me whether I knew of any disorderly houses. I told him I did. He told me there would be the price of a hat or a pair of shoes in it if I gave him the password [for entering the house of prostitution] and if he effected an arrest in the place, he would pay me for it. I gave him an address and the password of a place in Harlem and I haven't seen him for a week after that, and when he saw me again he paid me five dollars.

Q. This was the first case in which you had ever given information to any policeman, was it?

A. That's right.

Q. And you were paid for it?

A. That's right.

Q. Did you continue to give him information?

A. I did. . . .

Q. Have you known Quinlivan ever since then?

A. I have. . . .

Q. When was the first time you met him in the year 1927?

A. It was around February or March of 1927.

Q. Did you have conversation with him?

A. I did.

Q. And what was that conversation?

A. I was walking on 125th Street, incidentally, near the Harlem Opera House, where I had met him in 1915, and I heard somebody say, "Hello, Harry." I turned around. I saw Quinlivan. We shook hands. He asked me what I had been doing. I told him I had been driving a taxicab for the last six years. He said, "How is business?" I said, "Terrible. The police took over the supervision of the taxicab industry, and they took away my license." He said, "Did you hear I am in plain clothes now?" I said, "No, I haven't." I said, I thought that the Police Department had a Special Service, and he said that was eliminated, and that he had a new partner, and he said, "By the way, I will take you over and introduce you to my partner." He took me to an automobile in which was seated Officer William M. O'Connor, and introduced me.

Then I asked Officer Quinlivan if there was any chance of helping me get my taxi license. I told him I had driven a taxi in New York for six years and had never received a summons for a violation, and that the only reason they took my hack license away was because I had previous convictions.

He said, "I will try it, but I don't think there is any use. You can make plenty of money with me."

I said, "No, Jim. I am married now, my wife has just given birth and my baby has been two or three months in the hospital. I spent all my money on it, trying to get it [the license] through politicians, fixers and everything else." . . .

Then he asked me whether I had anything at the time I was speaking to him, anything in the way of a disorderly house. I gave him the address of a woman named Lopez on 116th Street near Lenox Avenue. He gave me the phone number of the Sixth Division office. . . .

Q. Did Quinlivan get you your hack license?

A. He did not.

Q. Then did you continue giving him information?

A. I did.

Q. Did you give him information frequently?

A. Very often for a while, that is, three or four times a week. . . .

Q. Were you paid for it?

A. I was. . . .

Q. What else did you do for Quinlivan in December of 1927? . . .

A. We went to a small night club or speakeasy owned by a man named George Bens, 145th Street and Broadway. We were admitted, that is, Officers Quinlivan, O'Connor, and myself. When we entered, there was a small night club on the left and a bar right ahead in the center of the place. We proceeded to the bar. There was a man there whom I later knew to be George Bens, shook hands with Officers O'Connor and Quinlivan, and Officer O'Connor at that time introduced me to this man George Bens and said, "Meet the boy friend, George," and I shook hands with him. . . .

Q. Did you go to any place after you went to George Bens'?

A. We did.

Q. Where did you go?

A. To a place on 103rd Street and West End Avenue, owned by a man named Dan McNamara.

Q. What happened there?

A. Also introduced at that place by Quinlivan.

Q. What did he say?

A. "Meet the boy friend. Any time he comes round, he is okay. Give him anything he wants," something to that effect.

Q. Any other conversation?

A. No, only about horse racing and things like that. . . .

Q. Go to any other speakeasies?

A. Yes, sir, every day, to some place, new places, apartment speakeasies, basement speakeasies, stores, night clubs. . . . We went to Dan McNamara's. . . . Officer Quinlivan did most of the talking at that time. He was sort of boss.

Q. What happened?

A. He told me to go in and ask for Dan, and Dan would give me something. I went in and saw Dan McNamara and he gave me $100 in cash.

Q. What did you do with it?

A. I came out and gave it to Officer Quinlivan. . . .

Q. What happened the next day?

A. The next day we continued on our program of trying to get houses of prostitution, gambling, bookmakers, and we made several stops that afternoon . . . and Stone's place . . . speakeasies under the same conditions. . . .

Q. Did you know what was in the envelope [from Stone's place]?

A. I do now.

Q. What?

A. Money.

Q. Do you know how much?

A. I think it was $75.

Q. How do you fix that figure in your mind?

A. The reason I remember Stone's place was this, Mr. Dewey, that there were very few of the people who ran speakeasies that marked the envelope, and he was one of them.

Q. What did he mark it with?

A. He had a habit of putting names on. One month he would put down Ginsberg and Cohen; another month, McCarthy Construction Company, something on the envelope. . . .

Q. What happened after you finished your collections on the night you are talking about?

A. I drove Quinlivan to his home.

Q. You were his chauffeur?

A. I was.

Q. You drove him home regularly?

A. Every night we worked.

Q. What do you mean by that?

A. Every night Quinlivan was on duty.

Q. You went to his home and got him?

A. I went to his home about twelve o'clock.

Q. At noon?

A. Noon. Met him there and drove to the office at one o'clock.

Q. What was the practice every month; you say you made these collections monthly?

A. I did. . . .

Q. Who was present with you at these times?

A. Every time I went out for collections of that sort Quinlivan and O'Connor were in the car.

Q. Where would the car park?

A. Twenty feet from the speakeasy, or fifteen feet.

Q. Did you drive from speakeasy to speakeasy?

A. Sometimes, in one parking, I would get twelve to fifteen places.

Q. You mean when they were in a small area?

A. That is right.

Q. What do you mean by small area?

A. Say, on Columbus Avenue, from 110th down to 104th Street, an area of six blocks, there is at least twenty-five places. . . .

Q. Did you ever have trouble making collections?

A. Many times, in small places only.

Q. What do you mean by that?

A. If I went to a small place, and I would be told by the bartender to come back tomorrow, or next week, we called them stragglers. . . .

Q. What happened?

A. If they persisted in withholding, and kept putting me off, telling me to come around the following day or week, and they showed no sign of paying, Quinlivan would give them an observation sale.

Q. What do you mean by that?

A. He would go down to the Federal Court and make affidavit that he saw an unknown man purchase liquor in the place, and in turn he would receive a warrant signed by the United States commissioner, or a judge, proceed to the premises with a Prohibition agent, and make the arrest. . . .

Q. What happened after the arrest, did they pay up there?

A. Some did and some did not. The smaller places went out of business. . . .

Q. Did you keep track of the money collected from month to month?

A. I tried it a couple of months until Officer Quinlivan got wise to the fact. . . . I continued keeping that book for three or four months until one day Quinlivan saw the book and punched me on the jaw.

Q. Did you stop keeping the book after that?

A. I did. . . .

Q. What would you say was the average a month that you collected?

A. I put the average at $6,500, Mr. Dewey, I am pretty safe in saying that.

Q. That would cover all the time you were collecting?

A. That is right.

Q. During this time, did you ever drive Mrs. Quinlivan around in a car?

A. I did.

Q. Where did you take her?

A. I used to take her to the Nadana Club.

Q. The Nadana Club?

A. A Hundred and Eighty-fifth Street and St. Nicholas Avenue.

Q. What was that?

A. A speakeasy.

Q. Who owned it?

A. Quinlivan and a man named Ross owned the place, and later on Ross was paid out by an ex-policeman named Jerry Quinn. . . .

Q. Where did the liquor come from?

A. At times, we would make a legitimate raid, or it was on complaint, from a bootlegger who had a great deal of stuff stored in a store or basement, or we would confiscate a car on the street. . . .

Q. Did you accompany them in, did you go in there with them?

A. I did. Mr. Harris was not in the place, so they searched the place, and we got an enormous amount of liquor, must have been about forty or fifty cases of rye whiskey. After [we had been] there for a while, Harris came in.

Q. Who is Harris?

A. The owner of the place.

Q. Do you know his first name?

A. George. And they began to talk to him—I do not know what they were talking about because they were off on one side and I was stacking up cases; and while they were talking Quinlivan asked me to take some and put it in the car which I had outside. The best I could do was to get about five cases in there. It was all in burlap bags, and he told me to drive it to his home and come back. When I came back I filled the car up again, and Quinlivan had a taxicab that he was filling up, and he drove that stuff up to the Nadana Club. He took it out of the cab, and the Chevrolet, and brought it up to the Nadana Club and came back again. We made three or four trips that way, and no arrest was made in the place. . . .

Q. That is in the late winter or early spring?

A. It was a spring day. Then there is one case during the summer of 1928, we heard of an automobile on 108th Street and Amsterdam Avenue, and we found about ten cans of alcohol in the car, and I took it up to the Nadana Club with the exception of one can. . . .

The Court: . . . I wish you would tell me something. You testified to thirteen months' work for Quinlivan and O'Connor and a hundred and twenty-five collections a month. On what basis were you paid?

A. My salary with them was $50 a week and every day that a collection was made, that is, the first four or five days of the month, if we received a large sum of money, and we counted it at Quinlivan's home, he would hand me $50, $40, or $25, whatever he saw fit. The money that I made outside of that was in calling up bondsmen when they made liquor arrests or prostitution arrests. If a bondsman bailed a defendant out, I received a fee from him for that. . . .

Q. [examination resumed]: What happened in January of 1929?

A. The first week of January 1929, I came up to Quinlivan's home as usual to pick him up with the car, and he told me that Lieutenant Shields, his superior officer, was very anxious to see me about something. I asked him what it was, and he said he didn't know. . . . We met Lieutenant Shields on the sidewalk. He got in the car. I said, "Lieutenant, you want to speak to me?" He said, "Yes, very important."

He seemed very angry. I asked him what the trouble was. He asked me if I knew two disorderly house madams by the names of Jennie the Factory and Sadie the Chink. I told him I did. And he said, "Harry, I don't believe this, at least I don't want to believe this, but Jennie the Factory came to me yesterday and told me that you came to her place of business and told her that I sent you there to get $100 and unless she gave you $100 for me, that you would see that her place was raided, and in addition, after she gave you $100 . . . she said she gave you $50, for yourself, a total of $150."

The only thing I thought—I told Lieutenant Shields after I heard that, I said, "Lieutenant, the best way to straighten this out, why not go up to Jennie the Factory's, and Sadie the Chink's house, and have her tell that to my face?" He said, "That's all right, that's a good idea," and in company with O'Connor and Quinlivan and Lieutenant Shields, I went to [Jennie the Factory's] home.

They opened the door and admitted us. We were all seated in the parlor, and I said to [Jennie], "Lieutenant Shields tells me you gave me $100 for the lieutenant and $50 for myself." So she got up, and looked at me, and said, "Yes, I did." I turned to Jennie and said, "Jennie, are you realizing the accusation you are making, do you realize that is extortion. If I am arrested for that I can go to jail for twenty years?"

She said, "You have been turning my place over for years and if I find out you are a stool pigeon with O'Connor and Quinlivan, I will fix you."

Lieutenant Shields said, "Do you want this man arrested?" She said, "No, I don't want him arrested, but keep him out of the district, because he is putting it over on Quinlivan too." Quinlivan said, "I think you are a God-damned liar," and she said, "Keep out of this, Jimmie, he is putting it over on you, and putting it over on everybody."

Q. You mean she addressed him as Jimmie?

A. Yes.

Q. What did he say?

A. He said, "Stop kidding me, I don't believe it." Lieutenant Shields said, "You don't want him arrested?" She said, "No, I don't want him arrested, keep him out of here." When we got down on the sidewalk Lieutenant Shields said, "Harry, you have been honest—"

The Court: Was this eulogy of your character in the presence of Quinlivan?

A. Yes.

The Court: Quinlivan hear it?

A. Yes, he said, "You have been honest and truthful for a long time, since you have been up here. My advice to you is, get out of this district and stay out. She is a dangerous woman. She sent a policeman to jail before. The best thing for you to do is to take the air."

Quinlivan said, "I think the lieutenant is right. I don't believe what she said. If I did, I would lock you up myself, but I don't believe it. The best thing is to blow. I will give you a couple of weeks' pay and call it off. Besides, Lieutenant Shields would not permit you to work for me anyhow. It is too cold to go back into uniform for the winter, and I have to do what Lieutenant Shields tells me."

He then gave me $100, amounting to two weeks' pay, and I shook hands with him and Officer O'Connor and was told by the three of them, if I knew anything, to call them up on the phone and tell them that way, but that they did not want any trouble with Jennie the Factory or Sadie the Chink, she was very dangerous.

The Court: Which was dangerous?

A. Both of them. [But by November 1930 the Seabury investigation was on and I saw Quinlivan again.] . . . I said, "Hello, Jimmie." He said, "Come here," and grabbed me by the coat and pulled me towards him, into the doorway of Liggett's drugstore. I said, "What's it all about?" He said, "I hear you have been down to Seabury's, and giving . . . Seabury information."

Q. What did you say?

A. I said, "Jim, it is a lie. I have never been down there, I have no reason to go down there, I have not been subpoenaed."

Q. What did he say?

A. He said, "Personally, I didn't think you would go down there and say anything against Bill and myself, but I understand you went down there and pointed out all the different stool pigeons and had them subpoenaed." I denied it, and said I did not. He stopped me and said, "Don't deny it, because we have some real good dope on that and know you did go down there. If I ever find out you went down there again, it will be just too bad for you."

He said, "I am not telling you this because I am afraid. I can take a slap in the face as well as the next man, but if I found out you have been down there, I will just knock the head right off your shoulders. Now, be a regular guy, and keep away." . . . [I went to Baltimore, where I received a telephone call from Quinlivan, who asked], "Where are you going when you leave there?" I said, "I didn't make up my mind, but I am going either to New Orleans or Miami." He said, "Keep away from New Orleans, there is too much racing there, and you will lose all your money, but keep going."

He said, "In about an hour, you will receive a money order for $200, and when you get to your destination, notify that party again, and I will send you some more." I said, "How will I identify myself to get the money from the Western Union?" He said, "Just tell them that you expect it from Harry Lewis, 3544 Broadway, New York, and they will give it to you, and, by the way, hereafter, if you send any communications to that party in Brooklyn, don't sign your right name, sign it Leo."

Q. What did you say then?

A. That was all. He said, "Good-by." Wished me luck.

Q. Did you receive any money following that telephone call?

A. I did.

Q. In what form did that money come to you?

A. I received a Western Union money order.

Q. I ask you whether *this* is the money order you received [showing money order]?

A. It is.

Q. How much is it for?

A. Two hundred dollars.

Q. Is that the figure Quinlivan promised you on the phone?

A. It is.

Needless to say, we knew that no jury would send a yellow dog to jail on the unsupported testimony of this miserable character Levey —so we had brought along plenty of corroboration. This had taken many months of hard work by the Internal Revenue Service and by Bernard Tompkins, the assistant working on the case with me, but it had all fallen into shape. We had located bondsmen and bookmakers who had sent money from Quinlivan to Levey while Levey fled from place to place until the long arm of the Seabury investigation finally caught up with him in New Orleans. Quinlivan's handwriting on the telegram blanks was also irrefutable.

We found one bank account after another in the names of Quinlivan and Mrs. Quinlivan, in both her married and her maiden names, and we tied the ownership of these accounts to the Quinlivans by the testimony of respectable witnesses. Quinlivan's purchase of a $16,500 house and two automobiles added to the picture, in the Depression, of what a policeman could do on his salary of $2,500 a year. There was a touching note of connubial harmony. Quinlivan always deposited one half of every Police Department salary check in one of his accounts and the other half in one of hers.

Specifically, we were able to prove that Quinlivan had banked from unexplained sources $18,200 in 1927, $21,757 in 1928, and $11,688 in 1929. These figures we had on ice and no tax had been paid on them.

Quinlivan was ably defended by James D. C. Murray, a charming and courtly leader of the Bar. His conduct of the defense was instructive to the young lawyers for the government, but the evidence was overwhelming. Quinlivan was convicted on September 4, 1931, and sentenced to three years in the federal penitentiary at Atlanta.

What good did this prosecution do? It was difficult to say. It was a miserable case which attracted widespread public attention when it was first exposed, and much more when the evidence was brought out in a court of law. It proved one or more policemen to be dishonest. Certainly it did not indict the whole Police Department, and certainly there was no profession without its share of bad apples. Moreover, in a city with a basically corrupt political administration, this disease affected everyone who served the city and the community as a whole. During Prohibition the graft was much worse, as the underworld and the respectable elements combined to invite corruption. But, happily, Prohibition would soon be gone, and Police Departments would be better organized and of finer caliber. I was to work with many policemen, and I always believed their integrity on the average ranked higher than that of the average citizen they served.

The Quinlivan case, along with many others, combined with the major thrust of the Seabury investigation to weaken the grip of Tammany Hall on New York City. In the summer of 1932, Judge Seabury filed charges of personal corruption against Mayor Walker, who resigned midway in his hearing before Governor Franklin D. Roosevelt.

The Quinlivan case also reinforced the lesson of the Al Capone conviction—that income tax evasion was a useful approach for the federal authorities to follow, whenever state or local prosecutors could not or would not move against crime.

In the course of the Quinlivan trial we developed at least a thousand instances of extortion, bribery and/or obstruction of justice. Each of these was a felony and might easily have been tried in state or local courts. But since the state prosecutors could not or would not move, the federal government obtained justice by exercising its authority in an income tax case. That this was necessary was in itself a severe indictment of the level of prosecution in the United States.

By now the Intelligence Unit of the Internal Revenue Service had moved into high gear under its chief, Hugh McQuillan, one of the finest men who ever served the government. My special staff of young lawyers was working day and night on rackets income tax cases. It was in this period, incidentally, that I acquired the habit of working six days a week, some Sundays, and most of the evenings. It took thirty years for me to get over that habit, and it never completely wore off.

At the outset our big guns were aimed at the then reputed kings of organized crime, Dutch Schultz (his real name was Arthur Flegenheimer), Waxey Gordon (real name, Irving Wexler), and Legs Diamond (real name, Jack Diamond). As I have said, Lucky Luciano was still in the shadows. All of these were infinitely difficult, long-pull investigations.

It was always a jigsaw puzzle. We would get leads and, bring in witnesses, often ordinary citizens who were employed in one walk of life or another. Even the most completely illegal outfits had to deal with legal businesses, and records had to be kept somewhere. So we would try to work backward, attempting to assess the volume of business, the profits and the amount of income tax we thought was being evaded.

Getting people properly identified, connecting them with bank deposits or with recorded commerce of some kind—this was usually the problem. We never got hold of the real records of the racketeers, but sometimes they had accountants who were half respectable and, half gangster, and sometimes we would learn something. These people would sometimes lead us closer to the bosses, sometimes not.

Incidentally, and this was important, it was not difficult to establish criminal intent. If these men did have income, and they did not file income tax returns, the intent was fairly to be presumed.

In any event, through this laborious process of piecing bits together, we were able to develop evidence of thriving businesses the racketeers claimed not to have. Sometimes we had wiretaps, sometimes the reports of special agents who had tailed the racketeers, sometimes the names of people who had seen the racketeers come and go.

Sometimes, we even got the bank records. And if banks were handed a grand jury subpoena, they had no privilege to withhold information. The banks had to supply the records and give the testimony they were asked for. In fact, most of our subpoenas were for bank and telephone company records, and they were hardly inclined to resist these subpoenas when the whole city knew we were after the hoodlums.

As our probing of the Dutch Schultz and Waxey Gordon empires proceeded, we found witnesses who were guilty of outrageous obstruction. What to do? We decided there must be some power in the courts to compel those with knowledge of crime to disclose it. So we set off to develop this vague field of law and to establish that there were valid sanctions against this kind of obstruction of justice.

Our principal test involved Frederick S. Lang, a senior clerk of a small bank in Hoboken, New Jersey. The revenue agents had found bank accounts at Lang's bank reflecting large transactions involving a brewery we were sure was operated by Waxey Gordon.

Although Lang as a bank officer had opened many of these accounts, he said he could not identify any of the men in whose names he had opened them. In most cases he told the grand jury nothing, although he did admit it was his handwriting on the account cards. Where references given by the new depositors should have been listed, the word "None" appeared. On one account card the words "Looks like liquor business" had been written down. Lang admitted he had written this, but he said he had no idea why.

Special favors and irregularities had been permitted in connection with these accounts, all of them under Lang's supervision, but he claimed he did not know why or on whose behalf. Repeated visitations to a grand jury for days and hours of testimony simply piled up evasive, impudent answers and probably perjury.

Of course Lang was given full assurance of protection if he was afraid of a mob. But nothing would persuade him to talk. So, he was cited for contempt and, given further opportunity to answer and, when he would not, he was sentenced to ninety days' imprisonment.

Throughout this exercise Lang was lavishly represented by counsel whose fees would have been far larger than his annual salary. He appealed all the way to the Supreme Court of the United States, to no avail. Lang served his time—and we never got his testimony even when we finally closed in on Waxey Gordon.

It was hard sledding, and there were many other cases like this before we got to the end. Our contempt weapon was effective but it had limitations. We could say "On the record, this man is obviously guilty of contempt," and he might be sentenced to prison. And when he came back after serving his time we could theoretically give him a new subpoena and begin the process all over again. But we could not repeat this forever without arousing sympathy, without creating martyrs, when our objectives were to stimulate honest testimony. At all times we had to keep public opinion on our side.

We did catch up with Legs Diamond quite rapidly. Diamond and his mob had reportedly kidnaped a farmer in the Catskill Mountains and tortured the man to make him tell the location of an applejack still. The farmer survived, and Diamond was indicted with one of his henchmen, John Scaccio, on charges of kidnaping and assault. Although Scaccio was convicted, Legs Diamond was acquitted for lack of proven connection between him and the kidnaping and torture.

Diamond continued to assert loudly that the territory for liquor and beer upstate north of New York City was his territory. Every so often one of his or somebody else's mob would be found dead of gunshot wounds. But all this publicity helped us build up a case connecting Diamond to the operation of a still. We had been investigating Diamond for income tax evasion, but we decided to bring in a very rare indictment of a known underworld leader on other than income tax charges.

On May 12, 1931, Legs Diamond was indicted for the operation of the still along with two of his henchmen, John Scaccio and Paul Quatrochi. The case fell to Arthur H. Schwartz, chief of the Prohibition Division, one of my closest lifelong friends. Schwartz, in his twenties, was a brilliant, thoughtful, humane Columbia Law School graduate who would subsequently become one of our very finest judges and a justice of the New York State Supreme Court.

We had a sticky ethical problem. Several years before, in the normal course of his private practice, Medalie had been retained by Diamond to defend him in a murder case. The case had never come to trial, and the indictment had finally been dismissed for lack of evidence.

But now our indictment against Diamond was from the office of United States Attorney Medalie. The indictment itself was signed George Z. Medalie. If Medalie should take the case, or try it, or even be responsible for the prosecution, this might give the defense a point on appeal. On the other hand, Medalie could hardly resign as United States Attorney simply because a former client had been indicted.

After long discussion we solved the problem. Medalie would take a vacation in Canada when the case was due to come on for trial. I would become Acting United States Attorney for the Southern District of New York. There was a daylong conference in the judge's chambers, and the defense advanced every possible argument for disqualification because of Medalie's previous representation of Legs Diamond. Arguments for changes of venue and for delay were all made one by one. On all these points we held firm, and we were upheld. Then, a major effort was made by the defense to obtain the promise of a light sentence in exchange for a plea of guilty. This tactic was also unsuccessful.

So we went to trial, with Arthur Schwartz in charge, and George Phann helping him. Legs Diamond was convicted, and he got the maximum sentence of four years' imprisonment and an $11,000 fine for operating the still. Quatrochi was sentenced to two years' imprisonment and a fine of $5,000. The case against Scaccio had been severed since he had previously been sentenced to a long term in connection with the kidnaping and torture of the upstate farmer.

When Diamond was sentenced his counsel asked that he be released on bail pending appeal. This bail was granted over the urgent objection of Arthur Schwartz, who pointed out to Diamond: "I think I am doing you a favor. If you get out on the street, you may not live very long."

Schwartz's words were prophetic. Within a few days Diamond was dead, shot down in a gangster killing. Legs Diamond had acquired too many enemies who were ready to take him over at the point of a gun, just as he had taken over others at the point of a gun before.

The Numbers Kings, the City Hall Cupid, the Labor Extortionist, the Stock Market Swindlers, the Artichoke Monopolist, the Cryptologist, the Chairman of the National City Bank

The two cases against Henry Miro and Wilfred Brunder, in which I participated in the Federal Court, were as far as I knew the only cases made against important numbers racket bankers in years. It was proven that the net profits of the lotteries run by these two men totaled close to a million dollars a year. And, since there were at that time between ten and fifteen other numbers bankers of equal importance in Harlem, there must have been total net profits of $10 to $15 million a year.

After the Miro and Brunder convictions, many of these games were taken over and concentrated in the hands of one or two gangs of organized racketeers, who were also the bankers and operators of some of the major business rackets in New York City.

If this was a fact, as it seemed to be, then the underworld was taking $10 to $15 million a year out of the numbers game alone to finance its depredations against legitimate businesses and the lives of the people of the city. With such a war chest, organized crime had abundant means for corrupting public officials and buying immunity from punishment.

The numbers game, or policy, or just plain numbers was apparently a simple device intended to bring some spice to the lives of the poor and to make them pay more for it than it was worth. The bettors could bet from ten cents to a dollar on a combination of three numbers—ooo to 999. As there were one thousand combinations, the odds were almost a thousand to one, but the winner was only paid at the rate of six hundred to one. Out of his winnings had to come an additional ten per cent for "the collector."

At that time the three winning numbers were certain digits of the daily totals of the New York Bank Clearing House. At other times the payoff was on three numbers in the payoff on the Daily Double at a given race track. The winning numbers were always given prominent display in the late editions of the evening newspapers.

Millions of people played the numbers game in the 1930s and, for every million dollars staked, some $400,000 went to the organization.

The collector was the corner newsstand operator, perhaps, or a porter, a local bookmaker, a taxi driver, or a messenger or clerk in a public office, anybody whose normal livelihood brought him into contact with large numbers of people. At the next level of the organization was the controller, to whom the collectors turned in their slips and their money and in turn received any winnings for their customers for payoff, less ten per cent commission.

The collectors rarely knew the banker, even though they generally knew his name. The controllers knew the banker and turned in the slips every day to his appointed agents.

But the Seabury investigation had unraveled the organization to the point that we knew who two of the numbers kings were. The Seabury staff even identified a number of large bank accounts that were traceable to Henry Miro, if not yet to Wilfred Brunder. But the local District Attorney did nothing, as he had been accustomed solely to prosecute collectors whenever it was impossible for him to avoid prosecuting them.

So our United States Attorney's office took the case on. We had to find Miro's collectors, then his controllers, and persuade them to testify. Our Intelligence Unit located them, one after another, until we had dozens of them. We told them we were not interested in prosecuting them and that we were after the larger fry. With this assurance, some told us the story. Others would not, and we put them into a grand jury where they were questioned at length under threat of prosecution for perjury. Over many months, the case developed well.

A bit of Miro's personal history emerged. The principal messenger in Miro's office had met him while they were both working as boiler scalers in 1922. Six years afterward Miro was a policy king and his old friend now worked as a messenger in his office. This man described the number of offices they maintained for receiving and checking the slips of the bettors, and told how the offices were moved around frequently to avoid detection.

Then Miro was tied in by the testimony of bondsmen he had hired to bail out his collectors whenever they were arrested and charged with the possession of policy slips. This was illegal, of course. Many of the collectors and some of the controllers tied their functions together, within the organization of the numbers king.

The inevitable bank clerks were found to identify the signatures of holders of accounts, and some identified Miro personally as the owner of accounts under various names. Most of the accounts, however, were in the names of his agents. Deposits in the banks that we were able to locate, less withdrawals, amounted to $1,083,154.73 for a three-year period. Since losses and salaries were usually paid out of current receipts, a fair inference was that a large portion of this immense sum was net income.

What to us was an even more sensational aspect of the case came late in the Miro trial in Federal Court, even though we could not stress it or identify the people involved for fear of risking a mistrial. It was part of a case of this kind to prove not only large income but a high standard of living or expensive gifts to others. To this end we offered as evidence a long list of sales slips charged to Miro ranging from shirts to silk pajamas to fitted suitcases and onyx ashtrays. These were gifts that had been made, and for what?

Some of the sales slips were highly significant—and one in particular showed delivery of one dozen shirts on July 22, 1930, to J. J. Hines, the price of the shirts being $14.85 each, and for twelve monograms an additional $18.10. The total was $196.30.

Who was J. J. Hines? We knew, of course, but could not risk a mistrial by naming James J. Hines, the most powerful Democratic Party political figure in the city of New York, and the real leader of Tammany Hall. But there it was.

What was this connection between Miro and Hines? What else

was involved? Was Hines in fact the man at the top who controlled the police who did not interfere? Did Hines control the judges who set free those who were arrested? Was Hines the man who controlled the District Attorney who looked the other way?

There were more revealing sales slips. On December 19, 1930, Miro had sent a dozen shirts of the same quality to "Sam Kantor, % the Owosco Club," and the same day a dozen similar shirts to none other than "Dutch Schultz, % the Owosco Club." Another dozen had been sent to "Honorable William Solomon, % the Owosco Club." We could not bring it out, but Solomon was a satellite of James J. Hines and a Tammany leader. There was only one Dutch Schultz and now we had a whole raft of new questions. Had Dutch Schultz muscled in on the numbers game? Was Miro's gift to him just a courtesy from one criminal to another, a gift from a local administrator to keep a very important racketeer happy?

J. Richard "Dixie" Davis was counsel for the defense. This man had also been the counsel for the defense of some of Miro's collectors when they had been arrested some time before. Was Dixie Davis the counsel to a large criminal organization, perhaps even helping to direct it? It would be four more years before the Dixie Davis mystery was solved and the amazing story spelled out.

Medalie tried the Miro case beautifully and all of us who had participated in the preparation and the the trial felt rewarded for a lot of hard work. Miro was sentenced to three years in the federal penitentiary in Atlanta, and the conviction was affirmed by the United States Court of Appeals. We were happy over the result but were not satisfied. We felt we had lifted only a corner of a curtain, raising more questions than we had answered. We had vindicated the law in the Miro case, but the gangster influence, the political sponsorship of organized crime, were as yet unexplored.

The trial of Wilfred Brunder, the second numbers king, followed shortly thereafter. He had been discovered at the same time as Henry Miro. Now Brunder pleaded guilty and received a somewhat lighter sentence.

These were the only numbers kings tried during our tenure of the United States Attorney's office. How many more bankers were left we had neither the time nor the manpower to determine. There were surely many we had not found, we would go on pouring tax-free income into the underworld to finance political corruption.

Should all forms of gambling be legalized and put into the hands of government? We researched that question repeatedly over the years. While I was Governor of New York a state lottery was proposed, with the claim that it would remove sources of corruption and produce enormous revenues for the state government. In response, I sent a special message to the legislature in which I reviewed the dismal history of legalized gambling in this country, and opposed the proposition.

Years after that, under pressure of a popular vote, the state did establish a lottery, which, or so it was hoped, would crush illegal gambling, make it possible for people in every circumstance to have the thrill of a small bet, and produce huge revenues for the state. There appeared to be considerable question whether it would in the end accomplish any of these objectives. Meanwhile, legalized gambling under theoretically stringent controls in the state of Nevada seemed primarily to be spawning more multimillionaire gangsters than ever.

During these and subsequent months our office was never busier. Our Criminal Division was handling its cases with an altogether new efficiency, keeping its calendar up to date, and recording the highest percentage of convictions in history. The New York *Times* summarized this period:

"Medalie doubles the speed of justice. Best results since 1911. Criminal cases disposed of faster than at any other time in the history of the office. The trial calendar is up to date for the first time in years. Verdicts confirmed on appeal in 19 out of 21 cases. Convictions obtained in 82.2 per cent of the trials, compared with a general average of 69 per cent in the previous ten years."

Our work was also heavy because we were launching major prosecutions against stock market swindlers, bucket-shop operators, and other financial offenders, and we were using the mail fraud laws. These mail fraud laws established a federal jurisdiction.

In *United States* v. *Brown*, Jack Rosenblum of our office prosecuted the Manhattan Electrical Supply group of crooked pool operators who ran the price of its stock up from $20 a share to $56. The manipulators had used false rumors, placed matched orders, and used wash sales in order to induce the public to buy. Then they sold out. The stock dropped to $6.00 and thousands of investors all over the country lost more than $10 million. After a two-month trial the defendants were sentenced to five years in the penitentiary and were heavily fined.

This case was accorded its true significance by A. A. Berle, Jr., in the March 1938 issue of the *Columbia Law Review*. He wrote:

> The past seven years have seen a surprising development in the law of manipulation of security prices. In part, this is due to to the definite provisions of the Securities Exchange Act of 1934. . . . It is erroneous, however, to assume that the statute constitutes the primary development in the field. . . .
>
> [Previously] the major difficulty with the common-law doctrine was that it placed the burden of bringing action on the plaintiff who had been defrauded. . . . The means of obtaining evidence was difficult. Particularly, it was troublesome where the false statement consisted in a series of "wash sales" and still more difficult with "matched orders" . . . where two or more confederates put in orders to buy and sell which are designed to meet orders to sell or buy placed by a confederate. . . . Only a wholesale study of many brokerage accounts would disclose the ultimate scheme. . . .
>
> Crystallization occurred in the now famous case of *United States* v. *Brown*. . . . Preparation of the case for trial and the handling of the evidence still furnish a model for similar cases in this field."

We had another major fraud, a $5- to $10-million venture to produce a motion picture to be called *The Life of the Blessed Virgin*. Those defrauded included cardinals and former Governor Alfred E. Smith.

We had a challenge of a different sort one day when I overheard the trial of a sixteen-year-old boy who had been seized as a drug peddler. It turned out that his elder brother had made him a delivery boy. He was headed for prison but we had the indictment changed and the boy was turned over to the Children's Court for protective care.

Life was full of frustrations, but occasionally it had its lighter moments. James J. McCormick, a leader of Tammany Hall, was then deputy city clerk at a salary of $8,500 a year. But he admitted to Judge Seabury that he owned thirty-four savings bank accounts into which had been deposited $51,000 in 1929 and $53,000 in 1930. This extra money came mostly, he said, from "nice people" who made "gifts" to him when he conducted their marriage ceremonies in City Hall.

McCormick was promptly dubbed in the press the "Cupid of City Hall," but he was a dour Cupid to the people he married. Moreover, a quick check showed that he had not paid any income tax in the six years of his marrying duties, and we considered that our federal business. We began rounding up some of the couples he had married and we learned that the "gifts" were not exactly that.

McCormick's system was direct and mean. After the bride and groom had paid their two-dollar city fee in the other room and waited in line, they were admitted into McCormick's office. There they stood before his desk while McCormick mumbled the marriage ceremony. Simultaneously, he pulled out a desk drawer full of one-, five-, and ten-dollar bills. Then, as he said the final words, he would reach into the drawer and pretend to fumble for a rubber band to put around the marriage certificate. The ceremony took at best about thirty seconds, but sometimes the fumbling took longer.

Many bridegrooms got the point, but if they did not McCormick was not subtle. According to one bridegroom's testimony at the trial, McCormick said "It is up to you."

Q. Then what happened?

A. I didn't get it at first, because I was a little nervous.

Q. What happened?

A. Then my wife nudged me.

Q. Then what did you do?

A. I produced a five-dollar bill.

Q. Then what?

A. He said, "God bless you."

But one bridegroom only gave him a dollar and, as the man walked out, McCormick mumbled, "One lousy buck." Another gave nothing, and McCormick called out, "Cheapskate!"

So it went. Of course we did not have all the bridegrooms in the courtroom, but we had enough to explain the sources of the bank deposits. Twelve days after his exposure by the Seabury investigation, McCormick had rushed down and paid income taxes for six years back, but this did not save him. After four days of trial and sixty witnesses he was convicted, fined $15,000, and sentenced to four months in prison. He was, incidentally, the first Tammany leader to be removed from office by our efforts.

By now I was feeling my sea legs as a trial lawyer growing firmer under me. Confidence, judgment, and skill in cross-examination are essential to trial work, and I now had at least a whole lot of exposure under my belt. McCormick's congressman, for example, had testified for the defense and he had turned out to be something of a test in cross-examination.

McCormick's congressman testified that he had, as a lawyer, advised McCormick that these "gifts" were not subject to income tax. That seemed like a pretty good defense for a jury even though, legally, it was no defense at all. Ignorance of the law was never a defense. But it was a strong argument to the jury from an impressive source, a United States congressman.

It was a tough decision for me whether to cross-examine this witness and risk offending some jurors, or whether to ignore it and rely on the judge's charge to the jury on the point of law the congressman had raised. In one of those instant decisions that have to be made in a courtroom, I decided to risk it. Courteous questioning of the congressman now developed that the man did know that money derived from extortion was taxable. He had not examined the law as to the differences in taxable status between extortion and true, voluntary gifts. The congressman had not even inquired how these "gifts" had happened to be made in such staggering totals. And he admitted that he did know that tips were taxable. That was all, and very brief.

In the end the congressman as a defense witness had done the Tammany leader no good. Instead, he unwittingly helped nail down our case against McCormick. Cross-examination, as I had learned it from Medalie, could be a delight and very helpful.

The really important event in the preceding few months had been the birth of our first son on October 2, 1932. While he was on the way we had spent a Sunday in the New York Public Library, researching names in a Dewey family genealogy which had been published after Admiral Dewey's victory at Manila Bay. There were all sorts of enchanting, old-fashioned names, and I had thought that Frances was in favor of one or another of them. If the child turned out to be a boy, I was against calling him a Junior because my father had found it confusing to be named George Martin Dewey, Jr., for his well-known father. I thought Frances agreed with that conclusion. All this lasted until the child was born, and then she promptly decided that he was going to be named Thomas E. Dewey, Jr. Who is going to argue with his wife in a hospital after the birth of his first son?

All this happened at a time when I was up to my neck in trials and investigations in the United States Attorney's office. Partly because we had no full-time nurse, and partly because it was the only way I could keep acquainted with my infant son, I got up every morning to give him the six o'clock bottle. This did get a little rough because it continued right through the trial of the McCormick case but it was an experience I would always cherish, particularly when it was in the past.

On another front, we were meeting rough going in an important investigation of Patrick J. Commerford, delegate and undisputed boss of Local 125 of the International Union of Operating and Hoisting Engineers and vice-president of the New York Building Trades Council. Commerford's union was in a key spot: nothing could go up or down on a construction job without the hoisting engineers.

This was the unusual case in which we had solid complaints. These came from men in the union who knew they were being exploited when Commerford called quickie strikes for no visible reason and then settled the strikes for no visible reason, with no change in conditions. The men fought to get elections and never got one. The officers selected themselves privately every year and any member who objected soon found there was no work for him in his trade. Some of the men had appealed to the courts for help and they lost. They complained to the District Attorney of New York County. It was said, however, that Commerford was a Tammany Hall man of some kind, and they got nowhere. So they came to the United States Attorney's office with plenty of complaints but no hard evidence.

We had one lead—to Patrick McGovern, a major contractor who was conducting a multimillion-dollar project on the New York City subway system. This inquiry focused on five checks McGovern had drawn on his own company over a period of eleven months, totaling $380,000. These checks were drawn to his own order. And we had two reports—one, that he had paid large sums to Commerford and, two, that he had paid large sums to the former Mayor Walker for his contracts. So the question was, what did he do with that cash?

McGovern had plenty of time and notice to consult his lawyers before we invited him to our office. He refused to tell us anything, so we subpoenaed him to a grand jury. There he refused to talk, this time claiming the protection of the Fifth Amendment. He refused specifically to say whether he had had any financial transactions with Commerford.

After hours of questioning before the grand jury McGovern was taken before a district judge, who formally advised him that the investigation was not aimed at him and that it was intended solely to ascertain who had received the money. The judge then ordered McGovern to go back to the grand jury and answer the questions. There McGovern was again asked what he had done with the $380,-000 and he replied, "I won't tell you that." Pressed further, he changed his tune and gave a variety of explanations, saying that he "never kept any record," that he used the money to "pay living expenses," and for "general expenses."

At the next session McGovern had to concede that all his family and living expenses were paid by check all the way down to items of five dollars for a doctor's bill. But the larger of the suspect checks was drawn for $160,000 and he said, "I must have drawn it for some personal reason. I don't remember just exactly what it was."

Next McGovern claimed he put the whole $380,000 into a safe deposit box and took money out three or four times a month for personal purposes. This sounded as phony as the other stories, but we had to check it out. At the next examination we produced the records of his visits to his safe deposit box. These blew up his last story. Then he said the tale was all a mistake and he must have kept the money in his desk.

He took refuge in the old story about "charitable gifts," but his income tax returns refuted that.

He said he must have spent the money on liquor and gambling, but he could not name a single place or circumstance in which he had done either.

After five prolonged sessions the record of this mass of evasion and perjury was presented to the court and McGovern was sentenced to sixty days' imprisonment for contempt. The sentence was affirmed on appeal and, after refusing a final chance to tell the truth, he served his time. We never did get his story and it was a heartbreak to Murray Gurfein, to another assistant, David Paley, and to me. Months of hard labor had come to nothing.

Other contractors were equally difficult, but over many more months we did get the story from some. We got pieces from one contractor, and we showed them to another, and we gradually built up more and more information as they felt the whole story was going to come out. Finally our indictment charged that Commerford had defrauded the government out of income taxes on $17,584 in 1929, on $20,000 in 1930, and on $26,000 in 1931. This was surely only a part of the total, but it was enough for us to prove that the complaints of the union members in the first place had been well founded. It was quite a story, another of those microcosms of the history of an era.

It turned out in court that a contracting firm, Gahagan and Canavan, had three jobs going until, one day, all the men on the job failed to show up. Canavan suspected Commerford and went to see him at the office of the Building Trades Council. There the contractor saw Commerford and Charles Johnson, a delegate of the Dock Builders Union. He was promptly told, "If you want service, why, it is worth something." They started the negotiation at $12,000 and after some haggling it got down to $7,000, which sum Canavan agreed to take up with Gahagan. There was no mention of wages or working conditions by anybody.

The contracting firm was in real trouble. They could not afford delays on the jobs because there was a penalty for every day they passed the deadline for completion. So Gahagan and Canavan told Commerford they would pay. He replied in Delphic terms, "Johnson is all right." They then drew two checks, one for $4,000 and one for $3,000, dividing their cost between two jobs, put the money in envelopes, and left them on the table in an empty inner office. Johnson came in and they left him alone in the office. When they came back the envelopes were gone.

All the men returned to work on the jobs the following morning with no change in wages or working conditions.

It was the same story with David Malzman, who was constructing a large office building at 120 Wall Street. All of a sudden one Friday afternoon all the men went off the job—the hoisting engineers, the bricklayers, the carpenters, the cement finishers, the plumbers, the electricians, the elevator installers, and everybody else. Malzman was desperate. He could not even find out why the men had quit, so Walter Swanson, his superintendent, did: it was Commerford. This time the shakedown began at $10,000 and they settled at $2,500. The payoff had a novel twist.

Commerford told Swanson to go to the office, get the $2,500 from Malzman, put it in an envelope, go to City Hall Park, and wait until a man tapped him on the shoulder. He did as directed, a man came up, tapped him on the shoulder and said, "I am the guy." Swanson gave him the envelope and the man went off in a taxi. All the men on the job came back to work the following Monday morning, again with no change in wages or working conditions.

The same thing happened to the Carlin Construction Company, this time for $5,000. Another victim was the Robert J. Murphy Company, this time for $5,000 which was handed directly to Commerford.

Two hoisting engineering companies found they had to pay Commerford $100 a week, and another found it necessary to pay him $320 a month or somehow their machinery did not work when it was installed. A laborers' union wanted to be admitted to the Central Trades and Labor Council. It took many months, but $1,000 to Commerford opened the door.

Out of forty-seven witnesses, most were reluctant or hostile, and Commerford put up a vigorous fight. But the evidence was irrefutable and he was duly convicted, fined $2,000, and sentenced to prison for a year and a day.

Commerford was the first defendant I helped convict whom I was to see afterward. At the time of his release from the federal penitentiary at Atlanta, I was engaged in private law practice and he came to see me. It seemed that, knowing the terms of his parole would keep him out of the union, he had learned stenography while in prison. Now he wondered if I could help him get a job as a stenographer! He got a job somewhere, and I never heard of him again.

Meanwhile, after two years of work, Murray Gurfein completed the investigation of Joseph Castaldo, known as the Artichoke King. Now the artichoke did not seem like a very important vegetable in the United States economy, but to Castaldo it became an empire. Most vegetable dealers brought their own artichokes from California until Castaldo decided to take over the whole business.

Dealers were warned to buy their artichokes from Castaldo. It was as simple as that. If they did not, the delivery of their artichokes was delayed until the artichokes were spoiled. Sometimes the delivery trucks were hijacked. Sometimes recalcitrant dealers were robbed or beaten or both. One by one they caved in, the artichoke racket was complete, and one Sicilian had a monopoly of a small business.

We indicted Castaldo for non-payment of income taxes on more than a million dollars of net income, which indicated he was getting most of the money from that small business. After Murray Gurfein had opened the case and presented his witnesses for two days, Castaldo pleaded guilty and went to jail for income tax evasion. None of the witnesses was harmed, and the racket was broken.

There was to us, of course, real satisfaction in removing this undesirable character from society and in the elimination of one racket monopoly. As so often happened, however, more questions were now asked than had been answered. Was Castaldo part of a larger mob? Did he have a higher-up boss? Outside his area, who delayed the other merchants' artichokes? Who hijacked their trucks? Where did Castaldo get the manpower from, the other gangsters, to beat up his competitors before they came into line?

On a broader scale, why did the District Attorney of New York County never do anything in areas of this kind? A truck hijacking, a beating up, or any other act of violence was always treated as an isolated incident. Was this the result of indolence? But all seventy of this District Attorney's assistants could not have been so indolent or anti-social. Was this because of a general relationship between organized crime, Tammany Hall, and the public officials?

My own curiosity, which I had brought to the office originally, was less and less satisfied.

By the spring of 1933 we had been in office more than two years. Despite all the successes, both major and minor, Dutch Schultz and Waxey Gordon were still at liberty, although we were coming closer to them every day. Meanwhile all manner of other things seemed to be happening in all kinds of directions, and I supposed this was the fundamental interest and the variety of the law.

An unusual visitor came to see me in the person of Major George P. Brett, the president of the Macmillan Company, publishers. He had in his hands a manuscript by Herbert O. Yardley, whom he called the greatest code expert of the century. The book, he said, revealed secrets of activities by our government in decoding messages which, if revealed, might endanger our security.

Brett said that he had not fought for his country to have its safety endangered later by anything he might publish.

After a brief look at the book I asked him whether he would mind if I gave him a grand jury subpoena for the manuscript, and he said, "Certainly not." So we went up to the grand jury, the manuscript was impounded, and I reported the facts to Medalie. He promptly sent me on a train to Washington.

Yardley had rendered invaluable service in World War I in organizing and directing desperately needed cryptographic services, and afterward he persuaded the State and War departments to set up a joint code and cipher office in secret quarters, later called the Black Chamber. Since all nations, friendly and unfriendly, used secret codes, and since our own nation had been incredibly naïve and neglectful in this area, Yardley had to proceed to break the codes of most other nations in the world.

In 1929, when Henry L. Stimson became the new Secretary of State, he learned of Yardley and the Black Chamber. Stimson was shocked. As he said later, "Gentlemen don't read each other's mail." Adhering to the high principles he attributed to all other nations, he canceled all support from the State Department for the Black Chamber. This closed the office. The files reverted to the Army Signal Corps, where a single officer with a tiny staff was in charge of cryptography.

Yardley was out of a job, and within a year his savings were gone. His talents could find no market. Gradually he became desperate, and he sat down to write a book, *The American Black Chamber,* one of the most famous books on cryptography. The book created a storm. The reviews were unanimously good, calling the book fascinating and of prime importance. Government officials tried to look the other way. Cryptographers were furious at this violation of the confidence of the government, terming the book outrageous, vainglorious, and full of exaggeration.

Yardley himself defended the book on the ground that, if decoding was to be abolished, it should certainly not be done unilaterally by our government. He pointed out that every other country was still doing it and that our State Department was guilty of gross negligence, using what he called "sixteenth-century codes."

Financially, the book was a great success, and it was followed by English, French, Swedish, Chinese, and Japanese editions. The

Japanese version created the greatest furor. Elements of the Japanese government accused Yardley of dishonorable conduct and one another of grave blunders. The Japanese edition seemed to have sold twice as many copies as the American edition.

The climax came a year later, when Yardley sat down to write another book, to be entitled *Japanese Diplomatic Secrets*. This time he really gave away secrets which could have embarrassed the United States Government. In his first book he had reported on his service in the early 1920s during the Washington Disarmament Conference, designed to limit naval armaments to certain ratios between the United States, Britain, France, Italy, and Japan. As this conference had dragged on, Yardley was decoding the messages of instruction from Tokyo to the Japanese Ambassador in Washington. The Japanese were struggling to obtain a sea power ratio of 7 to 10 vis-à-vis the United States and also Great Britain. The Japanese finally cabled in code to their ambassador: "It is necessary to avoid any collision with Great Britain and America, particularly America," on this subject. They instructed the ambassador that, if it was absolutely necessary, he should settle for a ratio of 6.5 to 10 and, if required to save the conference, he should yield and accept a 6 to 10 ratio.

Secretary of State Charles Evans Hughes and his staff were able to read these instructions every morning with their coffee, and they bargained from great strength. They knew all they had to do was to hold out to win, so they held out. There was achieved the five-power ratio of 10 for the United States, 10 for Britain, 6 for Japan, and 3.3 apiece for France and Italy.

David Kahn, in his remarkably comprehensive book *The Codebreakers*, reported that the Black Chamber had produced before the end of the conference more than 5,000 code solutions and translations. Yardley had to go to Arizona for four months to recuperate from overwork.

The American Black Chamber had been trouble enough, but if there was to be a new Yardley book entitled *Japanese Diplomatic Secrets* it might well precipitate a disaster for our relations in the Pacific. Kahn reported that Stanley K. Hornbeck, a Far Eastern expert in the State Department, heard of this new book and wrote a memorandum dated September 12, 1932, concluding: "I cannot too strongly urge that, in view of the state of excitement which apparently prevails in Japanese public opinion now, characterized by fear of or enmity toward the United States, every possible effort should be made to prevent the appearance of this book. Its appearance would contribute substantially to the amount of explosive material which seems to be piling up in Japan."

In any event, five months later Major Brett had walked into my office with the new Yardley manuscript in his hands.

All of this happened at the worst possible time since the Hoover administration was going out of office. On March 4 the brand-new administration of Franklin D. Roosevelt would be in charge. After my own secret train ride to Washington, my conferences began in the Attorney General's office, with representatives of the State and War departments on hand. It started first thing in the morning and lasted all day. We agreed that we had no legal power to suppress the book. Even if we could get its publication enjoined, the mere fact of the lawsuit would be harmful and would probably cause the secrets to leak out anyway. Finally, I was instructed to go back to New York, get in touch with Brett, Yardley, and his agent George Bye, and persuade Yardley himself to suppress the book.

After extensive negotiations, Yardley finally agreed to meet with us. The next problem was where. He would only meet in his favorite speakeasy. For obvious reasons, federal attorneys did not go to speakeasies during Prohibition. Nevertheless we ended up having the meeting in a speakeasy.

Yardley, Bye, and Brett were all there, and we had a difficult conversation. Yardley was no longer poor, as his first book had been a great financial success. He was bitter at the government for what he considered its incredible stupidity. He asserted his devotion to the country and his desire to do no damage to its interests. He believed that his new book would alert the nation further to the need to act like a grown-up, modern nation.

At a second meeting there evolved the idea that a letter of apology from Colonel Stimson might persuade Yardley to abandon the book. This looked to me like a pretty difficult letter to get, so I proposed an alternative possibility. I said we might get a letter from Cordell Hull, the incoming Secretary of State. Meanwhile, we had the manuscript, but we did not know whether there was another copy in existence.

On my next trip to Washington we canvassed the progress of the conversations, and it was decided to try Secretary Hull. After long negotiations over the language, Hull signed the letter of apology for the government's termination of Yardley's services. Yardley accepted the letter, and the book never appeared.

This, of all others, was the toughest negotiation I was ever involved in.

Yardley was never again employed in cryptography by our government and, after a varied career, he died on August 7, 1958, and was buried with military honors in Arlington National Cemetery.

As a footnote, Stimson had the moral courage to admit his error and reverse himself when he became Secretary of War in 1940. If he made an error in terminating support for cryptography, it was surely buried under the mountain of his patriotic dedication to the service of his country: United States Attorney for the Southern District of New York, 1906–9; Secretary of War under President Taft, 1911–13, under President Roosevelt, 1940–45, and President Truman, 1945; soldier, chairman of various international conferences, Governor General of the Philippines; Secretary of State under President Hoover, 1929–33; and a superb practicing lawyer in between.

Incidentally, he was especially kind to a very young man when he invited me to lunch in the early 1930s. He regaled me with stories of his work as United States Attorney under President Theodore Roosevelt, including his pioneer prosecutions under the Sherman Antitrust Act, in which he succeeded in breaking up the sugar trust. Few men in American history have served our country so well and for such a remarkable span of years.

Another footnote to the Yardley case was a long and bitter fight in the Congress over the effort by the new Administration to enact a statute containing criminal sanctions against unauthorized disclosure of official code material between a foreign government and its diplomatic mission in the United States. Actually we had drafted this bill in our office in New York for the Department of Justice. To our surprise, it kicked up quite a storm, and the debates in both houses produced more heat than light. The differences were finally ironed out in conference, and the bill was signed by President Franklin D. Roosevelt on June 10, 1933.

While the Yardley matter was still going on, President Roosevelt took the country off the gold standard, and Congress made it a crime for a private citizen to hold gold. This landed on our desk too. A good many people thought the statute was an unconstitutional violation of the government's contract to redeem currency in gold. A New York lawyer, Frederick Barber Campbell, announced publicly that he had $100,000 in gold in his vault and that he would not surrender it. So we had to act, and my memory is rather vivid of staying up all night to draft a new kind of indictment to present to the grand jury the next day.

Campbell pleaded not guilty and tested his theory all the way up to the Court of Appeals, where the statute was upheld. He surrendered his gold.

Only once during these years did a crowd walk down the middle of Broadway celebrating a defeat for the United States Attorney's office. A Senate hearing had exposed the fact that in 1929, during the stock market debacle, Chairman Charles E. Mitchell of the National City Bank of New York had "sold" 18,000 shares of his stock in the bank to his wife. This resulted in a loss of $2.8 million, which he had taken as a deduction on his income tax returns. Quite apart from everything else, his wife had not paid for the stock, did not have the money to pay for it, and Mitchell had made her periodic gifts of the money necessary to pay the interest on her indebtedness.

It looked like a paper transaction to create an artificial loss for an income tax fraud.

Mitchell also testified to other private transactions which appeared to some in Washington to be dubious, and Senator Burton K. Wheeler shouted that Mitchell "should be punished as Al Capone was." President Hoover, still in office, privately wrote a blazing letter to his Attorney General directing prompt and immeditate investigation and action.

Mitchell, of course, insisted that the transactions were thoroughly legal and proper, and his counsel affirmed that they had given him legal advice to that effect at the time. We had many days and nights of examinations of records, legal research, examinations of witnesses, and conferences with counsel. Shortly after President Roosevelt took office we were ready to go to Washington to lay out the results of our investigation before the new Attorney General. We did, and we were directed to proceed with an indictment for income tax fraud.

This turned out to be a famous case, delicately balanced as to the law and the facts, one in which any trial lawyer would have been overjoyed to have been involved on either side. Two leading barristers of the day were ranged against each other: Medalie for the government and Max D. Steuer for the defense. I had prepared the case and participated in a minor way at the trial. Steuer was assisted by a contemporary of mine, an old friend, Leonard P. Moore, who became a judge of the United States Court of Appeals. The case was fully presented and well tried on both sides. Mitchell was acquitted, and he walked in triumph down the middle of Broadway followed by Max Steuer and a large group of happy friends.

There were two factors that turned out to be decisive in this jury trial. First was a long series of deeply affectionate letters Mitchell had written to his wife, on various anniversaries, transmitting the checks for the money with which she could pay him the interest on her debt for the stock he had "sold" to her. Steuer read these letters to the jury with great effectiveness.

The second and probably the greater factor in the acquittal was Mitchell himself. He had been called the greatest bond salesman of the era, and it was probably true. He was a man of force and charm and, as somebody said, if Mitchell could not sell his side of the story to a jury, he was not the Mitchell who had built up a great bank. He surely did sell his side of the story.

As a postscript, however, many months later, after I had returned to private law practice, the Roosevelt administration asked me to serve as a Special Assistant Attorney General with Edward S. Greenbaum to try a civil tax case before the tax court. We set out before the tax court to collect the taxes Mitchell had been charged with evading. We won the case in that forum.

Waxey Gordon

By the late winter of 1933 we were finally able to seek income tax indictments of the top gang bosses, Dutch Schultz and Waxey Gordon. The Schultz case was a study in frustration. We managed to locate Abe "Bo" Weinberg, the head of Schultz's disciplinary forces, one of the most efficient and murderous gunmen in the business, and we issued him a subpoena. He was questioned repeatedly in the grand jury but he revealed nothing. He was sentenced to sixty days for contempt and he appealed all the way to the United States Supreme Court without success. Bo Weinberg served his time and said nothing.

Rocco Delarmi, another kingpin in the Schultz organization, ignored a subpoena and was sentenced to seven months' imprisonment. We spent months of valuable time on both of these mobsters and the only dubious satisfaction we got was that the trials and appeals must have cost "the Dutchman" a lot of money in legal fees.

Dutch Schultz himself was in hiding and, charged with evading payment of $92,103 in federal income taxes on an estimated income of $481,000, he simply stayed in hiding until our group no longer occupied the United States Attorney's office.

Incidentally, Bo Weinberg was paid back for his loyalty to Dutch Schultz in an exotic ritual. It was said that Weinberg, after his release, and while the Dutchman was still out of circulation, began to take over some of the rackets as his personal property. So Weinberg was taken out in a boat on the Harlem River and was made to watch while concrete dried out around his feet and ankles. Then, in his concrete shoes, he was dumped overboard.

But we did catch up with Waxey Gordon. This was the heavy-set, laconic former pickpocket who had served his apprenticeship with some of the toughest mobs in the East and was now a multimillionaire beer baron. Waxey Gordon had always employed the same murderous tactics that Al Capone had used in Chicago and we were now ready to put him away for income tax evasion, Capone style.

For two years under my supervision, six investigators had worked full time collecting bits and pieces of information that would stand up in court. For the final six months six lawyers and twelve Internal Revenue Service agents formed the task force, and we finalized the answers to the prosaic and all-important questions.

For example, who sold the beer barrels to the Gordon breweries? Who sold the malt? Who sold the fleet of trucks the Gordon organization used for distribution? Who sold the oil, the gasoline, the tires, the brewing machinery, the cooperage coating, the air compressors, the cleaning compounds, the kettles and pipes, the hops, the yeast, the repair parts for the trucks, and the materials for repairing beer barrels, the heads, shooks, and rivets? Who installed the piping and the electrical equipment?

How were all these goods and services paid for, and in whose names had delivery been taken? What did the sellers' books show about the checks and who had signed them? On what banks had the checks been drawn?

Sometimes we had a race with the Gordon organization to get to the records of the companies and the banks first. Sometimes we did not get there in time. Record books almost too large for men to carry walked out of banks in New Jersey and could not be located. One painstaking search of huge bundles of deposit slips in a Paterson, New Jersey, bank showed that every deposit slip from a Gordon account had been extracted before we got there, and only the Gordon slips were missing. Nobody at the bank ever admitted knowing why or how.

A large, independent trucker had brought thousands of dollars' worth of supplies to the Gordon breweries. When our agents got to him, however, his books had been completely rewritten. No sales to Gordon's breweries appeared at all. All sales of what had actually been sent to Gordon were listed in the rewritten books in fictitious names. But we finally traced the payments made by this trucker through the new names to Gordon's bank accounts. Our trail led from there to witnesses who had heard Gordon's men give orders for the books to be rewritten.

The hunt through the banks had virtually unbelievable aspects. There were times when our agents went into the New Jersey banks and were asked to sit down and wait. Then some of Gordon's men would arrive from nowhere, withdraw all the money in the accounts, and make away with all evidence of the ownership of the accounts.

In Hoboken, New Jersey, when our agents went to a bank they were arrested by the local police. These local policemen charged our agents with using forged credentials, and they held our men until the Gordon records could be spirited away.

In June 1932 our agents had caught up with Sam Gurock, a key Gordon employee, who had ignored a subpoena and was in contempt of court. Gurock was arrested in New Jersey and put in jail for a hearing the following morning. He was a potentially valuable witness for us because he had opened a variety of Gordon bank accounts under fictitious names, and we had never been able to locate him for questioning.

We lost Sam Gurock this time too. In the middle of the night a United States commissioner named Frank J. Pfaff came from his home to the jail in which Gurock was being held. Commissioner Pfaff secretly fixed bail for the Gordon employee at $500, whereupon Gurock posted the bail on the spot, walked out, and disappeared. We never saw him again.

Waxey Gordon had financed part or all of the construction of the Piccadilly Hotel in New York City through his Paramount Hotel Corporation. Checks from beer accounts were traced to its books but before we could examine them these books had been rewritten too.

But we gained ground nonetheless. Even though the New Jersey banks were proving less than co-operative, we were able to seek out the Recordak copies of checks which had passed through the big clearinghouse banks. With snapshots, rogues' gallery and passport photographs, we helped to identify men who had opened accounts in fictitious names. We obtained specimens of the handwriting of many of the Gordon mobsters, from drivers' license applications, automobile registrations, property leases, order blanks, insurance accident claims, telephone contracts, anything that long and patient research could turn up.

Scott Leslie, the handwriting expert, spent months enlarging signatures, comparing and analyzing them and identifying the dummy account operators who were otherwise established as part of the Gordon organization. Though Waxey Gordon had no bank accounts in his own name, he had been careless enough to sign his own or another name on the back of a number of checks for deposit in the dummy accounts. The handwriting expert tied these and the accounts to Gordon. In fact it was fair to say that handwriting analysis did more than any other single factor to tie the whole case together.

Telephone toll slips proved to be almost as useful. The irrefutable records of telephone calls from homes and offices, hotel suites, the breweries, the garages, and the washhouse tied the mob and the business tighter.

Meanwhile the District Attorney of New York County, the perennially inactive Thomas C. T. Crain, an aging Tammany sachem, now announced that he was investigating Waxey Gordon. Before long, however, he gave up, and he did so with the highly prejudicial comment that there were no witnesses brave enough to testify against Waxey Gordon. This was one of our blacker days. Naturally a number of our own witnesses got the message, and they forgot all they had told us. It took quite a while for us to get over that one.

Nevertheless, after our two and a half years examining 1,000 witnesses, 200 bank accounts, and several thousand hours of grand jury examination, and tracing of the toll slips of more than 100,000 telephone calls, we indicted Waxey Gordon. We indicted him for attempting to evade payment of federal income taxes on a net income of $1,618,690 for 1930 and 1931. A second indictment later increased this total to $1,338,000 for 1930 and $1,026,000 for 1931.

Gordon had other and perhaps more serious troubles at this time. The grapevine had told us that he was engaged in another gang war, and there was reason to believe that another mob was gunning not merely for his subordinates but for Waxey himself. The newspapers attributed sixteen murders in three months to this particular gang war. As a result Gordon had been missing from his usual haunts for quite a while before the indictment. Whether he was a fugitive more because of his underworld rivals or because of our own investigation was never clear. In any event, when our agents finally caught him in his summer cottage at White Lake, in the Catskill Mountains, his loaded gun lay unused under his pillow and he came quietly. His bodyguard, "Joey the Fleabag," made no resistance. Gordon was held in $100,000 bail.

Gordon was an old hand at gang wars, of course, and knew the rough underworld logic: what you take at the point of a gun you can lose at the point of another. He had not acquired his empire by purchase. Once, his Eureka Brewery in Paterson, New Jersey, and his Union City Brewery in Union City, New Jersey, had been owned by paper corporations controlled by a group led by James "Bugs" Donovan and Frank Dunn. Legal titles had been irrelevant, however, because possession was all that counted.

Late in 1929 and early in 1930, Bugs Donovan and Frank Dunn died suddenly. We could not develop the evidence that they had been shot in a gang war because it was considered that this might be prejudicial. But they did die, and Waxey Gordon was the man who took over a $5 million beer business. He had previously owned a whiskey business.

By the time we reached trial we had identified most of the Gordon mob's holdings, which were large indeed. They owned and operated no fewer than sixty Mack trucks. They had two breweries, washhouses, drops for the delivery and concealment of the beer, thousands of barrels, a complete automobile repair garage, five offices, two houses and various hotel suites in Paterson and Hoboken, and offices in the Fourth Avenue Hotel and Piccadilly Hotel in New York City.

All of this was not to mention Gordon's interest in backing plays on Broadway. Things were fairly wide open in those days, and one of our informants told us that Gordon had taken the entire cast of at least one of his Broadway musical productions up to Great Meadow Prison in upstate New York for the entertainment of the inmates. Gordon sat in a box with the warden.

By the autumn of 1933 we were ready—and then came a sensation. On November 1, United States Attorney Medalie, ready to return to private practice, said that he intended to resign. I began to serve as

United States Attorney until President Roosevelt appointed a successor. This unique and complimentary selection was made by the judge of the United States District Court under the provisions of a little-used and almost forgotten federal statute and it made me, at thirty-one, the youngest man ever to hold the office. Medalie commented: "Mr. Dewey is young, but he has the head of a veteran on his shoulders. He is a very good trial lawyer and a great administrator."

The trial of Waxey Gordon—his real name was Irving Wexler—began on November 20, 1933. I commented to the jury that ". . . there are a lot of dead men in this case whose names you will hear. In fact, almost everybody who doesn't want to tell the truth will point to a dead man and say he was the man responsible."

It was our job, of course, to establish the nature of the business and to prove that it belonged to Gordon. Then we had to establish that income had been earned and that income taxes on that income had been evaded. It was a technical process, and on one side of the courtroom we set up a huge chart locating each of the breweries, offices, garages, drops, and some of the homes of the Gordon employees. Lines between these places on the chart traced the flow of thousands of telephone calls between them.

On a second chart we traced the flow of checks made out in payment for beer and checks to suppliers and workers which passed through many hands on their way to the Gordon bank accounts. The Recordak films told a powerful tale on both the fronts and the backs of checks.

Still another chart listed suppliers, a long array of them, and our first witnesses—gasoline, oil, malt, truck tire, and other salesmen—tied their sales to Gordon's people, and a few to Gordon himself. One salesman said he went to the garage one day just before a cavalcade of three cars drove up, a Pierce Arrow in the middle. The men in the first car got out. Then Gordon himself, with some companions, stepped out of the Pierce Arrow and finally came the occupants of the final car. Waxey Gordon was well protected.

Another salesman was in the garage when Gordon and his entourage walked in. As they passed by, one of the garage workers called out, according to the witness, "Holy Gee, the Big Chief himself!" Nobody from the defense side denied this appellation.

Waxey Gordon's cars seemed to have been involved in frequent accidents, according to the testimony. This meant many casualty claims, many insurance adjusters. Gordon was known by the insurance companies to be a chiseler, and his insurance claims were always investigated. Those adjusters were helpful because they said they met him in offices that were identified with the beer business or in the Piccadilly Hotel.

Gordon was a showoff, at least where it was safe, and by 1931 he was notorious and well established in northern New Jersey. Once he became expansive and gave a dinner at a restaurant there for a party of more than a hundred of his managers and agents. He mixed in some local officials from nearby towns and villages. When he got up to make a speech, Gordon proudly introduced some of his associates. At his trial, however, his defense was shaken when one of our surprise witnesses turned out to be one of Gordon's own brewmasters. This man testified that Gordon had introduced him to the throng at the dinner, "Meet my brewmaster."

A Polish-American girl named Helen Delbeck was, to many, the heroine of the Waxey Gordon trial. Dozens of other respectable people had suffered from a serious loss of memory when we asked them to identify Gordon and his lieutenants. Other people had given statements under oath, and signed them, only to repudiate the statements before the trial. But not Helen Delbeck. She operated a restaurant across from the garage where the beer barrels were loaded on the trucks, and her business was poor. So one day in 1930 she sought out Gordon himself and told him her business was poor. She testified, in a heavy Polish accent, that she had asked him, "How about to give me a break and send your boys to my place?" Gordon told her his men were "too busy to eat."

Nevertheless, a number of Gordon employees did use her place, Helen Delbeck said, but the trouble was they also used the telephone and ran up some good-sized bills. Once again she went to Gordon personally and told him his men were running up big telephone bills. He said, "Just let my men know, let someone know, give them to him, so we will take care of the bills." She concluded, "So I always gave them, and they paid them." This testimony tied Waxey Gordon to an acknowledgment of "my men" and helped us substantiate the existence of an organized mob.

From one witness after another we got pieces of the picture of the operation of a beer empire during Prohibition. It was fascinating. First, an application had to be made for a federal license to make near beer. This application had to be filed by a corporation with real, living, respectable owners and officers.

Next books had to be set up which could be regularly inspected by the government, showing the amount of near beer made and showing the sales.

What these books did not show in Waxey Gordon's operation was that near beer amounted to approximately one per cent of the total beer produced. Near beer was made by dealcoholizing real beer. But the books had to show a balance between the dealcoholized beer and the amount that had been sold. None of the real beer was ever supposed to be on the books, and the bookkeepers had gotten badly mixed up a few times.

To get the real beer out of the brewery, they had erected a complicated system of pipelines. From the vats, the beer was taken underground to a machinery house adjoining the brewery. Then the pipeline turned and went under the street and into the basement of the house of the truck foreman, and thence by a detachable hose underground to the main sewer of Paterson, New Jersey.

Now the Paterson sewers were so big a man could walk along them. So the detachable line carrying the outflow of beer was connected with another line which ran down the sewer for several blocks to a point from which it was piped upward into a garage. There the beer was put into newly washed barrels, and the barrels were loaded on trucks. When the coast was clear the trucks were run out to bring the beer to the public.

The public had to be thirsty to drink Waxey Gordon's stuff. His brewmaster at the Eureka Brewery had been a brewmaster for thirty-three years and he knew his business. He testified that it took from four to six weeks to make good beer, and this should be kept in the vats from eight to twelve weeks, depending on the season and the demand. But the Gordon organization did not bother with such niceties, he testified. Their beer stayed in the vats exactly forty-eight hours, and down it went into the pipelines, under the street, along the line in the sewer, into the garage and the barrels.

After a year or so that garage had become so well known—probably everybody in Paterson knew what was going on—that the Gordon mob decided to move. It was not difficult. They just rented another garage about three blocks away and added another length of detachable hose running through the sewer into the new garage.

The brewmaster was helpful, too, in describing the volume and cost of making the beer—the malt, the yeast, the hops, the barrels, the cooperage coating, the brewing machinery, and all the rest of it. The beer cost about $2.00 a barrel, according to his figures, plus about $4,500 a week for the men and the brewery. He testified that they made 5,000 barrels a week.

Many of the Gordon bank accounts had been held in one fictitious name, and these gave an indication of the volume of the business. In six weeks checks totaling $270,000 had been deposited in that name. Then the accounts in this name were closed out. The same day the same individual opened a new account, at the same bank, but under another fictitious name. He deposited $529,000 in the next six weeks.

The income and expenditures were estimated by the government from all these sources of evidence, but no credit was allowed the organization for the money that was used to persuade Prohibition agents never to look closely at anything when they came around, or to provide for adequate notice of any visits by the chief inspector. In this last eventuality, the vats could be quickly emptied and the hoses detached. But the estimate was that Gordon had made net income from beer alone of $1,338,000 for 1930 and $1,026,000 for 1931.

Our job was also to substantiate this volume of income by showing that Waxey Gordon lived royally. He had four cars, the Pierce Arrow, a Lincoln, and two Buicks, all registered in the names of employees. His ten-room apartment on West End Avenue in New York City cost $6,000 a year, and it was filled with antique furniture. A library of un-opened book sets had cost him $4,220. The cost of his annual vacation trips to Florida and Hot Springs, Arkansas, could only be estimated, but dozens of sales slips for expensive haberdashery and suits were useful evidence of an impressive standard of living.

For the year 1930, Gordon had reported a net income of $8,100, on which he had paid $10.76 tax. By the time it came for him to file his 1932 tax return he knew that he was under intensive investigation and he was already a fugitive. So he had an accountant fill out an-other income tax return reporting "estimated income from various sources" at $35,000. That was still a long way from $1 million.

After nine days, 131 witnesses, and 939 exhibits, we rested our case.

Defense counsel then opened to the jury, describing Gordon as just a humble employee of other men, all of them dead, who had really owned the business. He called three employees of the Piccadilly Hotel to testify that they had not seen Gordon giving orders there.

Next the defense called a life insurance agent who testified that Gordon had had a $45,000 life insurance policy which he had recently canceled. Presumably the purpose was to show that Gordon was a poor man.

On cross-examination, however, we developed from the insurance agent that Gordon had been paying on this policy an annual premium of $2,427. That seemed to be a lot for a man who had declared his total income as $8,100 for the year 1930.

Next I showed this life insurance agent his own letter, written in 1927, in connection with this insurance policy. The letter certified to the insurance company that Gordon had a half interest in the Paramount Hotel Corporation, with a value of $3 million when completed, that he was also a twenty-five per cent owner of the Allied Hotel Construction Company with a value of $500,000 and a twenty-five per cent owner of the Mansing Coal Corporation with a value of approximately $900,000.

The insurance agent by now was thoroughly frightened. His own letter was proving our case for us. So he admitted his signature but claimed that the letter was false in every detail. So it went, item by item. This witness was a disaster for the defense—and they did not call any more.

But the defense did call Waxey Gordon himself.

Gordon was a chunky, confident, articulate witness. Under direct examination by his counsel, Charles F. G. Wahle, he started out candidly admitting that as a young man he had made a number of "mistakes." When he was nineteen years old he was picking pockets for a living. He was finally caught and sent to Elmira Reformatory, and was twice sent back there for violations of parole. After that he had been convicted in Philadelphia for grand larceny and sentenced to nineteen months' imprisonment. In 1915 he had been convicted of robbery and sentenced to two years. After he got out in 1916, Gordon testified, he had married and led a blameless life ever since. He had been in the real estate business, he said, but frankly his real business was liquor and bookmaking. He admitted owning the Fourth Avenue Hotel, a well-known fleabag.

Along about 1929, he testified, two very old friends, Jimmy Hassell and Max Greenberg, had approached him about working for them as a salesman in the beer business in New Jersey. It was a humble start, he said, and he was to get $125 per week and seven and a half per cent "of the organization." This explained everything. He knew nothing about the bank accounts. He could not possibly figure out how checks payable to him had been deposited in the beer accounts operated in fictitious names. All of his automobiles belonged to "the syndicate," of which Hassell and Greenberg were the bosses and he was a minor participant. He had to go to Florida and Hot Springs periodically "for his health."

Where were Hassell and Greenberg? Something very close to an inside description of a gangland murder came next. At least it was convincing because it explained the absence of the two men. In April 1933, Gordon testified, he was in a room in the Elizabeth Carteret Hotel in Elizabeth, New Jersey, near to another room in which Hassell and Greenberg had been sitting. Then he said he heard "sort of like a rattle of dishes out in the hall." He looked out and saw "some of the men that worked for Mr. Hassell and Mr. Greenberg running along the hall." He said, "What's the excitement?" The men replied, "Well, they just shot Max and Jimmy."

This was adroit, suggesting that the assassins were part of Hassell's and Greenberg's gang, and by no means employees of Waxey Gordon. The fact was, however, that nobody shot at Gordon. Try as he would, he could not possibly identify any of those men he saw running down the hall.

After these particular killings, said Gordon in continued direct examination, the business went along as usual for several months. One difficulty was that a good part of the staff, in addition to Hassell and Greenberg, "went away" after what he repeatedly called "the incident."

His counsel asked him about the Paramount Hotel Corporation and the Piccadilly Hotel. Gordon said that his friend Max Greenberg had asked him to join in the corporation, which was to build the new hotel, but that he had declined to go into the new venture. He "never put in five cents" and knew nothing about it. He was surprised when he learned that he had been elected secretary of the corporation, and he "told Mr. Greenberg" to take him off.

Gordon testified it was the same thing with the beer business. He really knew nothing about the Eureka and Union City breweries except that they produced the beer he sold. All those telephone calls were just times when he was calling one of the boys to convey a message for Hassell or Greenberg. When anybody called him, "it might have been to give me a message from someone."

He did go to the garage and the breweries on rare occasions, but as a visitor. When people came to him to get payment for deliveries, this was just because he happened to know them, and he interceded with Hassell and Greenberg to get them paid. He never heard about any books being rewritten, because he knew nothing about books, bank accounts, or any of the details of the business. He vaguely remembered the conversation with Helen Delbeck, and he remembered telling her he would ask the man who owned the garage to send the men over to give her some business in her restaurant.

Gordon told a touching story about the reason for the elegance of his home. His wife, he told us, loved beautiful things, and she wanted to sell her jewelry "in order to have a beautiful home." He added that she had said, "After all, I never wear the jewelry, I am mostly at home. I would sooner have a beautiful home than have the jewelry." So, he testified, she sold her jewelry for $4,900.

Gordon was so moved by her sacrifice that he borrowed $5,000 from Max Greenberg, he told us, and together with other borrowings they were able to put together the funds for his new home on West End Avenue, including the books, the decoration, the bar, and all the trimmings. He was willing to do all this on the strength of his new job at $125 a week plus his seven and a half per cent. It was a beautiful canvas he painted and, in Wahle's hands, from time to time he appeared an almost believable and sympathetic figure.

This turned out not to be the case on cross-examination. I began:

Q. Just to get the record a bit straighter, your first offense for which you were prosecuted and convicted was in 1905, right?

A. That is right.

Q. That was grand larceny.

A. That is right.

Q. And then you served a prison sentence.

A. I did.

Q. By the way, what name were you convicted under on your first conviction?

A. I think it was Benjamin Lustig. . . .

Q. And then we come down to 1908 and again under the name of Benjamin Lustig you were returned to prison, were you not?

A. That is right.

Q. What crime did you commit on that occasion?

A. No crime whatsoever.

Q. You were returned to prison for a violation of parole, were you not?

A. That is right.

Q. And were you sent back for no crimes at all?

A. The papers will say it was no crime.

Q. I am asking you.

A. I am telling you. . . .

Q. Your first explanation was not the case on that one, was it, that one just happened to be impossible? We agree on that?

A. You have about twenty arrests on here, so I don't remember them. . . .

Q. Now, we come down to 1915. This time, as Irving Wexler, for assault and robbery; right?

A. That is right.

Q. Two years in Sing Sing. By the way, is that where you met Max Greenberg?

A. No, sir. . . .

Q. Was Greenberg a member of the St. Louis Rats gang at the time you met him?

A. I met him in New York. . . .

Q. You claim you did not know anything about Greenberg's history?

A. I did not say. I did not claim. I wasn't interested.

Q. I am not asking you today what you are interested in or what you are not interested in. I am asking you for the facts, and will you answer my question?

A. I will answer the question.

Q. All right. Did you or did you not know Greenberg's history?

A. I did, to a certain extent.

Q. What did you know of it?

A. I knew that he had a bad record.

Q. And then you teamed up with Greenberg and shared offices with him, is that right?

A. That is right.

Q. Counsel said that, after 1916, you emerged from Sing Sing and settled down to live with your wife sometime after that, and reformed. Am I correct in my summary of counsel's question?

Mr. Wahle: Yes.

Q. Is that your testimony?

A. Not in 1916. I think I was married in 1913 or 1914.

Q. So that the event of your marriage did not affect your activities very much, did it?

A. Well, not at that time, no.

Q. On what date would you say was it that you did, as your counsel puts it, reform?

A. After 1916.

Q. After 1916?

A. That is right.

Q. How did you make your living after the year 1916?

A. For several years I was in the real estate business.

Q. Did you ever hold a license as a real estate broker?

A. I did not.

Q. What were you in the real estate game?

A. Broker.

Q. Broker for what?

A. Selling real estate.

Q. Real estate?

A. And whiskey. . . .

Q. As a matter of fact you were in the whiskey business, isn't that so?

A. That is right.

Q. And what else were your occupations?

A. Well, in 1924, I acquired that hotel.

Q. The Fourth Avenue Hotel?

A. Yes.

Q. Now, what kind of place is the Fourth Avenue Hotel?

A. More of an office than anything else.

Q. What?

A. More of an office than anything else.

Q. What kind of place were you and Greenberg conducting in that

place, which was marked and called a hotel, although you walk in
through a three-foot corridor across the street?

A. A legitimate hotel. . . .

Q. A legitimate hotel?

A. Absolutely.

Q. Did you know that your manager was arrested six or seven
times during the period you owned that hotel?

A. That is why they had a Seabury investigation. . . .

Q. Weren't you familiar with the fact that that hotel was running
as a house of prostitution?

A. That's a lie. . . .

Under cross-examination, Gordon held to his story that it was
Greenberg, together with Hassell, who had lured him into the beer
business in 1929. It was also Greenberg who had lured him into the
Paramount Hotel Corporation and induced him to sign the certificate
of incorporation, and he repeated his claim that he had absolutely no
interest in the hotel and never put up any money. One ledger sheet
that had escaped the rewriting of the books showed the hotel owed
him large amounts of money. But Gordon insisted this was not true at
all.

Gordon was in deep trouble when I showed him a building loan
for $1 million for the hotel which he had personally guaranteed, and a
second one for $795,000, each of which indisputably bore his signature.

He said this was all "just a favor" for his friend Max Greenberg,
and this was his testimony.

Gordon also admitted that, on an application in the state of New
Jersey for a pistol permit, he had answered "No" to the question
whether he had ever been convicted of a crime. The answers were all
false, including one in which he said he needed the gun because he
was accustomed to carrying large amounts of money from time to
time.

It was just a coincidence, he testified, that his office associate, a
man named "Blackie," and the missing witness, Sam Gurock, had
been in charge of the books at the Eureka Brewery when he "joined
the syndicate." He explained that Max Greenberg had hired them
and they, like all the others, were merely working for Max and
Jimmy. But the only people who could corroborate this story were

Max and Jimmy, who had been shot to death, and Blackie and Gurock, who were fugitives. He was in deep trouble.

He was in worse trouble when confronted with records showing that the president of his Union City Brewery, the man Gordon said was running the place, was in fact a Union City fireman holding down a city salary of $1,800 a year. Gordon said, "My understanding is that he is on that permit, and he owns that brewery."

He floundered more when I asked him next what he knew about Bugs Donovan and Frank Dunn, the previous owners. He volunteered the fact that their killing had nothing to do with the fact that his "syndicate" had taken over the Union City Brewery with all its business.

By now my assistants were suggesting that I stop cross-examining. We had been going only an hour, but they felt that anything more would create sympathy for a man who was on the ropes. So I continued only a few minutes longer. Briefly, I reviewed the names of the many he claimed could corroborate his basic story that he was really just a salaried employee. Everyone who could help him was dead or a fugitive and, curiously enough, he had made no effort to find any of the living ones to assist in his trial defense.

Gordon was looking physically sick, and I limited the rest of the cross-examination to pinning down the details of the income tax evasion for which he was standing trial.

Q. Now, very briefly, and I will finish. You filed no income tax returns for the years 1918 to 1924, did you?

A. Nineteen eighteen to 1924, I don't know if I did or not.

Q. Isn't it a fact that the first income tax return you ever filed in your life was in 1925?

A. That is possible.

Q. That return reported no taxable income, did it not?

A. I know that I had an attorney go up and see Commissioner Blair in Washington, and I made a settlement for those three years, I think. . . .

Q. Isn't it a fact that for 1926 you filed an income tax return which showed no taxable income?

A. It is possible. . . .

Q. In 1927 you filed an income tax return for $6,032.75 and paid a tax of $11.25, did you not?

A. That is possible.

Q. In 1928 you filed a return for $6,852.27 and paid a tax of $15.21, isn't that right?

A. That is possible.

Q. For 1929, $7,394.20, right?

A. I guess that is right.

Q. For 1930, $8,125, right?

A. That is right.

Q. Then, for 1931, after your conference with the agents of the Bureau of Internal Revenue, for the first time in your life, you filed an income tax return of more than $8,125?

A. That is right.

Q. Right?

A. That is right. . . .

Q. Did you or did you not have insurance on your household furniture for $100,000 in the year 1931?

A. I did.

Q. How did you acquire $100,000 worth of furniture with an income of $6,000 a year?

A. There was no $100,000 worth of furniture. That included everything.

Q. What did it include?

A. It included clothes, rugs, and children's clothes, everything in the place—books.

Q. How did you acquire $100,000 worth of property with an income of $6,000 a year?

A. I had had that since 1910.

Q. You mean you were a wealthy man since 1910?

A. In that year I lost $100,000 on a race track. Yes, I was a wealthy man in 1910.

Q. Were you broke when you lost that, or did you have a lot left?

A. Well, I had a little left.

Q. What do you mean by a little?

A. Well, I had enough to live on.

Q. Did you have $100,000 of household effects left in 1910?

A. No, I didn't, but I had a lot of beautiful things in 1910.

Q. Were they still worth $100,000 twenty-one years later?

A. Certainly, they are antiques. They are worth a lot of money.

Q. In 1910, how old were you?

A. I was only a young boy.

Q. How old were you in 1910?

A. Well, I was twenty-seven—wait a minute.

Q. How old are you now?

A. Twenty-seven, I guess I was in 1910.

Q. How old are you now?

A. I was twenty-three in 1910. I am forty-seven.

Q. You were twenty-three in 1910?

A. Or twenty-four.

Q. Is it your testimony that by the age of twenty-four you had acquired $100,000 worth of property?

A. Just a minute. I was twenty-four years old when I had that money, yes, sir.

Q. You were twenty-two, I believe. You were born in 1888, were you not? You were twenty-two in 1910?

A. That is right.

Q. You had been in jail how many years of your life prior to 1910?

A. Oh, I was in jail and out since 1905.

Q. How did you acquire $100,000 worth of property?

A. I won it on the race track.

Q. That is your testimony?

A. Yes, sir.

Q. Did Leah Wexler have a new Cadillac car in the year 1930?

A. She didn't.

Q. Was one registered in her name?

A. It was.

Q. Whose car was it?

A. A fellow by the name of Louis Parkowitz, who worked for Marks, Hassell and Greenberg, at the Elizabeth Carteret Hotel.

Q. Somebody else who worked for Hassell and Greenberg?

A. That is right, Louis Parkowitz.

Q. And the car was registered in your wife's name?

A. Wait a minute. He owned the car, and I bought the car from him.

Q. It was a 1930 car?

A. Nineteen thirty—well, it looked like a 1925 when I bought it.

Q. I show you Exhibit 494A [showing photographs] and ask you what kind of Cadillac that was.

A. I can't see it, the black is right over it.

Q. Isn't that a 1930 Cadillac sedan?

A. Whatever it was, I paid $500 for it.

Q. You paid $500 for a 1930 Cadillac sedan during the year 1930, is that your testimony?

A. That is right, that is my testimony. . . .

Q. How valuable was this jewelry you say your wife sold in 1929 to furnish this $6,000 apartment?

A. I don't know. She got about $7,000 or $8,000, $9,000, I don't remember.

Q. How much was the jewelry worth originally if she got $7,000 to $9,000 on sale?

A. I don't know what she originally paid for it, because jewelry was very high in 1929.

Q. At least $25,000 worth, right?

A. I would not say that.

Q. No?

A. No. In fact, the jewelry was worth a whole lot more, I mean a whole lot less, than she got for it.

Q. You mean to say that she went out and sold secondhand jewelry for more than it was worth?

A. It wasn't a question of the secondhand jewelry; it was a question of the stones, what type of stones they were.

Q. Is it your testimony that she went out and sold her jewelry for more than it was worth?

A. That is right.

Q. That is what you say, and you stand on it?

A. Wait a minute. When she bought it, it was worth a whole lot less than when she actually sold it. She bought it many years previous, and when she sold it, she got a whole lot more money than she actually paid for it.

Q. Did she buy it in any of these years when you reported $6,000 or $7,000 income?

A. She had that jewelry from the day we were married.

Q. You were paying $2,400 a year for life insurance, weren't you?

A. Twenty-four hundred dollars, yes.

Q. Where did you get the money?

A. Borrowed it.

Q. For how many years?

A. Well—

Q. From 1923 to 1930, right?

A. Oh, I made money in 1923, 1924, I think it was. Nineteen twenty-five and 1926 I borrowed some money to pay for that insurance.

Q. Nineteen twenty-seven, did you borrow some money?

A. I can't remember just what happened. That is, I can't define as to just what happened each year.

Q. Where did you get the money to pay $2,400 a year life insurance premiums in the years when you reported a $6,000 or $7,000 income to the government?

A. Why, I was borrowing it.

Q. That is your testimony?

A. That is my testimony.

In my summation to the jury on behalf of the government in this, the biggest rackets case ever brought to that date in the East, I said:

As I said to you in the opening, this is a case of fragments. This is a case in which the trial has been almost completely obliterated by the greatest criminal conspiracy that has ever come to my attention. Yet, despite that obliteration, they could not get into the vaults of the New York banks; they could only get into the vaults of some of the Jersey banks; and there were some witnesses who had kept records which we caught before they got to them to destroy them. It is because of those fragments which we have been able to find, and which these loyal and fine servants of the government, who have devoted two years and nine months of their lives to the collation of this evidence, have been able to gather together, that we could trace through these millions of bank documents, and present to you that concise summary which you saw upon these various charts.

I make no pretense that we have all the evidence available. All we have are fragments. The rest have been destroyed by this defendant, and you know it, and I know it, but from these fragments we have been able to spell out certain facts.

Before I forget about it, I want to say that this is not a beer case, it is not a murder case, it is not a case of any kind except an income tax case. I said that to you with all the sincerity and clarity at my command at the beginning of this case, and I repeat it. This is a prosecution for the most flagrant violation and the most flagrant conspiracy to violate the revenue laws of your government which has ever been committed in the history of the United States and I believe that that statement can stand uncontradicted.

While you heard, therefore, evidence about the beer and when you heard evidence about the almost incredible genius in the way in which these breweries and operations were conducted, that was not because there was anything in the indictment or in our proof which concerns that, except for the purpose of proving that this defendant made colossal sums of money and then descended to cheating the government on them. That is the point of this case, gentlemen. Do not be deluded into thinking that it is anything else. . . .

I want you to know, and I state it frankly, that I am not in the business of prosecuting the puppets of great criminals in this country. . . . I tell you that neither you nor I nor any self-respecting citizen expects the government to let the great criminals go, and prosecute the small fry. We have seen enough of that kind of thing in this country, gentlemen. We have seen enough of that pointing at the little fry, when they finally have to tell the truth about the men who made criminals out of them.

Now let us be honest. What is the honest situation? The great criminals of this country seduced honest businessmen and ruined them, and corrupted them, and took into their employ the weak and the foolish and the innocent and the criminal. We have had enough of prosecuting these cheap little front men in this country. . . .

The defendant, by his own admission, is a cheat, a fraud, a robber, a pickpocket, a professional criminal and also a man so low that, although he must have had a colossal income in those years, on the basis of the few things that got into the record, he paid the government a pittance and left the support of the government to the honest citizens of the United States. . . .

That brewery sold beer of the value of $2,800,000 and there isn't a shadow of a doubt about it. There has not even been an attempt to discredit the figures, and there is no question but that those are the facts. . . . You still cannot get the net down to the fantastic and impossible figures which this defendant was stupid enough to report to the federal government, and asks you to believe as his real income in years when he obviously was spending from ten to forty times the amount that he reported. . . .

As you retire to your room, gentlemen, I ask you to bear in mind that the people of this country look to you twelve men as to the course of justice in this country. Are we to have justice in the courts? Is justice to be effective in this country in the courts, or is it not? I ask you to bear in mind that the protection of the lives and the property and the liberties of the people of this country is in the hands of men like you, who under similar circumstances receive similar cases, and must decide them in accordance with their duty and their sense of obligation to the community in which they live, and to their fellow citizens.

The jury was out fifty-one minutes, and convicted Waxey Gordon on all counts. He was fined $20,000, with $60,000 costs, and was sentenced to ten years' imprisonment to be served in the federal penitentiary at Atlanta.

At the end of the trial I said, "This case could never have been presented or won without the brilliant and faithful work, for days and nights and on Sundays during several months, of Assistant United States Attorneys J. H. Terry, G. S. Tarbell, Jr., Barent Ten Eyck, Nicholas Rogers, Jacob Grumet, and the special agent in charge of the Intelligence Unit of the Treasury Department and his remarkable staff." Judge Frank J. Coleman was quoted in the press: "It is my firm conviction that never in this court or any other has such fine work been done for the government. If ever again I hear the criticism that there are no longer enthusiastic and able young men in the government service, I shall refer the speaker to this case."

I also warned:

"If any witness in this case is ever touched by reason of his testimony, the federal government will never stop until the responsible parties are punished to the full extent of the law."

CHAPTER VII

The "Runaway Grand Jury"
Demands a Special Prosecutor

Throughout these turbulent years in the United States Attorney's office, it was also politics as usual for our group of Young Republicans, at least on our evenings off. In 1931, in the old Tenth Assembly District, where I had gotten my start, Herbert Brownell was being promoted as a candidate for the state Assembly. The chances did not look good, but all of us felt that he could make a good campaign, and he agreed to run. I have scant recollection of why it fell to me to be his campaign manager, but that was the way it worked out.

In the three weeks, we brought life into a dead district with intensive campaigning, delivering speeches from the backs of trucks and distributing small plastic phonograph records of a talk by Brownell, which was quite a novel idea for those days. The fortunes of the Republicans were at a low ebb in this Depression year, but Brownell waged a fine campaign and came within 1,700 votes of winning out of 14,000 votes cast.

Brownell had made corruption in the city and support of the Seabury investigation his principal focus, and this went down so well that he was nominated for the Assembly once again the following year. In 1932 he was elected in the teeth of the Roosevelt landslide.

Brownell immediately became an effective and leading member of the state Assembly. He gave vigorous support to the Seabury investigation and to various proposed electoral reforms for the city. He successfully sponsored a second-degree perjury law, which was greatly needed. We had already lived through too many elections in which we had watched ferry boats full of drifters coming over from New Jersey, to vote again and again in district after district.

Brownell sponsored legislation to tighten the election laws. He also successfully fought through the legislature a new law requiring that all voting machines be recounted five days after elections. We had seen something of the amazing amount of larceny in vote-counting, and the new results were salutary. The election inspectors would no longer be able to make up their own figures and would have to conform at least to what showed at the backs of the voting machines.

I was not involved in Brownell's successful campaign of 1932 because in that year Medalie was nominated for the United States Senate on the Republican ticket to run against the popular Robert Wagner. All this was taking place the year before the Waxey Gordon trial. It was obvious that 1932 was going to be a Republican debacle but he accepted the nomination as a duty and waged an intelligent and constructive campaign. Since he took a leave of absence to run, I served for a while as Acting United States Attorney. I was also able to spend evenings as Medalie's representative at his campaign headquarters to take part in the management of the campaign.

This was an eye opener for me. The amount of pulling and hauling within the party organization, among the volunteers, the various friends of the candidate, not to mention between different points of view, was incredible. My experience had been primarily in well-organized and disciplined law offices. The campaign was chaos. There had to be a committee for every ethnic group, for example, and New York was a community of ethnic groups. Every one of them seemed to be squabbling with all of the others for money, for publicity in their particular foreign-language newspaper, for staffing, and for a share of the candidate's time. All of the elements of the political spectrum from left to right were similarly fighting to sell their views on the positions to be taken on various issues. For the big meetings, the squabbling over the seating, the order of speakers, advertising, and everything else was infinite and exhausting. Subsequently I was to learn that these chaotic conditions are standard for all campaigns.

Another trouble was that the Republican Party did not grow many political campaign managers. They were almost always amateurs, probably because, regrettably, few Republicans made a business of politics. They were usually new at campaigns. They had to learn the techniques, separate out the fakers who descend on all campaign headquarters, raise money, keep the other running mates happy, and make a thousand decisions on complex matters. The manager also had to nurse the candidate through the inevitable crises and strains.

The Democratic Party by contrast seemed to grow good managers. At least from the outside, it always seemed to me that they had plenty of people who lived for politics and were smoothly organized well in advance of the campaigns. Of course you always knew your own troubles better than the other fellow's, but that was the way it seemed to me.

In November 1932, as Acting United States Attorney, I issued several hundred warrants for illegal registrations and stationed scores of United States marshals at the polls with the statement: "Federal statutes make it a felony to solicit or accept bribes, or to offer or give them. It is a federal crime to oppress or intimidate a voter."

Franklin D. Roosevelt was elected President and Herbert H. Lehman was elected Governor with enormous majorities, as expected, while Wagner defeated Medalie by more than 700,000 votes.

During 1933, our last year at the United States Attorney's office, politics intruded little as we concentrated on prosecuting Waxey Gordon and his ilk. We did mount a campaign, however, to depose Samuel Koenig, who had been Republican county chairman for decades. There had been rumors about alleged trades between the two parties, with some Republicans getting morsels tossed their way by the Democratic Caesars. These stories were validated by the fact that Koenig's brother Morris, a Republican, had received a Tammany Hall nomination for judge of the Court of General Sessions, the highest criminal court in the city. Actually, Morris Koenig turned out to be one of the best judges on that bench, but that was not the point: he got the biparty nomination in a private deal.

Everybody was fond of Sam Koenig, and he was a fine district leader on the Lower East Side. Nevertheless, he had been chairman through too many disasters, and the party needed new leadership. So, together with many others, I did my share of doorbell ringing during the primary election in June 1933, and Koenig was replaced.

In the summer Judge Seabury (of the investigation) and Charles C. Burlingham succeeded in putting together a Fusion ticket, an alliance in effect against crime and municipal corruption. This move resulted in the election of Congressman Fiorello LaGuardia, the first Fusion Mayor of New York in thirty years. I was sure LaGuardia would make New York a better place to live in, although I did not know then that I was entering into a very important political relationship.

LaGuardia's heart was in the right place. He had as much personal charm as any man I ever knew, and he could be as rough as any man I ever knew. He devoted his extraordinary talents to running the city and, for me, he was a great Mayor. Of course he was petulant, and sometimes he was cruel, such as when he made his Commissioner of Hospitals eat an uncooked can of food before the reporters just to prove that the food was edible. He could be jealous in the extreme, as he was later, after I had become Governor. But I liked him, respected him, and we worked together happily.

LaGuardia was explosive and unpredictable. He concentrated all attention on himself. He could be utterly irresponsible in his statements and indulge in demagoguery of the most unbelievable character. But at the same time he tried to get good people in public office, and he expected the highest standards of integrity and proper administration.

He had a great musical gift, by the way. He really could conduct an orchestra. This was not a fake. He could not conduct it with the technical skill of a man who had given his life to it, but his father had been a bandmaster in the Army and he had a fine sense of music, a great love of music. Later, we used to go to the symphonies once in a while together, three or four times in the summer, to the open-air concerts at Lewisohn Stadium.

At this time of our lives, however, while LaGuardia was becoming Mayor, I was preparing to return to private life. I have related how, at the outset of the Waxey Gordon trial, Medalie had announced his intention to return to private legal practice, and how I served as the United States Attorney during this trial. On November 25, 1933, President Roosevelt announced the appointment of Martin T. Conboy as the new United States Attorney, and at the end of the year I too returned to private legal practice.

Meanwhile, upon his own retirement, Medalie had resumed practice in a brand-new set of offices. His brother-in-law and long-time associate, George Sylvester, had carried on the practice at Medalie's old office at 120 Broadway and moved with Medalie to the new offices. Now Medalie said that he would turn over the lease of the 120 Broadway office to me, together with its furniture and its library. This was a generous gift, and I gratefully accepted.

I think we all felt that we had done a useful job. Among other things, the underworld had learned it was dangerous not to pay its income taxes. It was established that with manpower and enough patience and skill the biggest criminal enterprises could be broken up. We had pioneered what we considered to be new techniques of combining investigative and legal skills in criminal investigation with new, investigative accounting procedures and extensive use of grand jury examination of hostile witnesses.

As far as I was concerned, this was to be the end of any full-time public service. I had an intense interest in the political process as well as an incurable passion for improving it. I despised the kind of government most of our big cities had been getting, and the exploitation of people by their political leaders. I guess I was a full-fledged reformer at heart, but with no desire or impulse to hold public office as an occupation.

Public service in the traditional sense of a part-time contribution of one's life was in my blood. But I think I knew even then that I had no gifts as a political campaigner, and certainly no desire to enter the lists as a candidate for any office—ever.

Private law practice had always been my first love and I opened my new office, alone, at the age of thirty-one, as a barrister to stay there for good.

Before I had opened the door on January 2, 1934, former Supreme Court Justice Joseph M. Proskauer had asked me to be associated with him in a major litigation. Another law firm came with a complicated suit on a $400,000 bond. Another firm came with a lawsuit involving the theft of trade secrets by a competitor.

The Association of the Bar also asked me to investigate charges of favoritism to special litigants allegedly shown by a municipal court justice, Harold L. Kunstler. This work was to be done without compensation and it was difficult. There was plenty of suspicion, but I had no power of subpoena to compel testimony. Kunstler had been appointed to the court by Mayor Walker over the protests of the Bar Association and the Citizens' Union. Among other things, he had been a close friend for many years of a well-known fixer named Leef, and he had actually let the man sit on the bench with him on occasion. Suspicion was not evidence, however, and it took three months before I was ready to file a petition for Judge Kunstler's removal.

It was not until we reached trial and the presentation of witnesses that I was able to subpoena the judge's bank accounts, but by the time he reached the stand we had them. The bank statements showed that in three years he had deposited $126,000 more than his salary. He pretended great surprise and made the astonishing claim that he had kept no records of his deposits, or indeed any check stubs. At his request the case was adjourned so he could examine his accounts.

Fortunately I had become acquainted with A. J. Goodrich, for whom I had acquired a high regard as an accountant. I hired him for this case at my own expense, and he made a brilliant analysis of the Kunstler accounts. As a result of Goodrich's work, when the trial resumed the cross-examination of Judge Kunstler became a massacre. Before I could finish it, Judge Kunstler asked for a recess—and he resigned from the bench.

This was my first trial experience with the grubby kind of judicial corruption that had been quite commonly suspected, because of the low quality of so many of our local judges. It shocked me. Also, in the United States Attorney's office, we had had an uneasy feeling that there was something wrong with Martin T. Manton, the presiding judge of the Court of Appeals, Second Circuit, but there was never anything definite to go on. We had complete confidence in the other federal judges, of whom many were of the highest caliber. But the judges in New York City were a different breed, and it was the general view that Kunstler was like many others.

The ridiculous part of it was that there was no machinery for investigating complaints or rumors of corruption, drunkenness, or indolence on the bench. The Bar Association had no power of subpoena and no money for staff, and no other agency had responsibility. In my final report to the Bar Association on the Kunstler matter I strongly recommended that it seek legislation conferring such powers on the

Bar Associations. It took five years, but that program became law in 1939.

As the months passed by, my office at 120 Broadway began to fill up. "Goody" Goodrich, who had done such a beautiful job in the Kunstler case, had done accounting work for one of my closest friends, Carl T. "Pat" Hogan. Goodrich's practice as an accountant had been hit by the Depression. He could not afford an office, so, after he mentioned the problem to Hogan, Pat asked me whether Goody might be able to hang his hat in my place. I let him, and Goody put his name on the door downstairs. Actually he made very little use of the office because he did most of his work auditing books for small companies on a retainer basis. But he did have some spare time and, in addition to working on the Kunstler case, he did some work for me that only heightened my opinion of this remarkable man.

One day while I was visiting with Goody and Pat Hogan at Pat's place, a salesman for an adding machine company came in and offered to give us a demonstration of the operating speed of his machine. Pat looked at Goody and offered to make a bet with the salesman that he had a man in the office who could add the same column of figures faster than the machine.

The bet was made and a long column of figures, each amounting to five or six digits, was made out for the race. At the starting signal, the adding machine salesman started punching away at his keys. Goody took up his pencil and, mumbling to himself, went down the list of the numbers. Goody finished well before the machine and wrote down a total, which was confirmed by the machine when it was done.

Early in November 1934, I took on a temporary secretary for a couple of weeks. She had been sent around from the Bar Association, and I admired her work so much that I asked her to return for a weekend's work preparing a brief. I asked her back the weekend after that. When she could not make it for a third weekend, I called her up and asked her if she would like to come and work for me permanently. She said she would.

Miss Lilian G. Rosse, a native of Birmingham, Alabama, was a graduate of Menninger High School in Charleston, South Carolina, and Cecil's Business College in Asheville, North Carolina, and she is one of the finest people I ever met in my life. She has served as my personal secretary for more than thirty years, with complete dedication, flawless professional competence, exemplary organizational and managerial skill, a splendid civic spirit, and profound humanity.

One of the happiest moments for all of us during these tempestuous years came when Miss Rosse married Goody Goodrich. They were to live happily ever after, and they both continued to serve our community in our struggle against lawlessness of all kinds.

Franklin P. Wood also came into my office. He had been with Cotton and Franklin and had gone to Hawaii to set up a practice, and now he had returned to New York City. Frank was determined to be an independent lawyer, and he was looking for space. I had an extra room and I rented it to him for a modest amount. In the event, I always had enough corporate work coming in, too much of it, and I assigned some of this to Frank. I was able to pay him something more, on the average, than the rent, and it was a satisfactory arrangement.

Frank Wood and I have been intimate friends ever since and, when I went to take over the rackets investigation in 1935, he took over my private practice at 120 Broadway. Many years later history more or less repeated itself. I had resumed private practice after leaving the district attorneyship and had taken an office at 20 Exchange Place. But, in 1942, I was elected Governor of New York. So Frank moved out of 120 Broadway and took over the office at 20 Exchange Place, buying my furniture.

During my private practice in the 1930s, I became chairman of the Committee on Criminal Courts Law and Procedure of the city Bar Association. During this tenure my associates and I proposed a wide-ranging program of improvement in the criminal law. In those days, as in subsequent years, the scales of justice were obviously tipped heavily in favor of the defendant and against society as a whole. We felt that our people were entitled to better protection.

Our program therefore included several features which were introduced somewhat ahead of their time. These included the grant of authority to a prosecuting attorney to comment upon a defendant's failure to testify in his own defense, a presumption of ownership when firearms were found in an automobile, the establishment of a central felony court, the denial of bail to an accused who had already been twice convicted, the acceptance of a verdict by ten out of twelve jurors, and a law forbidding lawyers to advise in the operation of criminal enterprises. This last was already deemed to be unethical, of course, but it had never been specified to be, on all occasions, criminal conduct.

None of our program was adopted.

A casualty insurance company retained me to advise in the handling of major accident claims and this became a revelation to me. I saw for the first time the kind of perjury that so often reeked in the courtroom in the trials of accident cases. In fact negligence cases were to occupy between seventy-five and eighty per cent of the time of all trial courts in New York State. It was much the same in many other parts of the country, and a large proportion of our lawyers were making their living from this kind of work.

One of the worst aspects of this negligence field was that, so often, laymen would get their impression of the Bar from watching lawyers hanging around the courthouses looking for automobile accident cases, or by meeting their lawyers through the medium of hired runners.

These lawyers would sign up the injured person as a client on a contingent basis for a third to a half of the recovered amount. After payment of the lawyer's fees and the hospital and medical bills, the claimant would be lucky to have one third of the award left. Juries were quite familiar with this system, and they began to give increasingly outrageous damages. Insurance costs skyrocketed as a consequence, and in many regions the insurance premium rates still did not keep pace with the costs. It was a heavy and unnecessary toll on everybody who owned an automobile and purchased automobile insurance.

As if this were not bad enough, the business also encouraged false claims, fake accidents, and grossly inflated claims of injury, medical and hospital expenses, and loss of earnings. There were even lawyers who went around the country giving lectures to the public on how to develop negligence cases against hospitals and doctors, and on how to increase the level of demand for damages.

The social waste of this negligence practice was equally shocking. One example occurred many years later in a case of a man who was employed near our home in Pawling, New York. While driving home one evening he came upon a battered car in the gutter and found that it contained his wife and daughter. He got them to a hospital, where they were found to be badly injured. The daughter recovered, but the wife would never be normal again.

A lawsuit against the other party was brought and was finally settled for $70,000. After payment of the lawyer's fees, the investigation costs, and the hospital and doctors' bills, there was about $22,000 left to take care of the wife for the rest of her life.

The husband used part of this money to pay off a small mortgage on their home and the rest to buy a restaurant, a business he had never been in. Within a year he had gone broke, and the net result of the whole accident was family tragedy.

Whenever such a substantial amount of money was left for the injured's family, it was usually more than they had ever seen before in their lives, and they might spend it, or invest it and lose it, ending worse off than they had been before the jury award. But there should be a simple solution. This would be to treat negligence cases the same way as accidents sustained in the course of employment. The cases should be placed in the hands of an administrative agency and the injured people should be compensated—regardless of fault—for the cost of their medical and hospital bills. They should also be paid a reasonable amount until recovery. If the injured had sustained injuries that would incapacitate for life, then the payments should last for life.

In such accident compensation cases, legal fees were usually small.

In the larger picture, the staggering costs to the public of automobile liability insurance would be radically reduced, three fourths of the court burdens would be eliminated, and three fourths of the judges theoretically could be dispensed with. The injured people would be far better taken care of, and promptly and fairly.

This conclusion was disputed by the lawyers who lived off the negligence cases and by some of the insurance companies. But I maintained that our society, sooner or later, would have to get rid of this cancer and restore dignity and decency to the compensation of accident victims.

Finally, in private practice, I could more nearly call my time my own, and we started taking a summer home at Tuxedo Park where the commuting was not too arduous, our neighbors were delightful, and I could engage in sailboat racing on the weekends. This was a happy refuge for a few summers.

The year 1935 was my second year back in private practice and it began peacefully enough and happily busy. Fiorello LaGuardia was the Mayor and Lewis Valentine, a thoroughly honest policeman, was the Commissioner of Police. There seemed to be less crime in the streets, and a young man could court his girl in safety in Central Park after dark. People of all ages felt somewhat more secure.

The occasional gang shooting or other outbreak of underworld violence even seemed to some to be encouraging news. It was a story of another hoodlum killed off by "one of his own." LaGuardia would then promptly denounce the killing and order the police to drive "the punks and tinhorns" out of town. This reassured some, but not the large body of people who knew that under the deceptively calmer surface New York was still becoming a mob town on the order of Chicago. There was a feeling of unease, a sense that organized crime was somehow, invisibly, pervading the community and the country.

Suddenly, in mid-February, Irving Ben Cooper, formerly on the Seabury investigation staff, exploded with a report for the Commissioner of Accounts that seventy-seven bail bondsmen had perjured themselves 1,584 times. He said they had done this while procuring the release on bail of runners in the numbers racket. He charged that none other than Dutch Schultz had put up the money for the bonds, and it was reported at this time that the Schultz numbers banks were collecting $100 million a year.

Outraged civic groups demanded action. William Copeland Dodge, who had succeeded Crain as the Tammany District Attorney of New York County, reacted by appointing counsel to one of these groups as a special assistant to conduct an investigation. A grand jury was empaneled. Before long this special assistant and Dodge were having a violent public disagreement. Dodge fired the special assistant and the whole matter seemed about to die.

At this time Martin Mooney, a reporter for the New York *American*, charged in a series of articles that the Dutch Schultz mob was getting its political protection at the highest level from none other than James J. Hines, the Tammany leader whose trail we had crossed during the trial of the numbers banker Henry Miro. But when Mooney was required to name his sources, he declined, preferring to go to jail for a short while for contempt.

The grand jury was under the leadership of one of the unsung heroes of the 1930s, its foreman, Lee Thompson Smith, a strapping, brave citizen who refused to quit. Smith startled the whole country with a declaration: "We have labored under the most difficult handicaps. Every conceivable obstacle has been put in our path." Relations with Dodge grew so bad that the grand jury would not let the

District Attorney's assistants into the room. Then the grand jury began to subpoena people on their own without reference to the District Attorney. They rejoiced in the title of the "runaway grand jury."

The runaway grand jury publicly demanded that Dodge appoint a Special Prosecutor of *their* choice, and by now the public uproar was so great that Dodge agreed. After consulting with the various Bar associations and others, the grand jury came up with a list of six lawyers. But Dodge refused to appoint any of them, and appointed his own man, a former associate of Max D. Steuer, the man who had defended the bank chairman Charles E. Mitchell long before. The runaway grand jury refused to accept Dodge's nominee, and there was another deadlock.

Meanwhile, William Fellows Morgan, LaGuardia's Commissioner of Markets, was telling the runaway grand jury that a poultry racket was milking New York City of $10 million every year, and he charged that Dodge was responsible.

Dixie Davis, Dutch Schultz's lawyer, was called in for a session with the runaway grand jury and, afterward, he told the press that the numbers racket was not taking in $100 million a year. He said that numbers was taking in $500 million a year. This wild estimate poured more fuel on the fire.

Finally the runaway grand jury stepped down with the peremptory demand that Governor Lehman move into the situation and appoint a Special Prosecutor. Civic groups stepped up the pressure by demanding that Lehman appoint a Special Prosecutor to supersede Dodge. On June 25, Lehman directed Dodge to appoint one of four leading lawyers: Charles E. Hughes, Jr., George Z. Medalie, Charles H. Tuttle, or Thomas D. Thacher. One of these distinguished citizens was going to be the new Special Prosecutor, so it seemed, and a start would be made to fight crime and corruption in New York.

Until now I had paid little attention other than as an interested citizen, even though my own name was being pressed publicly on Lehman by the New York State and City Bar Associations, and by the Association of Grand Jurors of New York County. Then I got a shock. Medalie telephoned me to say that the four lawyers intended to refuse the appointment and would make a joint public announcement recommending to Lehman that he appoint me. Would I accept? he asked.

This was a rough one. My practice was busy and I was happy in it.

Charles "Lucky" Luciano, seen here in original police "mug shot" taken after his arrest in April 1936, was the leader of the Mafia in New York City. A brilliant organizer of narcotics and assassinations, he was caught while organizing mass prostitution into "chain stores, like the A & P." In the trial of the decade, his reputation suffered when he was proved to have ordered the beating of madams and managed the operations of pimps. He was sentenced to thirty to fifty years' imprisonment.

Special prosecutor Thomas E. Dewey, at his desk early in his racket-busting career, told his staff he would be mad to go after prostitutes, but he wanted the top racketeers locked up. He thought of law as the basis of a happy society, fought to remove the pall of fear of the mobs that hung over Depression America in the 1930s.

James Frederico, one of Luciano's enforcers, beat a madam on the head repeatedly with an iron pipe until she was covered with blood.

Thomas Pennochio, alias Tommy the Bull, was one of Luciano's treasurers. He wanted to increase prices and profits by more than fifty per cent.

Little Abie Wahrman, a tintype for a prostitution racket gunman, was exactly that for Lucky Luciano, loving to put people to the wall.

Ralph "The Pimp" Liguori spent insurance money from Gashouse Lil, slugged syphilitic junkie Nancy Presser, found girls for Jennie the Factory.

Paternal grandfather George M. Dewey, one of founders of the Republican Party, became a fiery Michigan editor, a controversial campaigner for President McKinley, an inspiration to generations of Deweys in Owosso, Michigan. Poster *at right* was for a Republican rally in October 1880.

REPUBLICAN RALLY!

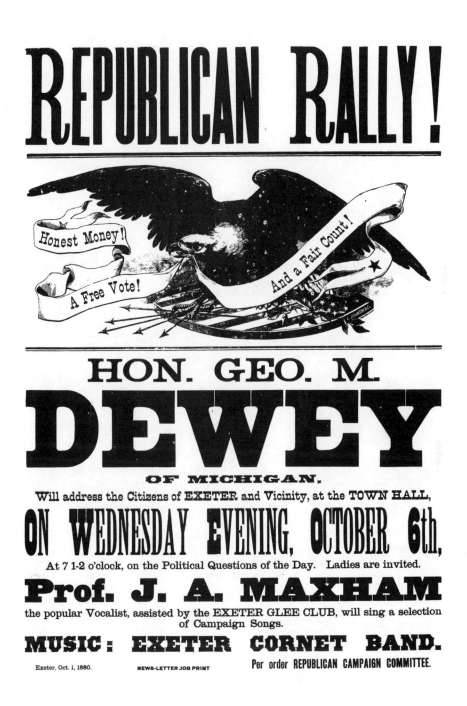

Honest Money!

A Free Vote!

And a Fair Count!

HON. GEO. M.

DEWEY

OF MICHIGAN,

Will address the Citizens of **EXETER** and Vicinity, at the **TOWN HALL**,

ON WEDNESDAY EVENING, OCTOBER 6th,

At 7 1-2 o'clock, on the Political Questions of the Day.   Ladies are invited.

Prof. J. A. MAXHAM

the popular Vocalist, assisted by the **EXETER GLEE CLUB**, will sing a selection of Campaign Songs.

MUSIC: EXETER CORNET BAND.

Exeter, Oct. 1, 1880.   NEWS-LETTER JOB PRINT   Per order REPUBLICAN CAMPAIGN COMMITTEE.

Dewey's birthplace was this apartment over his maternal grandfather's store in Owosso. In the store, "a mystic place . . . where my first boyhood memories took shape," eggs were stored in water glass, fat geese were hung at Christmastime, and Grandfather Thomas used to make mountains of popcorn for the youngsters.

George Martin Dewey, Jr.,
Dewey's father, was the lifelong
editor of the Owosso *Times*, employed his son Tom as a printer's
devil at ten cents an hour.

Annie Thomas Dewey, Dewey's
mother, had the financial mind of
the family, dealt with tenants,
made money on gold stocks in
the 1920s.

Ten-year-old Tom Dewey as Uncle Sam, with Margaret Ellis as the Goddess of Liberty, poses for a July Fourth portrait in the Bull Moose year 1912.

Dewey home on Oliver Street, in Owosso, Michigan, remained in the family throughout his life. There he had to weed the garden, tend the furnace, sweep the snow off the sidewalk, bring home cans of rich, warm, unpasteurized Jersey milk from Uncle Edmund's cattle.

Dewey on bicycle. As a teen-ager, he went on to his aunt Emily Warren's Hubmobile.

Dewey as Boy Scout. His mother saved this picture of Tom, at age twelve years and ten months.

Dewey at singsong at his cousin Harriet's in Owosso. Although he grew up to be an adequate *basso cantante*, his aunt Grace thought he should enter the legal profession. After the University of Michigan and Columbia Law School, he did what his aunt had recommended, reveling in "the majesty of the law."

The Dewey family, in the closest thing they ever had to a group campaign portrait, are seen here with friends and neighbors from Owosso on a summer vacation at Glen Lake, Michigan, in 1912. Young Tom is seated *at center* with his hands in his lap. Directly behind stands his father, and his mother is smiling happily *at extreme left*.

Tom Dewey and Earl Putnam on the Putnam farm at Ovid, Michigan. Tom did volunteer war work on the farm in World War I, cultivated crops, nursed calluses, never learned to enjoy the Putnams' Bible-reading after breakfast.

Top of the Mornin' was an Irish opera in which Tom Dewey, *second from right,* played a pretender to an Irish throne along with three other Irish pretenders at the University of Michigan.

High school student Dewey, seen at the age of sixteen, had made enough money as a *Saturday Evening Post* sales agent to pay for his first year at Michigan.

Tom Dewey as a young lawyer in New York. He said: "How
the law fits into the stream of life is a long distance away. The
rest of your life you are at the opposite end. You have a set of
facts, and the question becomes how to accomplish the desired
results legally, how to take the set of facts you have, or the
desired corporate reorganization if you like, or the lawsuit, and
how to appraise it against the law. Until then, you have done
it theoretically. Basically, you have been learning how to think
legally, not how to deal with people and practical problems."

I knew that even if I could get a free hand, adequate funds, legal and other staffing, police co-operation and, most of all, plenty of time, it would be a long and formidable task, unlikely to succeed.

Frances and I talked it over at length. Finally we concluded that, if the community was going to be worth living in, somebody had to clean it up or at least make a big start. I was only thirty-three years old and, though we knew the chances of failure were large, we thought perhaps I had a duty to try. Also, it did seem like an exciting challenge. I told Medalie that under proper conditions I would accept the appointment if it came.

The next day the four lawyers named by the Governor made their joint public statement declining the offer, and then urged Lehman to appoint me. But Lehman rejected the suggestion, expressed his resentment that none of them would accept, and asked them to come to his apartment the next day for a conference. He said he did not think that I was "sufficiently well known" for the task.

Governor Lehman's rebuke made the four lawyers pretty irritated. He was already irritated, so the prospects of a settlement between them looked dim. I was relieved. It seemed that I was off the hook after all.

The four lawyers' conference with Lehman the next day lasted long and, I was later told, acrimoniously. Nevertheless Lehman finally yielded and announced that he would direct Dodge to appoint me. Although I was "not well known," he said, I was "competent." He added that I would have his "complete confidence" and "full independence" of action.

It happened that on this day I was in Boston, giving away my cousin Elizabeth Dewey in marriage, her father having died some time before. The news of Lehman's announcement did not reach me until I bought a newspaper when my train reached New York City that evening. There being nothing for me to do about it for the moment, I got my car out of the garage and drove home to Tuxedo Park for the night.

The next day Governor Lehman called me on the telephone and invited me to accept the appointment. I was flattered by his telephone call but not by his ungracious choice of words in the announcement. Private pique is never seemly in public affairs, however. I said yes.

A day or so after that, District Attorney Dodge wrote me a letter advising that he would follow the Governor's direction, and he invited me to come to a conference. Following this conference, Dodge announced that I had been promised a totally free hand and the whole support of his office. This was a complete fraud, and we both knew it. He said I had accepted an appointment as Deputy Assistant District Attorney. This was the lowest title in his office.

So, with thoroughly mixed feelings, I found myself appointed Special Prosecutor to clean up New York—with no staff, no office, no police, no budget appropriation and, as I looked back on it afterward, no sense whatever.

In the United States Attorney's office we had been wielding the entire influence of the federal government. This time we were alone.

Part II | SPECIAL PROSECUTOR

CHAPTER VIII

All Were Able,
Most Were Stars

New Yorkers were used to investigations. We had them about as often as we had elections, and with greater benefit to civic progress. We believed, with good reason, that there was some larceny in the best of men, and that the island of Manhattan, with its concentration of wealth and business, provided an atmosphere in which that very human trait did and would continue to flourish. There was even in normal years some disposition to yawn politely whenever the investigators started on their journeys. After all, New York had become accustomed to rectifying in this fashion any mistakes made by the voters at the polls.

But our investigation beginning in July 1935 differed in important details from its predecessors. It took on none of the aspects of a purity drive, nor did it assume the partisan character of an inquiry into political corruption. It promised to be a frontal, and expert, attack on extortionists and gangsters. Its avowed purpose was to destroy organized crime and racketeering of all kinds.

There were long and busy days in this month of months. Applications for places on my staff came to my private law offices at 120 Broadway at the rate of one hundred a day. Civic leaders and delegations of citizens called with words of advice and encouragement. The size and make-up of the staff were agreed upon and a budget prepared. The Board of Estimate was presented with the desired amount and the Board of Aldermen prepared to vote on it.

A search for suitable quarters was instituted, and hours were spent poring over blueprints in an effort to convert available space into a leakproof office. Lawsuits designed to obstruct the investigation were fought off and won. An intensive investigation was begun into all members of the panel from which an Extraordinary Grand Jury was to be selected.

Late at night, hours were borrowed from sleep and devoted to a study of the 750 pages of minutes of the runaway grand jury, whose dedication to duty had brought forth the rackets investigation upon which we were now embarked.

Our basic headquarters plan was to take space in a large downtown office building where witnesses could come and go, unnoticed in the shuffle of thousands milling about in the lobby. After a thorough canvass we selected the Woolworth Building, on lower Broadway, a sixty-story structure with hundreds of tenants. The building lay directly across the street from the United States Attorney's office, a block from City Hall, and only a short distance from the Supreme Court Building in which the Extraordinary Grand Jury was to hold its sessions.

A chief justice of the Court of Special Sessions had once observed in an address to the Federal Bar Association: "Anyone can go down to the Criminal Courts Building any day, and see four or five district leaders hanging around the corridors. It is not hard to imagine what they are there for." Certainly we were also anticipating the difficulty of inducing witnesses to come to a building where they could be observed with ease by associates of the gangsters against whom they were giving information and evidence.

In the Woolworth Building there were seven entrances to the lobby, which was invariably crowded. Detectives familiar with underworld characters were assigned to lookout positions in the lobby. The elevator operators were investigated, as were the porters and cleaning women.

Our office space consisted of 10,500 square feet of the fourteenth floor, about three quarters of the whole floor. A railroad company and a law firm also occupied space on the floor, and their co-operation was solicited and obtained from the start. It was possible to enter the building from the West Side subway direct, without going to the street, and to ascend to our floor by any one of six elevators. But a uniformed police officer was stationed at our entrance at all hours of day and night.

On reaching the fourteenth floor, a visitor would go to a receptionist, who would contact the Deputy Assistant District Attorney in charge of the particular matter involved. The visitor would then be escorted along an inner corridor, which looped through the entire office, to the private waiting room of the assistant. These waiting rooms had frosted glass partitions. There was no general waiting room where witnesses could be seen and sized up by others.

In the offices—there were thirty-five all told—potential witnesses were not to be questioned unless venetian blinds were drawn. The blinds shielded the witnesses from any spies in adjacent buildings and generally helped them overcome their fears.

After the interview the visitor, if he chose, could ascend or descend to other floors by way of a seldom-used stairway connecting these floors with an office hallway. There were also freight elevators in the rear of the building, adjacent to my own private office, in which people could come up to see me and leave again without being seen by members of my staff.

A special untappable telephone cable was installed, connected directly to the main office of the New York Telephone Company. The operators were instructed to accept no outgoing calls unless approved by me or by a Deputy Assistant. All stenographic work was to be done in one large room under constant supervision against leaks. Special locks replaced standard locks on all the filing cabinets. There was no incinerator in the building, but arrangements were made to burn all scrap paper and other waste materials in the furnace.

Our proposed staff was twenty Deputy Assistant District Attorneys, ten investigators, ten accountants, four process servers, a chief clerk and three assistants, two grand jury reporters, twenty stenographers, and four messengers.

Our proposed budget, for the remaining five months of 1935, called for an appropriation of $121,456. This included the non-recurring item of $16,000 for furniture and office equipment. It included, also, $26,500 for rent, telephone, supplies, and contingencies.

Our lease was signed for two and a half years.

Throughout this period there were frequent meetings with Mayor LaGuardia to discuss personnel, budget, police, and other aspects of our investigation as they would relate to the various departments of the city government. LaGuardia, of course, was a Fusion, or reform, Mayor, and he owed nothing whatever to Tammany Hall. One of our most important problems was how to secure and retain the enthusiastic co-operation of the New York City police. During my first meeting with LaGuardia and Police Commissioner Valentine, I said, "There is a man in the department whom I consider one of the finest detectives in the country. I want him to organize and head my squad of detectives."

I shall never forget how LaGuardia replied: "Whoever he is, you can have him." And the Commissioner, without knowing to whom I was referring, also nodded his assent.

In this way I secured the services of then Acting Deputy Chief Inspector John A. Lyons, who would later rise to become New York State Commissioner of Correction. Lyons had been in charge of an under-cover squad, working with me on the Waxey Gordon case and on other federal cases in the early 1930s. His quiet, self-effacing, efficient co-operation with the federal agencies had been of the utmost importance. I thought he was one of the ablest and most completely trustworthy policemen I had ever known.

Lyons and I decided that we would need seventy-five men. We wanted young policemen, men with no bad habits to correct, who had not been dulled by precinct routine. We wanted men bright and willing to learn, who would see in the hard work ahead an opportunity equal to their ambition.

Lyons went carefully about the recruitment, and he began by selecting a dozen seasoned veterans from the bomb squad, the alien squad, and the under-cover squad. These had been under his personal supervision and the men were known in the departments as Lyons' men. Their loyalty to him was limitless.

In choosing the others, Lyons made note of and was guided by the education of the officers, their lack of political affiliations, and their police service records. Most of the men accepted were between twenty-one and twenty-five years old and had just completed their training at the Police Academy. These men were assigned to Lyons even before they reported to police stations. They did not look like cops. They had small feet, alert minds, and tough, wiry frames. All types were represented; laborers, clerks, professional men all had their counterparts in this police group. They were of many national extractions and spoke the languages of the countries of their fathers.

This, then, was to be known as the grand jury squad. To aid in directing its work, Lyons brought in Lieutenant Bernard A. Dowd as second in command and Sergeant William J. Grafenecker as third in command. Barney Dowd was a square-jawed officer of the old school who knew all there was to be known about the police business. He treated the men in his command as if they were his sons, and he was rewarded by their unswerving affection. All that could be said for Bill Grafenecker was, in the estimation of our Deputy Assistant District Attorneys, that he was the greatest detective in or out of shoe leather. Dowd and Grafenecker had both done fine work in the Lindbergh kidnaping case.

Then there were other fine detectives, such as James Canavan and James Cashman, both of whom had worked Broadway for years, who knew everybody, and probably knew more about the underworld than anybody alive. I shall always remember the way they approached the rackets investigation job when they learned they were to be assigned. They went together to Lyons and asked him one question: "Is this thing on the level?" Lyons told them it was. They said they would give it all they had. These two detectives were major sources of information, which we needed desperately. I doubted whether the investigation would have survived long enough for us to show results, but for the devoted information gathering of these two policemen.

Frank Hogan recalled: "At the outset, there were rumors to the effect that the police did not intend to exert themselves in connection with the investigation. So pronounced did they become that Dewey felt obliged to scotch them. He issued a statement ridiculing the imputations of lack of co-operation from the police.

"The danger was real, however, and Dewey realized it. Too often had the members of the Police Department watched similar campaigns against the big shots wind up in the prosecution of a handful of cops. They were accustomed to holding the bag and taking the rap for District Attorneys eager to shift their responsibility. Experience had taught them to be suspicious of lofty motives in public officials. This defensive attitude made it difficult to put every ounce of energy into the desired offensive on crime. It had to be changed.

"Dewey accomplished it in short order. He made the detectives feel they were working with him and not for him. If a plan went awry, it was his fault, not theirs. If they made honest mistakes, he was beside them, shouldering the responsibility. He was first to appreciate and praise good work, and quick to inform the Mayor and the Police Commissioner of it. In conversations, press releases, and public addresses he unfailingly lauded the detectives working for him. Typical of such remarks were these: 'The police force in the city of New York is one subject on which I am an expert. I want you to know that never in the history of New York has the morale, the integrity and the character of the New York police been as high as it is today.' The result was that the men on the squad slaved for Dewey. They had the utmost confidence in his fairness. They were inspired by his example. They told their brother officers that he was a square shooter."

Within our organization, the legal staff was top priority. They had to be the best we could get for our salaries, which ranged from $1,500 to $4,000. There had to be no possibility of undesirable connections. They had to be willing to work days, nights, and weekends. The spectacular origin and purpose of the investigation had made us a magnet for hundreds, then thousands of lawyers, and interviewing them was a massive job. But it was worth it. The nineteen men and one woman we chose were all able, most were stars, and there was never a leak from any lawyer in our office. We were all filled with idealism and supreme confidence that we could lick organized crime on a wholesale scale.

During the rackets investigation, I would say this was the ablest group of lawyers in the country—and I have felt that way ever since. The oldest was forty and the youngest twenty-five. The average age was thirty-two. Seven were members of Phi Beta Kappa. Practically all had won honors in the best law schools in the country. Columbia and Harvard Law Schools led with six apiece.

The political complexion of our group was also interesting, especially in the light of a forecast that had been made by a member of the Board of Estimate. In voting to approve the budget of the investigation, James J. Lyons, the Democratic Borough President of the Bronx, remarked, "I predict that Mr. Dewey will select his staff completely from Fusion ranks." But I said I would pick my assistants without regard to party and that there would be no politics in the investigation as long as I conducted it. A tabulation showed that seven of our lawyers were Republicans, six were Democrats, three belonged to the Fusion Party, and four were independent voters.

First off, I needed top-flight lawyers with experience in criminal work, and I found them among my old group at the United States Attorney's office. They were William B. Herlands, Murray I. Gurfein, Barent Ten Eyck, and Jacob J. Rosenblum. They had been through the wars with me under Medalie, and they became the four Chief Assistants. I chose Goody Goodrich as chief accountant. Lilian Rosse, my personal secretary, came to the rackets investigation with me and served throughout.

On July 26, 1935, Frank S. Hogan, Thurston Greene, Harold M. Cole, and Paul Lockwood were appointed Deputy Assistant District Attorneys. Paul Lockwood recalled: "I had discussed my interest in the rackets investigation job with two friends, two of the active Young Republicans, George Sibley and Dave Peck, and they told me they thought it was a great idea. One afternoon, when I was sitting in my office, the phone rang, and a deep voice said, 'This is Thomas E. Dewey,' and he invited me to drop around to his office at 120 Broadway the next morning. I walked around there at ten o'clock and found fifteen lawyers sitting on chairs including one of my fraternity brothers from Columbia, Frank Hogan, whom I greeted. Finally I had a talk with Dewey, and it lasted about an hour. He asked me about my legal training, didn't seem particularly interested in my political activity, and was not the least bit interested in my newspaper experience on the Brooklyn *Eagle*. We then talked price, and I'll never forget the rather direct way he went about it. He said, 'If I was to ask you to bring in a copy of your income tax return, how much would it show you made last year?'

"I told him. I explained my problem, which was that I had a going law office with some cases on the books, with a great many accounts receivable, with some clients, and that in joining with him I had no idea of what the duration of the prosecution would be. He responded, 'Neither do I.' He said that he had given up his own office and turned it over to one of his fellow lawyers, Frank Wood, and he said, 'Can't you do the same, turn your practice over to some of the other lawyers in the office, sort of keep your space there? The city of New

York has given us an appropriation for six months; you may be here longer, but I don't think that it will be much over a year.'

"I said I thought I could make these arrangements, with the result that we shook hands, and I was hired. He said, 'How soon can you start?'"

Of course, Frank Hogan's story would become better known than I could ever tell it. He was eventually to succeed me as District Attorney for New York County in 1942, and he would serve in this position longer than anyone in history, becoming known throughout the world as "*The* D.A." He was a native of Waterbury, Connecticut, a baseball and football player at Columbia University, and a member of Beta Theta Pi fraternity there. After graduation he had gone into law partnership with an uptown firm in the Forty-second Street area, and he had always been a Democrat, politically.

One of the assistants recalled his job interview with me. He was a registered Democrat and was living at the time in the Eleventh Assembly District. "'The Eleventh is Hines' district,' said Dewey. 'I suppose you are a member of his Monongahela Club?' 'No, I am not,' was the reply. 'Get this straight,' said Dewey. 'I don't care what your political views are but I don't want anybody on my staff who owes allegiance to any political leader. Two years from now, I may be prosecuting Jimmy Hines. I have got to know where you stand.' The applicant related in detail the nature and extent of his political activity. Dewey was convinced of his independence and appointed him. In the early summer of 1938, Dewey was prosecuting Hines, and one of the four assistants aiding him was the Democrat who had been cross-examined as to his fitness for this work in July of 1935."

Thurston Greene was a son of a very distinguished lawyer, a partner in Alexander and Greene, an old New York law firm. Thurston was a tall, slender, extremely gracious, somewhat reserved young man who betrayed his early law training and Harvard background by his reserve and by the fact that he always carried a green baize bag for his books, and an umbrella, most of the time. In fact Thurston's green bag, umbrella, and overshoes got to be a legend in the office.

Harry Cole came from an extremely well-to-do New Jersey family, was a graduate of Brown University where he had been a swimmer, and also from Harvard Law School. He had been in private practice briefly, but he liked the idea of the racket prosecution very much, and he wanted to serve. Although he was married, he gave up his law connection and came with us. He was a tall, husky, extremely able trial lawyer with a remarkable professional and business ability.

The announcement of Raymond Ariola's appointment to the staff was also made on July 26, 1935. Ariola had an unfortunate career. He was some five feet three or four inches tall, of rather distinguished Italian ancestry, and he had been practicing law in Brooklyn after graduating from New York University Law School. He was an intense fellow who worked with us for some months. Then we were astonished when William Copeland Dodge, the Tammany District Attorney, had Ariola arrested on a charge of ambulance chasing. This, Dodge thought, would be fatal to us. The charges were made that Ariola, in his law practice in Brooklyn, had split some fees derived from negligence cases with his brother, who was a doctor. Ariola resigned from our staff, was prosecuted and, in a spirit of vindictiveness, was sentenced to the penitentiary. He served a few months and then got out. He showed real character by starting all over again and going to dental school.

That was a very unhappy situation, and the only time we had anything like it. However, it had no effect on the status of our rackets organization.

On August 2, 1935, the appointment of Edward McLean was announced. He was a graduate of Harvard Law School who had been in private practice downtown. He was a medium-sized, rather serious redhead of obvious Scottish background, a brilliant lawyer with great professional attainments.

The next person to join the staff, on August 6, was Eunice Carter. She was already a successful lawyer, from a family noted for its YMCA work, with a fine academic record from Smith College and Fordham University Law School. She was the wife of Dr. Lisle Carter, a dentist in Harlem, and she had her own private legal practice until she joined the rackets prosecution.

Victor J. Herwitz, a graduate of Brooklyn Law School in 1932, joined the staff on August 15. Vic was a New Yorker who looked much more ferocious than he was, because he had somewhere sustained a broken nose that made him look like a prize fighter. He was an aggressive, able lawyer, something of a table-thumper, with experience in and around the city government under LaGuardia.

John A. Gleason, a Princeton graduate, also joined us on August 15. He had graduated from Fordham University Law School and had experience in negligence insurance type litigation. He was somewhat older in appearance than the others. He stayed for some months before he resigned.

The third lawyer who joined us on August 15 was Stanley H. Fuld, and there would be little I could add to ornament his distinguished career. Stanley graduated with honors from the College of the City of New York, and with honors from Columbia Law School in 1926. After working with a downtown law firm he joined one of the major New Deal agencies in Washington, the National Recovery Administration, the blue-eagle NRA. After serving there with distinction, he applied to us for a job. Stanley turned out to be one of the most brilliant men who ever turned his scholarly talents to the penal law of New York State.

He was to prepare practically every indictment in the office, to go over the points of law with the assistants in all cases, to find precedents for rulings for the admission of evidence in almost all cases.

Stanley was considered by his fellow assistants to be our real law man and brain. He was a wiry, medium-sized chap, with a charming sense of humor, rather reserved, with a penchant for outrageous puns.

Milton Schilback, Sol Gelb, and Charles D. Breitel were announced as members of the staff on August 20, 1935. Milton Schilback was a Harvard Law School graduate, a man of medium height and weight, sallow complexion, dark mustache, an excellent and experienced trial lawyer and a solid and substantial workman.

Sol Gelb, our prime trial strategist, was short, slender, a fellow who came up the hard way in New York. His father was a Hebrew scholar and teacher and, as Sol said, "They were all impoverished."

Sol had to work hard. He put himself through New York University Law School and got a job with a distinguished lawyer in Westchester County, Humphrey Lynch, while he was still in law school. Lynch had such a high regard for Sol that he told him to pick out any cases he wanted in the office, take them, and go out and open his own office because he would have nothing more to gain by working for Lynch. Sol took some of the cases, opened a law firm, and did very well at the Bar. In fact Sol had already developed something of a specialty in a peculiar type of negligence case that arose in the field of railroad law, and he had tried cases and argued appeals in state and federal courts of many jurisdictions.

Sol had an incisive mind and was able to separate the trivial from the substantial almost instantly. Lockwood commented about him: "His great quality is his ability to take a complicated set of facts and statements, together with the worries and apprehensions of other assistants, and, in a very few minutes, with almost what appeared to be casual attention, say, 'What this is is the following kind of case, and that's all there is to it. If you can prove that, you've got a case.' I might add that sometimes this quality used to drive Dewey with his passion for thoroughness almost nuts, but Gelb seldom if ever erred."

Charles D. Breitel was a New Yorker who had graduated from the University of Michigan. In his freshman year at Ann Arbor he had met and married a co-ed, Jean. They graduated together, went to law school together, and they were both admitted to the Bar. Charlie went with some of the downtown firms and, when the rackets prosecution came along, he applied and was hired. He was a short, bespectacled, charming, gracious person, in those days rather quiet and reserved, a brilliant legal scholar. He brought to the office a sharpness, perceptiveness, quiet intensity, and a lot of common sense and human understanding. Breitel recalled in later years:

"Dewey's a very direct person—sometimes too direct. He still is, you know. He sees my wife, and he tells her that he doesn't like the shape of her eyeglasses. He used to be worse, but he has these remarkable powers of observation and intensive, parental interest in his people. I remember some time later we were walking toward the County Court House. We already had one of the cases on, maybe it was the restaurant case. I don't remember what it was, but he said, 'Charlie, you speak in too low a register. It's not your proper register. It makes your voice crack. Try not to speak in so low a register. Let it come up a bit.'

"That was the end of the conversation. I had very little consciousness of what to do about this. I had no voice training of any kind. Two years later, maybe, we happened to be walking in the streets again, and he said, 'By the way, Charlie, you know your voice is much better now than it used to be.'

"Not only did he admire his men the way he did, with this excess admiration and this parental attitude toward them, but actually you could count on him, and, by the way, this is still a truth. For instance, I haven't any doubt about it that there's nobody in the world from an outside group that could get Dewey to do anything that would be hurtful to me. I have complete confidence about that. Now, when you get a group of men, and this started to develop in due time, that have this feeling about their leader, it is precisely like the quality of leadership you look for in an army."

Sewell T. Tyng, Charles P. Grimes, Jacob Grumet, Edward Joseph, and Harris B. Steinberg were announced as members of the staff on October 12. Tyng, of course, was my valued associate and great friend from my early days at Larkin, Rathbone and Perry, who was now signing up for public service against the rackets.

Charles P. Grimes was a tall, handsome Yale University athlete with curly hair, and high shoulders. He was a powerful man and an excellent lawyer. After working with one of the downtown law firms he joined Harold Ickes in the first, full days of the New Deal. But Charlie could not put up with Ickes, and he resigned and came back to New York, where he got a job with us. He used to cause a sensation among people in the office when he came or went with his squash racket under his arm, on the way from or to the Yale Club for some exercise. Charlie had a pretty good sense of humor but took a terrible ribbing about his Yale background.

Jacob Grumet, graduate of City College and Columbia Law School, was a New Yorker, medium-sized, rather thin and cadaverous, with a black mustache. Jack was a fine trial lawyer and a fine scholar and was soon considered to be one of the best trial lawyers in New York. He was one man who, like Medalie, always looked like ice when he was on his feet, and he was extremely capable and competent. He was also something of a hypochondriac. One of our jokes in the racket prosecution was that Grumet always wore a heavy woolen scarf of crimson hue and wrapped it around his neck carefully whenever he went out. I remember a staff conference when Grumet rose dramatically, looked around with an expression of haunted anguish, and said, "My God! Is there a window open in this room?"

Edward Joseph of Harvard Law School was one of our younger fellows who came on as a dollar-a-year man and then was moved onto the staff. He was too young to be in the headlines during the racket prosecution and he moved up, after that, to join the District Attorney's office.

Harris B. Steinberg also came in from Harvard Law School and started at the bottom. He was a rare combination of legal scholar and good trial strategist, and he demonstrated this in a junior role. He was also a dabbler in the arts, doing some remarkable cartoons and water colors of the courts and the people who infested them. Many years afterward, Steinberg recalled:

"I think they very carefully screened the applicants even for the dollar-a-year men. For one thing, Dewey wanted to know what my father did. My father had been a sign painter. He was dead now, but he was a sign painter, and belonged to a union. I think the particular union he belonged to had some gangster connections, and Dewey wanted to know what my father's connection with the union was. I told him he'd never been active in it. He just paid his dues, and Dewey said, 'Well, the hell with that. That's all right.'

"You had a bunch of bright young guys on the staff. Because there was a Depression on, and because there was this tremendous kudos attached to being a member of the staff, Dewey had a wealth of talent available to him at very low prices—Depression prices. Ordinarily, very bright boys have all kinds of jobs offered to them.

"Also, the Dewey investigation was offbeat for a fellow who wanted to be a corporate lawyer. Yet we had some of them on the staff, Ed McLean, Harry Cole, and a few others like that. They were the type of men—you know, Ivy League schools, wealthy families—the order of men who would become leaders of the Bar on the stuffy side of the profession. They took time to come with the Dewey investigation because it was exciting and worth while.

"Other fellows like myself were Jewish boys who could not get into a big law firm. There were pretty tight bars on the doors against a Jewish fellow who had quite good marks. I think today to some extent this has changed.

"Putting it all together, Dewey had the pick of men who would not normally be available to a prosecutor. He had a bunch of fellows like Charles Breitel, Stanley Fuld, Herlands, who all went on to the bench, and Rosenblum, Gelb, and others who became leading trial lawyers. They were all just as bright and energetic then, and they were all in one office. Compared to the kind of men there were in public life later on, there was a tremendous concentration of very good men on Dewey's staff. I think the times and the economics had a great deal to do with it.

"There was an air of cockiness in the office. Looking back, I would imagine that not many of them were likeable characters. There was a truculence, a swaggering toughness about them because they were doing a good job, and because they felt they had the imprimatur of integrity.

"If you were on Dewey's staff, you were ipso facto a man of great integrity, ipso facto a man of great ability. It was an interesting job and you had the world by the tail. It couldn't have been too easy to live with guys like that. They were a competitive, tough bunch and Dewey, I think, is the only man I've ever met who could have kept that team of horses running harmoniously together. He could quell any uprising with one look, and he was tough enough himself so that nobody fooled around with him.

"Later, it was the same—when he became a big politician, he was able to control appointments of judges. His appointments were very good, far better than those of Roosevelt. Roosevelt I consider a great statesman. LaGuardia was a great statesman. Both of them had the ability to appoint judges, but they appointed lousy judges. They appointed them as political deals. A judgeship was a political plum that you exchanged for something else you wanted. But Dewey always appointed good judges to the bench because he was molded in the federal court with John C. Knox, Learned Hand, that bunch, and Dewey felt that it was very important. Even later, when a guy who deserved some political recognition came to Dewey for an appointment on the bench, Dewey wouldn't go along with it. He'd make him something else, commissioner, maybe, but not a judge."

Three other dollar-a-year volunteer lawyers of early vintage were Richard K. Korn, Livingston Goddard, and Manuel Robbins. Dick Korn, whose appointment was announced on July 26, was an accomplished musician who became a composer and conductor of some note. He stayed with us for some two years before he resigned to devote his full time to a musical career. "Livy" Goddard came from Groton, Harvard College, and Harvard Law School. He was tall, rather lanky, with a gargantuan appetite and a very bawdy sense of humor. His legal ability was tops, and he was later promoted to Deputy Assistant.

Manuel Robbins, known as "Manny," or "Manny the Muscle," was a New Yorker by birth. His father was a partner of Louis Untermeyer, the poet, in the diamond business. At a very early age he had suffered from encephalitis, with the result that his hearing was slightly impaired. He graduated from Horace Mann, Harvard College, and Harvard Law School. Manny was good company and a brilliant lawyer, and he was always a worrier.

Robbins recalled: "There was also this staff question hour, with questions Dewey answered very bluntly. You got in the habit very early of never asking questions which you really didn't have to ask. If anyone asked a question just to hear the sound of his own voice, or to make his presence felt, he would get a very blunt rejoinder which dissuaded him from ever doing it again. Dewey at times was very crude with people who he thought were wasting time. You also learned never to say things that you hadn't thought out first, because you could get caught very badly, and he would press you very hard. If you asked that kind of unthought-out question, he would push you into a ridiculous position. You learned quickly that if you hadn't thought a matter out, if you didn't have a real problem that could be apparently answered, or quickly answered, you'd make a jackass out of yourself before the rest of the group.

"He had an air of inspiration about him that certainly got carried on to his staff. It was a crusade, and we were all young enough to be very ardent crusaders. His determination and doggedness, the care with which we felt he was selecting his associates and the veil of high-level integrity that was constantly apparent throughout the investigation had a tremendous inspirational effect—because we were battling the whole, organized underworld in New York City, and we were the forces of decent living."

Our non-legal staff was chosen with the same degree of care. Goody Goodrich, the chief accountant, a man with thirteen years' experience of investigative accounting recruited nine other accountants who, when racketeers refused to talk, were able to make their books talk for them.

This was the first time a Special Prosecutor or District Attorney had established an accounting staff as part of the office. Before, an accountant was hired for a particular case. But I felt the accounting staff was important, not only to investigate cases but also to bring pressure on witnesses to testify. This was extremely important in the racket investigation.

So much interest was aroused by this accounting staff that, in years to come, District Attorneys came from all over the country to look into that aspect—including Earl Warren of California—and they were given any information or help they wanted by my office.

Out of Goodrich's staff, six were certified public accountants.

Three of them had prior experience with state and city investigating authorities. Two of them had been employed by the NRA Code Authority in the cloak and suit industry, and they were to prove particularly helpful in our inquiry into rackets in the garment industry. One had served as chief accountant under Herbert Hoover for the American Relief Administration in Russia in the early 1920s. Two of Goody Goodrich's accountants were also members of the Bar, and their legal training would enable them to render the additional service of distinguishing between competent and incompetent evidence.

To head my staff of investigators I named Wayne Merrick. He had been born and brought up a farm in Iowa and, after graduating from high school there, had become an agent in the Department of Justice. For eight years he had worked on many of the most important cases of the FBI. His investigating skill was responsible for hundreds of convictions obtained by federal prosecutors in twenty states. Merrick was credited with solving the O'Connell kidnaping case, with breaking up the Scarnici mob of bank robbers, the leader of whom, Leonard Scarnici, was electrocuted for the murder of a New York City policeman.

To assist him, Merrick recruited nine keen and experienced fellow investigators. Five of them were lawyers. These five and a sixth, an accountant, had served as agents in the Department of Justice. Merrick had worked directly with four of these men and knew first hand of the excellent reputation of the others.

Lockwood recalled: "Merrick and one or two others certainly would have passed in the movies as investigators, but the rest of them, befitting a cosmopolitan place like New York, did not look like motion picture detectives at all. It was planned that way.

"In a great city like New York, of course, we had neighborhoods, and sections, which were inhabited by people of one national origin, or one racial origin, like Chinatown, Harlem, Little Puerto Rico or the San Juan Hill area on the East Side, or the Irish neighborhood down by the docks on the West Side, or the Italian neighborhood along Mulberry, Baxter, and Elizabeth streets downtown. But at that time the town was hot. Bookmakers, policy slip pushers, narcotics peddlers, anybody who had anything on his mind that was possibly illegal, say, in the Italian neighborhood, well, he would certainly be aware if two well-set-up Irishmen with snap-brim hats and hands in their coat pockets walked down the street.

"The street would close immediately. By the same token, two gentlemen looking like movie versions of FBI agents arriving in a questionable New York night club would strip the joint in five minutes. Everyone would just leave.

"The investigators, or some of them, had to be able to speak the foreign languages. Many of the people with whom we were in contact, if they wanted to conceal their activities, talked in their native tongues, Italian, Yiddish, Spanish, and other languages. Later on, we had a poll taken, and we found that one member of our staff could even converse in the manual language of the deaf and dumb.

"One of the detectives, a chap named Bob Goldstein, told me of his earlier days in the Police Department when he had been sent down to the East Side. Bob was Jewish and, while he certainly didn't look like an Irishman, he was very well set up, had a formidable carriage. He told me of being assigned to find an illegal distillery being operated down in a tenement block on the East Side. He said that he walked through a tenement house cellar out into a rubble-strewn back yard and looked around. He said that there were a lot of old crones hanging out of windows staring into space. One of them apparently looked down, and she saw him. She let out a loud screech: 'Becky, shamus.'

"'Shamus' in the Yiddish vernacular meant policeman and Bob told me that every window immediately bounced down. Every shade was drawn. That was the end of any activity on the block."

In general terms, I explained earlier how we had promised to keep absolutely secret the names and the testimony of witnesses and other informants. In order to keep this pledge, I now decided it was necessary to appoint stenographers and clerks of my own choosing, and this was by no means standard bureaucratic operating procedure. So my associates and I went to the state Civil Service Commission and asked for permission to go outside the competitive lists in filling these positions. The members of the Commission agreed that the work was of a highly confidential nature and granted the exemptions requested. The Governor of the state approved the resolution of the Commission in this regard.

So, for 20 stenographic vacancies, we now received applications from no fewer than 385 stenographers, and also from 75 others who described themselves as secretaries. A dentist, a chemist, two doctors, a psychologist, a bricklayer, and a hostess were included in another batch of 225 applications, marked Miscellaneous.

In the end, 20 stenographers were hired, who could take question and answer statements at the rate of 200 words per minute. Most of them were actually qualified to serve as court reporters. The scarcity of employment, however, enabled the rackets investigation to benefit by their services for as little as $1,500 a year. The head of the steno-graphic bureau, Lois E. Van Gordon, spoke Spanish, Portuguese, Italian, French, and German, had served as a court reporter, and was an acknowledged expert in deciphering documents. She even had a working knowledge of the science of handwriting and typewriting identification.

The chief clerk, Morris Schneider, was another find. A lawyer by profession, he had served as managing clerk for one of the largest firms in the city for twenty-four years. During that time he had taken care of the paper work in thousands of lawsuits without once suffering a default. His knowledge of court procedure and motion practice was such that managing clerks in other firms constantly called upon him for advice. But a year before the investigation started he had given up his job and opened his own law office only to find that, while lawyers eagerly sought his advice, they never quite caught the idea of paying for it.

A mild-mannered little man with the stoop and demeanor of a bookkeeper, Schneider ran the office with quiet efficiency. On the few occasions when it was his duty to administer a rebuke, it caused him such apparent pain that the person spoken to felt himself to be guilt-ier in that respect than he was for breaking the rules. Schneider was respected and beloved by all.

Frank Hogan recalled: "After the returns were in on Election Night in 1937, newly elected District Attorney Dewey called Schnei-der to an inner office in campaign headquarters. The little clerk edged his way through a crowd of political leaders and campaign strategists. Dewey took his hand, turned to the group around him, and said, 'Let me announce my first appointment. After January 1, 1938, Morris Schneider will be the chief clerk of the District Attorney's office.' It was a tribute richly deserved."

At the entrance to the rackets prosecution office I stationed Michael Monz. He had served as chief receptionist during the Seabury investigation, and he was on intimate if not cordial terms with most of the cranks in town. He spotted them as soon as they came in and gently turned them away with tact and dispatch. His skill in sizing up and handling people saved the assistants a great deal of time and energy. A moment's conversation, and Monz could tell with a real degree of certainty whether someone was genuinely distressed about something for which there was a legal remedy or whether he or she belonged in the observation ward at Bellevue Hospital. His mistakes, considering the thousands of people who passed his desk, were miraculously few.

The rackets investigation staff, as finally assembled, numbered seventy-six. Frank Hogan summed up:

"It was a versatile group, and as cosmopolitan as New York. Most were college trained, or completing equivalent education at night schools. There was a clerk who had left Wall Street after years with stocks and bonds. One of the process servers had studied pharmacy. Another, an expert photographer, often went out on his own time with detectives to get desired pictures. There was a stenographer from Tubbercurry, County Sligo, who could do with a bit of Gaelic, and a messenger born in Aleppo, Syria, who could lend a helping hand with problem children from the Near East.

"One, who started as a volunteer messenger, successively held the jobs of messenger, process server, and investigator. Another, a Princeton graduate, began as a clerk, completed a law course in evening sessions, and became a Deputy Assistant District Attorney."

Meanwhile, Governor Lehman appointed Philip McCook as the justice of the Supreme Court to be in charge of the special term. No finer man ever undertook such a delicate and heavy chore. He and his ancestors had been in every one of our wars, which was why they were known as "The Fighting McCooks." He had unlimited courage, dedication, and a total sense of fairness. The public was never better served by any judge than during the two and a half years Philip McCook presided over our turbulent investigation.

My radio address to the people of New York concerning the purposes of our investigation was well received publicly, but then I made a bad mistake. Having promised to prosecute any kind of racketeer, large or small, I now found I had one of the smallest kind. Nineteen-year-old Dominick Tossoni threw a stone through a plate-glass window of a store, and offered to protect the storekeeper for a price. Tossoni had done this before in his neighborhood and the storekeeper complained to us. We watched while the storekeeper paid Tossoni $30 in marked money. We arrested Tossoni and he confessed.

The underworld and a whole lot of people had a horse laugh at our expense. The mountain had labored and produced a mouse. But I did not see what else we could have done under the circumstances, and I issued a statement:

"This is a typical case of a small racket. While the case itself is petty, it must be remembered that all organized rackets are based on a long series of petty extortions and intimidations. The small shopkeeper and business are entitled to just as much protection as the large business. I have said we will prosecute every racketeering case that comes to us, large or small, and I meant it. By protecting the identity of the complainant and his testimony, we were able to make this case, as we will all others. We will continue to give the complainant the same absolute protection, now that the case has been broken, that we gave him before the arrest."

The New York *Post* commented: "The first fish was landed today in the Dewey racket net. It was a small fish—just big enough to keep— but it elated the special prosecutor as the first nibble always pleases a fisherman."

Meanwhile the tens of thousands of people who could have given us evidence against the rackets were staying away. We were twenty lawyers against the world, and we now knew something of the monstrous nature of our job. We were coming to realize that nobody really believed in us. The press said it did. Public figures said they did. The citizens said they believed in us. The members of the grand jury were willing to work long hours with complete trust. We never had a leak out of a grand juror, and we never had a fix in a trial jury, although some would be attempted. The hard fact was, however, that our principal enemies, cynicism and fear, seemed overpowering. The victims of organized crime did not believe that anything could be done.

It was at this time that a judge of the highest court of our state told me he was satisfied that nothing would break the hold of the underworld except a dictatorship. It was also at this time that Sol Gelb was asking Appeals Court Judge Manton whether he should seek a job with me. Manton told Gelb the investigation would amount to nothing and would be dead within six months. I was lucky that idealism triumphed in Gelb.

I had lunch with Arthur Brisbane, the noted columnist in the

Hearst newspapers, and with Bernard Gimbel, one of the leading merchants in America. Brisbane was filled with hope and confidence and exhorted all to help and believe. Bernard Gimbel had no faith in us at all. Gimbel was a man who knew everybody of all stations and was greatly beloved and respected. He did have one addiction—to gambling. He knew every big bookmaker, and he gambled regularly for very large sums at the places where it was legal. He had encountered and knew in person many of the leaders of the underworld.

Over this particular luncheon, Gimbel and Brisbane argued heatedly over my body, and the argument ended up in a bet. Gimbel bet Brisbane $500 that I would be out of business in six months. It was not encouraging.

Two of the most important and respected labor leaders in America were David Dubinsky and Sidney Hillman, the heads, respectively, of the International Ladies Garment Workers Union of America and the Amalgamated Clothing Workers of America. I knew—as everybody knew—from gossip that the underworld rulers in that industry were Lepke (Louis Buchalter) and Gurrah (Jacob Shapiro). I invited Dubinsky to dinner with me alone at my home. He was one of the most charming men I knew, and we had a delightful evening, but he knew nothing—absolutely nothing—about any gangsters or racketeers in his industry.

Over the years since then I have enjoyed a warm relationship with Dubinsky and respected him as a completely honest, progressive labor leader. The one subject I was never able to discuss with him was why he did not consider it feasible to help me in the racket investigation.

Sidney Hillman also came to dinner at my home, alone, and the result was another total blank.

Meanwhile our office was swamped with work of an unexpected kind. After my radio address, we received thousands of complaints, and we found that the word "racket" was loosely applied to almost any kind of shabby transaction, dirty trick, fraud, swindle, exorbitant selling practice, repossession of goods sold under a conditional sales agreement or chattel mortgage, sharp auction practice, and so on. Turning people away, or referring them to the magistrate's court, or the District Attorney, or the law enforcement agency with appropriate jurisdiction was often an unhappy or bitter experience for us. This was even more so because many of the victims had tried and failed in these agencies to get relief. Some of the situations were slimy and indecent, and it was more of the history of our times.

Paul Lockwood had a vivid recollection of a visit one day from a delegation of six men who said they represented the West Thirty-fourth Street Merchants Association and wanted to make a complaint against a racket. Lockwood recalled: "In response to my opening question, they said that their problem was the 'puller-in racket' and it soon became clear to me what was involved.

"These gentlemen were the owners of some small percentage of the retail stores on the south side of West Thirty-fourth Street, between Herald Square and Seventh Avenue, facing Macy's. There were all sorts of lingerie shops, show shops, women's hat shops, and notion shops of one sort or another there. It seemed that some of the stores not represented by this committee, but competitors of the committee, were employing 'pullers.' These were genlemen who stood on the sidewalk in front of their stores and pulled into their establishment any unwary women who might look in the windows.

"The merchants' association people brought a woman in, and she told me she had been shopping at Macy's, had crossed Thirty-fourth Street on her way to Pennsylvania Station, and had stopped to look in a store window over which there was a large sign announcing some sensational sale. She looked at shoes, and the next thing she knew she found herself in a chair, in the store, with an ice cream cone in her hand. She said that some men had taken her by the arm, whisked her into the store, seated her in the chair, while another man pulled her shoes off. The puller had given her the ice cream cone as a present. The idea was that she should buy some new shoes.

"I had to explain that we were not in the business of going after pullers, and they seemed very much disappointed, In fact, they threatened to write a letter to the Governor about it. But the suppression of this kind of nuisance was, of course, the job of the policemen on the beat. When I explained this, they indicated—whether they had any evidence of it or not I didn't know—that the policemen were induced to look the other way while the pullers operated. We referred the group in the end to the Police Commissioner with a view to getting better enforcement of existing laws."

Paul Lockwood told how an elderly, foreign-born woman had come in to complain about a labor racket: "According to her story, she subleased from the tenant in a retail store along one of the streets on the East Side her own small area of the sidewalk. There she erected a wooden trestle and she placed on it, every day, some fresh fish she had purchased from the market. She was in the retail fish business.

"One day a man identifying himself as a union organizer came along and told her the union insisted that she take on a clerk. Since she was barely making her own living, selling probably not more than a hundred pounds of fish a day, this request became a little ridiculous. But when she refused to take on a clerk at some union pay scale a picket line was put in front of the whole building.

"Well, of course, this raised hell with her tenant-landlord because, in a labor-conscious neighborhood, people would not cross picket lines.

"She came down to our office and asked for relief. The situation was one in which some labor union had deemed that she was a retail establishment, decided for itself that it had jurisdiction over retail stores, and concluded that she ought to hire a clerk. It meant that the woman had to go out of business. We tested her carefully by letting her tell her story over and over again. We wanted to find out, and we had to find out, whether there was any extortion involved. We needed to find out whether the alleged union organizer had said something like, 'Well, you either hire the clerk, or if you pay so much a week, we won't force you to hire the clerk.' That would have been extortion.

"That was the element that, unfortunately, in this and in similar cases did not exist. There was no extortion. Therefore this situation, sad as it was, was something over which we had no jurisdiction. The propriety or ridiculousness of union demands was not something within our scope."

There were other problems that took up an amazing amount of our time. For example, under the scheme of law enforcement in New York, the prosecution of a crime had to be undertaken in the county in which the crime had been committed. Not too many New Yorkers were familiar with the fact that the city of New York consisted of five counties, and their names are not always the same as the boroughs. The Borough of the Bronx is Bronx County, and the Borough of Queens is Queens County. But the Borough of Brooklyn is the County of Kings, the Borough of Manhattan is the County of New York, and Staten Island is the County of Richmond. On countless occasions we had to explain we had jurisdiction only over Manhattan, or, rather, the County of New York.

We also had to spend an inordinate amount of time with disappointed litigants, workmen's compensation cases, and potential plants who might have been attempting to infiltrate our investigation in some way.

Michael Monz, our receptionist, had what he called his "C" file. This was C for "crank" or "crackpot," and Monz had a genius for spotting them and sending them on their way. One man kept accusing him of denying "justice." One woman took her shoe off, pointed to her big toe, and said, "That's where the message comes in every night— the message that tells me every night to go out and do something evil."

Monz exposed us all for the first time to what is known in psychiatry as *folie à deux*, which is a madness of two. We found two elderly women, theretofore unacquainted and unrelated, who had run into one another while making their own separate rounds of prosecuting and police agencies. Each had delusions, and convinced the other that the delusions were true. After a while they tended to corroborate one another. Mrs. A. might say that a man had told her she had to pay so much money or else. Then Mrs. B. would supply corroborative evidence: "Yes, I was there, and I heard it."

Monz was sitting one day at the reception desk when an elderly woman leaped in and said, "I want to see Dewey right away. They're after me." Mike said, "Who's after you, lady?" She said: "Dutch Schultz and Luciano."

Mike Monz never batted an eye. He said, "Madam, just sit down. We'll take care of them." He called over Patrolman Tom Schaffer, a large, stout, elderly patrolman on detail in the office, and said, "Officer, I want you to go out and arrest those people outside. Take them off to prison." Old Tom was a very wise fellow. He said, "Yes, sir. I'll go out and arrest them right away. Don't worry any more about this, madam."

Tom went out on the sidewalk and walked around the block while Mike reassured the lady that Dutch Schultz and Lucky Luciano had been arrested. She felt much relieved, thanked him very much, and went on her way. The next day a young man came in, and he asked Mike, "Are you the man who interviewed my mother yesterday?" He described his mother, and Mike said, "Yes, I am." The young man said, "I want to thank you very much for what you did for her. She slept last night, and she hadn't slept in weeks."

Paul Lockwood noted the legend in our office that, every time there was a full moon, the C file people came out. He recalled: "You're familiar with the popular superstition that a full moon affects people suffering from mental disease. There's no scientific evidence to substantiate that. I even had the state Department of Mental Hygiene make a study of the effect of a full moon on those who suffer from mental disease in later years when in Albany, in response to a newspaper query.

"But according to the boys at the reception desk of the rackets investigation, there was some relationship between that phenomenon and the people who came in. Many of them were known as 'full mooners.'"

Intramurally, we set up Medalie's rules from the United States Attorney's office: no private practice by any assistant; no consorting with criminals and no photographs with defendants; no discussion of any case outside the office and—in this we went further—no discussion between any member of the staff working on one case with any member working on another case. Above all, there were to be no leaks to the press, no trial by newspaper.

The difficulty of maintaining this position vis-à-vis the press constituted a real problem. Each day they appeared, eager, intelligent reporters, and they bombarded us with questions as to our plans, the rackets we were investigating, and the latest rumors. Repeatedly I said I could not comment on any work being done by the office. I said information would come only from arrests and indictments when the cases had been fully investigated and were being prosecuted.

Frank Hogan recalled: "While the newspapermen appreciated the logic of Dewey's position, it did not fit with them. City editors were demanding copy. It was up to them to get a story. Since there was no material to be obtained at the Woolworth Building, they played up gossip and rumor, did some speculating on their own, and indulged in daily forecasts as to the current object of Dewey's attentions.

"The effect of this publicity was very damaging. Dewey realized that his policy of silence would be futile if the stories continued. The reading public would not take the trouble to look for quotation marks. They would say, 'I see by the papers that Dewey is investigating so-and-so.' A month or two of this, and Dewey would be credited with running a 'goldfish bowl' investigation—and prospective witnesses would be making their last wills and testaments before responding to request subpoenas.

"It was a ticklish problem. The newspapers, in large measure, had been responsible for the investigation. Their continuing support was of vital importance to it. Dewey decided that he must convert each and every one of them to his way of thinking. For months after making this decision, he utilized every spare minute of his time convincing editors, publishers, and owners of newspapers and press associations that the best way to help the investigation was to ignore it. The response was most gratifying."

On September 9, 1935, the Washington *Post* reported: "New York is now in the process of undergoing a widespread inquiry into current rackets, but you would scarcely know it from the papers. Stories concerning the investigation manage to get on the inside pages, chiefly because there appears to be so little to tell."

Then the Washington *Post* added: "All that seems to be known is that about 3,000 witnesses have been examined, many of whom have proved recalcitrant."

In our first sudden swoop, in a field nobody knew we were even looking into, our rackets investigation arrested twenty-two loan sharks in New York City. We held them on 252 counts in 126 meticulously prepared indictments. We knew they would not be able to beat the bail demands totaling $174,500. We issued a warning that, if anybody attempted to make reprisals against our witnesses against the loan sharks, we would see to it that offenders were sentenced to prison for life.

The New York *Times* wrote on November 3, 1935: "Bred to the hare-and-hounds tradition of racket investigation, New York was puzzled until last Monday by the silent procedure of Thomas E. Dewey, who undertook last July the gigantic job of ridding the community of organized crime." Then the *Times* told about our loan shark arrests.

Among his other activities, Sewell Tyng had conducted a study of loan sharking for the Russell Sage Foundation. This resulted in a report that loan sharking in New York City alone amounted to $1 million per week. Loan sharking was an individual crime, but on such a large scale it was estimated that one out of every thirty New Yorkers was in the clutches of loan sharks.

The loan sharks actually had one of the most vicious, rotten rackets that ever plundered our city. They got fat on the profits they took from poor, hard-working men and women, laborers and small businessmen, people who were hard up, who needed money to pay for doctors, for groceries, for rent.

Usually the loan shark would lend five dollars and demand six back the next week. Six for five sounded good when people did not know where to turn for ready cash, but if they were not able to pay at the end of the week, they soon learned they had let themselves in for a much bigger debt, which kept getting bigger and bigger. Threats made them easy victims for more and more extortion.

If they did not pay, they got the works. Many were beaten. Some even had to leave their homes to get away from the thugs hired by the loan sharks. Decent men and women, who were forced to borrow money to buy their children food and shoes, had gunmen come right into their homes and make threats against them in the presence of their children.

The loan sharks organized their racket into a big business. The gangsters broke heads and cut men with knives and made their victims lose their jobs. Thousands of people were caught in their net and this was the Depression.

I remember a letter carrier, a fine man, whose wife was having a baby. He borrowed $50 from a loan shark because he did not have enough money. He paid back $5.00 a week for twenty weeks, a total of $100, and then he still owed the loan shark $75 more. At least the loan shark said he owed him that.

Another time a man had paid $40 on a $20 loan and was still $8.00 behind in the payments. The loan shark walked right into the apartment with two thugs. He took the man's pants off the bed and took the money right out of the pocket. When the man's wife tried to stop him the shark threatened to cut her throat. The man pleaded, "My rent is due tomorrow. I have to pay $6.00 or I will be on the street." The loan shark snarled at him and, with the thugs, walked out with the money.

Chief Assistant Jack Rosenblum recalled: "A gray-haired lady and her husband, both seventy-two years old, had fallen into a loan shark's grip in order to pay rent for a small beauty shop that they were operating. When they were unable to meet one of the payments the loan shark and two of his thugs visited the beauty parlor, smashed the showcases, hit the old man on the head with a bottle, and punched and kicked the wife. They wound up by telling the wife that, if the payment was not made within two days, they would cut her hand off at the wrist."

Usury, of course, is an ancient practice and has been so universally condemned over the centuries that it must have arisen out of something fundamental in the human character. By the 1930s, however, the $6.00 for $5.00 formula meant an interest rate of a little more than 1,000 per cent per annum. The rate was lower for men who borrowed a hundred dollars. They could pay it back at the rate of $20 a week for six weeks, a mere 160 per cent interest rate.

We found out that the loan sharks were usually gangsters themselves and were often part of large mobs. The victims knew the penalty for non-payment was not a lawsuit but a vicious beating or cutting, and everybody who did business with a loan shark knew it. But would they testify to it?

Sewell Tyng was convinced that the field was important in the organized crime sense and that we ought to move. So we did. We got good identification from our own sources of twenty-two notorious sharks. We made our simultaneous, sensational arrests of all of them, all over the city, and we brought them to our office.

Then we brought in dozens of the victims, most of them poorly paid clerks and laborers who had fallen into financial troubles through illness, carelessness, or family misfortune. At first, they were eager to testify, but their courage oozed away when they were asked to confront their tormentors face to face.

For a while it looked as if we would have a real and very public failure on our hands. Then somebody had an inspiration. We put all the loan sharks, mixed in with some detectives, in one large room with a venetian blind hanging outside over the door. Then we brought the victims one by one to the door and allowed them to peer through the slats. When the victims realized they might testify safely, their fears were relieved. The victims were also impressed by the fact that we had so many witnesses against the loan sharks. Before the night was over we actually had multiple, solid identifications of every loan shark, every one of them.

With the cases parceled out among several deputy assistants, we brought the loan sharks to trial one by one. Within a month they had all been convicted, save one who escaped on a minor technical mistake made by one of the young assistants. During the trials, more complaints were brought in against more loan sharks, and we went out

and made more arrests. Before we were through, thirty-six of the
sharks had been convicted and sentenced to terms ranging from two
to five years' imprisonment.

This was scarcely a major investigation, but we thought it useful to
attack one of the slimiest of criminal practices, and to demonstrate how
comparatively easy it was to stop it if anybody took the trouble. We
had also proven that we could keep our preparatory work secret, that
we could protect our witnesses, and that we had indeed been extremely busy all these months.

Our sudden foray into loan sharking also gave us valuable leads
into our chosen major target areas of organized crime and political
corruption. We learned much about, but did not touch, the question of
loan sharking within the criminal underworld. This was the hardest
problem to deal with, because criminals rarely blew the whistle on
one another. A narcotics importer might need a large loan. A gunman
might be broke and need money to buy guns and ammunition. A
madam might need money to reopen a house of prostitution after a
raid at her old address. An arrested criminal might need more money
than expected for bail or for legal fees. Their only recourse was to
loan sharks, and the underworld was even more cruel to its own than
to others. Those in default might be beaten to a pulp or shot to death
to set an example.

Then there was the fact that the District Attorney of New York
County, Dodge, had done nothing about loan sharking. Why not?
He had a chance to do it, but he did nothing. There was even one
specific case on record in which a loan shark gangster named Sam
Faden had been brought right into the District Attorney's office. A
victim had demanded that Faden be arrested. But the victim was told
to go to the magistrate's court and tell her story there. Sam Faden
walked out of the District Attorney's office a free man, and nothing
happened at magistrate's court.

But Sam Faden was one of the loan sharks we sent to prison. He
was put away.

Smashing Lucky Luciano

As we looked over the racket situation, it often seemed to me that the Mafia was worse than the rest of the underworld. There was no honor among this breed of thieves, gunmen, robbers, narcotic peddlers, pimps, murderers, and racketeers. The whole lot of them were not merely anti-social. They were slimy, cheating savages, even in their relations with one another. They were members of the human race, but with few redeeming qualities.

Not long before we took office there had been a savage gang war for leadership of the various elements of the Mafia. Giuseppe "Joe the Boss" Masseria had been murdered in a restaurant where he was meeting with Charles Luciano and five others. Luciano was the only guest who remained after the shooting. When the police arrived, he explained he did not know the people who had come in, and he had not seen anything that happened because he was in the men's room washing his hands. This was one of Luciano's more brazen efforts.

Masseria was succeeded by Salvatore Maranzano, an educated man who had studied for the priesthod in the old country and spoke several languages. It was said that Maranzano was an enthusiastic student of the life of Julius Caesar and had a roomful of books on the subject. He called a meeting of Mafia leaders to announce a new organizational hierarchy. He said that he would be *Capo di Tutti Capi*, meaning Boss of All the Bosses, and the rest of the Mafia would be divided up into families, each with a boss, lieutenants, and ordinary soldiers. Maranzano reviewed the rules of the Mafia in which the death sentence was standard operating procedure. It would be death for talking about the Mafia, for violating another member's wife, even for talking with one's own wife about the Mafia. It would be death for a soldier who disobeyed the orders of a lieutenant. He proclaimed a new rule, that no member could lay his hands upon another member in anger.

Maranzano named five bosses of the families in New York, one of whom was Luciano. But this show of mastery seemed to have gone to Maranzano's head, because he began to talk about eliminating Luciano, Vito Genovese, and some of the others. He was going to start the gang wars all over again, and this did not sit well. One day four men posing as detectives walked into Maranzano's legitimate-front office, a real estate company in the Grand Central Building, and they killed him with six bullets. Some forty other Mafia leaders allied with Maranzano were killed elsewhere in the country on the same day.

Luciano became the absolute top boss of the Mafia in New York and, as far as we knew, in other cities as well. Luciano had been brought from Sicily to New York at the age of nine, attended public school on the Lower East Side, and quit at the age of fourteen. He worked for a few months in a hat factory and hung around poolrooms and crap games. He quickly learned that he could make more money even at the bottom levels of the rackets than by working for a living. He is said to have announced his philosophy at an early age: "If I had to be a crumb, I would rather be dead."

By the time Luciano was eighteen he had been convicted of peddling narcotics, and he served six months in the reformatory. After that he was more careful, acquiring a reputation as a gunman, a narcotics specialist, a gambler, and as a calm and determined leader. In 1929 he was kidnaped by a competing group of narcotics peddlers and taken on a ride to Staten Island. There he was hung up by the thumbs, taped across the eyes and mouth, and his throat was slit from ear to ear. But the knife had not cut deep enough to kill. Life came back to him. Somehow he crawled to a road where he was picked up by a cruising police patrol. "Don't know who did it. . . . I'll take care of this myself," he said, and then he lost consciousness.

The Mafia and others thought this survival was so miraculous that his underworld name became "Charlie Lucky." On the mend, Luciano said he got the name "Lucky" because he had a horseshoe tattooed on his arm. After Staten Island, he also had a scarred chin and a drooping eyelid, which fascinated the crime reporters of the 1930s. One of the ubiquitous crime magazines wrote:

> He was wily, rapacious. He was savagely cruel. For years, like some deadly King Cobra, this droopy-eyed thug coiled himself about the Eastern underworld and squeezed it implacably of its tainted gold. Nights were spent touring the Broadway hot-spots with gorgeous Gay Orlova, or another of the show-shop beauties he was partial to. Then, if Broadway palled, his powerful private Lockheed plane would roar him away to Miami, Chicago or Hot Springs, to be hailed there with open arms. He was the bookmakers' joy, the torch singer's delight, a Dracula masquerading as Good-time Charlie.

Luciano managed to avoid such publicity for the most part, and his importance in the over-all scheme of things was not known. One story was that a newspaper reporter who mentioned his name in a couple of articles was offered a bribe not to do it again. When the reporter declined the bribe he was transferred by his paper to Washington.

Luciano liked anonymity so much that he lived at the Barbizon-Plaza in New York City under the name of Charles Lane. By 1933 he was living at the Waldorf Towers, and he was known there as Charles Ross. His name had virtually vanished from the headlines and it was pretty well understood in the underworld that anybody who talked about him was likely to run into trouble.

To my certain knowledge even then, his business was far-flung and brought in a colossal revenue. This was estimated to be far, far in excess of $12 million a year. He was head of the gigantic Italian lottery. He was one of the largest beneficiaries of the policy racket, or numbers game. His henchmen operated a number of industrial rackets affecting the basic life of the city. He was one of the biggest illegal importers of drugs in the country.

One of the principal reasons for his power was that he was smarter

than the rest and had an excellent organizational sense. He knew
when and how to respect the territories of associated, neutral, and
hostile mobs, and they respected his.

He also had connections of all kinds, some of them in high places.
He had been seen at the 1932 Democratic National Convention in
Chicago in the company of Albert Marinelli, the county clerk of New
York County and one of the most important associates of James J.
Hines of Tammany Hall. Luciano's principal lieutenants were power-
ful and important. One, Frank Costello, a slot machine king, would
eventually become known as the "Prime Minister" of the underworld.

In our first months of operation, while we were concentrating on
the loan shark racket, another field was proposed for our investigation. Eunice Carter had been asked some years before to help out at
magistrate's court when it was swamped with work resulting from a
periodic "drive" against prostitution. Two of the "bookers," the men
who arranged for women to work in the houses of prostitution, had
been caught, convicted, and sentenced to prison. These were Nick
Montana and "Cockeyed Louis" Weiner.

But Eunice Carter observed on her rounds at magistrate's court
that prostitutes never seemed to go to jail if they were represented by
a lawyer named Abe Karp, a man who seemed to specialize in this un-
lovely practice. Somehow there always seemed to be a necessary fact
left out of the arresting officer's testimony, or the girl's story was so
convincing that she was acquitted. When Mrs. Carter checked into
the records she found her supposition was correct. Prostitutes represented by Karp never went to prison.

Mrs. Carter now definitely smelled a racket, and she took up the
question with one of my chief assistants, Murray I. Gurfein. I trusted
their judgment, but I had no enthusiasm for the investigation they
proposed. I thought it was our job to attack organized crime, and
specifically not to go after prostitutes who were social problems in
what was still called the oldest profession.

Both of my assistants stuck to their guns, however, and they were
convinced that organized crime had moved into prostitution in a big
way. So, quite reluctantly, I authorized them to commence a full-scale
investigation. Two other young assistants joined in—Harold M. Cole
and Charles P. Grimes—while Gurfein, who was buried in an investigation of major industrial rackets, kept a supervisory eye on the project

for me. With the help of informers, skilled police work, and discreet wiretapping, an astonishing picture emerged.

Until a few years before—and we did not know just how long be-fore—prostitution had not been organized into a racket. It was an age-old institution, and I thought I would be insane to try to interfere with it or stop it. It was an individual matter. Women were prostitutes, on their own in some instances, or in houses in other instances, run by madams. They were separate, isolated, and they kept the money they earned. They were not blackjacked by thugs and their money was not stolen by racketeers.

Then the bookers of women, or "bookies" or "books," appeared on the scene. They were men who knew numbers of prostitutes and numbers of madams and made their living from a fast-growing busi-ness of sending girls around from house to house. The girls would work there for a week at a time, perhaps more. Thus a whole chain of houses sprang into existence, and the industry was ready for consoli-dation.

By 1933 there were at least four big bookers who ran large chains of houses of prostitution, almost a sort of Orpheum circuit in the busi-ness of women. The bookers now had their first, second, and third as-sistants, and lobby guys, as we called them, the people who liked to help out just for their meals. One of the bookers was Nick Montana, who had been convicted and imprisoned, and his business had since been taken over by Jack Ellenstein, known as Jack Eller. The other convicted booker, Cockeyed Louis Weiner, had simply been suc-ceeded by his son Al Weiner, who was keeping the family business going.

The other two big bookers, Pete Harris and Dave Miller, would play a very large role in our investigation.

Now the girls in this newly organizing business went through quite a mechanical change. They usually lived in hotels and rooming houses with their pimps. They would go to work at the houses to which the bookers had assigned them at 1:00 P.M., 2:00 P.M., or 3:00 P.M., put in ten, twelve, or fourteen hours, and go home. At the end of their work week they would be paid. They had timecards, for the most part, in-dicating the number of times they had earned their two- or three-dol-lar fees per assignment. They might total an average of $300 per week, but half of that would have to be handed over to the madams on the spot.

The girls, left with their average of $150, would then have to pay over ten per cent to their bookers. That left their average at $135 per week. Out of that sum, $5.00 would have to be paid to the doctors who gave the weekly medical examinations. That left an average $130. Then the girls would make their contribution of perhaps $25, perhaps $35, to the madams as their share of operating expenses or client contact expenses. Even at this point the girls were taking home only $100 or so out of their $300 gross, before taxes, of course, which were never paid.

This must have been one of the most depressing ways of life of the Depression. As one of the girls would tell us: "All us girls got two meals a day from the madam, but we had to shell out about $18 a week. They worked us six days a week, the syndicate did, and we received all kinds of men from young punks trying to act like wise guys to old fellas no decent woman would have. Well, after six days of that, we had the seventh off. But then we telephoned the booker, and he gave us the address of the house where we'd work the following week. None of us ever stayed more'n a week at the same spot. The outfit made us see a croaker every week. And that was three bucks more we had to pay, sometimes five."

Another of the girls told us: "They worked us like dogs for a couple of years, and then they kicked us out."

So, by the year 1933, the booking business was flourishing to the point that it attracted the attention of major racketeers. About that time various groups of them proposed "bonding" the girls at the rate of $10 per week apiece. As there were at least two thousand girls who could be easily reached, there would be a million in it. In return, they would guarantee that any girl, if arrested, would go free. To be able to make that guarantee, the racketeers obviously had to have fairly thorough connections with municipal justice. To be able to make the girls pay, they also had to use strong-arm methods.

Whenever any of the girls were arrested, their bail would be put up from an over-all "bonding fund" to which the madams had also been forced to contribute. Along would come a bondsman, perhaps Jesse Jacobs, with his lobby guy Meyer Berkman, who would spring them on nominal bail. An attorney, perhaps Abe Karp, would coach them on the testimony they should give. As one girl told us, this might run like, "Why, just visiting a friend, your honor. I didn't know it was that kind of place."

In the unlikely event that this kind of testimony did not produce an acquittal, and if it was judged that the evidence against any girl was too strong, she would be told to "take a walk," "go take a bath," or "take it on the lam." This meant, in effect, "Skip your bond, and don't come back to New York until you're old and gray." The girls who took this way out we called "lamsters."

The next refinement of the system came when the racketeers decided to extract fifty per cent of the value of any forfeited bonds from the madams of the houses where the girls had been arrested. This was pure extortion and it would lead to much more violence.

By January 1936 we were hearing talk of a single "combination" that was pulling all the prostitution rackets together. There was talk of "control" of all organized prostitution in Manhattan and Brooklyn. There was ample evidence of its effectiveness. Our observant Eunice Carter learned that, out of the 175 arrested girls, not one of whom had gone to jail, every single one of them had been "bonded." Our investigators knew that tremendous pressure had been brought to bear upon the four major bookers, and they had been "taken over" by the one combination.

The apparent boss of the combination was Little Davie Betillo, one of Al Capone's former bodyguards, a smart and ruthless murderer and gunman. The treasurer was apparently Thomas Pennochio, "Tommy the Bull" or "Tommy Bull," a senior racketeer with a long narcotics record. The strong-arm squad was apparently led by James Frederico, "Jimmy Fredericks," an ex-convict, and Little Abie Wahrman, another gunman. Ralph Liguori was apparently a holdup man and pimp. Benny Spiller, another strong-arm man, was also apparently even running a loan shark racket among the other members of the combination.

"Apparently," because we knew only so much, but we decided that we now had enough information on a major racket in prostitution to justify a major move. So we prepared to move. We had little live, valid testimony against the madams. We had no testimony against the bookers. And we had only information against the mob. The only way we could break this kind of a case would be to get the prostitutes to testify against the madams and the bookers. Then we would have to get the madams and the bookers to testify against the higher echelons of the combination.

If we should raid a lot of houses and bring in the girls first as material witnesses, we would expect the madams, the bookers, and the gangsters to leave town for an indefinite period. We would be left with the girls on our hands.

But if we arrested the madams and the bookers, our evidence against the gangsters would not be sure enough without the corroboration of the girls. The girls, we expected, would take off, and the gangsters, if they bothered, would evaporate for a stay in other cities.

So we had to do the whole thing all at once—and nothing like this had ever been seen, done, or even dreamed of before.

And of course our probings had not gone unnoticed on the other side. A crime reporter, many months afterward, wrote:

> In a dingy basement of a restaurant in New York's Chinatown, three men and a woman sat at a table. The woman was Cokey Flo. She conducted a house of prostitution. Beside her sat a huge, swarthy man with slicked hair and the neck and shoulders of a stevedore. His name was James Frederico. Cokey Flo was his mistress. The second man at the table, Little Davie Betillo, had sharp features and a face as dead white as a dead fish's belly.
>
> The third man was the most striking-looking of any of them. Low off his forehead, curly brown hair started, falling back in thick waves. His swarthy face bore scars like pockmarks. His lips were a cruel, straight line. Incongruously, he had dimples. His eyes, set under bushy dark eyebrows, were the most arresting feature of a face that was definitely sinister. One was wide open, alert. The other, his right eye, drooped, giving him a singular appearance of sleepiness.
>
> He was known in the underworld as "The Boss."
>
> His lips twisted open as he spoke. "I don't like the racket," he said. "What the hell. There's not enough dough in it for the risk we take."
>
> The man with the dead-white face spoke pleadingly: "Try it a little while longer. We can make it go. There's big money in it if we handle it right."
>
> The Boss shook his head: "Maybe we'll only be sticking our necks out. This Dewey investigation is coming on. That may make it tough."
>
> The other man said, "What's that to be afraid of? You know

how these things go. He'll grab a bunch of prossies and a couple of bondsmen. And that'll be all."

The Boss considered this silently, then nodded. "All right, Davie. Let it go for a couple of months. Let's see what happens. But you haven't got the racket up well enough to make it worth while. Here's what we'll do. We'll put all the madams on salary. No more fifty per cent stuff. We'll syndicate every house in New York. We'll run them like chain stores. We'll . . ."

A Chinese waiter padded over toward their table. Cokey Flo beamed on him. "Chicken chow mein, son," she said. "A whole flock of it."

At the stroke of midnight, January 31, 1936, we moved. Our most trustworthy detectives had been keeping sixteen senior suspects under surveillance, and we knew where we could lay our hands on them. Quietly we arrested Little Davie, Tommy the Bull, Little Abie, and Benny Spiller after a party. We picked up the others in apartments, as they came out of restaurants, as they stopped for lights while driving home. We had Jimmy Frederico, Jesse Jacobs, Meyer Berkman, and three out of the four big bookers. The fourth was arrested in Philadelphia. We stashed all of these people away for the night in various police stations. We made no announcement of the arrests.

The following night was Saturday, a big night in the prostitution business. We assembled 160 policemen in secret to raid eighty houses of prostitution simultaneously. None of the policemen were to know what their assignment was until the last minute. They were even gathered at various spots and divided into pairs of men who did not know one another; each pair was given their orders in a sealed envelope not to be opened until 8:55 P.M. The police teams were told to enter the houses, take the names of the patrons and let them go, and bring the inmates down to an address, 19 Barclay Street, in Manhattan. This was the freight entrance of the rackets investigation offices in the Woolworth Building on lower Broadway.

To judge from the headlines the next morning, the raids were sensational in the extreme. The New York *Mirror* headlined:

DEWEY VICE RAIDS NET 7 CZARS, 87 WOMEN PAWNS

A crime reporter wrote: "Perfectly timed raids fell like a thunderclap on bawdy houses running full blast from Brooklyn to the Bronx. Half-naked women shrieked. Gangsters reached for guns, terrified patrons for clothing. Madams rushed frantically for hidden exits. But the raiders moved like lightning. Commandeering a fleet of taxicabs, they hauled out the swearing, struggling crew."

In a way, the results were disappointing. There were raids planned for the eighty houses. Somehow, for reasons we decided not to investigate, the raids on forty of them were failures. But we had a hundred prostitutes and madams jammed into our offices, including some of the best-known women in the business. Our madams included Polack Frances, Silver-tongued Elsie, Sadie the Chink, Nigger Ruth, Jennie the Factory, Cockeyed Florence, Max the Barber (a male madam), Fat Rae, and Jennie the Fox.

It was a terrible night. The women were all questioned, one by one, all night and into Sunday afternoon, and with ghastly results. We were told that the madams were innocent housewives. The girls were art students, or seamstresses, or telephone operators, or models. Some were simply visiting from out of town. They all expected to be bailed out any minute. After all, they always had been before.

Three of the madams were smarter than all the others. The scale of our arrests made them realize this was no ordinary pinch. They reasoned that they were not going to be bailed out so easily, and they might not get a simple six-month sentence if they did not tell us what they knew. These three madams were finally convinced that we had the whole mob in jail—and they might be able to get the mob off their backs. So they said they would respond to our questioning.

Still, with only three out of a hundred willing to testify, it was a gloomy prospect. It was possible that the other ninety-seven women might tell us nothing, the bookers might not even tell us the time of day, and the gangsters would walk out free. But there was nothing to do but go through with it. So about midday on Sunday I called Supreme Court Justice Philip McCook, the responsible judicial authority, and asked him if he would come down to the Woolworth Building to fix bail. After some persuasion he came down—and fixed bail at a whopping $10,000 each on the women as material witnesses and at much higher levels on the gangsters.

The arrested women were told, in effect, one by one: "We are not in the business of prosecuting prostitutes and madams and pimps and heels in this business. We are here in an effort to get the big shots." They were frankly told that, and they were just as frankly told, "If you don't testify and tell us what you know, we will send you back up to the magistrate's court, where you will get what is coming to you, if anything is. What you do, you are going to have to tell, and if you tell the truth and the whole truth, and it checks up with what we get from every one of dozens and fifties and hundreds of other witnesses, we will allow you to testify to it in the grand jury. In fact you will have to testify to it in the grand jury." And as we reminded them, when witnesses testified before the grand jury, they got immunity. That was the immunity business.

The girls began to testify and they told us what they knew. One said: "If I talked, they'd slit my throat, I know that outfit. God, how I hope you get 'em. If you don't, it's curtains for me. They'll grab me the minute I'm out of here." My assistant asked her: "How would you like to quit the racket and go home to Pennsylvania?" She replied: "Back? Me? Say, everybody back home thinks I'm holding a big job in a New York department store. Even my family don't know where the money I send them every month really comes from. The cadet who brought me down here said I'd model clothes, entertain the buyers, have a swell life where all you did was look beautiful and go on parties every night. I didn't know what I was getting into, see?

"When I did find out, it was too late. I'm sunk. If I stay in New York it's the streets for me. If I leave, well, what can I do? Who'd want me? No. My life ain't worth much now, maybe, but I don't want to throw up the sponge, and that's what I'd be doing if I testified against that gang like you want me to."

A madam whipped off her hat, pointed a finger to a scar on the crown of her head: "Look, look there. That's what Frederico done to me. Frederico himself. I want none of their bond racket. Things is tough enough as is. Why, down in that house, I was just making enough to get by. I charged a flat rate, see. I gave the janitor ten dollars a week and a tip to the booker. But I wouldn't go for this bond thing. So, after Liguori holds me up one week for thirty-six dollars, the next thing I know in crashes Frederico and a bunch of his men. 'So you won't bond, you ——!' he says, and he whips out a length of lead pipe and bashes me on the head. Oh, my God, the blood, I was all over blood, and they kept beating me with that pipe."

Sol Gelb now took charge of the case, with part-time and sometimes full-time participation from Frank S. Hogan. Deputy Assistant Charles D. Breitel joined the task force and so did Barent Ten Eyck, a chief assistant. Still very much on the job were Grimes, Cole, and of course Eunice Carter.

Frank Hogan took general charge of all the women, who were being kept in the New York House of Detention in Greenwich Village. For four months, he would be known around the office as "Father Hogan." Solemn of manner, but with real warmth and an elfin sense of humor, he took the troubles of every one of them seriously. He was adviser, confessor, errand runner, and always a star prosecutor. He and others interviewed the madams and the girls in the House of Detention, and he gradually convinced them that their position was hopeless unless they talked.

Every one of my assistants developed a different interviewing technique. One never interviewed any woman in his office without wearing rubber gloves. Some were tough and threatening, while others were warm and friendly. But all were fair, and few of those women had met such a group of men, who treated them like civilized human beings, for many years.

Meanwhile the girls' diseases were gradually cured and they withdrew from drugs. They were clean and well fed. With some, it was like pulling teeth, but one after the other they told us their stories and made plans to go straight once it was all over. The whole thing finally became under "Father" Hogan a sort of self-generating revival meeting. It was just as well, because people walking beneath the windows of the House of Detention would sometimes look up, draw their fingers across their throats, and hope new witnesses would get the message.

During the early stages of this procedure one of the girls took out a writ of habeas corpus, and she was brought before another justice of the Supreme Court. After the hearing this judge walked down the corridor to see Judge McCook. "You know, Phil," he said, "I have just had a long visit in chambers with this girl, and you have made a terrible mistake in holding her with all of these prostitutes. She is a nice lady, a graduate of Northwestern University, and is here in New York studying to be an opera singer." McCook was alarmed, to say the least. He sent for me immediately and asked for a full explanation. Within two hours I was back, and handed him the girl's medical record. McCook looked at it and walked down the hall to see his brother justice, who had signed the writ of habeas corpus. The medical record showed that the girl had four-plus syphilis, gonorrhea, lice, and crabs.

The writ of habeas corpus was dismissed—and this girl ultimately became one of our most impressive witnesses. She was well groomed, well mannered and well spoken.

Sol Gelb recalled: "Most of them were like opening oysters. They started out awfully tough, and in the course of just one night I learned more about questioning people than I did in my entire life. It was amazing. You'd get a person that seemed almost hopeless, and in fifteen or twenty minutes they'd opened up, and this soft, confidential approach was very important. Unqualifiedly, it was never with deceit. This was very important for long-run purposes, by the way, because the word was to spread throughout the prisons and throughout the rest of the underworld that was interested that we didn't lie, we didn't deceive, we threatened, and we delivered even on the threat, that it was not a bluff. When we said we had a case against someone, we had a case.

"Of course one of the important techniques of questioning was not to say what we knew, because they would then give us what we knew. So we just made them talk, made them talk, and once in a while you'd just throw out a little spear if you thought they were lying. Sometimes you did this by looking at the wiretap. You didn't let them know that you had wiretaps. And sometimes you'd give them rests.

"There was one particular girl, and while this was not too important an incident it became interesting. We weren't supposed to spend too much time on prostitutes. They just weren't worth it—there were so many of them, and all they could give you was madams and bookers. It didn't take us long before we had all we needed on madams and bookers, but there was one girl I was questioning who was quite young and almost pretty. She wouldn't give me the time of day.

"It became a challenge to me. I said, 'I've talked to a lot of you girls, and sometimes you try to protect a pimp. That's a silly business. These pimps talk faster than you girls, whether you know that or not. I know you have a pimp, but I don't think that's what's keeping you from talking. Some girls have family, and they're afraid that the family will find out what happened. I don't care about your family. I'll have to know your real name, but even that will be kept confidential. If it ever goes to court, as we hope it will, we'll see to it that your name is not brought out.'

"She said, 'It's not family.'

"This was a dividend, and I said, 'I don't know what's bothering you, then. Look, by any chance, is it a child?' She didn't answer, but I thought I had something, and I said, 'Look, if it's a child, we certainly don't want to hurt a child of yours.'

"She said, 'I didn't say it was a child.'

"After I repeated my assurances she said, 'That's what you say. A child have a prostitute for a mother. That couldn't hurt a child! That's what you say?'

"I said, 'Well, now you've told me. You've told me. Why don't you get it off your chest? I give you my word it will be in absolute confidence.'

"I began to take her story. She gave me the name and address. The child was a baby in a foster home on Staten Island. This was the only reason why she had not talked before. Now she told us all she knew, and we lived up to every one of the assurances we had given her."

With each of these material witnesses we did our best to make their material lives in prison as comfortable as possible. We went out and got their clothes for them. We let them see members of their families and friends whenever it was convenient. We took out a few of them to motion pictures. We helped the women on withdrawal, and when they were a mass of nerves, and asked for it, they got a drink of liquor. We did our best, for the people who testified and helped and told what we believed to be the truth within the legal proprieties.

On the first Saturday night of the raids we had one other break that was as sizable as it was unexpected. One of the big four bookers, David Miller, heard that we were running a major operation and he suspected that we really intended to put the racket out of business. He had a bad heart, a dependent wife, and three children. He had just come out of the hospital after a heart attack and his wife, who was a part-time prostitute herself, had run his booking business while he was in the hospital. Miller figured that, if we did have a case, he and his wife were facing twenty years' imprisonment. So he told one of his prison guards, "I want to talk to Dewey."

Chief Assistant "Jack" Rosenblum joined me in spending much of this first night with the booker. Miller wanted a promise that his wife would not go to jail and that his children would be placed in a proper home. In return for this assurance, he said he would take his own rap and tell everything he knew. On this basis, we made a deal.

This was our first inside break, and it was a long story. Miller said he had started out as a constable in a small town near Pittsburgh where he supplemented his salary by shaking down speakeasies and houses of prostitution on the side. Then he said he found out that a girl who was a roomer in his home was in fact a prostitute. Miller's wife began to substitute for the girl whenever she was out. In due course the Millers were caught and he was fired from his job as a policeman. The whole family moved to New York.

Miller now began to make a living peddling dresses to girls in houses of prostitution, and he learned a lot about the business. He became a booker and did well at it. But when the combination moved in, as he told us, he was shoved up against a wall one night by four men and a knife was held at his stomach. "Get out of town," he was told. When Miller tried to find out who was moving in he was told, "Those are our orders. You get out of town."

Miller tried to make a deal with the combination but they wanted $10,000 to let him stay in business. This was reduced to $5,000 but Miller would not pay it. A few days later, while he was getting into his car, another car drove by. A hail of bullets struck Miller's car. Not long afterward he got a phone call. "The cops won't do you any good. We will get you anyway." Miller left town with his family and moved to California.

When we pressed Miller as to who the bosses of the combination were, he replied: "Davie—and Abie—and Charlie Lucky." This was the thunderbolt. We now had testimony for the first time that Lucky Luciano, the top boss of the Mafia, was messing around with prostitution.

Before long two other bookers sent word to us that they wanted to talk with us. Pete Harris offered to plead guilty and take his chances on a lower sentence, and we knew he had a significant story to tell. Al Weiner, who had inherited his booking business from his imprisoned father, Cockeyed Louis, was less impressive as a witness, but helpful nonetheless. We now had three out of the four big bookers and the case was looking up.

The bookers apparently realized the game was up. They were telling what they knew. We had been on the wires of each of them for weeks and months. We had bales of wiretapping testimony and they said, "All right, we will plead guilty and tell you the truth in the hope of getting consideration from the court." I said personally to each one of them that if they pleaded guilty to all counts and told all the truth, "We will recommend that consideration be given."

Pete Harris told us he had been a gambler and had drifted into the booking business as something to do. In the fall of 1933 some of the combination men shoved him against a wall and told him he would have to pay them $250 a week to stay in business. He said he could not afford it. They came back again, this time with Little Abie Wahrman, a gunman. They all pulled guns on Pete Harris, took him to his apartment, and told him to pack. He surrendered and agreed to pay them. He also said his madams and girls would make no trouble about paying their bond money.

But Harris had a lot of trouble making his madams pay, and this and other signs of disorder forced the combination to use new methods. Harris and the other bookers were ordered down to a meeting in Little Italy, on Mulberry Street in Manhattan, where Little Davie Betillo read out some new rules. From now on no booker was to be allowed to take on a new house unless and until he was contacted by the madams. No bookers were to ask any madam to switch from one booker to another, and secure territories were therefore established Mafia-style. But whenever any bookers were short of girls, the others would have to help supply replacements at short notice.

There was also a new scale of punishment. For example, if bookers kept the names and locations of any of their houses secret from the combination, they would run serious risks. For the first offenses they would be fined $500. For the second offenses, according to Little Davie, the bookers would "get their bellies kicked in." All the bookers were ordered to write down the names of all their houses there and then.

Pete Harris told us he was surprised at the meeting when Jesse Jacobs, a bail bondsman, sidled over and asked him to withhold the name of a house of prostitution that Jacobs was running on the side. Even the bondsman had one.

Finally, according to Harris, Little Davie reminded everybody at the meeting that if anybody mentioned the name of Charlie Lucky he would "get his head busted open."

By now Pete Harris was living with a tall, statuesque, henna-haired thirty-year-old madam named Mildred Balitzer. She had started smoking opium some years before, had graduated to morphine, and was wholly hooked on heroin. Mildred had known Little Davie and Tommy the Bull socially before the combination moved in on prostitution. At one time Little Davie told her he worked for Lucky Luciano, but there was no discussion about the nature of their business together. Mildred told Pete about meeting Luciano casually a number of times, in the company of Little Davie and Tommy the Bull. On the first occasion Little Davie introduced her to Luciano, saying, "I want you to meet my boss."

After a year or so under the combination, paying out his $250 a week, Pete Harris was running into debt. He told Little Davie he would like to quit. Little Davie, unco-operative, remarked, "You can't get out unless you pay all you owe." Pete said he could never pay because he was in debt to loan sharks. Little Davie said that was his problem.

Next, Mildred went downtown to see Little Davie. She said Pete could not keep on paying out that kind of money, but she got the same answer. She asked, "Who is behind this? Are you still working for Lucky?" Little Davie replied that he was.

Mildred said, "Pete and I are going to be married, and I want Pete to get out of the business." Davie repeated, "He can't get out. He owes too much money." Mildred pressed him. "That is ridiculous. Every week there is something else. They constantly shake him. There is tickets; there is donations from week to week, and there is more and more money. Then he has to borrow back from your own Shylocks. There is no possible way that he can ever get out. He can't pay the money, because it goes around in a circle."

Mildred added, "I am going to see Lucky. I am going to make it my business to see Lucky."

Little Davie replied, "It won't do you any good, because anything I do is all right with him."

Mildred Balitzer was a brave woman and she later sought out Luciano. As she told our investigators, "I said to him, 'You know I am married to Pete now. I want Pete to get out of the business.' And I said, 'I have been to Little Davie, and he won't do anything for me. I told him I was going to see you, and he said it wouldn't do me any good.' Luciano said, 'He can't get out because of the money he owes. As long as he owes the money he can't get out. You know the racket.'"

Dave Miller, meanwhile, had been running a gas station in California for a few months. He had gone broke and had returned to New York City. He told how he had gone to see Little Davie and asked to be let back into the business. Little Davie told him that one or two of the smaller bookers, such as "Charlie Spinach," had not been doing too well. So Little Davie let Miller back into the business with these words: "You're working on a salary. You get $50 a week and expenses, and you pay Danny Brooks $50 a week, and he goes around with you to check up on you."

At another point, Joe Bendix, a three-time convicted thief, told us that he had served his term for his third felony and he wanted some kind of job where he was unlikely to be caught again. A fourth felony meant life imprisonment in New York State. Bendix was a somewhat accomplished painter and was well known as one of the top hotel thieves in the country.

He told us that he had once gotten an introduction, through Jimmy Frederico, to Lucky Luciano. He asked Luciano for a job as a "collector." Luciano said he thought Bendix was "too high-hat" for a job at $40 a week but Bendix said $40 a week was better than life in prison. Luciano said he would speak to Little Davie about it but never got back to Bendix. In time, the inevitable happened. Bendix never got the job from Luciano and he did get caught again at his trade. He testified to us in the candid hope that he might get help from us—and he helped us document the rapid expansion of organized crime in the once purely "social" area of prostitution.

"Good Time Charlie," an ambitious pimp, was another interesting fellow who told us what he knew. He said he and Frederico joined in 1933 to set up a bonding combination of their own. They were soon told to come downtown to a meeting. They went to a restaurant on Mulberry Street, where they sat down at a table in the back room. Then, according to Good Time Charlie, Little Davie Betillo walked in. He was accompanied by Lucky Luciano. "It was funny," Good Time Charlie told us. "We were sitting down and then, when Charlie Lucky came in, all the Italians stood up. Lucky made it short. 'You guys are through,' he said to all the bookers and others present. 'I am giving the business to Little Davie.'" Then Good Time Charlie added: "Luciano turned and walked out again. We were sitting down, but all the Italians were standing up."

We had heard this conclusive story from a number of sources but did not have the straight of it until we heard it from Good Time Charlie. He gave it to us. He was sore because he had been ordered out of the racket and also, particularly, because Little Davie had later hired Frederico to manage the bonding collections for the combination.

In the course of his inconspicuous high living, Luciano had met a lot of girls and, as is usually the case with gangsters, they were mostly prostitutes. Several of the girls told us that Nancy Presser was one of these, and they were urging her to talk, but she was one of the last to open up. We found out she was afraid of her then current pimp, Ralph Liguori, the holdup man who used to discipline the madams who were tardy with their bonds.

In the end Frank Hogan, the father confessor of the girls in the House of Dentention, was able to do the job. With his quiet persistence, he persuaded her to come down and talk with me. After an hour or so she told her story.

Nancy Presser left her home in Auburn, New York, as soon as she quit school at the age of fourteen. She went to Albany where she worked in a lunchroom, and before long she was in New York City. She is said to have been a remarkably beautiful blonde, and she worked for a few weeks as an artist's model. This was too tame for Nancy, however, and she was soon one of the most expensive and sought-after call girls in town. She became a favorite of the Waxey Gordon mob and also of visiting members of the Capone mob. She met Luciano, who took a fancy to her and sent for her repeatedly. She also learned how to make drugs herself.

By 1935, although she was only twenty-six, Nancy's charms had dwindled. She had been working too hard, living too hard, drinking too hard, and she was by now heavily addicted to heroin. She descended from the top-level gangsters to Ralph Liguori, the pimp, who forced her to go to work for Jennie the Factory at two dollars an assignment. She was working in Polack Frances' house when we picked her up on the night of the raid.

It took us days to get all of Nancy's story because she was suffering severely from withdrawal symptoms. She was hurting from a punch on the side given her by Liguori just before her arrest. She also had syphilis.

Nancy had a remarkably clear mind and memory for details, however, and when we checked the details we were convinced she was telling the truth. Much that she told us about narcotics peddling we had heard from others. Much about the meeting places we had previously learned from others. So we believed her when she told how she often had drinks with Luciano in Keen's Chop House, not far from Madison Square Garden. She told us how Little Davie, Tommy the Bull, Little Abie Wahrman, and Jimmy Frederico had been there on one occasion, talking about prostitution. Little Davie said to Luciano that they were still having trouble making the houses pay the bond money. Luciano said, "Go ahead and wreck the joints."

Nancy Presser then told us that Luciano, on several occasions, had sent for her to visit him at the Barbizon-Plaza and at the Waldorf Towers. She said he had told her how the prices in the houses were going to be raised. He had ambitious plans to put the madams and the bookers on salary.

A curious facet of the underworld emerged from the stories. The higher echelons would eat, drink, cohabit, and go out in public with their favorite prostitutes. That was a way of life. But the same men would never eat with a pimp. This was beneath them.

For example, Benny Spiller was a member of the combination who was running his loan shark operation. He was living with a part-time prostitute, and one day the leaders of the combination sent for him. Tommy the Bull, Little Davie, and Little Abie were present. So, on that occasion, was another senior member of the Mafia, Vito Genovese. We were told that Benny Spiller was told: "Listen, we can't have any pimps in this business. It is too dangerous. If you are going to take money from that woman, you have got to get out of the combination." Benny replied that he was not taking any money from the woman. So the combination called the woman herself and asked, "Are you giving any of your money to Benny?" She said she was not. They told her, "All right, but if you do, Benny has got to get out of this combination. We can't have pimps."

This strong feeling in the Mafia against pimps perhaps explained their shock when Luciano's involvement was revealed. *The Valachi Papers* was a firsthand story of murder, torture, extortion, and organized crime, which might include exaggerations and inaccuracies, but which I believed to be as authentic as it was horrifying. According to the *Papers*, Valachi said: "I was stunned! Charlie Lucky wasn't no pimp. He was a Boss!"

As our mounting testimony indicated, it did not appear that the prostitution business took anything more than a few minutes a day of Luciano's time. We heard his name mentioned only by very few, by those who by some rare accident or good fortune we found who knew him or who heard him give directions.

For example, Luciano, in the presence of one of our witnesses, said to Tommy the Bull: "That madam doesn't bond? Straighten her out." A few days later the Bull came back. Luciano asked, "Did you straighten out that madam?" The Bull said, "Yes." Luciano asked, "Where is she?"

Tommy the Bull said, "She is in the hospital." Luciano asked, "Is it very bad?" The Bull said, "I don't know." Luciano asked, "Do you know the doctor?" The Bull said, "Yes." Luciano said, "Find out how badly off she is."

Gradually the whole combination was growing tighter and tighter and larger and larger. All the people in the prostitution business were becoming the terrorized servants of the men at the top. We only had glimpses of the man at the very top, but we thought these would be sufficient to present to a jury and so I decided to move to trial.

In addition to all our hearsay testimony, we felt we had five solid witnesses to Luciano's participation. But we knew this could be a house built on sand as far as Luciano was concerned. Three of our witnesses were drug addicts, one was a four-time loser facing life, and another was little better than a common pimp.

At this point it suddenly occurred to me that if our witnesses, solid and hearsay, were in fact telling the truth there might be a simple way to corroborate their testimony. Surely some members of the prostitution mob might have been seen in the company of Lucky Luciano at the two highly respectable hotels he had lived in under his assumed names?

We were in luck.

We found that a whole lot of hotel employees had known Luciano, and had watched his comings and goings, and had taken mental notes of his visitors. Some were too scared to talk with us but others were fearless. Before long we had real, live, honest, decent witnesses who would swear in court that they had seen every single member of the prostitution racket leadership in Luciano's suites. This was to prove the decisive element in the Luciano trial. Our case was now resting on solid rock.

Meanwhile we were quietly putting out lines to locate Lucky Luciano himself, so we could be ready to place him under arrest.

The Trial

On April 1, 1936, Lucky Luciano was arrested in a gambling casino in Hot Springs, Arkansas. It was April Fool's Day. Within an hour three of the most prominent lawyers in Hot Springs secured an order for Luciano's release on the posting of a $5,000 bond. Luciano walked out of jail.

I had secured from Judge McCook a warrant for Luciano's arrest, with a request to the Arkansas authorities to hold him on bail until extradition could be arranged. Now, we burned up the wires and got Carl E. Bailey, the Attorney General of Arkansas, to intervene and take Luciano back into custody. The judge hastily raised the bail to $200,000 and Luciano was back in jail.

Obviously Hot Springs was no place to hold a gangster of Luciano's importance and the Attorney General promptly sent twenty state troopers at dawn to take Luciano out of jail and lock him up in Little Rock, the state capital. Here a small army of lawyers, city officials, and members of the state legislature rallied to obtain Luciano's release, and there were reports that Bailey had been offered $50,000 to let him escape. I had previously sent Deputy Assistant District Attorney Edward C. McLean of our staff to handle the extradition proceedings.

Now I sent two detectives to Little Rock by air with a certified copy of an indictment of Luciano on ninety counts and our formal request for extradition. Our request was granted.

Luciano's attorneys, meanwhile, had obtained a writ of habeas corpus from a federal district judge. But when our indictment was in hand the judge denied the writ and gave Luciano ten days in which to lodge his appeal with the Circuit Court of Appeals. The judge ruled that Luciano would have to provide twenty-four hours' notice of the application.

Incredibly, Luciano's attorneys appeared to miss the point of the twenty-four-hour notice. At one minute past midnight, with the permission of the Arkansas authorities, our extradition would take effect and we would be able to take Luciano out of the state. But the notice was not given. Attorney General Bailey arranged to hold up a midnight train for fifteen minutes, and Luciano was removed from his cell, locked in a compartment under guard, and sent on his way to New York.

Luciano's bail in New York was now set by Judge McCook at $350,000—the highest bail in the history of the state. He and his principal lieutenants were held in a total bail of $1,750,000, and this was adequate. The final member on our wanted list, Ralph Liguori, the pimp, had meanwhile been arrested, and we had the lot of them in the bag.

We introduced an indictment in ninety counts against sixteen conspirators. Each placing of a girl in a house of prostitution was a felony. Each acceptance of money for placing the same girl was a felony. Each acceptance from that girl of any of the proceeds of prostitution without consideration was a third separate felony.

This indictment form was a novelty in New York State law. Historically, a single crime could not be joined with other crimes in the same indictment. One robbery, for example, was a single crime resulting in a single indictment. A series of robberies by the same defendant would have had to result in separate indictments and, usually, separate trials.

All this procedure might have been suitable for an earlier day and age but was hopeless in the context of dealing with organized crime. In the first place, it would have been very difficult to connect all the defendants with the single act, or acts. Secondly, if the whole case rested upon the testimony of one girl, the whole case might collapse if the jury did not believe this one girl, or if she disappeared, or, more probably, if she was poisoned or stabbed in prison. This had happened in racket cases in which a single witness, or even two, had been critically important to the prosecution.

As soon as we began the rackets investigation in 1935 we recognized the defect in the state law. Federal procedure had authorized joinder of felonies for a hundred years, and so we simply prepared a similar bill for the state. Governor Herbert H. Lehman agreed to sponsor it, and the new bill passed in the state legislature only days before we handed up this first indictment of its kind.

After six weeks of hectic preparation the trial got under way and an impressive jury was sworn in after the defense had exhausted its allotment of twenty challenges. The jury, all men as was the practice in those days, was empaneled by Judge McCook. The foreman was Edwin Aderer, a manufacturer of dental gold. The other members were Theodore A. Isert, a trade magazine editor, Edward Blake, a salesman, Paul Mahler, a consulting engineer, Hewitt Morgan, a customer's man, Norbert R. Cagnon, a bank purchasing agent, Charles H. Jones, a bank vice-president, Robert Innes Center, a book publisher, Lincoln R. Weld, an accountant, Stephen J. Smith, an art importer, John McGowan, an Edison Company supervisor, and Martin Moses, a foreign language teacher.

The trial began with a sensation—for no word about our intensive interrogations had been permitted to leak out. Three of the four big bookers, Dave Miller, Pete Harris, and Al Weiner, pleaded guilty at the opening of the case. This meant that they were going to testify for the People. The defendants were now reduced to Lucky Luciano, Little Davie Betillo, Tommy the Bull Pennochio, Little Abie Wahrman, Ralph the Pimp Liguori, Benny Spiller, the bondsmen Jesse Jacobs and Meyer Berkman, and the fourth booker, Jack Ellenstein, known as Jack Eller.

I spoke briefly for the prosecution, describing the nature of the combination, its procedures, and the different functions of the defendants, whose names were listed on a chart on the wall. I left the rest to the proof.

Most of the counsel for the individual defendants waived their right to open to the jury but not George Morton Levy, the counsel to Luciano. He threw down the gauntlet with an attack on the prosecution and the flat assertion that Luciano had nothing whatsoever to do with the combination. Then he made what turned out to be a fatal error, based, of course, on what he had been told by his client. He denied that Luciano knew any of his co-defendants: "All of these men, from what Luciano tells me, every single man on that sheet over there," he said, "are complete strangers to him, with one exception of the man they call Little Davie, or David Betillo. There is not another man on that entire list that Luciano even knows."

Counsel Levy continued: "There is not a business matter that Luciano has had in connection with any of these men. Even Little Davie has never worked for him at the race track or in any gambling game, and has never had any connection with him at all."

The courtroom was tense as we called our first witness. She was a prostitute who candidly told her story, how she started out as a street-walker and, after five years, started work in a house of prostitution. She had been working in houses for two years when she was arrested in our raid of February 1. She named Pete Harris as her booker and a series of madams for whom she had worked, describing the financial arrangements, which varied only slightly from witness to witness.

She described an arrest which had occurred the previous year and a meeting with the bondsman Jesse Jacobs in his office, together with Meyer Berkman, the bondsman's lobby guy. Also on hand at the meeting were Jimmy Frederico and Abe Karp, the lawyer Eunice Carter had watched operating with such success years before. Karp had since been disbarred, and other lawyers were doing the work. But our witness now told the Luciano jury that Karp had indeed coached her, and told her to say she was a visitor from Philadelphia where she worked in a department store. She told how the case had been dismissed.

The defense gave her a savage cross-examination. They forced her to tell her real name, Rene Gallo, which like most of the other women in the profession, she hated almost more than anything else to reveal. She was made to tell some of the disgusting details of her work. She was then harried about her treatment in the House of Detention and her treatment by my staff in the Special Prosecutor's office, but it was to no avail. Miss Gallo stood by her story all the way—and she had given the jury a record of the operations of the lower levels of the organized prostitution racket.

I took another of the girls myself through direct examination, and this was a typical episode of the Luciano trial:

Muriel Ryan (residing at Hotel Emerson, Seventy-fifth Street, New York City) called as a witness on behalf of the People, being duly sworn, testified as follows:

Q. . . . Miss Ryan, how old are you?

A. I will be twenty-five, August 9.

Q. You are twenty-four now?

A. Yes.

Q. Where were you born?

A. New York City.

Q. Where were you educated?

A. I went to school in Indiana for two years. Then my parents moved to Port Huron, Michigan, where I finished my education.

Q. Did you graduate from high school?

A. Yes.

Q. At what age?

A. Fifteen.

Q. Then what did you do?

A. Then I ran away from home and got married.

Q. After that, what did you do?

A. My parents got me back and had the marriage annulled, and I stayed home for six months, and I ran away again and started to work as a prostitute in Indianapolis, Indiana.

Q. How old were you when you started working as a prostitute?

A. Seventeen years old.

Q. When did you come to New York first?

A. In the spring of 1932, four years ago.

Q. Did you commence working as a prostitute then?

A. Yes.

Q. And did you first work the streets, or did you get a booking?

A. I stayed in New York two months, and then I got a booking. . . .

Q. Whom did you meet?

A. I met Nick Montana.

Q. And did he place you in a house?

A. Yes.

Q. And did you thereafter continue to work in houses in which Nick Montana booked you?

Defense counsel: . . . We object to this. . . . We object to it upon the ground that the person mentioned is not a defendant in this case, and that this testimony is not germane to the issue, not within the issues, highly improper and prejudicial.

The Court: Is he claimed to be a co-conspirator?

Dewey: Yes, your honor, although the first booking was at a time prior to the commencement of the conspiracy here involved. I am stating this because it continued into the time when this conspiracy did commence.

Defense counsel: I press the objection.

The Court: The objection is overruled.

Defense counsel: We except.

Q. . . . You booked with Montana until the spring of 1934?

A. Yes.

Q. Then did you change bookers?

A. Yes.

Q. Whom did you change to?

A. Pete Harris.

Q. Did somebody arrange an introduction for you?

A. I called him on the phone and—an Academy number, and he told me to meet him at Jamieson's Bar and Grill on Fifty-fourth Street, where I met him that same evening. . . . I told him . . . I thought I could make more money working for him. . . .

Q. Did he send you from house to house every week?

A. Yes. . . .

Q. Do you remember the names of any of the madams for whom you worked?

A. Yes.

Q. Will you give us the names of as many as you can now remember?

A. Jennie Fox, Molly Leonard, Dixie, Jennie Benjamin, Jean Bradley. . . .

After we had brought out the testimony of the prostitutes we brought on two of the bookers, Al Weiner and Dave Miller, who told how the combination had taken over. Al Weiner, known as Dumb Al, rocked the defense. A defense counsel demanded to know what I had promised Al in return for his testimony. Al said I had promised to recommend leniency and to put him "in a jail where I won't be murdered." The judge overruled the objection and Al's blast went into the trial record.

After more prostitutes, we brought on Danny Brooks, a minor

booker, and he told an interesting story. Born Daniel Caputo, he was forty-two years old, and he had been brought to the United States from Italy at the age of one. He got as far as the eighth grade in public schools. After that he was a truck driver, an assistant pipe fitter, a young bootlegger, and an operator of cheap night clubs.

In 1913, Danny Brooks had been convicted for the possession of a revolver; in 1914 he was convicted for possession of narcotics; in 1915 he was convicted on assault charges. He had vanished for a long time but he was caught again in 1935 and convicted on charges of enforcing compulsory prostitution. He was serving a sentence of seven and a half to twenty years' imprisonment at Dannemora, in upstate New York, the Siberia of all our prisons. When we heard about Danny from some of our witnesses, we invited him down.

Danny did much, in his testimony, to fill in the picture of the combination as a soulless, ruthless thing that preyed most relentlessly upon its own. He told how the combination exacted its tribute from the bookers and he confirmed he had been told he would be protected by "Davie and Abie and Charlie Lucky." Then he told how he had been arrested in Westchester County while he was delivering a couple of girls to a house of prostitution up there. The combination let him go to jail, paid something for his lawyer's fees, and gave his chain of houses to Pete Harris. They gave him no compensation whatever. Danny Brooks said the combination agreed only to pay his wife five dollars a week to live on while he was serving his time.

After four more of the women testified, Pete Harris told his definitive story of the workings of the combination. Then Joe Bendix told his story succinctly, and he pointed the finger at Luciano. But the defense came back strongly when it produced Morris H. Panger, an assistant to the Tammany leader, the District Attorney of New York County, William Copeland Dodge. Panger showed a letter Bendix had written to his wife asking her to "think up some real clever story to tell." How had the District Attorney obtained this letter? It had been misplaced in a letter Bendix sent to Panger—whom he was trying to persuade to help him get a lighter sentence.

This was a critical moment but, as the historian Rupert Hughes commented later in his *Attorney for the People:* "Joe's little mistake in envelopes looked to be an intentional ruse. But would the jury think so? Would the jury wonder why Mr. Dodge should have given

the letter to the defense, and said never a word to the Special Prosecutor until after Bendix left the stand?"

A surprise witness followed Bendix to the stand—none other than
Cokey Flo, one of the best-known madams in the business, a tough,
smart narcotics addict. We had missed her in the February 1 raids
and we had assumed she was one of those who had been tipped off
and left town. When we learned from some of the other madams that
Cokey Flo was Jimmy Frederico's mistress, we wanted her badly, but
she stayed out of sight. Now we found her in, of all places, the House
of Detention.

Cokey Flo had decided to take a narcotics cure a few weeks before February 1, and the withdrawal was so rough she had to quit the
cure and go into the hospital. She was very sick and she had to spend
six weeks in the hospital recovering. She had been there during our
raid. When she was discharged she thought there was too much heat
on the business for her to open up her house, but she had to live. She
tried some street soliciting, and she had been arrested, tried, and
convicted on minor charges in the week before the Luciano trial. In
the House of Detention she somehow managed to keep her identity
secret, or so we were told, and she was living under the name of Kay
Marston.

Cokey Flo wrote to Frederico upon her arrest and was furious
when Frederico's lawyer would do nothing for her. She was still feeling poorly after the unsuccessful withdrawal. She was also desperate
because she faced a fugitive warrant on a previous arrest for possession
of narcotics and maintaining a house of prostitution. She had also
heard about the friendly way we were treating the other madams and
prostitutes in our charge.

She sent a letter to Chief Assistant Barent Ten Eyck, who went to
see her at once. She told him her life story. She went into detail about
her relationship with Frederico, about her meetings with the rest of
the leadership, specifically including Lucky Luciano. She talked and
talked while Ten Eyck took dozens of pages of notes in longhand.
These longhand notes turned out to be extraordinarily important.

Ten Eyck came to see me, and we were both worried and suspicious. Any volunteer witness, at that stage of a carefully prepared trial,
could be dynamite. She could be a plant. She could blow up on the
witness stand and make all kinds of false charges against the prosecu-

tion. She was dynamite because she knew a great deal about the inner workings of the combination, but she could be dynamite in reverse.

Ten Eyck questioned her repeatedly for three days in a row, until he was satisfied she was telling the truth. Her story checked out at point after point with everything else we knew. Then he brought her down to see me and, with five assistants present, I spent three hours questioning her. We decided she was telling the truth. We also decided to put her on the stand the very next day before any friends of the defendants might be able to have her killed in prison.

Cokey Flo made a sensational appearance at the Luciano trial and, under my direct examination, she told how she had been brought up in Pittsburgh and had gone to a small coal mining town near Youngstown at the age of fourteen.

Q. What did you do there?

A. Well, we sold—

Q. Just a minute. Will counsel stop moving their chairs? Will you try again?

The Court: There is an awful lot of noise here. Everybody possible, while this witness is testifying, will keep still, unless it is something very emergent [sic]. I do not refer to the counsel so much as I do other noises around back there. Proceed.

A. We enlarged small photographs and had them hand-painted and then the men that went around later to deliver them had a racket of selling the frames for them, and that was my first job, to get those photographs. . . .

Q. After that, where did you go?

A. I went to Cleveland, Ohio.

Q. What did you do in Cleveland?

A. Well, I lost track of my first girl friend, and met another girl friend, and we started a speakeasy there. . . .

Q. Were you fifteen by then?

A. By that time I was fifteen. . . .

Q. How long did you run the speakeasy?

A. Three years.

Q. And after that where did you go?

A. I left Cleveland and went to Chicago.

Q. What did you do in Chicago?

A. Well, I lived between three different men.

Q. You were kept by three men simultaneously?

A. Yes, I was.

Q. Is that all you did at that time? I mean, did you work as a prostitute at any time?

A. No, I didn't.

Q. How long did you continue to live in Chicago and being kept by various men?

A. Over a year.

Q. These men were various underworld figures, were they not?

Defense counsel: Objected to as incompetent.

A. They were.

The Court: Sustained.

Q. What were the occupations of these men?

Defense counsel: Objected to as immaterial.

The Court: Sustained.

Cokey Flo was in pitiful condition, but she answered firmly when asked if she knew Lucky Luciano, "I do." She told candidly how she had started smoking opium, then moved to morphine, and was hooked on heroin. She had been taking three injections a day and, when we put her on the stand, she was only five days off the cure. She told how she had arrived in New York early in 1929, opened a house two months afterward, and had been served by the bookers. Charlie Spinach had sent her girls, then Jimmy Frederico, and then Nick Montana, Danny Brooks, Dave Miller, Jack Eller, and finally Pete Harris.

Cokey Flo told how she had become Frederico's mistress, and she gave firsthand testimony of his expressed intention to form a combination. She said she had asked Frederico "whether it was illegal to do it like that," and this caused some amusement in the courtroom. She confirmed how Little Davie Betillo had moved onto the scene. Somebody named "Diamond Tooth Eddie" had suggested to Little Davie that he hire Frederico, and Frederico got the job.

With Frederico, she met Luciano and Tommy the Bull, and dined one evening with them in a Chinese restaurant uptown. Much of the conversation was in Italian. In a car on the way home Frederico began to talk about prostitution. He remarked, "I think some of the bookies are holding out joints on us." There was some discussion, which Luciano ended by saying, "Well, have them all come down and we will straighten the matter out." This set up the meeting with the bookers on Mulberry Street which other witnesses had described. She confirmed the testimony independently and perfectly.

Another evening, in another Chinese restaurant, she testified: "We saw Charlie, Davie, and Tommy sitting at a table and they asked us to join them. This time the men were talking about madams who were giving them trouble. Jimmy mentioned that "Peggy Wild" refused to open the door when the collector came for the bond money. Lucky said, 'Oh, I suppose she is a wise guy.' And Davie replied, 'We will take care of it, don't worry.'"

And another evening, in this same Chinese restaurant, Cokey Flo was at the dinner at which Luciano expressed his concern about the progress of the Dewey investigation and said they ought to hold up for a while. She testified in court how Luciano had finally acceded to the pleas of Little Davie to stay in the business, and had said how the houses ought to be organized like chain stores. She added a nice Luciano touch, quoting him as saying, "The same as the A & P stores are, a large syndicate."

One reason why Luciano had been so successful in the past, as I have said, was that he was so much smarter than the others. If they had followed his hunch, they might have been out of business before we made our raids and began collecting the testimony from the bookers, the madams, and the girls. We probably would never have been able to pull the case together.

Cokey Flo, our surprise witness, had come through, at least for the moment.

Now a defense counsel named David Siegel began a nauseating cross-examination that brought the Luciano trial to a new low.

Siegel: Are you called Cokey Flo?

A. Yes, I am.

Siegel: And have you been having narcotics for a long time?

A. Yes, I have.

Siegel: And how do you take it?

A. Hypodermically.

Siegel: And you usually carry your needle with you?

A. No, I do not.

Siegel: As a matter of fact, while you just had the recess, did you take anything, liquid of any kind?

A. Yes, I had coffee.

Siegel: Coffee?

A. Yes, sir.

Siegel: Was there anything in the coffee?

A. Yes, sugar and cream.

Siegel: Did you use the hypodermic?

A. No. I did not. There weren't any.

Siegel: And you put it into your left arm or your right arm?

A. Put it into my left arm?

Siegel: When you use the needle, where do you shoot the stuff, into your arm?

A. In my muscle.

Siegel: Where?

A. Of the leg.

Siegel: Just show us where you use it.

A. In the muscle of the leg.

Siegel: Oh, you shoot it into the muscle of the leg?

A. Yes.

Siegel: And how often do you take these shots?

Dewey: Objected to; the witness testified that she has not had any in a week.

Siegel: Oh, I have a right, your honor, I can give you authorities—

Dewey: He had no right to assume that she is doing it now. He says 'do.'

The Court: The objection is overruled.

Siegel: May I have the question read, your honor.

Defense counsel Siegel pressed his attack all the way home, and he demanded that she submit to a doctor's examination there and then so that it could be determined whether she was off drugs or not. Judge McCook granted this request and she was examined in the corner of a room adjoining the courtroom. She was not on drugs. She was putting on an amazing performance, frail, twenty pounds underweight, sick, and testifying against the most fearsome mob in the underworld. As she left the witness stand, however, we all felt relieved. We all felt a lot better. Cokey Flo was not a plant and was on the level.

For our dramatic change of pace we now shocked the defense to its very marrow. Out of nowhere we produced Marjorie Brown, a decent, hard-working girl who traveled to Manhattan every day from Union City, New Jersey, to work on the thirty-ninth and fortieth floors of the Waldorf Towers. She was a real surprise witness, and she was a breath of fresh air. She was also completely fearless and completely believable. Under my direct examination the testimony went like this:

Q. Will you speak a little louder, please?

A. [I work] on the thirty-ninth and fortieth floors . . . the Towers.

Q. In apartments?

A. Yes.

Q. What are your duties there?

A. To clean the bathrooms and pantries.

Q. On the thirty-ninth and fortieth floors?

A. Yes.

Q. Do you see anyone in the courtroom who was a guest at the Waldorf during the past year?

A. Yes.

Q. Will you point him out, please?

A. This man right here [pointing].

Q. What is the color of his necktie?

A. Black.

Defense counsel: You mean this gentleman here?

Q. Indicating the defendant Luciano?

A. Yes.

Defense counsel: Yes.

Q. Under what name did you know him there?

A. Charles Ross.

Q. During the time that he was there, did you see a number of people going in and out of his apartment?

A. Yes.

Q. And did you see some of those people inside his apartment?

A. Yes.

Q. Will you stand up now and see if you can point out anybody in the courtroom whom you saw? Can you see clearly sitting down?

A. Yes—the fellow in the gray suit with the polka dot tie.

Defense counsel: Wait a moment.

Q. Wait a minute, please.

Defense counsel: Please, no.

Q. In the gray suit with the polka dot tie. What color is his necktie?

A. Dark blue, in the back on the left-hand side, right there.

Q. What is the color of the suit of the man next to him?

A. Green.

Q. Indicating the defendant Wahrman. Have you seen him there on several occasions?

A. Yes.

Q. How many times?

A. Oh, I can say about twenty.

Q. In the apartment of the man you knew as Charles Ross?

A. Yes.

Q. Who else do you see in the courtroom that you know? . . .

Q. Indicating the defendant David Betillo. . . .

Q. Indicating the defendant Berkman. . . .

Q. Thank you. That is all.

The defense was thrown into total confusion and no wonder, because Luciano's lawyers had said at the outset of the trial that he knew Little Davie Betillo and none of the others. Now an unimpeachable witness had tied Luciano to two of the "nuts and bolts" operators of a prostitution racket. They could have had no business with Luciano other than prostitution.

Then the defense, as I said, "got worse." Marjorie Brown had not picked out Jimmy Frederico in the crowded courtroom. So Frederico's counsel stood up quite gratuitously to nail down the point that she had never seen his client in Luciano's apartment. The counsel asked her whether she had looked at everybody in the room carefully. She said she had. Then he went on, "There is positively in your mind nobody else that you saw in that apartment?" Marjorie Brown then replied, "And the other man, with the green suit, that dark fellow in the back there, yes."

There was a roar of laughter in the courtroom. Frederico's counsel had managed to nail down Frederico right in the room with Lucky Luciano. And so much the worse for Luciano, because Frederico had been clearly named as an operating head of the discipline and collection forces, and this tied Luciano to the violence.

After these cross-examinations ended, the defense subsided. They indicated they thought Marjorie was confused in her identifications. So, on my re-direct examination, I asked her if she would be willing to step down from the witness stand and put her hand on the shoulder of each of the men she had described. She did this without hesitation and without fear. Lucky Luciano had been placed squarely in the middle of the prostitution racket on the testimony of an observant, respectable, and clearly honest witness.

From then on the defendants and their lawyers changed places, shirts, and neckties before every witness. They expected that we had more Marjorie Browns. Some of the defendants wore glasses for the first time in their lives. Some who regularly wore glasses left them off.

They changed the ways they parted their hair. They changed suits every day, and sometimes even during the recesses.

But it did not help them much. Our next witness was Joseph Weinmann, a waiter at the Waldorf-Astoria, who remembered serving dinner for four in Luciano's apartment. When he arrived in the suite there was only Luciano and one other. The other two were in the next room, from which he heard voices. He easily identified Jimmy Frederico as the man with Lucky Luciano.

A prostitute named Thelma Jordan was our next witness, and she provided more colorful details about life within the organization. Thelma was a girl friend of Benny Spiller, the loan shark man, and Benny had told her in the past what all the functions of the defendants were. Then Thelma was pressed hard by the defense on her own life as a prostitute, the way she worked, her acquaintanceship with members of the combination. Persistently, they asked her why she had held out after her arrest, and why she had not told us all we wanted to know on the spot. This was true. Thelmas had not been one of the first to talk with us.

But now Thelma Jordan was a witness before the Luciano trial and this persistent line of questioning finally blew it. Her nerves were raw from the cross-examination, and she answered: "All right, I will tell you."

The defense counsel made the mistake of his life. He said, "Go ahead."

Thelma said, "I was afraid to talk, because I knew what happens to people that talk and who tell things about the members of the combination, about racket people. I know times girls have had their feet burned and their stomachs burned with cigar butts because they talked, and their tongues cut, and things like that, and I was afraid of it, and that's why I didn't talk."

Desperately counsel tried to dig himself out by asking Thelma why she was testifying now. She answered acidly that it was because she had confidence in our office.

Outside the courtroom a shocked public read headlines like:

SAYS GANGSTERS SPLIT GIRLS' TONGUES
TORTURE IS LAID TO VICE BOSSES
GIRL SAYS SQUEALER'S FEET WERE BURNED WITH CIGARS
VICE WITNESS TIGHTENS EVIDENCE NET ABOUT
LUCKY AND HENCHMEN

Next, we had a bad break. We were all ready to call Good Time Charlie to the stand to tell the jury his memories of Luciano in the prostitution racket when he suddenly said in the witness room, "I can't tell that story. It isn't true." He was reminded that he had told it voluntarily, and also that he had testified under oath to that effect before the grand jury. Good Time Charlie made it perfectly clear that he was scared out of his wits and he was not going to testify to anything in the Luciano trial.

This hurt us, because he was one of our witnesses who had direct rather than hearsay testimony to offer against Luciano himself. It also hurt us because Good Time Charlie was corroborating Luciano's presence as described by some of the other witnesses. But no more. We were pretty sunk about it.

Things looked up when Mildred Balitzer took the stand. She told her life history simply and directly, and of her repeated efforts to persuade Luciano and Little Davie to let her husband Pete Harris out of the business, without avail. The defense threw every weapon in their arsenal at her. They dwelt on the details of her narcotics addiction and the gruesome details of her life as a prostitute and madam. They raked her with dirty words and ugly insinuations for eight solid hours, but they did not shake her testimony.

Then we had another very bad time of it. We called Frank Brown, the assistant manager of the Barbizon-Plaza Hotel, one of our scheduled respectable witnesses. He knew Luciano as Mr. Charles Lane and knew him well, often taking drinks with Lane in his room at the hotel. In our office Brown had unhesitatingly picked out the photographs of a number of the defendants as regular visitors to Luciano. He got on the witness stand. And there, in full view of the jury, his memory collapsed.

Brown looked over the thirty-five people in the courtroom enclosure, a group which included the defendants and their counsel, and said, "Well, I can't say I remember any particular one. I have seen a lot of them come in and out."

When we pressed him he said, "I see men that looked like I have seen them," but he would go no further toward an identification. Referring to the photographs he had been shown in our office, I asked, "Have you told me that you recognized among those pictures a number of men whom you saw in the room of Luciano or in his company in the lobby of your hotel?" He answered, "That is right."

Brown admitted further that he had identified them in person from the witness room just the day before. The furthest he would go was to say, "I said they were men that I thought I had seen."

In short, Brown ran out on us completely, ending up, "But I didn't swear that I had seen them."

It was a miserable setback, and our only consolation was that it must have been pretty obvious to the jury that he was lying in his teeth.

Of all the witnesses, only two ran out on their testimony. Both were men. The prostitutes and the madams had more courage and integrity than many of the men in or out of the rackets.

The next witness was William McGrath, a bellboy at the Barbizon-Plaza. McGrath had no trouble identifying Luciano, and also Little Davie and Tommy the Bull, whom he termed frequent visitors.

McGrath was followed by a procession of other hotel people, both from the Barbizon-Plaza and from the Waldorf-Astoria Towers, all of humble occupation and free of fear. Before we were through, every member of the mob, all the way down to the bondsmen, had been firmly and frequently identified as occasional or frequent visitors to Lucky Luciano. Their business had been overwhelmingly established as running the prostitution combination. There was no other visible reason for their sessions with Luciano. The case was looking stronger and stronger.

Nancy Presser was in frail condition when she took the stand because she had just finished withdrawal from narcotics. But she gave her testimony about her contacts with Lucky Luciano bravely and without a tremor. The cross-examination of Nancy Presser lasted eight and a half hours, and once again every type of nauseating, insulting question was thrown at her. Hours were spent dwelling on the details, especially, of her narcotics addiction. Finally she became ill on the stand and had to leave the room to vomit. But she managed to come back, and, on further questioning, she explained that talking about the details of drug addiction always made her sick. There was no one in the courtroom ready to dispute that.

A few scraps of paper were finally put into evidence to tie up some loose ends. A notebook taken from Tommy the Bull when he was arrested contained the word "Mildred," and the telephone numbers of Mildred Balitzer and the bondsman Jesse Jacobs. Also found on Tommy the Bull was a card of one of the eating places which had been mentioned in testimony, the Café de Capri, as well as written notes with the names of Pete Harris and Benny Spiller, with their telephone numbers.

Found on Little Davie when he was arrested were similar cards from Keen's Chop House, where Nancy Presser had testified she had sat with the mob leaders a number of times. One of these cards bore the penciled names and telephone numbers of Benny Spiller and Jimmy Frederico.

Wrapping it up, we felt that sixty-four out of the ninety counts of the indictment had been so thoroughly proven that further testimony would have been merely cumulative. So we moved voluntarily to dismiss the remaining twenty-six counts.

We rested the People's case on May 29, 1936. Sixty-eight witnesses had testified on the People's behalf.

Over the weekend we braced ourselves to meet the formal defense presentation. We had asked the New York City Police Department for everything they had in their files about Lucky Luciano. We had been shocked to learn that they had nothing, absolutely nothing except his formal criminal record. They had almost as little about the other defendants. We were all tired, but we spent long hours over the weekend with the madams and prostitutes who knew most about the defendants. We developed more facts that might come in handy in our cross-examinations of the defense witnesses. We even gathered our most knowledgeable witnesses in our office as an informal brains trust. They would be on hand when the first defense witnesses opened up on Monday morning.

It was also pretty clear that an all-out defense operation was taking place outside the courtroom. It was reported in the press that one of my assistants had been offered $250,000 to disclose our legal strategy, and that he had contemptuously declined the offer and reported it to me. A lawyer had been arrested trying to bribe a woman to contradict Cokey Flo. Four men and a woman were arrested for allegedly offering witnesses choices between bribes and death. One of our witnesses was said to have been offered money and a gambling house in the Adirondack Mountains. So we moved our witnesses around from place to place, so they could not be pinned down.

But when the defense opened up on Monday morning things broke our way. The fourth major booker, Jack Ellenstein, joined his mates Miller, Harris, and Weiner, and switched his not guilty plea to guilty to all counts. It seemed a little strange for him to plead guilty at this late date, because he had nothing much to gain. I guess he and his lawyer decided that there was no chance of acquittal, so he might just as well get out of the courtroom and save any more laywers' fees. Actually, this did help Eller a bit in his sentence, too.

From there on out, the defense presentation struck me as a dead giveaway. It was all designed to help Lucky Luciano. All the other defendants were so deeply buried under our mountain of testimony that they must have known they had little chance of acquittal. Their only remaining object was to help the Boss.

Their first witness was Ralph Liguori, the pimp. He turned out to be alternately brash, embarrassed, confused, and insulting. He was absolutely innocent of everything, he insisted. He did not know a single one of the other defendants. He had never even seen one of them, except Jimmy Frederico. He said he had "seen him around."

Then Liguori launched into a long story about how he had been picked up and brought to my office and pressured to perjure himself. He told a terrible tale of threats by the lawyers on my staff, and he apparently was hoping to persuade one or two jurors to disregard the testimony of our witnesses. As for himself, Liguori said he was just a hard-working son who worked in his mother's butcher shops until they were sold. Then he "worked around" other shops part time.

Liguori testified that he was indeed a friend of Nancy Presser. He fell in love with her, lived with her, and took her twice to sanatoria so she could try to get off narcotics. He took her home and introduced her to his mother and brothers, and she stayed there for a week, at one time. He really believed Nancy was a hard-working model. He had no idea where she got the money for her narcotics, and no idea where or from whom she contracted syphilis, which Liguori denied giving her.

Then the cross-examination began. He grudgingly admitted he had no job at all in 1933, which was when he was claiming he was buying clothes for Nancy Presser and entertaining her. So I showed him a registration card for a Cord automobile made out in his name. I asked him where he got the money to buy the Cord. He replied he had swapped his old Cadillac for the Cord.

Under cross-examination Liguori now admitted that, before meeting Nancy, he had been living with a prostitute named Josephine Gardella, also known as "Gashouse Lil." He thought she was a model too. I showed him a life insurance policy on Josephine's father which

Liguori had cashed in for $414.18. He admitted that he had got her father to cash it. He had done this by telling the man, falsely, that Josephine was sick in the hospital and needed the money. Liguori got the check and the cash, and he claimed that everything he did was on Josephine's orders.

Pete Harris had testified that Liguori introduced Josephine to him. This was a lie, said Liguori. Thelma Jordan and Nancy Presser had both testified that Ralph Liguori threatened to kill Nancy if she testified against him. Jimmy Russo, a male madam, had testified that Ralph ordered him to put Nancy to work in his house, "if you know what's good for you." Another madam, Joan Martin, had testified that Liguori held up her house when she had trouble with the combination. Liguori kept on saying lies, all lies, but he looked sicker every minute of the cross-examination.

When I confronted him with a Motor Credit Corporation card, Liguori first denied knowledge of it, then admitted he had paid for one of his cars out of Josephine's money. He took the money in the name of Langer.

Liguori's sister took the stand and loyally said he was a butcher, that she believed Nancy to be a hat check girl, and she denied that Ralph had ever done anything wrong in his life. She then accused one of my deputy assistants, Harry Cole, of having tried to get her to testify falsely against Lucky Luciano.

Liguori's sister also tried to help Ralph by explaining how she might have been able to support his Cadillac—or his Cord. He did earn some money, she said, and she also gave him some of the twenty-five dollars a week she earned in her respectable work. But she was no more help to the defense than her brother had been.

During the parade of defense witnesses, what looked like serious trouble erupted when a New York City patrolman named George Heidt took the stand. A uniformed officer, he had been assigned to help guard our witnesses. He confirmed what everybody knew and what I had said in my opening statement, that we had tried to make life as pleasant as possible for our witnesses within the legal proprieties. Now Heidt testified that one evening, accompanied by our senior trial strategist Sol Gelb, he had escorted Mildred Balitzer into Leon and Eddie's, to the Dizzy Club, and to the Club Richman. Heidt testified that Mildred was "pretty well intoxicated."

Years after this bombshell, Gelb recalled: "When I finished talking with this witness, we'd leave the office, take a taxi and ride uptown. I remember one night that this woman trembled in the cab, and she insisted that she had to get a drink, so I said to the cop, 'Stop off someplace and get her a drink.' He mumbled something to the effect that he wanted me with him, so I said, 'All right, I'll go with you.'

"He picked out a spot, and we got out. It was Fifty-second Street, and he goes into Leon and Eddie's. Now I have never been in Leon and Eddie's in my life. I had barely heard of it. I said to the cop, 'Is this the place you have to pick out to get a drink? You couldn't walk into any old bar?'

"We go in, sit down, and she gets a couple of drinks. We get through at Leon and Eddie's and walk out. We hail a cab, and she refuses to get into it. She says, 'I've got to have another drink.' So I said to the cop, 'Take her someplace and get her a drink.' She was trembling. No, the cop insisted that I be with them. He takes her across the street, and we walk in right off the ground, a brownstone house, and she had a couple of drinks there. I'm sitting there with her and the cop. Comes later the motion for a new trial, and the affidavit says that we then took her to the Dizzy Club. Well, I'd never heard of the Dizzy Club."

The fair question was, Who was the cop who was now a witness for the Luciano defense? Gelb recalled: "Georgie Heidt was a real wise guy who knew everybody on the wrong side and I was told then, 'My God, what kind of office are you fellows running when you allow the Police Department to send you a ringer like Georgie Heidt to guard witnesses?' How the hell did the defense know that she had gone with the cop and me to Leon and Eddie's and the Dizzy Club? The cop must have told them, and he was a member of the police force of the city of New York."

At approximately this same point in the defense, one of the girls now said that Frank Hogan pulled her by the hair to try to persuade her to testify.

Well, Frank Hogan made an affidavit denying that.

Meanwhile, Luciano's formal defense was rolling along predictably. One after another, bookmakers and gamblers testified as character witnesses that he was often at the track and was a fun-loving, roistering good fellow. They said they saw Luciano a lot and knew him well and they had never seen him in the company of any of the co-defendants in the prostitution case. Then Luciano's counsel called a

"Grace Doe" as a witness, who said she was a nurse and she knew our witness Bendix's wife, who had given her a piece of paper, the relevance of which was not made clear. On cross-examination, she admitted she had lived with one man after another, was in show business, singing at banquets. She remembered one banquet when she said she was paid twenty dollars. Then she had run out of banquets.

Luciano's counsel now produced a more serious witness, a housekeeper at the Waldorf-Astoria Towers brought on to counter the testimony of our star witness, the bath maid, Marjorie Brown.

The housekeeper testified that the maids were not permitted to stand out in the hall while they waited to get into the apartments to clean the bathrooms. Her implication was that the maids had been doing some unauthorized snooping. On cross-examination, the housekeeper said that she had often found the maids waiting outside Luciano's apartment. She said she had rebuked them for it many times. However, from our point of view, the housekeeper was confirming that the maids had actually been in a position to see what they said they had seen. The housekeeper also testified that the maids were girls of excellent reputations. She was another boomerang for the defense.

Finally Luciano's counsel called Lorenzio "Chappie" Brescia, a character who lived with Luciano part time at the Barbizon and the Waldorf and accompanied him to race tracks every now and then. Brescia said he had never seen any of the other defendants except Little Davie Betillo.

But on cross-examination Brescia had trouble remembering anything he had worked at during the previous twelve years. Luciano's counsel, George Morton Levy, tried to help by interjecting, "Give him a chance, he is a little dull."

Brescia said he had been in the real estate business but never sold anything. He said he had a gun permit so that he could "carry money around" but could not remember ever collecting any money to carry around. He was obviously nothing but a gunman-bodyguard.

Lucky Luciano then said, "I'm ready for Mr. Dewey," and he prepared to take the stand in his own defense.

The Duel

Under direct examination by his senior counsel, George Morton Levy, Luciano said he had attended school on the Lower East Side of New York City until the sixth grade. He quit to work for a while in a hat factory. Soon after that he quit to gamble and run dice games. In 1919, Luciano was convicted and sentenced to eight months' imprisonment for peddling narcotics. Since then, he swore, he had had nothing more to do with narcotics and no more convictions, except one for maintaining a gambling house in Miami, Florida. For this offense he had been fined $1,000.

Luciano said he had never seen or heard of any of the other defendants in the prostitution racket case—except that Little Davie Betillo had come to see him a couple of times about joining a venture about a gambling ship. He had refused to go into the venture.

Luciano said he had never met Nancy Presser or Mildred Balitzer, or any of the other women in the case. He swore, "There has not been a witness that got on this stand of Mr. Dewey's that I ever saw in my life." He excepted the hotel employees who had testified, and he admitted he did know them. His counsel Levy asked at one point: "Did you ever receive the earnings of a prostitute?" Luciano answered

"I gave to 'em. I never took." There was no laughter in the court-room at Luciano's remark.

I started the cross-examination by asking about the gambling con-viction in Miami to which the defendant had just referred. Was it not true that he had also been convicted of carrying a gun? "Yes," Luci-ano said, "but Mr. Levy didn't mention no gun." Luciano said there was "no law against a gun in Miami," but I showed him the record of his conviction and, for the first time, he admitted that he had been convicted on that occasion of "carrying a concealed weapon."

A newspaper clipping I introduced did not refresh his recollection of one interesting aspect of that arrest. He had told the press that he was carrying the gun for "a little hunting trip to the Everglades." But Luciano denied saying this, and then he could not remember.

Then, together, Luciano and I moved into a question-and-answer delineation of how he had gotten started in crime. It was a fascinating story, and it had to be drawn out of him, like pulling teeth.

Q. How old were you when you were convicted of selling nar-cotics?

A. Eighteen, around eighteen.

Q. How long were you selling narcotics before you got caught?

A. Oh, about three weeks or a month.

Q. It was not the first transaction, however, was it?

A. What?

Q. You did not get caught on the very first ounce of morphine that you handled?

A. No.

Q. Was it the second, perchance?

A. No.

Q. Was it the third?

A. I told you, about three weeks after.

Q. I am asking you, how many transactions had you before you got caught?

A. That I can't remember.

Q. Had you as many as a hundred, or just two or three?

A. I didn't have no hundred, and I had more than three.

Q. Would you say you had more than fifty?

A. No.

Q. Whom were you getting your dope from?

A. Who did I get the dope from?

Q. Yes.

A. That I couldn't remember.

Q. Did you do business with that fellow for the whole three weeks?

A. That is right.

Q. How many transactions would you say you had with him—as many as twenty-five?

A. No.

Q. As many as ten?

A. I had about three transactions with him.

Q. In other words, you were in the business of selling dope for three weeks, and on the third transaction you got caught?

A. I didn't get caught making a transaction with the fellow I was buying it off.

Q. Yes, he got caught?

A. No, I got caught.

Q. Yes. Where did you get caught?

A. On Fourteenth Street.

Q. Were you buying or selling at the time you got caught?

A. I was selling.

Q. Whom were you selling to?

A. To a dope fiend.

Q. What was his name?

A. That I don't know. . . .

Q. And you were guilty, weren't you?

A. Yes, I was.

Q. The man you were getting the dope from—he did not get caught, did he?

A. No.

Q. Will you make one more effort to tell us any part of his name at all?

A. I don't remember his name.

Q. Not the slightest recollection?

A. No.

Q. Of the name of the man from whom you bought dope?

A. No. . . .

Q. Some of your associates told you, "Here is a man who sells dope," right?

A. Not some of my associates. I didn't have no associates.

Q. Weren't you running around with any boys at that time?

A. I might have, yes.

Q. Didn't you have a little gang of your own at that time?

A. No gang.

Q. Did you belong to a little gang?

A. No.

Q. Just a few friends, hanging around the street corners?

A. That is right.

Q. And somebody told you, "Here is a man you can buy some dope from"?

A. That is right.

Q. And you went up to him, and what did you say to him?

A. I wanted to buy some stuff. . . .

Q. How many dope addicts did you know that were buying dope at that time?

A. I didn't know any of them, but I knew who they were, who the dope addicts were.

Q. How did you find out who they were?

A. You could see some of them.

Q. You could tell by looking at them?

A. That is right.

Q. You were an expert at that time, weren't you?

A. I was no expert.

Q. And you mean anybody can look at a person and tell whether he is a narcotic addict?

A. Them kind of addicts, certainly.

Q. You mean, the kind you had down in your neighborhood?

A. The few that they are around there, you could tell easy . . . a few was pointed out and I knew that there was dope addicts and that is why I approached them.

Q. Yes. Now I asked you, and I still have not been answered, did you go up to them and say, "Will you buy your dope from me?"

A. That is right. I told them I had some.

Q. Was that before you had it or after you had it?

A. After I had it.

Q. In other words, before you had a single customer, you went out and bought some dope?

A. Right. . . .

Q. When you walked up to them they said, "Sure I will buy it from you." You did not make any threats and say, "You better buy it from me," no?

A. No.

Q. They just suddenly said sure, they would buy it from you. Did they say anything about the fellow they had bought it from before?

A. No. . . .

Q. And then, on the third transaction, you got caught?

A. Right.

Q. And then you went away for eight months and did it in six months?

A. That is right.

Luciano next attempted to convince the jury that after he came out of prison he lived through the 1920s without any kind of business, profession, or means of livelihood other than gambling and helping manage a series of floating crap games.

Q. Let us see, did you have any pretense of a business of any kind or nature whatsoever?

A. No.

Q. You did not have anything else in the world that you were doing but running a crap game?

A. That is right. . . .

Q. You mean you ran a crap game night in and night out?

A. That is right. . . .

Q. Did you do anything else at all during that five-year period [from 1920 to 1925]?

A. I don't remember anything else, that is all.

Q. Did you go to the horse races a little?

A. What?

Q. Did you go to the horse races a little?

A. I did that.

Q. Did you do a little bookmaking on the side? . . . Was it between 1920 and 1925 that you did a little bookmaking?

A. Well, around that time, around 1925, something like that, yes.

Q. From 1920 to 1925, did you ever at any time in that entire five-year period earn an honest dollar?

Defense counsel: That is objected to as calling for a conclusion, calling for an opinion of a man.

The Court: He may give us his own view of what is honest. I overrule it.

Defense counsel: I respectfully except.

Q. Were you for a moment employed anywhere?

A. No. . . .

Q. You have to remember events four or five years back, if you are a bookmaker, don't you?

A. Bets?

Q. Events. Horses. History.

A. Well, no, I wouldn't say that.

Q. How far back does a good bookmaker's memory have to go on horses? . . .

A. I couldn't tell you who won last week's race.

Q. You can't tell me who won last week's race?

A. That is right.

Q. By the way, are you one of those people who cannot tell me what he had for dinner last night?

A. No. . . .

Q. All right. Now, coming from 1925 all the way up to 1930, a five-year period, did you do anything in that period of time except shoot crap and book horses?

A. Nineteen twenty-five to 1930?

Q. Yes.

A. That is all I did. . . .

Q. Well, did you have any device or gag fixed up in that period of time so that you could make it look as if you had a legitimate occupation? . . .

A. Yes, I think I did.

Q. Well, now. Can you remember what happened in between 1925 and 1930 with reference to that?

A. Yes, now it comes to me, yes.

Q. All right, now tell us.

A. Well, I was bootlegging for a while, about a year and a half.

Q. Yes.

A. And I pretended I had a real estate business.

Q. Where was the real estate business you pretended you had?

A. Right here on Centre Street.

Q. And what is the address?

A. Centre and White.

Q. And did you have a sign, "Real Estate," in the window?

A. On the window.

Q. And you had the office there?

A. I did, one of them.

Q. What is that?

A. I was one of them.

Q. And did you have some partners?

A. That is right.

Lucky Luciano was fighting one of the duels of his life, admitting just as much and only as much as he thought we could prove, asseverating until he appeared to be out on a limb, then conceding in inches. I next moved into a series of showings to him of his arrests, mostly for traffic violations, between August 28, 1922, and February 2, 1931. There were thirteen of these, all told. Since I could not properly refer to the charges involved in these arrests, all I could do was to use the sheets to refresh the recollection of the witness. The net effect of his answers was to cast doubt both upon his credibility and upon his story of how he had spent the 1920s.

As to the first sheet, I asked whether he had told Patrolman Clay, on August 28, 1922, that he was a chauffeur? "Maybe I did," Luciano said. As to the next, on June 25, 1923, did he tell W. J. Mellon, a Secret Service agent, that he was a chauffeur? He "might have said that." When pressed, Luciano said he had never been a chauffeur for anyone. Only after the trial, of course, could it even be hinted that Luciano made his way up in the Mafia as a chauffeur of bosses and as a particularly ruthless gunman-bodyguard.

On August 25, 1924, did he tell Patrolman Harris that he was a salesman? He "might have said it." Did he tell Patrolman Harris that he was born in Italy? "I don't know."

Did he tell Patrolman Hunt, in December 1924, that he was a fruit dealer? He would not admit it or deny it, claiming he did not remember.

On June 24, 1925, did he tell Patrolman Carter he was a salesman? "I may have said it, but I don't remember." Anyway, he definitely was not a salesman.

On June 20, 1926, did he tell Patrolman O'Connor that he was a salesman? He studied the arrest sheet a long time on that one, and his answer was, "Yes, but I don't remember these traffic violations," and "I am trying to think where this record comes from." He was not sure whether he said he was a salesman or not.

Again, on February 7, 1926, had he told Patrolman Lofrisco that he was a chauffeur, which he admitted he was not? He admitted that five months later he had told Detective Kane he was a salesman, and he admitted this was false. He then claimed he always told the truth when he was under oath. He added that he would not perjure himself "for anybody."

With the jury looking on, Luciano, when pressed, said, "I didn't say I told the truth all the time, but now I am telling the truth." Had he lied under oath? "Well, maybe if I am looking to get something, yes, not on the stand here."

Q. Yes, you lied about things, didn't you?

A. Yes. I probably told them that I had an occupation, and I didn't have it. . . .

Q. On how many occasions did you perjure yourself when you were trying to get a pistol to carry around?

Defense counsel: That is objected to, if it please the Court, the word "perjury" under the old law is ambiguous.

The Court: It may be so.

Defense counsel: It depends on a great many situations.

The Court: Better be more specific. I have heard of such things.

Q. On how many occasions did you lie under oath in order to get a gun to carry around the streets of New York.

A. Once, I think.

Q. Only once?

A. I think so, yes.

Q. Did you get the gun?

A. Yes. . . .

Q. If it was a little thing like a pistol permit, you are willing to lie; is that it?

Defense counsel: I object to that characterization of "a little thing like a pistol."

Dewey: Withdrawn.

Q. If it was a big thing like a pistol, would you lie to get a pistol permit?

Defense counsel: I will withdraw the objection. Let him answer.

A. That is the only thing I lied about, is to give them an occupation.

Luciano, at another point, had been asked a little more about his real estate business. He denied they were running a fence operation, even though his partner had been arrested, tried, and convicted for receiving stolen goods.

The struggle was now focusing on whatever we could bring out in court about Luciano's rapid rise in the Mafia as a chauffeur and gunman. The atmosphere in the courtroom was thick and tense. Finally the break came and it convulsed the audience with laughter.

Q. On July 27, 1926, were you with a man named Joseph Saleeze?

Defense counsel: Again objected to as irrelevant, immaterial, incompetent.

The Court: Overruled.

Defense counsel: Exception.

Q. Were you?

A. That is right.

Q. And did you have two guns and a shotgun and forty-five rounds of ammunition in the car between you?

Defense counsel: Just a moment. That is objected to as irrelevant, immaterial, incompetent, and improper cross-examination.

The Court: Overruled.

Defense counsel: Exception.

Q. Did you or didn't you?

A. I just come back from the country, and I had a hunting outfit in there.

Q: Yes?

A. Yes.

Q. You had two revolvers?

A. Yes.

Q. And a shotgun?

A. Yes.

Q. And forty-five rounds of ammunition?

A. And a couple of boxes of cartridges.

Q. Yes, and what were you shooting on that day?

A. What?

Q. What were you shooting on that day in the country?

A. On that day, I wasn't shooting nothing.

Q. What were you doing out in the country?

A. I wasn't up the country. I just come in.

Q. Came in from where?

A. From the country.

Q. What had you been doing in the country that day?

A. Shooting.

Q. Shooting what?

A. Birds.

Q. What kind of birds?

Defense counsel: That is objected to.

A. Pheasants.

Luciano pronounced this word "peasants," and this occasioned the roar of laughter.

Defense counsel: This is back ten years.

The Court: Overruled.

Defense counsel: Irrelevant, immaterial, incompetent. Exception.

Q. Shooting pheasants?

A. Yes.

Q. In the middle of July?

A. Yes, that is right.

Q. Shooting pheasants in the middle of July?

A. Yes, that is right.

Q. Is that your answer?

A. That is right.

Defense counsel objected once again on the grounds that this question had been answered, and once again the objection was overruled. Never mentioned in the record, but understood by many in the courtroom, was the basic point that pheasants are out of season in July.

Q. Do you shoot pheasants with a pistol?

A. No.

Q. What were the pistols along for?

A. I had a permit for a pistol.

Q. Yes. What did you have it along for?

A. I carried it. . . .

Q. Were you both on this pheasant shooting trip in July?

A. I guess so.

Q. Both of you, you and Joe Saleeze, right?

A. Maybe, yes.

Q. Well now, you really don't know whether he was along or not, is that your testimony?

A. I don't remember whether he was there or not.

Q. You remember that he was in the car with you?

A. That is right.

Q. Do you remember whether he was out shooting pheasants with you in July? . . .

A. I think he was, yes.

Q. That is your best recollection, now?

A. Yes.

Q. Why couldn't you remember before whether he had been along on the pheasant shooting trip or not?

Defense counsel: That is objected to as argumentative.

The Court: Sustained.

Q. What has called it to your mind now, that you now tell us he was along?

Defense counsel: Same objection.

The Court: Overruled.

Defense counsel: Exception.

A. It comes to me, that is all. . . .

Q. What shotgun did he use, or did you pass it from one to another?

A. . . . We just had one gun, that is all. . . .

Q. One shotgun between you pheasant shooting in July?

A. Yes.

Q. Right?

A. Yes.

Q. And you passed it from one to the other so you could alternate taking shots at the pheasants? Is that it, is that your testimony?

A. No.

Q. No. Which one of you used a shotgun on the pheasants?

A. What?

Q. Which one of you used a shotgun?

A. I did.

Q. And what was he doing along?

A. We had another shotgun up in the country.

Q. Oh, you left the shotgun up in the country?

A. Yes.

Q. Where did you leave it?

A. Where?

Q. Yes.

A. Up in the country on the farm.

Lucky Luciano's answers were becoming so faint, at this point, that Judge McCook told him his voice was dropped, and offered to declare a recess if Luciano was tired. But he opted to continue. Having drawn forth some glimpses of his role as a chauffeur and gunman, we now attempted to elicit some sense of his specialty within the Mafia —narcotics. After all, he had been in this business since the age of eighteen, as we had drawn out at the beginning of the cross-examination.

Q. And that drugstore up on Forty-ninth Street and Seventh Avenue, you heard Bendix [a prosecution witness] tell about meeting you there?

A. Yes.

Q. And isn't it a fact that you were hanging around that drugstore pretty often?

A. No, sir.

Q. That is Dukor's drugstore, isn't it?

A. Yes, sir.

Q. And you own half of that drugstore, don't you?

A. No, sir.

Q. You had no interest in it?

A. Never.

Q. Do you know Dukor?

A. Yes, sir. . . .

Q. Are you just a passing acquaintance of Mr. Dukor?

A. That is right.

Q. No business relations with him at all?

A. No, sir.

Q. Never had any?

A. No, sir.

Q. Why do you telephone him, then, from the Waldorf?

A. Why did I telephone him?

Q. Yes.

A. I don't remember telephoning him at all.

Q. Do you deny that you telephoned him from the Waldorf?

A. That is right.

Q. Do you deny that on May 3, 1935, at 10:58 A.M. you telephoned Dukor's drugstore?

A. I never telephoned for him, Mr. Dukor.

Q. You were just telephoning the drugstore for some other reason?

A. No. There was another boy hanging around there. I probably called for him . . . Georgie Burns.

Q. Who is he?

A. A boy that hung around the drugstore. . . .

Q. What was he hanging around the drugstore for?

A. That is his business.

Q. You would not know anything about that at all?

A. No, sir.

Q. What was your business with him?

A. No business at all.

Q. Just a social conversation?

A. That is right. . . .

Q. Isn't it a fact that he is a professional dope peddler?

A. Don't ask me.

Q. You have not any idea?

A. No, sir. . . .

Q. You know that is what he has been convicted for, don't you?

A. I don't know that. . . .

Q. You have known him ten years, but you do not even know whether he has been convicted of dope peddling or not?

A. That is right.

Q. Did you ever know anybody but yourself who had ever been convicted of dope peddling who did not go right back into it?

Defense counsel: That is objected to as argumentative, if it pleases the Court.

The Court: Sustained.

Q. You claim that after you were convicted of dope peddling you never sold any more at all?

A. That is right.

Q. Did you ever hear of anybody else, or do you know anybody who had been convicted of it who, like yourself, ceased dealing in it?

Defense counsel: That is objected to.

The Court: Sustained. A very skillful distinction, but not good enough. . . .

Q. Do you recall a little incident on June 6, 1923? Does that mean anything in your life?

A. I don't remember what you mean.

Q. No recollection at all?

A. No.

Q. All right. Do you remember first, on June 2, 1923 [this was some five years after his narcotics conviction], selling a two-ounce box of narcotics to John Lyons, an informer for the federal Secret Service?

Defense counsel: Objected to as irrelevant, immaterial, and incompetent.

The Court: Overruled.

Defense counsel: Exception.

A. Nineteen twenty-three?

Q. Yes, sir.

A. I was arrested—

Defense counsel: Now I object—

Q. I did not ask you that. I asked you whether on June 2, 1923, you did not sell a two-ounce box of narcotics to John Lyons, an informer in the Secret Service?

A. I was arrested, but I never sold anything like that.

Q. I am asking you whether you did not on June 2—I ask you for the third time—

Defense counsel: I submit it has been answered, if it pleases the Court.

The Court: He answered him something else. He may have included that, but I will allow it again so that we get a sole answer to that.

Defense counsel: Exception.

Q. I want to know whether—

The Court: Yes or no is the answer.

Q. Whether on June 2, 1923, you did not sell a two-ounce box?

The Court: If you will take the negative out of it, it will be a little better, Mr. Dewey. Then we can get an answer yes or no.

Q. Isn't it a fact that on June 2, 1923, you sold a two-ounce box of narcotics known as diacetyl morphine hydrochloride to John Lyons, an informer for the Secret Service of the United States?

A. I don't know who they were, but I was arrested, and if I was charged with them, that I didn't do.

Q. I did not ask you anything except: Didn't you sell the dope to John Lyons on that date?

A. No.

Q. You deny it?

A. No.

Q. Flatly?

A. I don't deny that I was arrested.

Q. I did not ask you anything except whether you did not sell dope on that day.

A. I didn't sell it to him.

Defense counsel: It has been answered, your honor, that he did not.

The Court: We finally got an answer.

Q. Your answer is no?

A. No.

Q. Positive? Isn't it a fact that, three days later, on June 5, 1923, you again sold one ounce of heroin to informer John Lyons of the Secret Service of the United States?

A. No, sir.

Q. You did not sell him anything?

A. No, sir.

Q. Isn't it a fact that at 133 East Fourteenth Street in the city of New York narcotics agent Coyle saw you sell narcotics to John Lyons?

Defense counsel: That is objected to.

The Court: Sustained.

Q. Isn't it a fact that on that date your apartment was searched?

Defense counsel: Objected to as irrelevant, immaterial, and incompetent.

The Court: Overruled.

Defense counsel: Exception.

Q. Was it or was it not?

A. It might have been.

Q. Was it or was it not?

A. Yes.

Q. Why did you say "might have been"? . . .

A. I wasn't there when they searched it.

Q. You are not quite sure about whether it was searched or not, is that it?

A. That is right.

Q. Isn't it a fact that in your apartment were found two one-half-ounce packages of morphine, and two ounces of heroin, and some opium?

A. No, sir.

Q. Absolutely false?

A. Absolutely.

Q. Isn't it a fact that, thereafter, you gave to Joseph Van Bransky, narcotics agent in charge of New York City, a statement that at 163 Mulberry Street they would find a whole trunk of narcotics?

Defense counsel: That is objected to as irrelevant, immaterial, and incompetent.

The Court: Overruled.

Defense counsel: Exception.

Q. Didn't you give such a statement to Mr. Van Bransky?

A. Yes, I did.

Q. And isn't it a fact that, thereafter, a whole trunk of narcotics was found by the Secret Service at 163 Mulberry Street, New York City?

A. Yes, sir. . . .

Q. And you still testify under oath before this Court and jury that you have not dealt in narcotics since the year 1919?

A. That is right.

Q. And that is your testimony now?

A. That is right.

Q. That is all on the subject. What were you—a stool pigeon?

A. I told him [Van Bransky] what I knew.

Q. Were you a stool pigeon?

A. I says, I told him what I knew.

Q. For a consideration?

A. I don't know what you mean by that.

Q. You got something for telling him what you knew, didn't you?

A. I didn't get anything. . . .

Q. But, as a good citizen, you went in and told them where they could get a trunkful of narcotics . . . is that your testimony?

A. I told them, yes.

Q. Just as a good, honest citizen?

A. [No answer was given by the witness to this question.]

Q. Is that your testimony?

A. Yes.

Luciano's credibility was one of the most important aspects of the trial because of the fact that his counsel, George Morton Levy, had stated that Luciano did not know any of his co-defendants, other than Little Davie Betillo. Within this tactic, if the other defendants were convicted, Luciano himself might survive. Under cross-examination, Luciano now denied once again that he had ever met Tommy the Bull

Pennochio. He held to this denial while conceding that Tommy the Bull and Little Davie used to hang out together in Luciano's own district of Little Italy. Then Betillo had gone to Chicago.

Q. Isn't it a fact that he was working with Al Capone in Chicago for five years?

Defense counsel: That is objected to. . . .

The Court: Objection sustained. . . .

Q. Well, you were fairly well acquainted with Capone, weren't you?

A. No, sir.

Q. You mean to tell me that you were not a good friend of Capone?

A. No, sir.

Q. Well now, after Capone went away, didn't you have a conversation with him about Davie Betillo?

Defense counsel: Just a moment: that is objected to.

A. Who?

Q. Capone?

A. No, sir.

Defense counsel: Just a moment please. . . .

Q. Did [Betillo] come back and work for you after 1931?

A. Work for me?

Q. Yes.

A. He never worked for me.

Luciano next denied that he knew the defendants Jimmy Frederico, Ralph the Pimp Liguori, and Little Abie Wahrman.

Q. All totally unknown names to you?

A. That is right.

Q. And you knew a good many people down in Kenmare, Mott, and Mulberry streets, didn't you?

A. Quite a few.

Q. You had a great many friends down there, didn't you?

A. Well, I guess so.

Q. And none of them even mentioned the names of any of these men to you?

A. Not that I know of.

Q. You never bumped into them on the street?

A. No, sir.

Then the cross-examination moved directly to the testimony of the

"respectable" witnesses, the hotel employees who had testified that
Luciano had been visited on frequent occasions by the co-defendants.

Q. Now, do you remember the little girl, Marjorie Brown, from the
Waldorf, the bath maid?

A. Marjorie Brown?

Q. The bath maid who testified here.

A. Yes. I seen her here, yes.

Q. Did you ever see her before in your life?

A. I might have seen her at the Waldorf, yes.

Q. You have seen her up there?

A. Yes.

Q. Do you remember hearing her testify that Davie Betillo was in
your apartment at least twenty times?

Defense counsel: Just a moment, please. That is objected to as an
improper method of cross-examination, attempting to compare and
argue the relative value of someone else's testimony, or refer to it.

The Court: On the same side only.

Defense counsel: I beg your pardon?

The Court: On the same side. It is not—on the same side.

Defense counsel: On either side, I urge it, your honor.

The Court: No, sir, that is not true, as I understand it. I overrule
your objection.

Defense counsel: I respectfully object.

Q. Do you remember her testimony?

A. I remember the testimony.

Q. And you say it is all false?

Defense counsel: Wait a minute.

Defense counsel: I object to that as to form.

Defense counsel: I object to the question.

The Court: That objection is sustained. We will find out by other
methods, without that question.

Q. You say that Betillo was in your apartment once—during the
entire time you lived there?

A. That is right.

Q. And do you remember hearing her testify that Jimmy Frederico
was there most of all?

A. Yes.

Q. And you say that there is not a word of truth in that?

A. No, there ain't.

Q. Did you ever have any trouble with that girl?

Defense counsel: Objected to, if your honor please.

A. I never had no trouble.

Luciano went on to testify that he remembered the other members of the staffs of the Waldorf and the Barbizon-Plaza who had placed him with co-defendants, and he said he had never had any trouble with any of them.

Luciano's defense was also posited on the basis that he knew nothing of the downtown meetings held to organize the prostitution racket. Various prosecution witnesses had placed him there, by direct testimony, and others had in hearsay testimony.

Q. You heard all that testimony about the meetings of these defendants at Celano's [Celano's Gardens, a restaurant], is that right?

A. Yes.

Q. What were you doing telephoning to Celano's?

A. Celano's?

Q. Yes.

A. I go in there and eat once in a while.

Q. Oh, and what were you doing telephoning there from the Waldorf, if you had no business down there?

A. I don't remember. I go down there to eat, there is a friend of mine owns that place. . . .

Q. Isn't it a fact now that on April 17, 1935, you telephoned there at 12:15 P.M.?

A. Celano's?

Q. Yes.

A. It may be so.

Q. Do you deny that you did it?

A. I am not denying it.

Q. Isn't it a fact that on April 29, 1935, you telephoned Celano's at 12:25 P.M.?

A. Maybe I did, yes.

Q. Do you deny that you did?

A. No.

Q. Isn't it a fact that on May 14, 1935, you telephoned Celano's at 2:44 A.M. in the morning?

A. Not me.

Q. Not you?

A. No.

Q. I show you a slip from the Waldorf, from 39D, and ask you if that refreshes your recollection that you were calling Celano's at two forty-five on that morning?

A. I never saw those slips until now. . . .

Q. Do you deny that on May 16, 1935, you called there at nine fifty-one in the evening?

A. I can't remember what calls went out, to call Celano's, but I—

Q. Well, if the slip shows it, do you deny it?

A. I am not denying it. . . . I don't remember when I put in calls. I don't keep track of calls. . . .

Q. You won't contradict records of the Waldorf, will you?

A. I don't keep track of calls.

The cross-examination brought forth the fact that there had been calls made from Luciano's apartment to Celano's Gardens on May 20, May 21, May 24, May 27, June 4, June 18, June 27, July 23, and from Saratoga, in upstate New York, on September 10, and also on September 16, September 21, September 30, October 25, October 29.

Q. You were not telephoning to Davie, or Abie, or Tommy Bull about business, were you?

A. They never came in there.

The Court: In where?

The Witness: Into Celano's.

Q. You want to testify that these defendants were never in Celano's?

A. No, they never hung out in there.

Q. You want to deny all the testimony about all the meetings that took place back of Celano's?

Defense counsel: That is objected to as irrelevant, immaterial, and incompetent.

The Court: Sustained.

Q. Well, you see, you testified that these men never hung out there?

A. That is right.

Q. Do you know that of your own knowledge?

A. Yes, I believe I have been, I mean I have, I have been in there, they never hung out in that restaurant. . . .

The cross-examination now brought forth Luciano's statements that he did not in fact know other key prosecution witnesses.

Through these doors every day walked the men and women of the most professional, orchestrated, expert investigation and prosecution of crime ever seen in America. Although civic leaders were saying that only dictatorship could solve the problem of the mob, with its terrifying domination of industry and labor and social life, Dewey's people set about to accomplish law enforcement within the system.

Judge Charles C. Nott, Jr., dean of the judges of the Court of General Sessions, swears in Dewey in the presence of his wife and mother as district attorney of New York County. Second from left is Judge Philip McCook. It was 1938. By now, Lucky Luciano, Legs Diamond, and Dutch Schultz were down, but Lepke, Gurrah, and James J. Hines were still to go.

A. J. "Goody" Goodrich, the epitome of the cool accountant-investigator, pioneered Dewey's techniques of making books talk when men would not, undermined the garment empires of Lepke and Gurrah. He was the one who married Miss Rosse.

Dewey's personal secretary, Lilian Rosse, served from 1934 throughout the rackets investigation, his three terms as governor of New York, his partnership in Dewey, Ballantine, Bushby, Palmer & Wood. She preserved Dewey's papers for the University of Rochester and for this book.

In the vanguard of social change, Dewey with brilliant assistants who made justice a Depression-weary nation's crusade. In historic photograph by Barney Stein of the New York *Post, from left,* Sol Gelb, articulate trial strategist, Charles P. Grimes, hunter of Hines, Dewey, and Frank S. Hogan, who succeeded Dewey as D. A., and served until February 1, 1974.

In little-known aspect of public career, Dewey consulted closely with his mother during his career as prosecutor and governor, exchanged telegrams during the restaurant racket and Hines trials in New York.

Paul Coulcher, restaurant racketeer, took control of waiters' union
local to promote massive extortion.

Louis Beitcher, restaurant extortionist, managed to stay free until
the eve of the epic trial.

Irving Epstein, transcontinental
traveler, sprang at his wife's throat
after Jewel told about Baltimore,
the night club in Vicksburg, and
the big bill they could not change
in Needles.

Heroes of the restaurant investigation were Chief Assistant William B. Herlands, *left,* who pulled together the most complex case of the 1930s, and Benny Gottesmann, *center rear,* head of Local 1 of the waiters' union, who defied the mob under threat of death.

Austere quarters were keynote of Dewey investigations. Behind desk
at left is Harold Keller, who kept file of piquant reminiscences.

Duces tecum is Latin phrase for subpoenas that enabled Dewey's staff, *at rear,* to move into racket-affected offices and bring away financial records in these typical fireproof storage crates. New reforms permitted them to bring out the documents "forthwith."

Executive assistant Paul Lockwood, holding putter *at right,* moved onward and upward from the Brooklyn *Eagle* and Young Republicans to become Dewey's alter ego and personal representative. The other golfers are friends from Owosso.

Thomas E. Dewey, Jr., lands direct hit on father in snowball fight. Hidden behind Tom, then aged seven, is John Martin Dewey, then aged four. The lady in coat is Mrs. Thomas E. Dewey.

John M. Dewey, in later picture, takes on his father at checkers. In *center* is Thomas E. Dewey, Jr.

Frances Hutt Dewey, of Sapulpa, Oklahoma, studied voice under Percy Rector Stephens and sang in a road company of *George White's Scandals* before she married Dewey in 1928. One of the worst moments came during the Dutch Schultz crisis when a caller told her on the telephone to come down to the morgue to identify her husband's body.

Jimmy Doyle, alias James Plumeri, blackjacked garment truck drivers into new syndicate war.

John Dioguardi, the "Johnny Dio" who later became a very important racketeer, compared himself to J. P. Morgan.

"Tootsie" Herbert, perhaps the meanest poultry racketeer of all time, even raided his union's death benefit fund.

Lepke (Louis Buchalter), seen here in original police mug shot, was a mass murderer and racket emperor who went to the electric chair. Dewey said, "No man deserved it more."

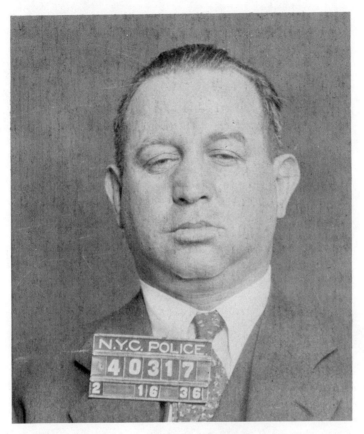

Gurrah (Jacob Shapiro), the terror of New York City's garment industry, broke down and blubbered convulsively when he was sentenced to fifteen years' to life imprisonment. He died in prison.

Thoroughly enjoying life are Mr. and Mrs. Thomas E. Dewey, shown here on the terrace of their cottage at Paget, Bermuda, on a two-week vacation.

Q. Now, you remember Nancy Presser, who was here on the witness stand?

A. Yes.

Q. And you say you never met that girl in your life?

A. That is right.

Q. And she was never in one of your rooms, is that right?

A. Right. . . .

Q. You never met her at Dave's Blue Room?

A. I never saw the girl in my life.

Q. And you didn't hang out at Dave's Blue Room either?

A. No.

Q. Did you do any business at Dave's Blue Room at all?

A. No.

Q. Why were you telephoning Dave's Blue Room?

A. I was telephoning Dave's Blue Room?

Q. Yes.

A. If I telephoned Dave's Blue Room, it was not for Dave's Blue Room, it was not for Dave, and I don't remember any telephones to Dave's Blue Room. . . .

The telephone slips were now beginning to saturate Lucky Luciano as he dueled on. The prosecution witness Cokey Flo, the madam, had placed him at the Standard Garage repeatedly, and Luciano denied knowing anything about the garage. But he was confronted with telephone calls made from his suite to the garage, and he could not remember making them. Another madam and prosecution witness, Mildred Balitzer, had placed him at the Villa Nova restaurant, and now Luciano admitted that he "might have telephoned" there because he knew the owner.

The telephone slips were useful, finally, in helping define Luciano's place at a very high level of the underworld.

Q. Now, you are pretty well acquainted with Lepke, aren't you?

A. I wouldn't say I am pretty well acquainted; I know him. . . .

Q. Doesn't he have to pay tribute to you to operate his businesses?

Defense counsel: I object to it. . . .

The Court: Overruled. . . .

Q. Any business relations with him?

A. None whatsoever.

Q. Why do you call him on the telephone from the Waldorf?

A. From the Waldorf—call who?

Q. Yes.

A. Call who?

Q. Lepke.

A. Where?

Q. At his home?

A. At his home?

Q. Yes.

A. I never called Lepke at his home in my life. I wouldn't know where he is.

Q. Isn't it a fact that on April 10, 1935, you called Lou Buchalter at 11:48 A.M. . . . [and] you know that is Lepke's right name, don't you?

A. Buchalter?

Q. Yes.

A. Yes.

Q. Now let me show you this slip from the hotel and ask you if that refreshes your recollection.

A. I don't remember calling that. Maybe somebody else at my house called it. . . .

Q. How about Gurrah?

A. Yes.

Q. [His real name is] Jacob Shapiro?

A. I know him.

Q. You know him pretty well, don't you?

A. I know him just like I know Lepke.

Q. What is his business?

A. I don't know his business either.

Q. You have not any doubt what his business is?

A. That is right.

Q. You do not know that he is the biggest racketeer in the clothing industry in the city?

Defense counsel: Just a moment. That is objected to, if it pleases the Court.

The Court: Sustained.

Defense counsel: Will you instruct the jury to disregard the question and the import of the question, please.

The Court: Disregard the question and everything pertaining to it.

Q. Now, can't you give us any idea as to what Lepke and Gurrah's business is?

A. I don't go into their business.

Q. No conversations on the subject at all?

A. No. . . .

Q. Did you think maybe they were restaurant proprietors?

A. I don't know. . . .

Q. How about Bugsy Siegel? . . .

A. I knew Bug Siegel.

Q. A pretty good friend of yours?

A. He is a friend of mine, yes.

Q. A fellow resident at the Waldorf?

A. That is right.

Q. What is his business?

A. His business? I know he has been putting on a couple of shows. . . .

Q. How many times in your life have you been taken for a ride?

Defense counsel: That is objected to.

The Court: Overruled. . . .

A. Just once.

Q. Just once; when was that . . . about 1929, 1930?

A. I would not say positive.

Q. Do you recall that you were found in Staten Island?

A. That is right.

Q. By a police officer?

A. That is right.

Q. You had been pretty badly beaten up and cut up?

A. That is right.

Q. Tape over your eyes and mouth?

A. That is right.

Q. And you told the police officers you did not want to give any information, that you would take care of that in your own way?

Defense counsel: That is objected to.

A. I did not.

Defense counsel: As irrelevant, immaterial, and incompetent.

The Court: Overruled.

Defense counsel: Exception.

A. I gave them all the information I knew about it. . . .

Q. Isn't it a fact that on or about October 18, 1929, you told Detective Gustav Schley of the New York police force to forget about it, and you would take care of it yourself?

A. I did not. I gave him all the details, how I got picked up, they grabbed me, and everything.

Q. You were questioned before the grand jury, weren't you?

A. Yes.

Q. Under oath?

A. That is right.

Q. Do you still want to say the only times you lie under oath are when you are getting pistol permits?

A. Yes . . .

Q. On that occasion, you told them you did not have the slightest idea who the four men were who took you on that ride?

A. No, that is right.

Q. You did not have the slightest suspicion?

A. That is right.

Q. And you did not know of any motive in the world, right?

A. That is right.

Q. As a matter of fact, you had $300 in your pockets, and they were left there, weren't they?

A. That is right.

Q. And you had a platinum wrist watch on, didn't you?

A. Maybe I did.

Q. That you had paid $400 for, didn't you?

A. I paid $400 for it?

Q. Yes.

A. For what, the wrist watch?

Q. Yes.

A. I never had a wrist watch worth $400.

Q. Were you asked [before the original grand jury] these questions:

>"*Q.* You had some jewelry?
>"*A.* Yes.
>"*Q.* Consisting of what?
>"*A.* Watch and chain. . . .
>"*Q.* Have you got it with you?
>"*A.* Yes.
>"*Q.* Let's look at it. Is it genuine?
>"*A.* Yes.
>"*Q.* Pretty valuable, isn't it?
>"*A.* Yes.

"Q. What did you pay for it?

"A. About $400. . . ."

Q. You gave that answer?

A. That was not a wrist watch, though.

Q. That was another kind of watch?

A. A pocket watch.

"Q. Five diamonds in the chain?

"A. Yes.

Q. Pretty good crap games that year, weren't they?

A. That was all right.

Q. How much income tax did you report that year?

A. I didn't report any income tax that year.

Luciano finally admitted that he had filed federal income tax returns for the previous six years, just eighteen days after our investigation had started. He had done this not from a sudden rush of conscience but because he thought he should pay. Why did he pay for only six years? Luciano replied: "How much do you want me to pay?"

Q. Six years is the statute of limitations on indictments, isn't it?

A. Yes.

Luciano testified that he settled on $15,000 to $16,500 for each of the years, something he thought was an estimate, and he had no records of any kind to rely upon. He had no idea in his mind at all about attempting to escape prosecution on tax charges. He had settled his accounts in full.

Q. All right. Now, after that, did you keep any books and records so you could be honest with the government? . . .

A. No, I don't keep books or records even from my business. . . .

Q. You filed income tax return for the year 1935 [after the settlement], didn't you?

A. Yes.

Q. And you still did not have a scrap of paper, did you?

A. I don't carry a scrap of paper in my business. . . .

Q. You paid on $25,000 for last year, didn't you?

A. Yes, for this—yes.

Q. Twenty-two thousand five hundred?

A. Twenty-five, yes.

Q. Where did you get that figure?

A. What?

Q. Where did you get the figure of $22,500?

A. Just an idea of what—

Q. Just out of the air?

A. An idea of what I made, yes.

Q. And you swore to it?

A. That is right.

Q. Did you pay state income taxes for those years?

A. No.

Q. Your rush of conscience is only with respect to the federal government, isn't it?

Defense counsel: That is objected to.

The Court: Read that question again. [Question read again.]

The Court: Sustained.

Q. You have not paid a dime to the state government in income taxes yet, have you?

A. That is right.

Defense counsel: Objected to. . . .

The Court: Overruled.

Defense counsel: Exception. . . .

Q. Your answer was, you have not paid a dime to the state government yet, right?

A. That is right.

Q. And that is because the federal government prosecutes big gangsters and the state does not, by income tax, isn't that so?

Defense counsel: That is objected to. . . .

The Court: Overruled.

Defense counsel: Exception.

Q. Isn't that so?

A. I don't know. . . .

Q. You do not know?

A. No.

Q. That is all.

The defense had cross-examined our principal witnesses seven to nine hours apiece. Four hours of this with Luciano seemed enough to us. Apparently his counsel agreed, because he asked Luciano only twenty-nine more questions on his re-direct examination and then dropped it.

The duel was over—and the summations were about to begin. One of the defense counsel and I were visiting in a corridor during a recess just before the defense summation to the jury was about to begin. He summed up for me his own problem about our case rather neatly. He said he was trying to figure out how to convince the jury that the testimony of fifty prostitutes and madams was no better than the testimony of one, just because there were a lot of them.

"How can I convince that jury," he asked, "that a mountain of manure is no better than a cupful?" I told him he had my sympathy.

Thirty to Fifty Years'
Imprisonment

May it please your honor, Mr. Foreman, and gentlemen of the jury, my summation to the jury began, I shall waste little time on formalities and preliminaries, other than to express to you my appreciation for the terrific patience you have displayed in . . . this four-week trial. I did not expect it would be four weeks and I certainly hoped that it would not be. . . .

There have been something like thirteen hours of [defense] summations in this case so far. My best estimate would be that, approximately, an hour and a half of these thirteen hours of summations were devoted to the case, and eleven and a half or twelve hours of these summations were devoted to vilification, abuse, and dirt throwing. . . .

I have heard myself described as the greatest actor in America and the stupidest dolt. I have heard myself described as an irresponsible child of thirty-two, and as Machiavelli's lineal descendant. If one tenth of the things that were said could have been true, I would not be wasting my time in a courtroom. The fact is that my staff and I are lawyers, trying to do a job as lawyers, in accordance with our oaths of office, and that is all.

I shall not debate here the ethics of anybody, and it is not my intention. I shall not debate here how any lawyer could put on the witness stand a shocking spectacle of perjury such as that witness Brescia, the defendant Luciano, the defendant Liguori. I shall not even bother to answer the vilification I got for exposing a defense witness put on the witness stand as a nurse, when counsel knew she was a prostitute. None of my witnesses took the witness stand under false colors, so far as it was within my power to have them tell you what they were. If I put on a prostitute, she said she was a prostitute. If I put on a booker of women, he said so. . . .

There has been a great deal of implication in this case, sometimes frankly stated, usually by innuendo, that I have been running a subornation-of-perjury factory over in the Woolworth Building. Well, let us see what that testimony rests on. There were some sixty-six witnesses called for the People in this case. Each one of those sixty-six witnesses, as I recall it, or say about fifty-five of them, were professional criminals of one kind or another, very minor, medium, and of more importance. Every single one of those witnesses with the exception of three defendants had been given immunity. Every single one of them had his immunity before he walked into this courtroom. Otherwise, I would have been unable to call him as a witness because, as has been repeatedly pointed out in this case, you cannot compel a man to testify against himself, and there is no power on earth by which any prosecutor or lawyer of any kind can make a man take the witness stand and say, "Yes, I did so and so," which is a crime, unless that man has first been given immunity.

He can say, "I refuse to answer," and that ends it. That is a fundamental of law as to which, if any of you have any doubt, I am sure his honor would be happy to respond to an inquiry. That being true, I could not call any witness to this witness stand, against his protest, to testify to his participation in this criminal enterprise, unless that man first had immunity.

Let us see the effect of that. Every one of those witnesses, before he walked on the witness stand, had received all of the consideration the People could give him, except for the three defendants, and Danny Brooks and Bendix, as I remember it. There may be someone else. I do not recall him. From the moment they received that immunity, they could have come into this courtroom and said anything they liked. They could have come into this courtroom and accused me of the things the defense accuses me of.

Gentlemen, they are not my witnesses, these people I put on the witness stand. I did not put them into the business of prostitution. I did not take their earnings. I did not associate them with these defendants. If the People of the state of New York are to receive the protection to which the law entitles them, if they are to have criminals prosecuted, and criminals convicted, and removed from the community, then there is only one way you can do it, and that is on the testimony of the people who have knowledge of the facts. That is a proposition which is beyond dispute.

You cannot convict a booker of women on the testimony of anybody but the people he booked, and corroborating witnesses.

You cannot convict a gunman on the testimony of anybody but the people he used his gun on, or saw use his gun.

You cannot convict a criminal bonding conspiracy, except on the testimony of the people who know about it.

You cannot convict the men at the very top of a criminal enterprise, who deal through criminal subordinates beneath them, except upon the testimony of the people who were their associates, their subordinates, or their intimates.

There is not any other way known to the law under this system of jurisprudence.

Let me say, therefore, that not a single one of these witnesses who were in this criminal business were people for whom I have to accept the slightest responsibility, and I told you that at the opening day of this trial, and I am sure you will all remember it. I said to you on that day, "We cannot get bishops, we cannot get clergymen, we cannot get bankers or businessmen to testify about gangsters, pimps, and prostitution." They just don't happen to be available as witnesses, as I said, and I say it now.

We have to use as witnesses such of the associates of these defendants as we can compel to tell the truth. You don't think that any professional criminal who has been evading the law all his life, and hiding behind doors, and running illegal enterprises and avoiding or corrupting police, walks into a prosecutor's office and says, "I want to confess my crimes and testify against my associates"? That happens once in a thousand times. The only way you get a man in that position to talk is because he has got to talk.

Now, the great complaint of the defense in this trial is that the first and only commandment of the underworld has been broken, "Thou shalt not squeal."

There is only one commandment in the underworld, and that is the one that has been broken, and that is the complaint of these defendants, and the only complaint.

If a prosecutor does less than seek out, analyze, and do everything within his power to get the testimony of people who know of crime, then he shirks his duty. He doesn't belong in any public office. And if I did less than that, you would have a right to say to me, "You are yellow, get out!"

Now, I will tell you this right now. This case has been no pleasure to me or to my assistants. If anybody thinks it is a picnic to work for four and a half months of actual work and months in preparation, on a case involving prostitutes, pimps, gangsters, and bookers of women, and to examine them, and spend time with them, and persuade them to testify, and to hold their hands and keep them from saying they won't, and for the pitifully small staff of lawyers, seven or eight of them, who have worked on this case continuously with this army of witnesses, to work days and nights and Sundays, they are badly mistaken. . . .

But I will tell you this, apropos of the only, or rather of the greatest, point the defense has tried to rely upon, and that is that Mildred Balitzer was allowed to have some brandy, and that on a Saturday night one of my assistants, dead and exhausted after working every night of the week, stopped in and had some drinks in a night club.

I recall something to your attention. Do you remember [Defense Counsel] Levy in his summation for the defense yesterday? He said, "I don't blame anybody for that. I don't blame Mr. Gelb for dancing," which is not the testimony, there is no testimony to it in the case. Mr. Levy said, "Pay no attention to that, it isn't of any importance." Why in heaven's name did he call that witness [the patrolman], then? Sheer, rotten hypocrisy. Why in heaven's name is a witness called, with a great flourish, and then counsel in his summation tries to be nice and say, "Don't pay any attention to it, gentlemen"? Just consider that, when you are trying to find out what the issues in this case are.

Now, on that whole subject, gentlemen:

Have you ever dealt with sheer, stark terror?

I wonder if any man on this jury—and I hope somebody has—has ever been faced with complete, paralyzing terror.

I hope that there is somebody on this jury who has endeavored at some time in his life to sit down and reason and persuade and alleviate the frame of mind of a person who is paralyzed with terror.

When the only underworld commandment has been broken, what do you think started happening in this case, gentlemen? When witnesses by the dozen, by the score, who had never been known to talk, to squeal, finally began breaking—and the word leaked out, as everything seemed to leak out, what do you think started happening behind the scenes? . . .

I could not break the entire underworld. I guess probably we have in this case more underworld testimony than has ever been produced in any twenty cases before in American history. More people have broken that unwritten rule, "Thou shalt not squeal." . . . We must use the testimony of bad men. Otherwise, there would be no rule of law, there would be only the despotic, terroristic rule of the underworld, and the sacred commandment would never be broken, and your Lucianos and your Abie Wahrmans and your Little Davies and Tommy Bulls and all the others would run unchecked around this town, and there would be no safety for life, liberty, and property. . . .

And let me ask you something: Why was Spiller using Luciano's name? Why was Frederico using Luciano's name, as they say? Using his name, using his name? What does that mean? . . . Why did Pete Harris, when he was telling a madam that from now on she had to bond, say, "You have got to bond, Lucky is behind it"? You know and I know why that name was used when it was needed: because it was his business, and his name carried such colossal weight, as you have seen between each line of this case, as you have seen in beckoning his finger right there, before your very eyes, and the lawyers all come running to the master. You have seen that going on every day. Those are facts. Those are internal things which are indisputable. And, again, do you recall the terrible confusion which prevailed [in the defense] when the identification witnesses [from the hotels] came on? Do you remember how one lawyer leaned away over, like this, to cover up his client? Do you remember that Betillo's hair was different for two days? I hope you observed those things. I merely call these things to your attention, because these are things which have happened in the courtroom, and they are what are classed in legal terminology as consciousness of guilt. Those are things, little things, which show what is going on, why the terror is there, and who is the boss.

. . . What business are they in, what do they do for a living? Where do they get all this money? How do they live? If they had any kind of legitimate business, any source of income of any kind or nature wouldn't every one of the people who could testify about it have been brought here? If they had a candy store, if they had anything, any excuse in the world, they would have brought them here, as Luciano did on his cooked-up defense that he was just a gambler.

No doubt about that in any of your minds, is there? Now—what is their business? As I said before, we don't contend that the only thing these defendants do is prostitution, but some things have come out in the course of this case, particularly with reference to Luciano. . . . Now, he takes the witness stand, after a parade of people have testified here that he made bets with them and that, once in his past, about six years ago, he ran a crap game. They want you to believe that all these people who go around intimidating the underworld and taking over prostitution in the name of Luciano are doing it because he is a bookmaker?

That is one of the inherent facts in this case that just cannot stand up. But he says he is just a bookmaker and crapshooter.

Now, let us see. He takes the witness stand and he testifies that he sold some narcotics . . . that he was convicted and that after his conviction he went straight. He worked a year or two, he says, and then he became a gambler. Now, I am not talking, gentlemen, at this moment, about the lies he had committed in the past, about his perjury in a grand jury after he had testified he would not lie under oath, about his perjury on the pistol permits. I am talking now about the perjury and sham performance that was staged here to kill you, to deceive you, to betray you into believing something which was not the truth.

He takes that witness stand, and he testifies, "I don't know anybody in this case except a couple of hotel witnesses, and I saw Davie Betillo once at my house." And they prove that Davie Betillo once had a gambling boat. Of course he did. I don't know how many interests he has. He is a big shot, next only to Luciano. . . . Now, on Luciano, you remember that I went over his life very carefully with him on cross-examination. I asked him if he had any other real or ostensible occupations. . . . Now, that after four weeks of trial in this case, after all the time a man could consume in deciding what kind of lies he was going to tell, what kind of a pretense he was going to make, to escape the mountain of damning testimony, of damning circumstances.

In the first place, it is a bad lie, because on its face nobody would believe it, since if it were true his name wouldn't be magic in the underworld, as it has been proved it is. In the second place, the lie was bad because he had forgotten about some things that might be proved. . . .

On that kind of testimony, on that testimony, and on that alone, you are asked to say that Marjorie Brown, the bath maid at the Waldorf, is a liar. Now, what does Marjorie Brown say? She was cross-examined at length. She says that we laid out a large number of pictures before her and asked her if she knew any of them. Do you think anybody could buy or intimidate the testimony of that girl? You saw her, that nineteen-year-old bath maid. Nobody in God's world could do it, and you know it, and I know it. You can't refute that kind of testimony. . . .

Of course, we cannot prove that Luciano was putting women in houses. Of course, we cannot prove that he was going out sticking men up. He graduated from that. It was back in 1927, when he had the two guns and the shotgun and forty-five rounds of ammunition in his car. That was nine years ago. That was before he got conscience-stricken and began filing federal income tax returns for six years back all at once for $20,000 more or less per year, beginning with fifteen or sixteen, going up to twenty-two in those years, conscience which was so terribly stricken that he filed federal but not state, and never kept a record, not a scrap of paper showing his source of income or his overhead—the man who says he is a bookmaker, the man who says he is a crapshooter! A bookmaker whose name is law in the underworld, and it is proved in this case, and it is used everywhere, and obeyed, with fear.

Those are the facts, the testimony of this case. And then they come in and offer you a defense which is just so rotten that it smelled to high heaven before it was half through.

What a shocking, disgusting display of perjury right here, gentlemen. I have adverted practically none to perjurious criminal past [sic]. I am talking about that act, that sanctimonious, lying, perjurious act on the witness stand, at the end of which, gentlemen, at the end of which, I am sure every one of you had not the slightest doubt there stood before you not a gambler, not a race-track man, but, stripped stark naked, the greatest gangster in America. You know that and I know that.

Gentlemen, we have had enough of that in this country. Isn't it time that the Boss is convicted, instead of the Danny Brookses, and the Spike Greens, and the Nick Montanas, and the Cockeyed Louises, and the bookers and the pimps and the prostitutes and the partners of stolen goods and all the others?

Isn't it nearly time that the Boss who stands behind, with Tommy Bull and Little Davie standing out front, and in front of them Abie, and in front of them Benny Spiller and Jimmy Frederico and Ralph Liguori and Jesse Jacobs and Meyer Berkman and the bookers, be convicted?

Gentlemen, I say to you, let us have no more of this nonsense. When a few witnesses have gone through what these have, when they have submitted to the terror which you know there is in this case, and have testified, then for heaven's sake, in heaven's name, do not turn these men loose.

Now—I say to you in all seriousness that, so far as I am concerned, unless you are willing to convict the Boss, turn them out. Say there cannot be any administration of justice in this country. Say to the world and the public the boss gangsters can go free. It is only front men who are going to be convicted, and announce it to the world. I say, gentlemen, that you know and I know that we have had convictions of tools and front men for years.

You saw what happened in this business. You know when Cockeyed Louis was convicted, somebody else came in. When Nick Montana was convicted, somebody else came in. And Danny Brooks is convicted, and they don't even miss him. And the bookers walk up and plead guilty and, gentlemen, the racket, the rotten vile racket of ruling prostitutes and taking the money from their bodies by guns, which is the effect of this case, will go on, and you can see it is no town to live in.

I say to you, gentlemen, unless you are willing to convict the top men, you might just as well acquit everybody, and let everybody laugh at the bookers for having pleaded guilty.

I submit to you that the proof in this case establishes every element in the case beyond a reasonable doubt. I submit to you that the witnesses on Luciano, directly, with the testimony as to the use of his name by his proved subordinates, his association with these defendants which he denies perjuriously, his intimate daily contact at his place of residence, his own conduct on the witness stand, and the attempted, rotten sham that he tried to put on to get out of it, convict him. Convict him beyond any conceivable doubt, gentlemen, not a reasonable doubt.

And I ask you for a conviction in the name of the People of the state of New York, and in the name of the safety of the People of this city.

It had been a long case, six days a week from nine-thirty in the morning until eight and nine in the evening, and it ended much the same way. My own summation lasted from the beginning of court until six in the evening, and then the judge charged the jury. Not until nine-thirty P.M. did the jury receive the case. It was a Saturday.

Then the long wait started. It was a monster case for these twelve men to go through. They had to examine the evidence as it affected each of the defendants, and it would take them many hours. Everyone on both sides of the case was nervous and exhausted. I never understood how Judge McCook stood the strain of it, kept his temper, and made his rulings so thoughtfully and wisely. I was so worn out I simply went up to the deserted judges' dining room and fell sound asleep.

According to a court reporter, the scene in the courtroom itself offered a sharp contrast. "The whole picture became something out of a weird New York version of *Alice in Wonderland*. The eight defendants on trial with Lucky became hilarious as the jury took the case. They were almost dancing with confidence. Ralph Liguori, the clown of the group, who sacrificed himself on the stand for his boss, even gave Jimmy Frederico, lumbering, giant general manager for Lucky, the 'hot foot.' He set a box of matches on fire at the toe of Frederico's shoe.

"Guards who stood around during the trial, alert against a threatened jail delivery [rescue attempt], immediately pushed into the scene, even while the defendants began mimicking their own attorneys. They were hustled back into the bullpen, where they played pinochle because they were broke, and couldn't play the poker they'd been enjoying up to that time.

"As the jurors went out to dinner . . . Justice McCook had gone to his chambers on the sixth floor. A coffee percolator and complete comfort, such as razors and toilet kits, were awaiting him, since he was determined to remain there until the jury reached a verdict.

"In the corridors of the building, the wives of the vice gang waited through the night. Hundreds of other spectators were shunted out of the building.

"But outside, a block away in Mulberry Park, the breathing place of Little Italy, more than a thousand watchers came and went through the night. In Foley Park, hundreds of others waited, watching the windows of the Court House, darting up to everyone who left the building, to ask for news."

A little after 5:00 A.M. on Sunday I woke up and came to the door just as an attendant was coming to tell me the jury was returning. They had, it was said, agreed on a verdict. Everybody gathered in the courtroom beneath the eyes of Justice McCook.

Court Attendant Leddy: The defendants are all present, your honor.

The Court: Are all the attorneys present? Let us check up on that; let us check up on the attorneys for the defendants, that is the important thing.

The clerk called the roll of the jurors, and all answered present.

Court Clerk McNamara: The foreman will please rise. Gentlemen of the jury, have you agreed upon a verdict?

Foreman Edwin Aderer: We have.

Court Clerk McNamara: How say you, gentlemen of the jury, do you find the defendant Luciano guilty or not guilty on Count No. 1?

Foreman Aderer: Guilty.

As to each of Counts Nos. 2, 3, 4, 5, 6, 7, 11, 12, 13, 14, 15, 16, 23, 24, 25, 26, 27, 28, 29, 31, 32, 36, 37, 38, 39, 40, 41, 42, 49, 50, 51, 52, 53, 54, 55, 56, 57, 58, 59, 60, 61, 62, 63, 64, 65, 66, 67, 68, 69, 70, 74, 75, 76, 77, 78, 79, 80, 81, 82, 83, and 87, the foreman answered in each instance, "Guilty."

Court Clerk McNamara: Those are all the remaining counts of the indictment, your honor.

The Court: Next defendant.

One after the other, Pennochio first, the other defendants were called and were found guilty on all counts, the monotonous drone of the words "Guilty . . . guilty . . ." accompanied now by moans and screams of wives who were waiting outside the courtroom.

As these words "Guilty . . . guilty . . ." were being uttered, my bodyguard, Frank Hnida, noticed a little man at the back of the courtroom straining forward with great intensity, his right hand inside his coat. This was all Hnida needed. Very quietly, he motioned to another detective and they ushered the man out of the room with his arms pinned to his sides. He made no resistance. When they brought out his hand, they found it held a silver crucifix.

Leaving the courtroom was a problem. The families were still on hand and outside the courthouse there must have been five hundred people standing there silently. They had been on the front steps all night long. The police told me we should leave by a back door. I did not think so. If we ever showed fear, how could we ever convince potential witnesses in the future, who had no bodyguards, that they would be kept safe from harm?

The question therefore answered itself, and I walked out quietly through the crowd on the steps, to go home and get my first full night's sleep in a month.

The top Mafia leader in New York and his whole mob had been convicted in a single case, and I felt the majesty of the law had in truth been vindicated.

The next day I issued this statement: "While this is the first felony conviction with which I am familiar of any top-ranking racketeer in any state court, it is in no sense a personal victory. The men who prepared this case through months of grueling hard work, and who presented more than half of the evidence, are responsible for these convictions.

"The verdict is the result of the untiring efforts of Barent Ten Eyck and Jacob J. Rosenblum, chief assistants, and my assistants Sol Gelb, Eunice Carter, Frank S. Hogan, Harry M. Cole, Charles P. Grimes, Stanley H. Fuld, and Charles D. Breitel. Their ability, loyalty, and the heavy sacrifices they made during the five months of day and night work brought about this result.

"I am also deeply grateful to Captain of Detectives Bernard Dowd and the devoted efforts of his staff assigned by Police Commissioner Valentine. I cannot adequately express my gratitude for their devotion and hard work. I also wish to express my admiration and appreciation of the co-operation of David Marcus, Deputy Commissioner of Corrections."

I invited a few members of the press to our apartment at 1148 Fifth Avenue and made an additional point: "This, of course, was not a vice trial. It was a racket prosecution. Control of all organized prostitution in New York was one of the lesser rackets of the defendants.

"It is my understanding that certain of the top-ranking defendants in this case, together with other criminals under Luciano, have gradually absorbed control of the narcotic, loan shark, policy numbers racket, Italian lottery syndicate, and certain industrial rackets."

After a few days, after studying the pre-sentence reports, Justice McCook was ready to pronounce sentence.

Court Clerk McNamara: Charles Luciano to the bar.

The Court: I would like all counsel seated except the counsel for this individual defendant. . . .

Court Clerk McNamara: Charles Luciano, alias Charles Lucania, alias Lucky Luciano, alias Lucky, alias Charles Lane, alias Charles Ross, alias Charles Reid, you have been found guilty of violation of Section 2460 of the Penal Law and all remaining counts of the indictment. What have you to say why judgment should not be pronounced against you according to law?

Defendant Luciano: Your honor, I have nothing to say outside of that—I want to say it again—that I am innocent.

The Court: Has your counsel anything to say?

Mr. Levy: Nothing.

The Court: . . . The evidence upon the trial, and reliable information since received, have convinced the Court that these defendants will be responsible for any injury which the People's witnesses might hereafter, by reason of their testimony, suffer. Let the record show that, should any witness for the People be injured or harassed, the Court will request the parole authorities to retain in prison the defendants against whom such witness testified, for the maximum terms of the sentences now about to be imposed.

I now proceed to sentence. Each defendant sentenced will be credited with the time already served since his arrest in connection with the case.

Lucania, or Luciano: . . . The crimes of which you stand convicted are of placing females in houses of prostitution, receiving money for such placing, and knowingly accepting money from their earnings without consideration. An intelligent, courageous, and discriminating jury have found you guilty of heading a conspiracy or combination to commit these crimes, which operated widely in New

York and extended into neighboring counties. This makes you responsible, in law and morals, for every foul and cruel deed, with accompanying elements of extortion, performed by the band of co-defendants, whose records and characters will shortly be discussed, or some of them. I am not here to reproach you but, since there appears no excuse for your conduct, nor hope for your rehabilitation, to administer adequate punishment.

Judge McCook then sentenced Lucky Luciano to thirty to fifty years' imprisonment. He gave Little Davie Betillo twenty-five to forty years. He gave Tommy the Bull Pennochio, a third offender, twenty-five years, and Jimmy Frederico, also a third offender, twenty-five years. Judge McCook gave Little Abie Wahrman fifteen to thirty years and Ralph the Pimp Liguori seven and a half to fifteen years. Of the four bookers, Jack Eller, who had pleaded guilty after the presentation of the People's case, was sentenced to four to eight years' imprisonment. Two other bookers, Pete Harris and Dumb Al Weiner, who had helped the prosecution from the start, received two to four years' imprisonment. The booker Dave Miller, who had been the first to mention to us Luciano's name, got three to six years.

This, of course, was not the end. Deputy Assistant Stanley H. Fuld, an authority on matters of law, took charge of the appeal. It was a massive undertaking. We jointly wrote the briefs on appeal for the Appellate Division and the Court of Appeals, where the convictions were upheld.

But the Luciano sensations were far from finished.

That summer of 1936, not long after the Luciano conviction and sentencing, I was peacefully sailing about on Long Island Sound. We came into Huntington Harbor on the North Shore to take on board some supplies. There we found a copy of the New York *Mirror* with a screaming headline:

LUCIANO WITNESS CUT UP

The girl claimed to be a Margaret Louise Bell. I had never heard of her, but her story could do us great damage with future witnesses. I went back to New York right away to find out what it was all about.

It turned out she was a prostitute who had not testified in the trial. She had been a witness before the grand jury but we had never used her testimony at the trial because we did not believe her. She claimed that, after the trial, a lawyer had offered her $500 for an affidavit that would say her grand jury testimony was false. She said she took the $500 and skipped away with it. The gang had caught up with her, she cried, and "they did it because I had welched."

There were scratches on her abdomen—not slashes as had been reported—making the initials "C.L." Further investigation showed that the same girl, some time before, had gone to the police in Florida with a flesh wound from a bullet in her arm, claiming that her uncle was responsible. The wound turned out to be self-inflicted. The girl was a fake, probably psychotic. We were glad we had been careful about the witnesses we called.

The unfortunate aspect that lingered was that the average newspaper reader never saw the whole story, which appeared several days later. It was printed on the back pages and, as so often happens, the denial never caught up with the original inaccurate story. But for years people asked me, "What happened to that poor woman who was tortured because she testified against Luciano?"

Nine months after the conviction the defense filed lengthy affidavits by none other than three of our most important witnesses, Nancy Presser, Mildred Balitzer, and Cokey Flo Brown. The defense demanded a new trial. At first this seemed like a stunning blow, but we went to work, hard. Our three former witnesses were now swearing that all their trial testimony had been false, and they were charging us with alternated coddling and threats. They swore we had kept them under the influence of liquor and rehearsed their testimony of lies. They swore that Luciano had been telling the truth all the time, and they had never even met him.

I issued an immediate statement:

"Over the past nine months, witnesses have complained to my office of efforts to intimidate them by threats of murder into giving false affidavits of recantation, and also making false charges against lawyers of my staff. They have also reported large offers of bribes and regular supplies of narcotics. Among these witnesses were Nancy Presser, Mildred Balitzer and Cokey Flo Brown, whose affidavits apparently have been procured by agents of this criminal. My office has 128 affidavits from witnesses showing that more than $100,000 has been offered for the corruption of witnesses. These will, of course, be presented to the Court."

In this context, it was fortunate that Judge McCook, on his own initiative, had made it his own business after the trial to interview every witness for the People privately, and under oath, and on the record. This was a large undertaking, but this responsible jurist personally went through the basic testimony of every one of the witnesses and confirmed their veracity. To each of the girls McCook pledged to do all he could to place them in whatever social or religious organization they seemed most ready to work with. The girls indicated they wanted to make a new start in life, although in many cases it was clear this would not last long.

Our assistants examined the new affidavits of Nancy Presser, Mildred Balitzer, and Cokey Flo Brown, and found that the statements were filled with perjury. The girls said they were completely off narcotics. But our investigators found they were all back on narcotics at the time they signed the affidavits. In fact, they were in private hospitals at the time they signed, and agents of Luciano had them there. We learned that Mildred Balitzer had made one statement merely withdrawing some minor points and adding further details about her acquaintance with Luciano. But Luciano's agents had gone back to her and procured a stronger recantation.

Cokey Flo was now saying that she had made up her trial testimony on the basis of things Jimmy Frederico had told her. But we were able to produce Barent Ten Eyck's longhand notes, page after page of them of the interview he had held with Cokey Flo over a period of many hours. These notes coincided with the testimony she had given at the trial.

Finally, all three of the girls had been in touch with our office since the trial. They had written us letters about how they were getting on, telling us what they were doing, and reiterating that they had told the truth in their testimony. They also had written to us about their fear that the mob would eventually catch up with them.

By the time our investigation was finished we were able to file 382 pages of affidavits, all from respectable witnesses, in defense of our position. We also had documentary evidence that the girls' recantation was possibly perjurious. After full argument before the Court, the motion for a new trial was denied. These motions were consolidated with the defendants' main appeal against their conviction. But the conviction was affirmed by a unanimous Appellate Division and by the Court of Appeals.

The moment the courts refused to accept the recantations, the value of Nancy Presser, Mildred Balitzer, and Cokey Flo Brown dropped to zero for Lucky Luciano and his men. The girls were told they would receive $50 a week for another year, but they never even got the first check.

Deputy Assistant Frank Hogan, the "Father Hogan" who had helped the girls through their rough days in the House of Detention, kept in touch with the three girls for a while longer. Two of them fell back to narcotics and disappeared. One of them settled down to a decent living and, after a year, got married.

Ten years after the conviction of Luciano, I was Governor of New York when the Mafia leader applied for a commutation of his sentence. This was a long and fascinating story and I shall detail it at the appropriate chronological moment in the second volume of these memoirs. Briefly it appeared that, early in 1942, Captain Roscoe C. McFall of the United States Navy, the officer in charge of intelligence in New York Harbor, had asked to have Luciano moved from Dannemora down to Sing Sing where the Navy could have easy access to him. The Navy feared that the harbor was in peril from enemy agents, and thought that the underworld would be willing to help in the war against the Nazis. At any rate, there was no question that Luciano still had powerful influence on the waterfront. Governor Lehman, who was still in office, granted the Navy's request, and for three years intelligence agents regularly visited Luciano in prison.

The Navy sought Luciano's assistance, so went the story, in the preparation for the Allied landings in Sicily in 1943. Once again, it was reported, Luciano co-operated.

After the war was over Luciano's counsel made a strong plea to the Parole Board for his release on the basis of the help he had given the country. The Parole Board reviewed the record and recommended commutation to me as Governor. It was also noted that, in the Court of Appeals, one of the judges had indicated that he thought the sentence was excessive. Finally, it had been established that Luciano was in fact a native of Italy, and a warrant for his deportation was in hand. Under all of these circumstances, it appeared to me that I should accept the Parole Board's recommendation, and I granted the commutation.

Since the commutation was a reduction of sentence, and not a pardon, Luciano was deported to Italy and exiled from the United States, for the rest of his life.

At the time, there was little public comment about the commutation, but whispers subsequently reached me. It was being said that there might have been something crooked about my action. This was infuriating, but I could think of no immediate way to answer ill-founded gossip. I decided that we should find out everything we could about the details of Luciano's help to the Navy, however, and I asked William B. Herlands, then the Commissioner of Investigations, to undertake such a study.

This turned out to be a longer job than we had thought it would be. Before he was through, Herlands had taken the sworn testimony of Captain McFall, three other Navy captains, five commanders, two lieutenants, and one ensign of the Navy, one colonel of the Marine Corps, and one Army colonel. The testimony and documents ran to a total of 2,883 pages, and the conclusions were that Luciano had indeed rendered all the assistance of which he was capable, and that it had been of real value to the war effort.

Since the Navy allowed the officers to testify only with the expressed wish that the report not be made public, I never released it. A few years afterward, Senator Estes Kefauver's investigation into organized crime asked for a copy and they received one.

It is anticipated that the Herland report will be summarized in volume II of these memoirs.

One postscript came for me in 1957, when Mrs. Dewey and I were spending a few days in Rome. A sleazy-looking little character, whom I did not recognize, came up to me and put out his hand. He said, "Governor, don't you recognize me? I am Ralph." It was indeed Ralph Liguori, Ralph the pimp, who had served out his sentence and gone to Italy.

Liguori explained he had read that I was in town, and he said, "I had to come and find you. Please do something to help the Boss. He will do anything. He will go back to jail if necessary, if you will only let him back into the United States."

I told Liguori I was sorry, that this was a matter of law, not of grace, and there was nothing I could do.

Lucky Luciano died in exile a few years later.

CHAPTER XIII

Dutch Schultz—and
the Restaurant Racket

It always seemed to me that the press and the underworld often underestimated the imagination and creative abilities of the famous racketeer Dutch Schultz. Born Arthur Flegenheimer in the Bronx, he grew up to be such a savage character that he was named "Dutch Schultz" after a well-known bully of that name who had been a member of the infamous Frog Hollow gang. His personal brutality and his reputation as a mad dog killer concealed, in my opinion, what must have been a brilliantly inventive mind.

Dutch Schultz was the son of a saloonkeeper and a devout, dedicated woman who adored him and grieved to the end that her son had chosen a life of crime. At the age of seventeen he was already serving fifteen months for burglary. As he grew through his twenties Schultz put together his own gang and built up a bootlegging empire with his guns and his fists. Well before the demise of Prohibition he moved toward new and richer sources of income while other bootleggers fell by the wayside or were killed off by other mobsters. It will be recalled how we had caught and convicted Waxey Gordon, but that Dutch Schultz remained at large.

On November 28, 1934, while I was in private practice, Schultz had given himself up in Albany, New York, and pleaded not guilty to federal charges of income tax evasion. On December 21, even though New York City Police Commissioner Valentine had charged that Schultz paid for police protection, and got it, Schultz was released on $75,000 bail.

On April 15, 1935, Schultz went on trial in Syracuse, New York, on charges of cheating the government out of $92,103.34 in taxes on a total income of $481,637.35 allegedly derived from illegal enterprises in the years 1929–31. Twelve days later the jury proved unable to agree and was discharged, with a retrial set for May 14. Amid reports of jury tampering, the retrial was reset for July 23 and was moved from Syracuse to, of all places, a town named Malone on the Canadian border.

On August 1, 1935, Dutch Schultz was acquitted by the jury in Malone. The jury was given this send-off by Judge Frederick H. Bryant: "Before I discharge you . . . I will have to say that your verdict is such that it shakes the confidence of law-abiding people in integrity and truth. It will be apparent to all who have followed the evidence in this case that you have reached a verdict based not on the evidence but on some other reason. You will go home with the satisfaction, if it is a satisfaction, that you have rendered a blow against law enforcement and given aid and encouragement to the people who would flout the law. In all probability, they will commend you. I cannot."

Malone residents said they felt that Schultz was a victim of "government persecution." Their attitude seemed to be, "Schultz isn't our problem. If New York thinks he's so dangerous, why don't they get rid of him down there?" Some Malone citizens noted that Schultz had been spending money all around town, sending gifts to hospitalized children, entertaining easily and expansively. One said flatly that Schultz was "a swell guy."

When word of this incredible verdict reached New York City, Mayor LaGuardia said, "He won't be a resident of New York City. There is no place for him here." Dutch Schultz told the press, "Tell LaGuardia I will be home tomorrow." And he was. Schultz put it another way to another interviewer: "So there isn't room for me in New York? Well, I'm going there." And he did.

This brought Dutch Schultz very much within my province as Special Prosecutor, even though it seemed that all the law enforcement authorities were chasing him in something like a mass pursuit. I let it be known that I regarded it as a matter of primary importance to get Dutch Schultz—also that, in view of the failure of the federal income tax prosecution, I had decided to go after Schultz in connection with his domination of the numbers racket.

The numbers racket was worth anything from $20 to $50 million, depending on whom you listened to, and Schultz was using the proceeds to infiltrate legitimate industries and pay off law enforcement people. Even the 1,000 to 1 odds against the individual numbers players did not satisfy Dutch Schultz. He hired a mathematical wizard named Otto "Abadaba" Berman to rig the final odds so that it would bring out the most lightly played numbers. And at Dutch Schultz's right hand sat "the boy mouthpiece," the lawyer Dixie Davis who had succeeded so well in keeping his leader out of jail.

On October 10, 1935, the federal authorities moved in ahead of us. A federal grand jury in New York accused Schultz on eleven counts of failing to file income tax returns for 1929, 1930, and 1931, a misdemeanor. There was no double jeopardy because the charges that had been dismissed at Malone were for willful evasion of income tax laws, which was a felony. Since Malone, Schultz had been arrested in Perth Amboy, New Jersey, and had been released on bail, re-arrested, and re-released. Schultz was in Newark in October awaiting hearings before the federal courts in removal proceedings designed to bring him back to New York City.

Around this time my wife Frances began getting ugly telephone calls at home which were by no means crackpot. Finally one call, which Frances took, instructed her to come down to the morgue and identify my body. She was pregnant at the time and that blew it. We got an unlisted telephone number which we have kept ever since, by necessity. This was just in time because, on October 18, 1935, our second son was born. John was a lusty boy, and we were happy indeed.

My only real worry was that things growing out of our investigation were getting pretty tense, all of which indicated that we were beginning to strike some soft spots. My detectives began bringing underworld gossip that there was a $25,000 price on my head for anybody who would assassinate me. The director of the FBI, J. Edgar Hoover, wrote me a letter warning me about it. There was nothing to do but accept a bodyguard, who drove the car I used, and rely on our faith that ordinary hoodlums would be scared off by the detective with me, and that the top gangsters would be too smart. It almost did not work that way.

In his book, *Murder Inc.*, a subsequent assistant district attorney, Burt Turkus, said that Dutch Schultz was beginning to spread the word that I had to go. Schultz said his lawyer had told him that I would be his Nemesis, and Schultz believed it. After all, Schultz felt, I had been responsible, in the United States Attorney's office, two years before, for the original federal charges. And now I was looking into the numbers racket in a systematic manner.

All this had become a fixation with the paranoid racket leader, according to Turkus, and the pressures built up within the underworld to the point that Lucky Luciano, Lepke, and some of the others had held a meeting on the subject with Schultz. These leaders were supposed to have told Schultz they believed it was more dangerous to have me killed than to leave me alone. At least, they concluded, even if they lost their business in New York County, they would be able to maintain it everywhere else in the country outside New York County. This was better, the leaders argued, than assassinating the Special Prosecutor, getting the whole country up in arms, and risking a nation-wide crusade against organized crime.

Schultz said it was well to be prepared anyway, and, according to Turkus, he was even ready to have the job done on his own. Turkus gave an elaborate description of how I was watched every morning as I came out of the house, and the setup was complete for an assassination.* I had no idea whether these stories were true. They might have been just underworld gossip.

---

* In *Murder Inc.*, Turkus and Feder, Farrar Straus & Young, 1951, the chapter entitled, "The Almost-Assassination of Thomas E. Dewey," reads in part:

"In those days, Dewey never moved without his two bodyguards. The caser would have to be especially adroit to avoid attaching suspicion to himself. Someone got the idea for the perfect subterfuge. A child was to be borrowed from a friend to accompany the caser. What could be less sinister than a devoted father romping with his offspring.

"For four straight mornings, this 'proud parent' with his decoy child pedalling a velocipede, took up an innocent stand in front of Dewey's apartment building. Each morning, they were already there when the prosecutor and his guards emerged. It must have been a fine show of parental devotion to Dewey and his companions—this man willing to rise early enough to spend a bit of time with his heir before heading off for the daily toil.

"Given four days of uninterrupted observation, the 'father' noted that Dewey's daily routine followed a pattern. The prosecutor and his guards left the apartment at practically the same minute every day. They headed for the same drugstore a couple of blocks away. There the guards took up a stand outside the door

Dutch Schultz, whatever his final intentions, told at least one associate that the edict of Luciano and Lepke that I was to be spared did not sit well with him. He boasted that he would do the job by himself, and then he said he would do it within the next forty-eight hours. Luciano and Lepke were shocked at the assassination plan and at the defiance of their wishes that it not be put into effect. Lepke was reported to have said that Schultz was disordered enough, mentally speaking, to do it. In any event, there was no question that Luciano and Lepke from their different perspectives now agreed that Dutch Schultz was out of control. The news got around to the other bosses of crime that they could not risk this crazy man any longer.

After discussion as to who should have charge of the job, the leaders of the syndicate arranged to have Schultz assassinated at once. They proceeded to have him shot in a restaurant in Newark on October 23, just two days before he was supposed to have had me shot.

---

while Dewey went inside. He remained for several minutes, then reappeared, and the trio would be off.

"The pharmacist could hardly be suspicious of the proud parent and his child who dropped in on two different mornings just after Mr. Dewey left. The man was very disarming, seemed interested, mostly, in seeing that the tot did not ride his tricycle into a floor display of beauty soap. It was no trouble for the man to learn that the prosecutor's regular stop in the drugstore was to make the first phone call to his office each day. Later, when someone mentioned it, Dewey recalled that morning call.

"'I did not want to disturb Mrs. Dewey by using the phone in our room at the apartment so early,' he explained. Besides, it was very likely that his home phone was tapped, once his probe began.

"By the fourth morning, the caser felt he had established that Dewey's actions were regular habit. The prosecutor could be counted on to do the same thing every day. Meanwhile, the other necessary details were being handled with the same efficiency. The report of the caser showed exactly how it would be done. On the day selected, the gunman would get to the drugstore a few minutes before the regular time for Dewey's arrival. He would be inside, and waiting, and the bodyguards who always remained outside would not know there was a stranger even in the neighborhood. Keeping his back to Dewey, the triggerman would be 'buying' a tube of toothpaste or a box of cornplasters, or something, until the prosecutor went to the phone booth, as usual.

"'Dewey will be a sitting duck in there,' it was pointed out. Out would come the gun, equipped with silencer. That was a must. The flat crack of the silencer would never carry enough to be audible to the guards through the closed door of the store, above the street noises.

"The assassin would turn and blast Dewey, cornered there in the booth. The druggist would be drilled where he stood, behind the counter. There would be no outcry, no sound of gunfire, no alarm—and no identification later. Having completed the contract, the killer would ease out. The guards, having heard nothing, would barely look his way as he ambled past. Casually, he would turn the corner to the waiting getaway car, which he would abandon with the untraceable guns wherever convenient."

Turkus gave Lepke the credit for saving my life. *The Valachi Papers* gave the credit to Luciano. As I said, I have no idea whether these stories were true, or whether they might have been just underworld gossip.

But there was no question what happened to Dutch Schultz—and from the screaming headlines, the sensational news accounts, this was one of the most horrifying murders of the 1930s.

The hit man, said to be Charlie "the Bug" Workman, strolled into the Palace Chophouse in Newark, around the corner from the Robert Treat Hotel where Dutch Schultz was living. The hit man knew he would find the Dutchman there. There was a bar in the front room and a men's room off to one side at the end of it. Beyond, there was a back room where Schultz and his lieutenants were holding their meetings and going over their accounts while they fought off the federal indictments. The hit man walked down the length of the bar and turned into the men's room. He apparently wanted to make sure he could not be taken from the flank while he attacked the men in the back room.

The hit man was surprised to find somebody in the men's room. He pulled out his pistol and fired. The man dropped without a sound. Outside, there was a mad scramble as patrons got out of the bar. The bartender went down behind the long bar and took cover. The hit man ran out toward the back room. The three men there opened fire on him. The hit man fired back and shot all of them. He was not touched himself. He kicked over the prostrate bodies and did not find Dutch Schultz among them. Then he realized that Dutch Schultz had been the one in the men's room. He ran out into the night.

Somehow Schultz staggered out of the men's room and had the bartender call for an ambulance. He was taken to Newark City Hospital in critical condition. His three lieutenants also were taken to the hospital. There, one by one, they died. First to go was Abadaba Berman, the human computer, followed by Abraham "Misfit" Landau, one of the Dutchman's gunmen and "Lulu" Rosenkrantz, the Dutchman's chauffeur and bodyguard.

Throughout October 26, Schultz lingered on. His mother and sister were at the hospital, and so was his wife. The Rev. Cornelius J. McInerney, of Livingston, New Jersey, baptized Schultz and administered the sacrament of extreme unction. Detectives of all jurisdictions hung close to Schultz along with the doctors and nurses, but he incriminated nobody by name.

All day the newspapers told astonishing stories of the Dutchman's life and near death. They focused on one known fact of the shoot-out at the Palace Chophouse. The adding machine on the table in the back room carried a long list of figures, among them entries of $313,711.99 and $236,295.95.

Then, in the evening, according to a copyrighted story by George Carroll in the New York *Journal American*, Schultz spoke these last words:

"George, don't make no bull moves. What have you done with him? Oh mama, mama, mama. Oh stop it. Oh, Oh, Oh. Sure, sure, mama. Now listen, Phil is fun. Ah, please, papa. What happened to the sixteen? Oh, oh. He done it. Please.

"John, please, oh, did you buy the hotel? You promised a million— sure. Get out. I wish I knew.

"Please make it quick, fast and furious, please, fast and furious. Please help me get out. I am getting my wind back, thank God, please, please, oh please. You will have to please tell him. You got no case. . . .

"Oh, oh dog biscuits and when he is happy he doesn't get snappy—please, please to do this. Then, Henry, Henry, Frankie, you didn't meet him, you didn't even meet me. The glove will fit what I say, oh, kayiyi, kayiyi.

"Sure, who cares when you are through? How do you know this? How do you know this? Well, then, oh, Cocoa, know, he thinks he is a grandpa again, he is jumping around. No hobo and pobo, I think he means the same thing.

"Q. (by Sergeant Conlon) Who shot you?

"A. The Boss himself.

"Q. What did he shoot you for?

"A. I showed him Boss. Did you hear him meet me? An appointment. Appeal stuck. All right, mother.

"Q. Was it the Boss shot you?

"A. Who shot me? No one.

"Q. The big fellow gave it to you?

"A. Yes, he gave it to me.

"Q. Do you know who this big fellow was?

"A. No."

Dutch Schultz's wife approached his bedside and said, "This is Frances." Schultz wandered on:

"Then pull me out. I am half crazy. They won't let me get up. They dyed my shoes. Open those shoes. Give me something, I am so sick. Give me some water, the only thing that I want. Open this up and break it so I can touch you. Dannie, please get me in the car.

"Please help me up, Henny, Max. Come over here. French-Canadian bean soup. I want to pay. Let them leave me alone."

Then he died.

Dutch Schultz's empire would surely pass into other and, perhaps, even stronger hands. So we pressed our investigation into the numbers racket and into the politicians who were protecting it. We also knew that, even while most of our resources were now concentrated on the Luciano case, we were making headway in our investigation of Dutch Schultz's racket in the restaurant and cafeteria business. This very large racket was said to involve a combination between two restaurant and cafeteria workers' unions and a restaurant owners' and managers' association. If this operation could be proven to exist, we would be well on the way to exposing a classic industrial abuse.

Not long before, large, gilded plaques had appeared in the windows and plate-glass door fronts of restaurants and cafeterias all over Manhattan. They proclaimed the establishments to be members of the Metropolitan Restaurant and Cafeteria Association, which looked like a sort of honorary society. The plaque showed the American eagle spreading its wings at the top, a montage of the New York skyscrapers below, and at the bottom a motto said, "United We Stand."

The racket seemed to be no secret. Articles had appeared in some labor and other publications flatly calling the association an extortionist racket. Protests had been made at international union conventions but nothing had been done.

At one point a few disaffected waiters complained that they were being betrayed by their union leaders and they took their stories to the office of District Attorney Dodge. This time Dodge's office did bring in an indictment against some of the front men in the restaurant racket, but no real investigation was conducted, no real evidence was collected. After a trial lasting just three days, all the defendants were acquitted. Then the waiters who had complained were fired. The restaurant mob appeared to have some kind of immunity from legal processes.

As soon as I had mulled over all this information, I assigned Chief Assistant William B. Herlands to take command of a major investigation. I assigned to him Milton Schilback and, part time, Edward McLean and Charles D. Breitel.

At an early stage we developed information about a man named Abraham Finkel, who had a small cafeteria where he served the food himself. We brought Finkel in, and he denied any knowledge of a racket, but when we examined his books we found unexplained disbursements out of all proportion to his income.

Finkel then invented one story after another to explain these discrepancies and, after five sessions before the grand jury, his obvious evasions brought him a sentence for contempt of court. His conviction was appealed to the Appellate Division and then to the Court of Appeals at an expenditure of more money for counsel fees than his whole cafeteria was worth. Obviously there was a lot of money committed to Finkel's defense, and it was clear we had located a whopping racket. But it would be almost a year after his original questioning that his sentence was affirmed on appeal. Then he came to our office in secret and told us the truth about a shakedown.

Finkel told us he had been forced to pay $250 initiation fees to join the association and an additional $30 per year in dues. Then he was forced to pay an additional $1,500 "association dues" so that he would be able to avert a threatened strike.

Every witness we caught up with in the restaurant investigation was almost a lawsuit in himself. We had to assure every witness that we would never use his testimony until there was such an overwhelming number of witnesses that they would all be safe. Yet none told their story until we forced them right up against the wall.

Herlands and his assistants learned that, early in 1932, Dutch Schultz had conceived this restaurant racket. One of his lieutenants was a smooth character named Jules Martin, who opened a cheap little restaurant as a front and entering wedge into the industry. Two of the waiters in Martin's little dirty spoon were named Retek and Baum. Together with a close friend named Paul Coulcher, another waiter, they schemed under Martin's direction to take over their own Local 16 of the Hotel and Restaurant Employees International Alliance, the waiters' union, which covered the district of Manhattan north of Fourteenth Street.

With the tough support of the Dutch Schultz mob, Coulcher ran in the next union election for secretary-treasurer, the salaried office with the real power in the local. Baum ran for president and Retek ran for delegate. They stuffed the ballot boxes so well that they received thirty-eight more votes than the total number of members of the local. This was too clumsy, and the local held another election. This time, Coulcher, Baum, and Retek were elected by a handsome majority, allowing a few negative votes to make things look more acceptable.

The next outfit to be taken over was Local 302 of the waiters' union, and this time Jules Martin and another Schultz handy man named Sam Krantz handled things another way. The properly elected leaders of this local, Max Pincus, John J. Williams, and Irving Epstein, simply joined the mob.

Only one step remained, and this was to create the employers' association to which the restaurant and cafeteria owners would be compelled to pay tribute. It was Martin who now formed the association. He installed a former silk salesman, Philip Grossel, in charge, aided by two lawyers named Harry Vogelstein and Abraham Cohen. Grossel actually ran the association, and the lawyers saw to it that every new member signed a certificate that he was joining of his own free will, without any coercion of any kind. Martin personally called on a few restaurants, telling them to join the association or else. These initial calls were so successful that Martin retired to the background, leaving Sam Krantz and another Schultz mobster, Louis Beitcher, in charge.

This industrial racket had thus, with incredible speed, assumed its classic form in which the boss, Dutch Schultz, was never seen by anybody except Jules Martin, and Martin was far enough in the background not to be connected to the unpleasant run of the work.

Of course, many restaurant and cafeteria owners resisted the pressure. The average scale of pay for a waiter in those Depression days was $6.00 per week, and his tips might have run up his total earnings to $35 or $40 per week. The owners were told that union would demand a doubling of these wages, but this would not happen once they had paid tribute and joined the association. They were told they would have to pay, or else the waiters would walk out at mealtimes. Or there might be picket lines. Or there might even be stink bombs.

TWENTY AGAINST THE UNDERWORLD   281

Nothing could do more damage to a restaurant business, without structural breakage, than a stink bomb. Nothing was easier to use. One of the Schultz mob could enter the restaurant, sit down at a table, put the bomb on the floor, step on the trigger mechanism, and walk out. Or he could toss the stink bomb from the doorway among the customers.

The stink bombs consisted of valerian or butyric acid, and they gave off an extremely offensive odor which got into the carpets, draperies, the wood of the tables, even into concrete floors and plumbing fixtures. They ruined almost everything in a restaurant, and places had to be closed for months.

For example, Hyman Gross had invested $100,000 in his new Girard Cafeteria, and he was not about to pay tribute to the Schultz mob. So, one of them climbed up onto the roof and dropped a stink bomb down the chimney into the kitchen. Hyman Gross lost his cafeteria and his entire $100,000 investment. Others also learned this hard way.

Herlands and his assistants found out that the initiation fees for the more substantial places in New York ranged from $5,000 to $25,000 and the annual dues were heavy. Almost a million dollars was being poured into the racket, and the totals were rising rapidly. The racket was a huge success. Such was the climate of the times that Coulcher, in his capacity as secretary-treasurer of Local 16, even became a big man in labor. He made speeches at NRA meetings in Washington and was appointed a member of the NRA board. He went to Albany to advocate legislation before various committees of the state legislature, and public dinners were tendered in his honor.

Meanwhile none of the violence was ever recorded in the police statistics, and nobody dared complain.

Then, suddenly, Jules Martin was murdered. There had been a matter of $30,000 which had not been turned over to Dutch Schultz. There was talk within the mob that Martin had been chiseling on his boss and Dutch Schultz was demanding payment of the money.

Herlands found out that, early in 1935, Dixie Davis had made a phone call to Jules Martin. It was on a Friday night. The following morning a young man bought with a single $100 bill five chair car tickets on the train to Albany. On board were Davis, Martin, Bo Weinberg, and two others. They went to Albany, where they were joined by Dutch Schultz himself. Davis took the train back to New

York, where he arrived on Saturday evening. All the others journeyed on.

At about 1:00 A.M. a telephone call was placed from Albany to Dixie Davis in New York. At the same time, Jules Martin's stabbed and mutilated body was deposited in a ditch, in the snow outside his home at Troy, New York. His body also contained one bullet wound. The bullet had been fired by Dutch Schultz.

But the restaurant racket now had so much momentum that it survived the death of its organizer, Martin, and it also survived the death in Newark of its creator, Dutch Schultz.

Herlands followed up some clues in the murder of Jules Martin and we had our first real bonanza. He examined the papers that had been found in Martin's office at 1819 Broadway, found letterheads of the Metropolitan Restaurant and Cafeteria Association and some bills for the manufacture of the gold plaques from a plant in Elkhart, Indiana. There were some photographs of restaurant owners smiling as they signed their non-coercive contracts. There was also a telephone message, "Call Jimmy Hines."

Taking Sergeant Grafenecker and other detectives with him, Herlands traveled west to Elkhart, Indiana, to see the plaque manufacturing operation for himself. In Elkhart, Herlands learned that the factory belonged to Martin himself, who had used it, in an almost unbelievable sideline, to assemble automobiles out of secondhand parts of old ones. And he had sold at least some of these to union locals under mob control.

Herlands found witnesses who had seen Coulcher and Retek in the town. Coulcher and Retek had spent the night with Martin, visited the plant, and advised changes in the drawings for the plaque design. This was a major breakthrough—we had tied the association, the union leaders, and the racketeer Jules Martin tightly together.

This, of course, did not solve the murder of Jules Martin. It took us more than three years before we learned that Schultz had shot his lieutenant with his own hand.

All the techniques we had developed to encourage witnesses to co-operate were now brought into play. Goody Goodrich's accountants were swamped with work as they searched the books of restaurants and cafeterias for clues to the concealed payments they had made to the mob. Sometimes the book entries were amusing—the payments had been made for "Hold Up," or "Labor Trouble," or "Professional

Services." One poor man was so hard pressed to explain large, disguised payments that he invented a mistress. The man was happily married, but, rather than face the vengeance of the mob, he tried to persuade us he had a mistress for whom he provided an expensive apartment, mink coats, and diamonds. When he finally "broke," the man confessed this was all sheer invention. Another of our potential witnesses explained an expense item of $4,000 as "Expenses" incurred at the birth of his child.

However sure we were of our ground, we could not get convictions, or even impede the racket without testimony, and we had a desperately frightened group of potential witnesses. Breitel recalled his problems as he investigated a shakedown of the famous Lindy's Restaurant on Broadway. The Lindy's lawyer had been in the office and talked frankly to Herlands. But when this man came to the grand jury the next morning to tell it under oath, he denied that he had told Herlands anything of the kind. So he was turned over to Breitel.

Breitel recalled: "I knew nothing about investigating, you realize, when I went into the Special Prosecutor's office. Some of the chaps who had been in the United States Attorney's office knew a little bit, but we had a lot to learn, and I developed my own strategy.

"I didn't call the lawyer in at all. He was the last man I wanted to talk to, and I never did call him in. When he went before the grand jury he claimed that he had been taking sleeping pills the night before he talked to Herlands and was all confused.

"Where did he get the sleeping pills? Well, he had testified that he had got them from a drugstore through a Dr. S. Surfine.

"I decided that the first man I would work on was the druggist, on the theory that he was the humblest man in this drama, with a lot of risk if he had done anything wrong. Of course we did not believe the sleeping pill story, so first of all I had to find out whether the lawyer took sleeping pills.

"The druggist lied. He said, yes, he had sold sleeping pills to the lawyer. He said he had received a telephone call, but no prescription. He had no prescription on file, so he could not justify the sale under the law. He said Dr. Surfine had said it was all right to give him the sleeping pills, and they were in a hurry because the son of the lawyer needed them. He remembered all this because he had made an entry in the books and charged the pills.

"Then we got the book in, and it showed a patent alteration as to the charge. I advised him quietly and in the most friendly way that this was bad business. He had altered the books and violated the pharmacy law. I insisted on the truth.

"It took three sessions with him before he finally broke down and said he had delivered the sleeping pills on a date long before the one shown on the book, and that the pills were in fact for the son. He finally explained that the lawyer had called him up and told him, 'Look, I am in a kind of difficulty. Don't lie about anything. All I am asking you to do is just move the date.'

"Dr. Surfine was next. He was a smooth fellow who was giving me wrong dates too. Of course we now had the right dates. The next important question was how many tablets had been prescribed for the son, and the doctor tried to cover this one. He admitted he had never backed up his order with a written prescription, and finally, after two more sessions, he cracked and admitted there were not enough tablets in the prescription for any to be left over for the lawyer who claimed he had been taking sleeping tablets the night before he talked to Herlands.

"At this point I decided to try a little different tack. I called in the lawyer's secretary, who was one of those real loyal secretaries. I had my assistant in, and we asked her about the office diary, and all about the data regarding bills sent out for services, and the way records of them were kept. 'There weren't any such records,' she said. So I asked her how they could possibly know how to do their billing. She replied, 'You just go through the files.'

"Getting nothing more out of her, I proceeded to subpoena every employee in the office. Many of them we knew wouldn't have any knowledge of this, but we wanted to let the lawyer know we were going to get the truth if it was the last thing we did. The reason we were pursuing this angle was that we assumed that his fee was probably heavily inflated to include the amount of the money he paid to the mob.

"Finally the lawyer's secretary did come up with a book which purported to show the way they kept track of legal fees. It was full of erasures. You could almost see them under a magnifying glass. The police laboratory then put the book under ultraviolet ray, and it showed the original entries.

"By this time the lawyer must have realized we were getting closer and closer to a first-class perjury case against him. Then I thought of a

short cut. The son of the lawyer, for whom the pills had been prescribed, was a boy of sixteen, at Columbia College, and I issued a
subpoena for him. I couldn't imagine a father telling his sixteen-year-
old son to go in and lie.

"It worked. The boy came to the office with his father. I made the
father stay outside and questioned the boy. He told me the truth about
the number of tablets and the number he had taken. There were none
left.

"His father's story was exploded. That afternoon I got a telephone
call from the lawyer. 'Mr. Breitel, can I come in?' I replied, 'Certainly,
are you ready?' He answered, 'I'm ready.'

"He came in and told me the facts just as he had orginally told
them to Bill Herlands, but this time it went on the record under oath
in the grand jury. He had arranged the deal through a man named
Brook, who had negotiated with Jules Martin for the labor contract.
A large part of the lawyer's fee was passed on to Brook for Martin.

"The next thing was to get Brook in. He was a much rougher
character. He was a real fixer. He lied at the first two sessions, but
with all the corroboration we already had, he broke before long. I was
pretty pleased with this result, and I went in and reported to Herlands
that we had the story and the corroboration.

"Then I got a shocker. What Herlands had not told me was that
they already had the story from Lindy himself. That is how secretly
we operated. I thought I was breaking the original story. I wasn't. I
was building up the corroboration of Lindy's story without knowing
what he had said, and it all jibed."

Throughout this investigation we had the fine word of Benjamin
Gottesman, one of the bravest men I met in my life, testifying to the
terror of the racket. Benny was a thin, middle-aged family man who
peered at the world through thick glasses. Life to Benny had meant
hard work, his wife, three children, a movie now and then, and his
labor union. Benny Gottesman was a waiter. And the job of improving
the lot of his fellow workers in Local 1 of the waiters' union was one of
his principal objects in life.

When the Dutch Schultz mob seized control of Local 302 and
Local 16 of the union, they attempted to break Benny's Local 1. One
day in January 1933, Julie Martin himself, along with three gorillas,
came to see Benny and lay down the law. Benny felt a gun stuck up

against his ribs and he heard the order to get out of that part of town
or else. Martin said the territory belonged to the mob, but Benny protested. Then Martin said, "Your executive board and the two thousand
members of your union don't mean anything to Dutch Schultz. We'll
send our men down with machine guns and take over your whole union if you don't play ball."

Benny Gottesman had risen to the leadership of Local 1, with
jurisdiction covering all of Manhattan south of Fourteenth Street, and
he did not give easily. For a whole year the mob kept after him. They
threatened him, tried to bribe him, warned him that soon he would
not have a union any more. Benny said, "I've been married twenty-two
years. Today you take my union away from me. Tomorrow you tell me
to divorce my wife. Go ahead, do what you want to, but I won't take
your orders."

Benny turned out to be too tough for the mob to crack easily. They
put picket lines on restaurants which had contracts with Local 1, and
they tried to frame Benny with a bag of marked bills. But Benny went
early on to the District Attorney's office. He got in to see District Attorney Crain in person. He told an Assistant District Attorney his
whole story on two separate occasions. The Tammany officials did
nothing to help, but Benny was too senior to harass any more. In the
following year, Benny went to see newly elected District Attorney
Dodge. He went to Dodge three times and told him the whole story of
the racket we were now unraveling. Dodge did nothing.

In time Gottesman came in to see us—in fact he was one of the first
to respond to my radio appeal for help—and he told us the whole story.
He helped us all through the investigation, and he agreed to be a witness at the trial.

And so it went on, for fourteen months, while we built up a case
as massive as the restaurant racket itself. Local 302 of the waiters'
union passed resolutions demanding that I cease my "vicious attacks
on the unions." The Communist Party's *Daily Worker*, beneath large
headlines, charged me with conducting "an anti-union drive behind a
racketeering charge." The Electrical Workers' Union held a mass
meeting, at which my name was booed.

Finally, on January 18, 1937, the restaurant racket trial began in
Supreme Court under Justice McCook. We were indicting ten defendants. We were charging two lawyers, six labor leaders, and two
gangsters with conspiracy, forty-one counts of extortion, and seven

counts of attempted extortion. We also named four co-conspirators, who were dead, among them Dutch Schultz and Jules Martin.

Bill Herlands and his staff had developed this case with very little help from me, and I put him in complete charge of the trial. Louis Beitcher, who had been a fugitive, was captured just before the trial started, and he promptly pleaded guilty. Max Pincus jumped out of a fifth-floor window and was killed. Sam Krantz was in hiding. Herlands then brought on forty witnesses, restaurant and cafeteria owners, who told the story day after day of the extortion they had been forced to undergo.

There was considerable public interest in a question we asked every potential juror in the empanelment procedure. We asked if they knew James J. Hines. This brought sensational headlines all over town: DEWEY NAMES HINES.

Also there was much interest in the fact that Jack Dempsey, the former world heavyweight champion, had been forced to bow to the racketeers to keep his restaurant on Broadway strike- and trouble-free. *Time* magazine reported that Dempsey "had encountered an enemy more formidable than any Firpo or Tunney. It had appeared in the person of hard-faced men who accosted him, snarled that it would be 'healthier' for his restaurant if he joined the Association. . . . Jack Dempsey could have trounced any two of his extortioners single-handed. But behind them was something that could not be reached with fists, something huge and vague and sinister. He dodged that fight, paid his forfeit." Jack Dempsey co-operated fully with our investigation.

Herlands presented our case and asked me to undertake the cross-examination of the defense. The defense called sixty witnesses in all, and five of the defendants themselves took the stand. Our case had taken four weeks, and that of the defense was to take six. On the stand the defendants in effect sang the same song: "I didn't do any of those things that all those restaurant people and others testified to. They are all liars. But if I did do those things, it was because I was forced to, and I was in fear of my life."

Irving Epstein, the operating head of Local 302, was the defendant who typified this entire line of defense. After giving his history as a counter man and then as a union organizer, Epstein testified that three men from "the Dutchman's mob" came into the union office and told him, "We come to take over the union. From now on, you will take orders from us. You'd better do as we say. You wouldn't look very good without your ears."

In fear of his life, so Epstein said, he went to Buffalo to see the international president of the waiters' union, who told him he could not help. The president told him to go back home and see Joe Ryan, the head of the Central Trades and Labor Council, or the police, or the District Attorney. After repeated efforts to get help. Epstein said, he resigned his job with the union and left town for a trip across the country. He said he was in fear of losing his ears, or worse.

Epstein explained that he had later resumed his work with Local 302 after he had finished his cross-country trip and returned to New York. He said the members all demanded that he resume leadership.

Under cross-examination, Epstein admitted that he had told none of this story to Herlands when he had been brought into the office for questioning before indictment. He had never said he was coerced, or threatened, that he had appealed for help, and he certainly had never said anything about losing his ears.

Before long Epstein's story was in such obvious trouble that his wife Jewel was brought to the stand to confirm that he had left New York because he was in fear of losing his ears.

It was always very hard to cross-examine a woman. It was even more difficult when her testimony was mostly truthful. I had no doubt the Epsteins had made the trip from New York and that Mrs. Epstein, in fact, kept an honest diary of the trip. The diary was even offered in evidence. The difficulty was that, if her testimony was not explored on cross-examination, the jury might believe her husband's story.

So I took a deep breath and began a thorough cross-examination. Mrs. Epstein had told about her previous life, about how the Epsteins had moved from one small apartment to another, sharing with her mother, her brother, and a boarder. Under the direct examination of her husband's counsel, David Goldstein, she presented a graphic picture of almost abject poverty. Then she briefly described how they moved about the United States after leaving town, presumably broke and in mortal terror. Was this true?

I confined myself to exploring the details of the journey. I had no basis for challenging her story of their family life, and about the trip I asked questions gently and in the friendliest manner possible. Mrs. Epstein had her travel diary in her hands, and I held a transcribed copy in mine.

Yes, she said, they had left New York on April 4, 1933, at 4:00 P.M. by automobile, and they had spent the night in Baltimore with friends.

Did she go shopping the next day? She did not remember. Her diary refreshed her recollection. She did go shopping.

Did she go sight-seeing? No, Mr. Epstein went sight-seeing, while she went shopping with friends.

Did they go to the movies? Yes, they went to the movies, that night.

Did her husband look for work in Baltimore that day? No, he did not look for work.

The next day they went to Washington, saw the cherry blossoms, and spent the day sight-seeing around the nation's capital. From there they went to Norfolk, Virginia, where they spent the night at the Hotel Monticello. They visited various friends and went sight-seeing. Her husband did not look for a job in Norfolk.

After two days they went on to Durham, North Carolina, and then to Asheville, North Carolina. Again, they visited a friend, and went to the Grove Park Inn for dinner. They saw as many of the sights of Asheville as they could in a few hours, and her husband did not look for work.

So it went. From the Towers Hotel in Asheville they moved on to Atlanta, where they had a nice dinner at the Pig 'n' Whistle, went sight-seeing, and generally "enjoyed the day." Her husband did not look for employment in Atlanta.

Then they started on the Mississippi route, and "enjoyed the scenery very much" on their way to the Gulf of Mexico. The trip was delightful there, too, "with the Gulf on one side, and the scenery on the other." They did some sight-seeing on the way and arrived in New Orleans on the seventeenth, where they did some more sight-seeing before going on to Gulfport. There they stayed several days, sight-seeing every day, or going fishing, and going to the movies at night. Her husband did not seek employment there.

In Vicksburg they went to a night club because "we wanted to see what it was like," and they were disappointed. On through Texas they traveled, sight-seeing as they went, stopping on the twenty-fourth at the Carlsbad Caverns in New Mexico for more sight-seeing, and on to El Paso, where they went to look at "the architecture and the various types of quaint dwellings." She testified, "Whatever there was of interest we didn't want to miss." She said her husband did not look for a job.

Traveling into Mexico, they hired a guide so that they would not miss anything, and then it was on from Las Cruces to Holbrook, Arizona, and the Petrified Forest. After more sight-seeing there, they went to the Grand Canyon and spent three days going down the canyon and seeing all of the sights of the area.

At Needles, on the California border, they were running short of small dollar bills, she testified, and could find no one to change "a big bill." So they scraped up enough change to get on to where they could change the bill. They drove to Los Angeles, enjoying the orange groves which, she said, were "very delightful." Her husband did not look for a job in Los Angeles or any place else on the entire trip across the continent.

Mrs. Epstein testified that her husband had paid a visit to the president of his international union, who was visiting Los Angeles at that time. They also did some sight-seeing and had a charming trip to Catalina Island, watching the fish from the glass-bottomed boat.

Then they started home via Las Vegas, Salt Lake City, Cheyenne, Omaha, Des Moines, and on through Illinois, Ohio, Pittsburgh, Atlantic City, and home.

That was all. I did not ask whether her husband was still in fear of losing his ears or his life. It seemed too obvious that he was not. She had wrecked her husband's testimony and undermined his whole defense.

As my cross-examination proceeded, Epstein's counsel, David Goldstein, who was sitting in a chair nearby, slumped lower and lower until his enormous stomach was higher than the arms of the chair. His eyes were closed, and he was feigning sleep.

At the end of the cross-examination recess was called, and the defendants and Mrs. Epstein went to the room set aside for witnesses. There Epstein leaped at Mrs. Epstein's throat, screaming epithets at her. He shouted that she was deliberately trying to convict him. This was, of course, untrue. She simply told the truth.

After the defendants and their witnesses were all through I turned the case back to Herlands and left him to suffer through the summations of the defense counsel. Then he made his own summation, which, I was told by all who heard it, was a masterpiece. Herlands concentrated on this key point:

"This is the first time that a full industrial racket has been presented in a single case. If there is anything that is important to the community today, it is a warning that rackets can be prosecuted and broken. If we cannot get a conviction in this case, there never again will be a like opportunity."

The jury took only six hours to reach a historic verdict, finding the defendants guilty on all counts. I felt so good about it that I sent a telegram to my mother in Owosso:

MRS. GEORGE M. DEWEY
421 WEST OLIVER STREET
OWOSSO MICHIGAN
ALL CONVICTED ON ALL COUNTS LOVE
TOM

At the time of sentencing I produced an envelope which one of the witnesses had given me. This man had told us that Paul Coulcher had left it with simple instructions. If Coulcher was acquitted, he was to be given the envelope back at once. If Coulcher was convicted, he was to be given the envelope when he came out of prison.

Judge McCook opened the envelope and found $3,300 in bills. I said I had reason to believe that the labor leader had passed out at least a dozen of these envelopes, although only one had been apprehended.

Judge McCook then said: "I don't know what the laboring men and women of the world, who have struggled for a hundred years for their rights, would think if they had witnessed this scene."

Judge McCook then sentenced Coulcher to fifteen to twenty years' imprisonment in a state penitentiary, and the other defendants to lesser sentences, all in excess of five years' imprisonment. The convictions were upheld all the way on appeal.

As far as I was concerned, this result also put a stop to the ugly charges of union-busting, and I seemed to be labor's friend once more. A happy postscript came when Locals 16 and 302 elected honest men as their new leaders, sued Coulcher and the others for embezzlement and collected damages, and more than doubled their membership in the next six months.

Benny Gottesman went right on running Local 1 the way he always had.

Into the Half-world
of Lepke and Gurrah

With the Lucky Luciano trial satisfactorily completed and the restaurant racket investigation well on the way, I had my first real opportunity to lift my head above water and see where we stood. By now the prestige of our investigation was such that we were getting more and more complaints against racketeers and alleged racketeers, and it was somewhat easier to obtain information. But the solid testimony of real, live witnesses under oath was hard to get indeed.

Terror still sealed the lips of the essential witnesses in all the essential rackets. We still had the unhappy task of making the witnesses more afraid of us than they were of the vengeance of the gangsters.

We had long since learned that subpoenas for the books of suspected victims of the rackets often caused the books to be suddenly lost. So we adopted a practice of serving subpoenas requiring the production of the books "forthwith." Two policemen and an accountant from our staff went along with the process server, and they brought the owners and the books before the grand jury then and there. This procedure gave Goody Goodrich and his accountants the best opportunities they had ever had to make columns of figures talk on behalf of the law.

Aside from the Luciano and Schultz successes, we were running up some useful accomplishments. Chief Assistant Barent Ten Eyck, assisted by Frank Hogan, was plowing into the flour trucking and baking industries. Soon they were convinced these industries were being dominated by another very large industrial racket formed of gangsters and corrupt labor union leaders.

Deputy Assistant Paul Lockwood developed information on a combination of a truck drivers' union and some gangsters that had built a monopoly in the salvaged brick industry. This combination was so tight that the expenses of city housing projects alone had soared by more than $170,000 a month, Independents who refused to join the monopoly found destructive emery in the motors of their trucks, or their trucks would be burned. Ten firms had been forced out of business during the formation of this monopoly.

Lockwood handed out some of our new "forthwith" subpoenas for the books of the remaining trucking companies and of the truck drivers' union. These were served simultaneously all over the city, and the result was a rare example of the collapse of a racket overnight. The leaders of the monopoly simply suspended operations—and stopped so completely that we felt we simply did not have the manpower to spend months proving crimes of the past since our objective had been achieved.

Chief Assistant Murray Gurfein was striking pay dirt despite the terror that dominated the clothing industry, New York's second largest, and the garment trucking industry. Gurfein brought one case after another, not against gangsters, but against the victims to compel them to testify. With some of these businessmen, the only recourse was a contempt case, brought after they had lied or evaded before the grand jury. With others, there would be charges for filing false certificates of incorporation, or income tax violations, or inaccurate entries in their books of account, anything, really, to encourage them to testify against the mobs.

Our first grand jury had been exhausted by December 1935, after having examined more than five hundred witnesses and handed up twenty-nine indictments and informations. An information was a charge of a misdemeanor, as distinguished from an indictment, which charged a felony. By the end of June 1936 the second grand jury reported it had sat six hours a day for six months and asked to be excused. This grand jury commented that our investigation had "just started," and they recommended that we should have two grand juries sitting simultaneously, instead of just one. They were released with high praise for their labors and with even higher admiration for their public service.

I now asked Governor Lehman for the appointment of a second Special Term Court and a second grand jury, and my request was granted. The Governor authorized the second Special Term to be presided over by Justice Ferdinand Pecora of the Supreme Court. Pecora had received widespread public attention in his conduct of a Senate investigation a few years before and had been rewarded with his place on the Supreme Court. He had been a political regular all his life, however, and his background as a long-time assistant in the offices of Tammany-backed District Attorneys sent a chill through our office. If we had then known that an accident of fate would bring the most important political case of our investigation before him, our forebodings would have been still deeper.

Chief Assistant Herlands subsequently made these comments about our work with the grand juries: "There were certain expressions that epitomized this method, this technique, and which later on became part of the working vocabulary of all the Dewey-Medalie men. First, there was the concept that the grand jury should be used as an investigative body not only to get a near *prima facie* case sufficient for indictment but also to 'freeze' the defense witnesses.

"Every prosecutor knew that if we got an indictment quickly there would be many witnesses who knew about the crime who might be approached by the defendants or by certain types of lawyers. Therefore it was important for the prosecutors not to be content with getting only two or three witnesses necessary to show *prima facie* the existence of a crime, but to bring in as many witnesses as possible who knew anything about the crime.

"By so doing, we were trying to anticipate who the witnesses were that the defense would call, and then we were 'freezing' them. This meant getting their story on the record under oath before the grand jury. So when the indictment was handed down, and the defense started to go around to look, they found that all of the witnesses who knew anything about the case had already been before the grand jury and were committed to a story under oath.

"Now, there could be no injustice to a defendant in that technique because, if witnesses in fact exculpated or exonerated the potential defendant, the man would never be indicted. It was a very fair way of dealing with the defense.

"On the other hand, if the defendant was truly guilty, and all of the witnesses who had any material information about the case were brought before the grand jury, he could not complain because later on he could not suborn perjury.

"That process of 'freezing the witness' meant that the prosecutors had to anticipate the defense. We were not only preparing the prosecutors' case. We were preparing the defense, and it was part of the Dewey-Medalie school that we did that.

"In other words, don't be in a rush to get an indictment. Sit on the egg until it hatched.

"The second purpose of this method of utilizing grand jury technique was that, if we had a longer grand jury investigation, word got around that a grand jury had been on this particular job for weeks and weeks. Then many complaints, or victims, or people who knew about the situations and whom we might have overlooked, would tend to be persuaded that a serious effort was being made to uproot the situation that had victimized them.

"This created a psychological atmosphere of confidence as distinguished from fear and intimidation, and this was of very great value in the subsequent works of Dewey."

Throughout this period, also, we were perplexed by comments that our investigation might be infringing upon civil liberties. One of our youngest deputy assistants, Harris Steinberg, recalled: "There were great pressures on Dewey to break laws because the temper of the people then was a lynching temper. They were mad. They were mad about the Depression. They were mad about racketeers. They wanted to find somebody to blame and, if Dewey had ridden roughshod over civil liberties, he would have gotten away with it.

"He did not do it. I don't pretend to know whether it was because he had an abiding affection for civil liberties. I don't know that that's so. But he was trained as a good lawyer, and if you're trained as a good lawyer, you don't make phony short cuts.

"There were lots of lawyers who hated Dewey, hated everything he stood for, and would tell you that he was the greatest violator of civil liberties in the world. But I don't believe that is true. These guys were talking through their hats. They were the same lawyers who, when Dewey would get an indictment against a restaurant racketeer, or somebody like that, would sneer, 'That's a lot of crap. Why doesn't he get Hines?' Then, when he did get Hines, they said, 'Poor Jimmy.' They just didn't like Dewey and were against everything he manifested, that's all."

Deputy Assistant Stanley Fuld recalled: "I was alone with him, or maybe one or two others, and Hitler was getting stronger and stronger. I said, 'It looks pretty bad for us Jews. We'll probably all be in concentration camps if this continues.' He said, 'Not as long as there are people like me who feel as I do.'

"I've never forgotten that. It made an impression on me, but I think he felt the same way with regard to the rights of all people. If he were prosecuting someone like Lucky Luciano, or Hines, he'd hit very hard. But he'd be very much aware of what doing it here in this case might mean later on to the detriment of somebody who might not have been as bad as Luciano. He was a prime lawyer. A very fine lawyer."

Stanley Fuld at this time, incidentally, was performing his inestimable job of developing the pure law resources that we needed in the Special Prosecutor's office. Fuld recalled: "I thought there should be a greater sense of what facts ought to be looked for. Dewey said to go ahead, so I started devoting myself a little more to law than to facts, going to the library, and preparing some memoranda, and letting the other assistants know that there was this service available. They would be digging for facts, but the facts might not have had too much importance, unless they knew what the law deemed operative and what the law deemed important.

"So I started getting requests, or questions as to law, from this or that assistant, and that started our law department. Then, when the law department became too much for me, I had another talk with Dewey—it might have been with Gurfein first—on the desirability of having others assigned to help me in the development of law.

"At that time, if we were not able to look the law up, I would more or less suggest to the one who posed the question how he could go about finding answers to law questions. That's the way the law work started. Before that, and even while I was doing it, I had been working on the brick racket, the kosher poultry racket, loan sharks, probably, and one or two others. I worked on the law in those usury cases."

With Luciano in Dannemora Prison for thirty to fifty years, and with Dutch Schultz dead, we now pointed increasingly toward Lepke and Gurrah. We were investigating flour trucking and the bakery industry, the poultry and poultry trucking industry, men's and women's garments and the garment trucking industry, and we knew that all the trails were leading to Lepke and Gurrah.

Louis Buchalter (Lepke) and Jacob Shapiro (Gurrah) had been partners for a long time. Lepke was the brains of the team. He started to build up a police record as early as 1915, when he was arrested for burglary and assault. He served three years in prison but had not been arrested since.

He was slim, handsome, and he acted like a respectable businessman. He lived in a luxurious apartment overlooking Central Park. He traveled about town in a high-powered automobile driven by a chauffeur, and he was a frequent patron of race tracks and night clubs.

Gurrah was a short, beetle-browed, bull-necked thug who had once been a petty thief. Coarse, hoarse-voiced, and violent, he was also arrested for the first time in 1915, on malicious mischief charges, but he was discharged. He was again arrested in the same year, and again he beat the rap. Third time around, still in 1915, he was sent to the reformatory as a burglar. After that he served three other jail terms, but never for major offenses, nor long sentences.

Gurrah also lived a life of luxury. He became a familiar figure at race tracks and night clubs, and he also enjoyed hockey games. His clothes were costly, and all his habits were expensive.

A sinister partnership between Lepke and Gurrah grew through the late 1910s and early 1920s. They teamed up, simply, as free-lance sluggers who sold their services in industrial disputes to the highest bidders. They became ranking members of the Little Augie mob in New York in the late 1920s. One day its leader, "Little Augie" Pisano, was left to die under a rain of bullets and Lepke and Gurrah, with a third partner named "Curley," had a clear field. Then Curley disappeared and, according to underworld gossip, he was encased in cement and dumped into the East River.

Over the bodies of Little Augie and Curley, Lepke and Gurrah now built up and dominated great industrial rackets. Their names became a legend. Whenever a gorilla called on a businessman and said, "I am from L & G," the victim asked no questions. He paid whatever he was asked to pay. He did whatever he was asked to do.

Lepke and Gurrah were no longer police characters. They would not have thought of carrying guns or getting into trouble. They had graduated from all that years before. They would not even think of getting into an argument with anybody. If somebody caused them any trouble they might drop a hint to one of their subordinates that they did not like that person, but they would not dream of being direct participants in his murder.

That would be the private venture of one of the boys on the payroll who would never squeal, even if caught.

As their power grew, Lepke and Gurrah had decided in 1931 to take over the flour trucking and baking industries in New York City. The machine-controlled District Attorneys with their politically picked assistants were sleeping peacefully. Nobody would want to trace the operations of rackets up to their bosses. It was safe for Lepke and Gurrah to expand.

In 1931, Lepke himself sent for a businessman in the baking industry and told him he was going to be the new partner. The businessman refused. After Lepke's agents revisited their prospect the businessman broke all the rules and courageously made a complaint to the law. Extortion charges were brought against Lepke and his henchmen, but Lepke disappeared for a while and never showed in court. But there was read into the record, in sworn testimony, a statement made by Lepke himself. It read: "It means to us a lot of money, maybe millions of dollars. In the flour industry, we have got the jobbers and the truckmen, and the next will be the bakers, and we are going to make it a big thing."

Public notice was thereby served that an industry was about to be taken over. The promised was fulfilled. Lepke returned and operations went ahead. The gorillas invaded a labor union in the flour trucking field and gave out new orders. From then on strikes would be called whenever they said so. Strikes would be called off only after the businessmen had paid out a large extortion. The rights of the workers were to be ignored. The gangsters intended to set up a trade association in every field of the industry with lawyers and front men protecting them from harm. And they did.

But there was trouble, and this time a murder could not be concealed.

It happened on the night of September 13, 1934, in Garfein's Restaurant on Avenue A, on the Lower East Side of New York City. The public dining room was nearly deserted, but in the large room adjoining it members of the Flour Truckmen's Association were meeting with the bakery racketeers who were dominating them.

It was a strange place for such a conference. It was a hall about eighty feet long, used mostly for weddings, banquets, and festivals. It had a parquet dance floor, and the ceiling was set with crystal chandeliers. The room was dark, except for one small pool of light in a front corner. Under that light two small round tables were shoved together, and around them sat fifteen men, discussing the threat of a strike.

Twelve of these men were connected in one way or another with the Flour Truckmen's Association. This was the business front for the Lepke and Gurrah racket. Among them were Max Silverman, a senior associate of Lepke and Gurrah, and Meyer Luckman, who, only a few months after this meeting, would murder his own brother-in-law. Three other leaders of the bakery racket rounded out the fifteen.

They had left one vacant chair, with its back toward the door. This was for William Snyder, president of Local 138 of the Flour and Bakery Drivers' Union. When Billy Snyder arrived he was greeted by the vice-president of the union, his friend "Wolfie" Goldis, a racketeer. The men around the table were displeased with Snyder because he had been refusing to follow the orders of the mob.

Toward 10:00 P.M., as the conference droned on, Wolfie Goldis got up. He went out the front door and opened a casement window from the street. As he stood on the sidewalk, he was visible to the occupants of any car which might have been parked out there.

A moment later another man appeared in the restaurant and advanced out of the darkness toward the conference tables. He raised a pistol and shot Billy Snyder in the back.

Snyder sprang up, glanced at the gunman, and wheeled around. The assassin fired twice more. One shot went wild. But as Snyder staggered away the second shot found its mark, ripping from back to front through his vitals.

The killer walked calmly out of the restaurant, jumped into a car which was waiting with its engine running, and made his escape. Billy Snyder was taken to the hospital by his good friend Max Silverman.

But the trigger job had been bungled. Snyder lingered two days before he died.

The police questioned the men at the table, who failed to identify the assassin. They all said they had dived under the tables at the first shot and had not seen his face.

But the police did not stop at that. They traced the getaway car through its license plate. They found it had been rented that night by a young man named Tratner, whom they found at his home. Police records showed that Tratner had once been arrested with another fellow named Morris Goldis. Morris was the younger brother of Wolfie Goldis, the man who had come out of the restaurant and opened the casement window. Tratner readily admitted that he had rented the car with money given him by Morris Goldis. A picture of Morris Goldis was taken from the police files and shown to two men who had been dining in the main room of the restaurant. These two witnesses identified Morris Goldis as the man who had walked out of the banquet room, gun in hand.

The police rushed to the home of Morris Goldis but he was gone.

This is what happened while Morris Goldis continued to be a fugitive from justice. Tratner, the man who had rented the murder car, was under arrest. He and his family were penniless. But somebody retained a well-connected lawyer to represent him.

A few weeks later this same lawyer appeared in the case as counsel for Morris Goldis as well. The lawyer surrendered Morris Goldis to the District Attorney. But something strange now happened to the two witnesses who had identified Goldis from the police photographs. When they were taken to look at Goldis in the flesh they refused to identify him. Something strange happened to Tratner too. He now denied having rented the car for Goldis, and he made up a feeble tale that he did this favor for somebody neither he nor the law enforcement authorities could prove ever existed.

So—there was insufficient evidence, and Morris Goldis was set free. Wolfie Goldis was elected president of the local, succeeding the dead Billy Snyder, and Wolfie put his brother Morris on the union payroll.

I had documents brought to me which threw light on how this murder was committed with immunity in our county of New York. The first was a formal police detective's report of his work on the Billy Snyder case, written five days after the murder. He reported on a conference with one of the then responsible Tammany Deputy Assistant District Attorneys. The detective requested the Tammany man to present the evidence to the grand jury immediately. There was danger to witnesses, danger to the case. The detective reported: "These two are willing to testify now as to the facts in this case, but the question that confronts us is whether they would do so at a later date."

Here was an official warning. What happened? In spite of it, the detective reported, the Assisant District Attorney told him he wanted the case to go through the "regular procedure." This involved waiting for the fugitive to be found, and then proceeding through the homicide court in which cases were aired in public.

That was how, after due notice, the witnesses were left to change their minds about testifying. No wonder that the case was dismissed.

The second document I obtained after I became Special Prosecutor was longer. It was a letter written by a relative of the murdered man. It had been written to the District Attorney himself after Morris Goldis had been turned loose and the murder case whitewashed. It read:

> Dear Sir:
> Have recently learned that Morris Goldis—the man you were holding for the murder of Wm. Snyder—was dismissed for lack of evidence, and because persons present on the night of the tragedy refused to identify him.
>
> I was one of those sent for when he [Snyder] was brought to the hospital, and heard him say that Wolfie's brother had shot him. I was under the impression that a statement of this kind carried no weight unless given in the presence of an officer of the law, or signed by the victim.
>
> I have never seen Wolfie's brother, so I can only repeat what I heard from Mr. Snyder's own lips.
>
> If you think this testimony will have any bearing on this case whatsoever, I am more than willing to divulge this information to the right party.
>
> I would like to see justice take its course, and have those people that were the instigators and also his murderer put away where they couldn't harm anyone else.
>
> If you care to investigate, you will find the statement I have made to be true.

I sincerely hope this information will be of some benefit to you in building a case against Morris Goldis.

Kindly let me hear from you in regard to this matter.

Yours sincerely

P.S. I haven't given you my home address as I do not want my people frightened. If they knew I wrote this letter, they would worry and believe that my life was in danger. But I do feel that someone should speak up so those murderers would not be sitting in a dead man's shoes.

And so—for the second time—the murder of William Snyder had been laid on the doorstep of the District Attorney's office. And the case remained dead.

Now, how about the lawyer who was hired to represent Tratner and who, seven weeks later, surrendered Morris Goldis to the District Attorney? That lawyer was none other than Charles A. Schneider, then and since an Assistant Attorney General of the state of New York, a law enforcement official of the state engaged in private practice.

Schneider was also a powerful politician of the Eighth Assembly District of New York County and within a few months he became the district leader in name as well as in fact.

Who had retained this politician Assistant Attorney General to represent Tratner? Who paid him to represent Morris Goldis? He was paid with part of the money collected by racketeers from the flour trucking industry. I had in my possession two of the checks by which that money was passed. They bore on their backs the endorsement of Charles A. Schneider. Now, it was not a crime in the state of New York for an Assistant Attorney General in a private capacity to represent a man accused of murder. But it was a shocking betrayal of the people of the state, which could only be rebuked by the people.

The members of that union never had a chance, and no employer ever had a chance. The Lepke-Gurrah empire was marching on. Another industry had been subdued. The price of flour trucking went up. Employers were forced to pay shakedowns totaling more than $1,000,-000. The mob added the pastry and pie divisions of the baking industry to the monster racket, and all New Yorkers paid the higher prices.

Every worker in the baking industry felt the terror and knew that he was helpless. Why? Because he knew that the politically controlled District Attorney of New York County would not, dare not, or could not lift a finger. He knew that public notice had been served that Lepke and Gurrah were taking over. He knew that every union head-quarters and every phony trade association was operating brazenly, openly, and as a matter of public notice, and the District Attorney did not lift a finger.

He knew that a murder had been committed with impunity, and the brother of the man arrested for the crime had then succeeded the murdered man as the subordinate of the gangsters in actual opera-tion of the racket. He knew also that Max Silverman, the general in charge of that racket for Lepke and Gurrah, lived in luxury and walked the streets with apparent immunity.

For ten years Lepke and Gurrah had been industrial racketeers in New York. They had gone uninvestigated and untouched by the District Attorney.

Not long after we began our rackets investigation, however, we re-ceived letters from none other than the mother and the wife of the murdered union official, Billy Snyder. I assigned Chief Assistant Barent Ten Eyck to the special tack of investigating the details. Ten Eyck decided to reopen the case of the Murder on Avenue A. He found in the Bronx the records of the abortive trials of Lepke and the others, and the testimony that Lepke had sworn to take over the in-dustry. He was struck by the presence of both management and labor people around the table at Garfein's, a combination that indicated a double racket.

Rupert Hughes, the historian, reported: "Letters sent into the office and a few bits of luck in securing testimony from a truck-owner who was sick of submission gave Ten Eyck evidence that proved Silverman to be the organizer and boss of the combined group of truck-owners and truck-drivers, and also the terrorist of the bakers and the small and very numerous manufacturers of pie and pastry and the drivers of their small delivery trucks. Silverman had driven one pastryman out of business by burning his trucks, and the rest had concluded that New York City was no longer the land of the free or the home of the brave."

When Ten Eyck subpoenaed and seized the books of the Flour Truckmen's Association, Silverman left town and went into hiding. Indictments were brought against Wolfie Goldis, Silverman's son Har-old, and Benjamin Spivack, the attorney for the association, charging conspiracy, and they were all found guilty. But the Goldis brothers now feared that murder charges were about to be brought against them. They learned, also, that an associate of Silverman's, named Max Rubin, was one of the people talking with our investigation.

One afternoon, on a New York City street, Max Rubin was shot in the back. The bullet struck his neck, passed through his head, and narrowly missed his brain. He had turned down our offers of a police guard He had survived by inches, and he lived on to testify against the whole mob.

On the radio, I told the people of New York "The shot which struck down Max Rubin was the frightened act of a desperate criminal underworld. The racketeers have flung down their challenge. I accept that challenge."

In November 1937, Morris Goldis was indicted for murder, and in the following year Wolfie Goldis was joined to his brother in the capital charge. The Goldis brothers, however, offered to plead guilty to first degree manslaughter and they were sentenced to just one-and-a-half years' imprisonment.

Chief Assistant Murray Gurfein, assisted by Victor J. Herwitz, found increasingly as he explored the Lepke-Gurrah garment racket that he was conducting a sort of sociological study. He was finding out more and more about the infiltration of organized crime—whose ultimate power was violence—into a legitimate industry almost by general consent. What was missing here was the usual evidence of threats and extortion. What was mysterious was that Lepke and Gurrah did not need to use force in their domination of this huge industry.

In this investigation we found our first leads in the structure of the garment trade itself. By agreement between labor and management under the NRA, wages and prices were officially agreed. Where, then, was the room for the racket? We found out that the very attempt to impose a universality of labor standards was what made non-conformity profitable.

Gurfein learned that there were now "protected" shops. These were manufacturing or contract shops, which did not have to adhere strictly to union requirements. They cut corners for that margin of their operating costs that might make the difference between success and survival, or between survival and failure. The union leadership was not supposed to tolerate this kind of thing but, in practice, it often looked the other way.

Gurfein found out about the "runaway" shops. These were generally contracting and subcontracting shops, located in New Jersey, Pennsylvania, Maryland, or upstate New York, which supplied materials to garment manufacturers in the city. Many of these were not unionized at all.

Lepke and Gurrah had developed a new technique with regard to the bulk of the industry. In addition to moving into some of the unions, they declared themselves to be partners of the manufacturers. They did not ask. They simply said this was so. Their reputation was so frightening that formal threats were not necessary. For those who benefited from violations of the NRA wage-price system, silence was golden. For those who suffered unfair competition, silence was their best protection.

Lepke and Gurrah found one specific life line between the "runaway" shops and the garment district to be the garment trucking industry. So they moved into partnership with the truck owners and truck drivers. Gurfein and his assistants probed an organization called the Five Borough Truckmen's Association, and they managed to find that rare prize, a real, live, willing witness. His name was William Brown and he told a typical story.

Back in 1932 a pair of rising gangsters named James Plumeri, alias Jimmy Doyle, and Dominick Didato, alias Dick Terry, decided to take over the downtown trucking industry. They started by forming the so-called Five Borough Truckmen's Association at 225 Lafayette Street, which happened to be the building in which a leading Tammany official, Albert Marinelli, kept his offices and maintained a personal association. They elected themselves president and treasurer of their Five Borough Truckmen's Association and were ready for the business of recruiting truckmen for the association by means of intimidation and violence.

Plumeri/Doyle and Didato/Terry took on two others to help with the rough work. These were Natale Evola and John "Johnny Dio" Dioguardi, the latter at the beginning of his racket career. The four racketeers made a success of their recruitment campaign with beatings, stench bombs, and the destruction of trucks. They also boasted of their political connections.

William Brown, our willing witness, was a typical victim. Together with his wife, Brown ran a small trucking business on West Twenty-first Street. The Browns had three trucks. They were struggling along in 1933, making a go of it, until the racket got after them.

One night Brown and his wife were sitting in their trucking office working on their books. They had just gotten a new customer. Then Doyle and Terry walked in. Doyle looked at the new order and demanded: "What's the idea of your taking this account? We are from the Five Borough Truckmen's Association. You can't get away with any of these accounts around here."

Brown had courage, and he told them to get out. Doyle threatened, "You know what happens to guys that don't play ball with us. They are pretty soon out of business."

Then they shoved Brown up against the wall and told him that, unless he gave up the new account, they would put emery in his truck motors and beat up his drivers. Doyle said, "We had a lot of complaints against us in the last year and we've beat every rap." He named the Tammany leader James J. Hines and said, "He's the man we got higher up that's protecting us."

Brown defied Doyle and Terry and within three weeks there was emery powder in the crankcase of his best truck. It wrecked the motor. Then seven gorillas entered the office one night, threw monkey wrenches at Brown's brother and beat him with an ax handle. The brother was in bed for two weeks after the attack. Another of Brown's workers was slugged at the same time.

Brown and his wife were terrified. They remembered what Doyle had said about protection. Then Brown heard a speech by the man who was then the Police Commissioner, who said that racket victims should come into the office and they would be safe. Brown went in the next morning and was sent to tell his story to a grand jury. Indictments for coercion and conspiracy were voted against Doyle and Terry, and also against Johnny Dio. Brown and his wife went home believing they would get justice.

But the case dragged on for another year and there was no trial. Finally Brown got a subpoena calling him to the Court of General Sessions for the trial. He handed his subpoena to the clerk and was told, "Why, that's a wrong date on that subpoena. Your case was dismissed yesterday."

The record showed the dismissal was on the recommendation of the District Attorney.

In August 1933, it was Terry's and Doyle's turn to be jumped by gunmen in the office of the Five Borough Truckmen's Association. When the smoke cleared away Terry lay dying on the floor and Doyle was seriously wounded. Doyle lived to keep the racket going strong.

A truckman named Blackoff had meanwhile put more evidence into the record when he called the police to arrest Terry, Dio, and Evola for threatening him with violence. The police found right in the car of the defendants a bottle full of emery. Here was another rare find, an actual instrument of crime. When the case was brought to court the bottle of emery was brought into the courtroom. Twice the judge asked the prosecutor what was the significance of the emery. The stenographic record of this trial showed that the Assistant District Attorney failed to advise him. The instrument of the crime was there, and the prosecutor stood silent. The best information the judge could get the prosecutor to disclose was that emery was used for grinding valves. So the Blackoff case ended with an acquittal, and the racket went on strong.

With the murdered Terry out of the way, Doyle and Dio were ready to expand, and they moved uptown. Although they were still faced with the pending Brown indictment, they brazenly served notice on the Garment Center Truck Owners' Association: "We are taking over your association. If you don't pay, we are coming uptown, and there will be busted trucks and broken heads."

The president of this association consulted his directors. They were worried. Somebody suggested that they should go to the District Attorney but everybody agreed that would be too dangerous. The directors agreed to pay up and shut up.

When our own rackets investigation began in the summer of 1935, William Brown came in and told us what had happened. Gurfein assigned Deputy Assistant Jack Grumet to work with him in developing the case. Gurfein and Grumet thought it was not desirable, for all of his courage, to have Brown as a sole witness.

So Gurfein and Grumet began to talk to truckmen and to subpoena the books of truckmen's associations. They found that the Garment Center Truck Owners' Association had disguised its payments to the mob with simple skill. Gurfein recalled: "Checks were drawn each month to the directors of the association as salary. The directors had never gotten salary before. The directors would turn these checks over to a man who would cash them and skip the cash to one of the gangsters on the street. This had been going on for three years before we got into the case.

"How were we going to break down the fear of these men who had lived in the midst of terror and who had been afraid to go to the District Attorney's office? Jack Grumet and I called them in one by one. At first we talked to them in a friendly way, tried to sell them confidence by telling them we would not break the case until we had a substantial number of them as witnesses. They froze up. 'It's all a mistake,' they said.

"Most of them even denied they had turned back their directors' salaries. They insisted they had kept their salaries and even paid income tax on them. Indeed, some of them actually had paid tax, so that, if called to testify, they would have the perfect alibi.

"Then began a long job of confronting each of the witnesses with the directors' checks that were cashed, of continued questioning of the signers of the checks, and of the men who had delivered the cash. We then began to play one against the other. We used parts of the truth told by some to break the lies of others. Finally we pieced together enough to prove that the directors' meeting had agreed to pay the mob.

"As they became aware through subtle hints that enough of them had broken secretly for all of them to be safe in testifying together, we called them in together. That was a strange meeting. We went over the ground, turned to the one, then to the other, and we got admissions and additions.

"Finally the tension eased. These men began to laugh when they realized that each had been afraid to talk because the others might not. At one point I stepped out of the room and came back to find them lightheartedly pitching pennies on the floor."

It was still possible that we might never have broken that case except for one amusing incident. We felt that we needed the president of the association. He was extremely reluctant to testify. Off the record, he would tell us the whole story, and how everyone had fit into the mosaic. He did everything he could to persuade Grumet to get Gurfein to leave him out because of his position, and because of the great danger he would be in if he testified.

Finally negotiation produced a remarkable result: the president agreed to meet Grumet and Gurfein in a restaurant, but not in the office. He made a wager with Grumet that, if Gurfein could outdrink him, he would be a witness for the People. After considerable discussion, we decided we had nothing to lose, except possibly Gurfein.

So the meeting was held, and as the drinking went along the president of the association became more and more relaxed under the ministrations of my two assistants. He finally gave his pledge that he would become a witness for the People and tell the truth.

By this time we had a large number of witnesses to extortion other than William Brown. We went to trial—and the testimony was overwhelming. After the president of the association took the stand, Doyle and Dio threw in the sponge and pleaded guilty.

Judge McCook sentenced Doyle to five to ten years' imprisonment in the state prisons, and Johnny Dio, who was then twenty-three years old, to three to five years.

These two thugs were not important gangsters and we were absolutely convinced that they had important racket sponsorship. Gurfein used all his wiles to persuade them to turn state's evidence against higher-ups, if there were any, and they were both defiant. Gurfein told me he was naïve enough to believe that perhaps if he could persuade Johnny Dio to talk he could turn the young man toward a straight life.

Johnny Dio was a racketeer on a long way up to "success" in organized crime. He gave Gurfein a typical exposition of his philosophy when he commented that though guilty in the legal sense, he was not guilty morally. He said, "What did I do that J. P. Morgan didn't do?" Gurfein wondered out loud what J. P. Morgan had to do with it, to which Dio responded, "It's all a racket. Isn't Wall Street a racket where the strong take advantage of the weak? Every industry needs a strong man. After you put us in jail, another strong man will come up to keep the industry from becoming a jungle."

The sponsorship of Doyle and Dio was logically that of Lepke and Gurrah. But Doyle and Dio kept their silence, went to Sing Sing, and served out their terms.

Chief Assistant Gurfein's next lead brought us to a segment of the garment industry we scarcely knew existed—the coat front business. We learned that in every suit of clothing there was a canvas coat front which kept the jacket in shape. This was a relatively small part of the industry but it aroused our interest.

A competitor in this small but strategic trade came in to tell us that

Lepke and Gurrah were partners in a company named the Perfection Coat Front Company. This business had been run by Murray and Weiner, who had once been competitors but had been forced into a merger by Lepke and Gurrah. Once the merger had been consummated, Lepke and Gurrah became their partners.

The Perfection Coat Front Company gave an advantage to Lepke and Gurrah that went beyond mere profit. It gave the gangsters a legitimate business. It enabled them to file ostensibly legitimate income tax returns. Most important, it enabled them to use the firm as a banking vehicle through which they could funnel checks received by the mob.

Gurfein decided not to tip our hand by premature action. We proceeded to study the operation with all the means at hand for a number of months before subpoenaing the books or asking any questions. Gurfein recalled: "We put a wiretap on the Perfection office. Out of this wiretap, through several months of patient listening, we began to compile a list of the characters involved. It was like writing a play by finding the actors as a first step. We puzzled day after day over the cryptic references that had to be interpreted and the unknowns who had to be translated into real people. We also gleaned the information that checks were being cashed at the Perfection office, and that we might find their source.

"From the wiretap we also had learned that another mob connection was with a ladies' coat house, Fierman and Kohler, in which a Lepke and Gurrah associate named Benny Levine was a partner. Also, a men's clothing manufacturer, A. Saffer and Sons, was a hangout for 'the boys.'

"The wiretap on Perfection led us to get the account books of Perfection and Saffer, and then Fierman and Kohler. In the books of Perfection and Saffer there were exchange accounts which reflected the cashing of checks for Lepke and Gurrah and their cohorts. Some banks in those days had Recordak pictures of checks that had been drawn on a particular branch. We sent accountants to the banks of deposit of Perfection and Saffer. There we traced the clearinghouse number of the bank on which the check had been drawn.

"Where the drawee bank had Recordaks, our accountant investigators went through the tedious job of matching amounts that had to be cleared to the Perfection or Saffer banks, and ultimately came up with the names of the bank customers who had drawn the checks that ended up in the house of Perfection and Saffer.

"In this way, one of our first developed leads brought us, tangentially, into the pocketbook manufacturing firm of Goldsmith, which we later found out had been compelled to pay a steady stream of tribute to the mob.

"The head of the Saffer firm, Oscar Saffer, was subpoenaed after we found he had been making regular payments through an account labeled 'D.F.' Saffer kept insisting that 'D.F.' stood for Disbursement Fund. We suspected strongly that 'D.F.' stood for Danny Fields, a lieutenant of Lepke's, and if the payments had been made to him, we wanted to know why.

"Saffer remained consistent in his story, incredible though it seemed, and it was not possible to make a contempt case against him. Contempt of the grand jury as we had developed it in the rackets investigation involved a series of evasive stories, in which it could be judged that the purpose of the evasion was the obstruction of an inquiry. When a witness stuck to the same story, one could only get an indictment for perjury by bringing forward two witnesses to testify to the falseness of the testimony.

"We bombarded Saffer with questions about the 'D.F.' payments. Finally, he was persuaded to co-operate with us by an attorney, Henry Gerson, who had once been an Assistant United States Attorney. But we had to accept an agreement that Saffer's testimony would never be revealed until we had compiled many counts in an omnibus indictment. The mob was relying on him not to talk.

"In the process of the investigation, we had found out that Saffer has violated state income tax laws, and we had filed a misdemeanor charge against him in the Court of Special Sessions. This had gotten publicity, and it was 'good' publicity for Saffer because it was a signal to the mob that he had not talked. Indeed, it was such good publicity that Saffer insisted that we follow through on the state tax charges and actually prosecute and convict him.

"Accordingly, we therefore arranged to try the most bizarre case in our rackets investigation. We informed Chief Justice William R. Bayes of Special Sessions about the whole situation. Then we tried the case before a panel of three judges of whom Bayes was the presiding justice. Everything was arranged. I tried the easiest case of my career and Saffer was convicted and given a suspended sentence.

"This was perfect protection for Saffer against the mob. Obviously, he had held out against us all the way and had not squealed. However, we had an anxious moment when we heard that one of the three judges, in the intimacy of a social gathering, had recounted the story as an anecdote. Fortunately, no word of this got to Lepke and Gurrah, and no more harm was done."

Around this time Danny Fields was shot down in the streets. He might have been an essential link. The prime suspect in the killing was none other than Charlie the Bug Workman, who supposedly had done the job for his boss, Lepke, in the murder of Dutch Schultz in Newark. So we located Danny Fields's girl friend in upstate New York and Deputy Assistant Herwitz and a police officer were assigned to find her. She said she knew nothing about Danny Fields's murder, but she did know a great deal about Charlie The Bug. The girl friend told us that Workman had boasted to her that he had indeed killed Dutch Schultz. We sent her to the New Jersey prosecutors.

In the meantime, in a trial brought by the federal government, Lepke and Gurrah along with many others had been convicted for a misdemeanor violation of the anti-trust laws. They were now about to take their case to the United States Court of Appeals. It seemed ludicrous to me that these two absolute rulers of a large share of New York's underworld and, the owners of huge garment businesses in New York and Baltimore should be convicted of a mere misdemeanor and get a sentence of a few months.

Our own indictments, in preparation for two years, were almost ready. I was sure that Lepke and Gurrah, if they were at liberty when the indictments were handed up, would then become fugitives.

They were about to apply to Presiding Judge Manton of the Court of Appeals, Second Circuit, to have their bail fixed on the federal misdemeanor case. I decided to go and see Manton.

Manton was cordial and gracious, as always. I told him that within a few days we would hand up an indictment against Lepke and Gurrah and the rest of their mob on many counts of extortion. This could send them to jail for the rest of their lives. It would remove the worst remaining mob from the New York scene.

I asked Manton to deny bail until our indictment could be completed, or at least to fix bail at a high enough level to hold them.

Presiding Judge Manton assured me that he certainly would not like to see Lepke and Gurrah escape, and that he would bear in mind all that I had said.

The following day he turned both Lepke and Gurrah free on $10,000 bail.

A week later we handed up our indictment of Lepke and Gurrah and fourteen others for extortions in the garment industry totaling $17 million. Later we would bring similar charges in connection with the baking industry.

Eleven of the sixteen were arrested, but the others had fled, including Lepke and Gurrah. This was quite a blow to the morale of our team, but we knew that sometime they would show up, and Murray Gurfein and Victor Herwitz would be available to try the case.

So—Lucky Luciano was in Dannemora and Dutch Schultz was dead. Now Lepke and Gurrah were, as they would say, "on the lam."

Running for District Attorney

Arthur Herbert was a man who worked his way up from bouncer in a dance hall to czar of a $50 million industry, and levied a tax on every man and woman in New York. This bouncer was no ham-fisted Bowery bruiser. He was a slim, slick-haired fellow who cowed the noisy with a cold eye or a crippling, unexpected blow. His liking for barbershops and liberal use of sweet-smelling hair oils and tonics won him the nickname "Tootsie."

Herbert was a truck driver by day and a bouncer at night, and he had the ambition to become a big shot and make the money that came quickly and easily outside the law. He succeeded and for more than ten years he also seemed to have an immunity from the law.

At the age of twenty-four Tootsie Herbert bullied his way into a job as delegate for the chicken drivers' union. This gave him a chance to study the inner workings of the poultry industry. Soon he brought in a mob of strong-arm sluggers and quickly took over the union. From then on the members never had a chance to choose their own officers. Tootsie reigned, and the frightened members did his bidding. He chose a convicted thief for secretary-treasurer. He had himself elected head of the union for life, and he abolished elections alto-gether.

While Tootsie was conquering this segment of the poultry industry, he struck up a partnership with an old friend named Joe Weiner. Now, Joey was an experienced man. An expert safecracker not long out of prison, he was looking for larger and safer fields. He wanted to maneuver behind the scenes while front men did the dirty work. So Joie took over the job of invading the chicken killers' union.

By 1927, Tootsie and Joey had control of the unions and the industry was to come next. They began to tell merchants where and with whom they could do business. For that privilege, they had to pay the new mob one cent a pound on every chicken they sold in New York. Fifty million live chickens were being sold every year in New York, weighing approximately 160 million pounds. With this source of revenue, the racket was big money.

Some of the poultry dealers had the courage to complain, but not for long. Their trucks and their chicken coops were set on fire. The home of one was bombed one night, while his wife and child were asleep. Paving stones were dropped on another dealer's truck as it passed under a bridge, and the truck was wrecked.

Quickly the industry was subdued, as the unions had been. All of this was no secret. It was public property. The District Attorney of New York County did nothing. It was rumored, but could not be proven, that Tootsie Herbert was somehow an offshoot of Lepke and Gurrah. But the poultry racket was so notorious that the federal government decided to step in and take a hand. The federal govern-ment had no power to prosecute the many crimes that had been com-mitted against the state and the People of New York. The only thing it could do was to exercise the anti-trust laws against the excess gathering of power in the poultry industry.

The federal prosecution authorities won convictions against sixty-seven out of ninety-nine defendants who sat through the anti-trust trial in a specially constructed grandstand. It was a misdemeanor and Tootsie served a total of eight weeks in jail. When he got back to work he decided that the old penny-a-pound racket was too crude. So Tootsie and Joey developed more refined methods.

Chicken dealers had to buy feed for their chickens. Tootsie and Joey decided that all the chicken dealers in the city should buy feed from them. So they moved in on the Metropolitan Feed Company.

The industry knew their reputation by now, and they had no trouble. They made themselves stockholders in the corporation. Then they made themselves vice-presidents of the corporation at $150 a week each, and put a president in charge of the office at $75 a week.

As the new vice-presidents of the Metropolitan Feed Company, Tootsie and Joey did the field work, and that was what counted. The chicken dealers soon found it was safer to buy their feed from Metropolitan. True, the prices at Metropolitan were about double those of the old dealers in the business, but it was good insurance. And, after all, the increased costs could always be passed along to the public.

Before long the old feed companies found they had almost no customers. They cut their prices still further, delivered secretly in the night, but before long they began to fold up, one by one. Things looked better and better for Tootsie and Joey as the competition diminished. They began to take fat salaries from their unions and from their feed business, in addition to their dividends from the racket money.

There was more to come. Dealers in the chicken business also had to have crates, the coops, in which live chickens were transported to market. A dealer could buy a coop for $1.65, and he could use it perhaps two hundred times. But Tootsie and Joey thought the dealers ought to rent the coops, and rent them from Tootsie and Joey. Soon the dealers found it safer to rent the coops from Tootsie and Joey at the rate of 65 cents per day. This worked out to cost them approximately $130 for a coop which was really worth $1.65.

The rules of business in the poultry industry were being turned upside down. But it was cheaper to pay than to have your skull fractured, your truck burned, or to have rocks heaved into your drivers' cabs, or your engines ruined with emery. And the District Attorney did nothing.

Once again, the federal government stepped in and put out an injunction for Tootsie and Joey for violations of the anti-trust laws. This time it was more serious. Joey was sentenced to two years' imprisonment. Tootsie was also found guilty, and sentenced to six months' imprisonment.

Tootsie saved money during his six months' vacation. By this time he had jacked up his union salary alone to $200 a week, and before he was sent away he ordered his union to keep him on the payroll during his temporary absence. He also took the union's entire $5,000 death benefit fund out of the bank and put it away in his personal funds for a rainy day. From his cell, he sent out orders which raised the members' dues from $5.00 to $10 a month.

Back from his vacation, Tootsie returned to the poultry business at the same old stand. He regained his healthy tan, sitting in his regular, reserved seat in the stands behind third base at the Polo Grounds and Yankee Stadium. His pockets bulged with money, and he was a willing bettor. His voice rang with the old authority as he called his challenges: "Lay you five hundred! Lay you a grand!"

Tootsie's apartment on West Eighty-sixth Street was richly furnished with the guidance of an interior decorator. He frequented race tracks, night clubs, and hockey games along with the really big racketeers, such as Lepke and Gurrah. He was an easy spender. When one of his underworld friends, a man named "Ziggie," sailed off to Europe, Tootsie sent him a $16 basket of flowers, paid for out of union funds.

What need for Tootsie to worry about spending other men's money? He had an annuity insurance policy that would pay him $1,000 a month after he reached the age of sixty.

But Tootsie wanted still more. The money was easy now, and he wanted to put it where nobody else could get at it. He applied to insurance companies for big life policies. But by this time his reputation as a racketeer was so widespread that he was turned down as a bad risk. He went to Canada and applied there. Even in Canada he was well known and was turned down.

Everybody in the United States and Canada seemed to know who Tootsie Herbert was and what his business was. Everybody but the District Attorney of New York County.

Where were the successive District Attorneys during all these years? For more than ten years the poultry racket had ruled one of the great industries of the city and controlled the lives of thousands. Bombings, beatings, arson had marked its growth. Three times the whole ugly record of larceny and violence had been made available in sworn testimony, produced in public by federal law enforcement authorities.

Not once did the District Attorney protect the people who lived and bought their food in his jurisdiction.

This incredible immunity Tootsie enjoyed in New York was the kind of law enforcement which emboldened the criminal underworld everywhere. So brazen had the underworld become that it even attempted to gain control of an international labor union. In 1933 the notorious Tuohy gang of Chicago went to the parent union of the chicken drivers' local, the International Brotherhood of Teamsters, and demanded $300,000 in cash. They said, "Pay up or else." But they got a courageous refusal. The executive board of the Teamsters met, and backed up the officers with advice that went part way to solving the problem. "Spend what you must for protection [defense] but not a dime to the gangsters."

Shortly after this a Teamsters delegate in Chicago was shot, and he survived with a bullet near his brain. His wife was shot twice, and recovered.

Again, the Tuohy mob pressed their demands, and again the Teamsters stood firm. The Teamsters were tough, too, and they bought an armored car and grilled steel gates for their headquarters. The Tuohy mob was broken, not long after that, by multiple prosecutions in the Middle West.

Not until 1937 was Tootsie Herbert's immunity from justice finally ended in New York. He was an obvious target for our special rackets investigation, and we went after him at once. Chief Assistant Jack Rosenblum and Deputy Assistant Sol Gelb took charge of it, and Goody Goodrich's accountants accumulated the evidence from hundreds of sets of books subpoenaed throughout the poultry industry going back over the years. We found all the evidence we needed of payoffs, extortion, and union larceny. We also learned that one of his lieutenants had even been operating a loan shark concession in the union, lending money to workers who were hard up for cash, and charging them enormous rates of interest.

Tootsie at first thought our investigation was a joke. We heard that the boys were offering odds of ten to one that Tootsie would succeed, as he always had in the past, of beating yet another rap.

We brought an indictment against Tootsie charging many counts of grand larceny—a felony—and we started the proceedings by putting the loan shark on trial. Tootsie even then had the brass to walk into the Court of General Sessions where his lieutenant was on trial and right there he attempted to intimidate the witnesses. But his power had begun to wane. The witnesses held for us, the loan shark was convicted and sent to prison, and the next on the list was Tootsie himself.

Formally, Tootsie Herbert, his union president, David Diamond-stone, and the secretary-treasurer, Harry Frankel, were accused of embezzlements and thefts from their unions amounting to just $40,000. Rosenblum and Gelb, assisted by Louis Rosenshield, had piled up such mountains of evidence to support even that charge that Tootsie Herbert was astonished and dumbfounded. In fact he was so shocked that, midway in the trial, he threw in the sponge and pleaded guilty. Diamondstone and Frankel followed his lead.

So—Tootsie Herbert was sentenced to four to ten years' imprisonment, Diamondstone to one to five years' imprisonment, and Frankel to one and a half to five years' imprisonment. Before he went away Tootsie returned to the members of the union a sum of $25,000 he admitted taking from them.

The downfall of Tootsie Herbert was another heavy blow to the underworld. To see pretty-boy Tootsie stand up and plead guilty was to see another public enemy removed.

The Metropolitan Feed Company was dissolved, and the coop manufacturing company resumed the delivery of coops at reasonable prices. Not long afterward the city Commissioner of Markets said, "I cannot remember in the past year receiving one complaint similar to the hundreds received before. I venture to state that the elimination of the racketeers has effected savings in the neighborhood of $50 million a year."

Yet all these years the Tammany District Attorneys had done nothing.

There was another touch to the story: we found photographs of Joey Weiner, the partner who had been imprisoned, with the Tammany leader James J. Hines. Hines always used to make Thanksgiving presents of turkeys to the poor. It was Joey Weiner who gave Hines the turkeys without charge.

At this time $5,000 reward was offered by the city of New York. Not for Jesse James. Not for Billy the Kid, not for the holdup of the Deadwood stage, but for a young New York lawyer who had betrayed his profession and turned gangster. He was a fugitive from justice.

The man was Dixie Davis, the counsel for and confidant of Dutch Schultz. That last night in Newark, Schultz and his lieutenants had been going over their books, and the adding machines had shown a take of more than $850,000 for a five-week period. These figures

applied, as we learned, only to the numbers racket segment of their
empire. They showed every expense, from the property taxes paid on
a store used as a numbers front for the mob, down to an underling's
bill for fifteen cents for a package of cigarettes.

After Schultz's death, we believed that Dixie Davis had taken
over. We were not sure, and there were probably many others involved. But Davis was the brains behind the new muscle men, whoever they were. And the numbers rackets were being carried on as if
the Dutchman still lived and breathed.

Dixie Davis was an improbable figure to be a top commander of
a New York racket. He came from Tannersville, a hamlet in upstate
New York, worked his way through Syracuse Law School and was
admitted to the Bar in 1927. This made him the professional contemporary of many of the men on our staff. Davis was given a clerk-
ship in an honored law firm, but he soon went into business for himself.

He was a clever kid, on the way to success, and he started hanging around the magistrate's court. He began to handle some small
numbers racket cases. He came to meet the little fellows in the racket
and he saw that it would pay for him to meet the higher-ups. He
established a law office in the back of a bail bondsman's office and,
from a professional "fixer," he learned the ropes.

Soon he became known around the mob as "the Boy Mouthpiece."
His work pleased his ignorant clients. In court he talked loudly and
waved his arms, putting on a good show. He shouted in the courtroom,
but in the back rooms he whispered. And his clients seemed to go
free with increasing regularity. The usual fee for a lawyer in numbers
cases in those days was $25. Dixie Davis cut the fee to $15 and did a
wholesale business.

By 1930, in three short years, this youngster had become the
leading lawyer for the numbers business. He also thought that his
own brains, along with Dutch Schultz's muscle, ought to be able to
divert the golden stream of profits from the little bankers into a
massive numbers racket. In two more years, as I described it, Dutch
Schultz was running a multimillion-dollar operation. It will be recalled that Dixie Davis was the defense counsel for two of the policy
bankers, Henry Miro and Wilfred Brunder, whom I succeeded in
sending off to prison during my days in the United States Attorney's

office. Among Miro's papers we had found direct evidence of that gift of silk shirts made to James J. Hines.

Since the murder of Dutch Schultz, Davis had risen to new levels of affluence. His law office, so called, was a whole floor of a skyscraper at 1450 Broadway. His rent there was $13,000 a year. He was a home-loving fellow, with three separate establishments, one on Park Avenue, one on West End Avenue, and a third, a penthouse, on East Ninety-second Street. Dixie Davis' wardrobe included sixteen suits, for which he had paid $165 each. His overcoats cost $190 apiece, and his shirts from $8.00 up. A well-known patron of the night clubs, he had also become a friend and associate of Hines.

So—the power of the numbers racket kept on growing, and where was the District Attorney? Thousands of people, in fact, were arrested year after year because they had the numbers slips in their possession. One poor fellow was held in court for betting two cents on the numbers game. This case prompted Magistrate Frank Oliver to remark: "The District Attorney can't break up policy rings that way." And he threw the case of the two-cent bettor out of court.

Even before Schultz's death, Deputy Assistant Charles P. Grimes had been in charge of one of our task forces investigating the numbers racket. We ascertained the names of some of key bankers such as Alexander Pompez, the brothers José and Masjo Ison, and a friend of Hines named Maloney. We learned the structure and the personnel, located the addresses of the drop stations, and filed the evidence for use against the leaders. We found out about the system the late Otto "Abadaba" Berman, shot to death along with Schultz, had used to narrow the odds in the Dutchman's favor.

It turned out that Abadaba was an official handicapper, and he had access to the computation rooms at some of the race tracks. The winning number was often chosen on the basis of the race results. Once the bankers all over town had made up their lists of the policy slips brought in by their collectors, they could find out which number had been most heavily played. A Schultz associate named George Weinberg, brother of the Bo Weinberg who had been dumped into the East River with concrete overshoes, would call Abadaba at the race track and give him that number. Six races would have been run, with the seventh remaining. Abadaba had ways of finding out the final betting odds, and the grosses, and if things looked bad for the

Dutchman, Abadaba would make enough last-minute bets on the seventh race to change the number.

In this Depression decade, Abadaba was paid $10,000 a week.

In January 1937 we decided we had better gather in some more of the evidence, all at once, to see where it would lead us. So, the night Tootsie Herbert was arrested, we launched a series of numbers raids in a midnight sweep through Harlem. Seventy persons connected with the various numbers banks were picked up and taken to the Claremont Inn, a delightful restaurant on the Upper West Side, closed for the winter and opened up only to accommodate our necessities.* The sweep was successful.

* In *Attorney for the People*, Rupert Hughes wrote this description of the Claremont Inn episode:

"The policy men were the most wary of criminals. They knew all the tricks of detectives, all the wiles of shadowers. The seizing of one had always sent the rest off in all directions. Hence, the first problem was to find a cage for those who were to be captured, so that they could send no warnings to the others. Police stations were out of the question, since newspapermen were always there and the neighborhood always interested. Dewey resolved to create his own station house. A study of upper New York provided the ideal spot, and it was owned by the City, the famous Claremont Inn, on Riverside Drive near Grant's Tomb, a popular resort in summer but boarded up in winter.

"With fine help and cooperation from Park Commissioner Robert Moses, under whose wing the Claremont was, Dewey provided the old inn with the necessary telephone service for his men and with necessary comforts for his expected guests. It was a large place, and the captured could confer with one another, but with no one else. They would realize how completely their army had been absorbed. Each would be tempted to be the first to turn State's evidence to save his own hide.

"Dewey concealed the grand rendezvous, even from most of his own detectives, and had them meet at another spot supposedly for a raid on another racket. Since he needed reinforcements of policemen, Commissioner Valentine gave him a squad of rookies from the Police Academy, who would presumably have no political or racketeering connections. They were told to telephone their families that they would be absent for the night, then were taken to the Claremont in small groups.

"Sergeant Grafenecker divided the detectives and the rookies into squads, each under a detective with sealed instructions to be at a certain place at exactly 6:00 p.m., read the letter, and strike sharply. At Claremont Inn, Dewey and some of his staff, Captain Dowd, and Grafenecker waited for telephonic news from the battlefront.

"First came word that the Pompez bank had been seized but, by an unlikely chance, Pompez was absent. Later learning that his bank had been captured, he fled all the way to Mexico. Ison was known to be already in France, although his bank had continued in business.

"The few motorists who passed Claremont Inn that night must have assumed that a private reception was being held there, as car after car swirled into the driveway and deposited its freight of men and women. Each guest-in-spite-of-himself or -herself was questioned at once by a member of Dewey's staff. Each lied, of course, but all grew anxious as they saw what a convention of old associates had gathered.

While we were at the Claremont, Goody Goodrich talked to an accountant for one of the numbers banks and was told that the books on a bank—or banks—were in a certain building in Harlem. I sent Goodrich and a detective to that address to pick up the books and question anybody they found there. Goody and the detective proceeded to the heart of Harlem in the middle of the night, went into the building and up several flights of stairs, knocked on an apartment door, and entered. One man ran away up the stairs and was caught by the detective. A second man in the apartment would say nothing—but Goody found the books under the floor of a closet. The books not only gave us amounts but also names.

After this breakthrough I assigned Sol Gelb, Harry Cole, and Eunice Carter to help Grimes develop the case. Six months of intensive questioning of the men and women detained at Claremont Inn brought out a mass of evidence. These men and women were held as material witnesses and they talked against the higher-ups.

On July 14, 1937, the grand jury handed up a dozen numbers racket indictments, and the name at the head of the list was that of J. Richard "Dixie" Davis. Also indicted were George Weinberg, a former Schultz treasurer named "Big Harry" Schoenhaus, and the bankers Pompez and Ison. It took three more months of detective work to locate Pompez somewhere in Mexico, but he was eventually arrested and held on extortion charges there under the terms of our extradition treaty with Mexico. He then commenced an expensive legal fight to be allowed to remain in Mexico.

Dixie Davis, meanwhile, was nowhere to be found. Along with George Weinberg and a beautiful, red-haired, former rodeo rider named Hope Dare, he had simply disappeared.

At my instance a $5,000 reward was offered by the Board of Estimate, and a nationwide manhunt for Dixie Davis got under way. Rewards of $5,000 were also offered at this time for Lepke and Gurrah.

"The deserted inn on Riverside Drive had seen many throngs in the ancient days and nights, but never an assembly quite like this. A few of the guests at last began to chatter. Little by little, they gave evidence enough to convict Pompez and Ison, and strong evidence against other members of the Schultz mob.

"Dewey now had a fairly complete picture of the whole racket, but he still had to convince most of the ladies and gentlemen that they were not the objects of prosecution, and their eventual freedom depended on their frankness and honesty. Refreshments were served and, when the party was over, the guests were taken in batches to prison cells, Claremont Inn went back to its sleep of hibernation, once more a haunted house where only ghosts walked."

Throughout this sequence of events, as I have said, the elected District Attorneys of New York had done nothing. Who were they? Before 1933, it had been Thomas C. T. Crain, the old Tammany creature, and after 1933 it had been William Copeland Dodge, a former magistrate. Throughout these years the real power was that of James J. Hines, who even termed Dodge "my man."

Now it was another election year, 1937, and Dodge's conduct in office had been so widely criticized that he did not offer himself for re-election. Instead, Tammany put up a decent fellow named Harold Hastings, one of Dodge's assistants. This was an adroit tactic but it could be easily seen through.

If I had been a racketeer, the first thing I would have tried to do would be to arrange for a man to be elected to the office of District Attorney who was respectable, but stupid and incompetent. If he happened to be old, and to have occupied at one time a seat on the bench, so much the better. For nothing added to the appearance of respectability so much as ermine once worn.

If I had been a racketeer, I would have seen to it that the next District Attorney was a man who had long been in public office and could not earn a real living as a lawyer if he had to. His fear of being out of a job would make him quite willing to accept suggestions as to the conduct of his office. Above all, I would avoid letting a real trial lawyer who amounted to anything hold that place.

If I had been a racketeer, I would then have seen to it that this prosecuting officer would appoint some sixty assistants, whose names had been suggested to him by district leaders, some of whom were intimate friends of gangsters. I would also have liked to see him choose three or four assistants from members of the opposing party, to be used as window dressing, but who would never be permitted to take part in the prosecution of any of the real racketeers.

If I had been a racketeer, I would then have known that, with this kind of setup, no matter what racket I headed, I would be safe in carrying out my plans. It would not matter if I decided to hold up an industry or get rid of my rivals. I could have gone along sure that I would be immune against the law.

On August 14, 1937, I accepted a draft from the Republican Party to run for District Attorney of New York County. I said:

"As a result of the work of the rackets investigation, it has become clear to me that there is an alliance of long standing between crime and certain elements of Tammany Hall. For twenty years Tammany Hall has controlled criminal prosecutors in this county, and for twenty years the power of the criminal underworld has grown. This alliance must be broken.

"I have become convinced that the only way to carry on the fight against the underworld and its allies, and achieve permanent results, is through a completely reorganized and effective District Attorney's office. Accordingly, I have accepted the nomination for District Attorney.

"I propose to serve no group or class. Decent municipal government in New York City is the only issue."

Judge Seabury, who, along with Thomas D. Thacher and Charles C. Burlingham, had previously asked me to accept a nomination from the Fusion Party, announced that I would have the Fusion nomination.

Mayor LaGuardia was running for re-election and he had also been eager to have me run. We had two or three sessions, but he was a curious fellow. He made it clear that it was a very good thing, and that I ought to do it, but he never came around and said, "Won't you do it?" He did not want to get himself in any position of feeling obligated. We were fairly good friends and we became better friends even though he had a little green monster in him. In any event, we were running mates.

The American Labor Party, through its spokesman Alex Rose, also endorsed La Guardia and me. Rose was a sort of mechanic who later ran the Liberal Party for Dubinsky. Rose was the head of the hatters, and he loved being a conspirator and exercising some political power, as do most people, and he was very active in the original American Labor Party, subsequently the Liberal Party.

The Progressive Party also nominated me for District Attorney. So I was the Republican-Fusion-Labor-Progressive candidate against Harold Hastings. My opponent was so confident about his Tammany connections and about his inevitable victory in the overwhelmingly Democratic city that he went off on vacation and stayed there for most of the campaign.

Meanwhile LaGuardia was taking on a Democratic opponent, state Supreme Court Justice Jeremiah T. Mahoney, who had actually overcome a Tammany nominee in a primary and was now going around saying that LaGuardia was "a red."

I had also given up, incidentally, arrangements I had concluded with Sullivan and Cromwell to become their senior trial partner at the conclusion of my rackets investigation. I had had lunch there with John Foster Dulles and a number of his partners. I think my participation might have been worth $150,000 a year.

During my campaign for District Attorney I was endorsed by most of the New York City press and by many powerful unions, including those of David Dubinsky and Sidney Hillman. The New York Bar Association endorsed my candidacy, and then we had a lot of volunteers, fine fellows with whom I had grown up in the Young Republicans. There was an enormous lawyers' committee, a thousand or more. It was a sort of municipal revival session.

Kenneth F. Simpson was the chairman of the Republican County Committee. A Phi Beta Kappa graduate of Yale, honor graduate of Harvard Law School, with many years of wheeling and dealing in local politics, Simpson had succeeded Chase Mellen, Jr., in this job in September 1935.

William M. Chadbourne, the treasurer of the County Committee, had been LaGuardia's campaign manager in 1933. It should be noted, however, that LaGuardia was running city-wide and I was running for District Attorney only of New York County, meaning Manhattan only. Two other Republicans, Newbold Morris and Joseph V. McGoldrick, were running with LaGuardia on the city-wide slate.

Millard H. Ellison, a prominent attorney who had once been an Assistant District Attorney, was my campaign manager. Murray Gurfein was in charge of a group of lawyers who went over all the campaign materials. This was also the time Harold Keller first showed up. Harold, a former newspaperman, performed superb services as head of a research staff and as a writer and editor. He was a fine, steady fellow with a good mind, and he was to stay with me with increasing responsibilities for most of the rest of my career. Hickman Powell, a newspaperman and friend, became publicity director. He had a bit of genius, and he did a good job. Keller and Powell both had precise minds, imagination in speech writing, and there was plenty of material. It was straight, factual information.

We also had the first foreign language division ever put together in a campaign of this type. It was run by Bernie Yarrow, a Russian.

As a young man, he had escaped from Russia, swum the icy rivers, got into Central Europe, worked his way to the United States, and landed without money. He was without English, but he learned it, and he worked his way through law school. He acquired workable English, became a friend of some of my assistants, and turned up in this campaign.

Yarrow did a superb job with the minority groups. There was a special organization for the Yiddish press, which was much larger in those days, a special organization for the Italian press, and Bernie was in over-all charge of everything but the Jewish group, which was always independent. Bernie organized the Byelorussians, White Russians, Czechs, Slovaks, Germans, Swedes, Norwegians, Syrians, Hungarians, and Poles.

Meanwhile Eunice Carter and another greatly valued associate of our rackets investigation, Frank Rivers, were doing splendid work in the black community. As I said, it was all like a revival meeting in municipal government.

Accepting the American Labor Party nomination formally on September 30, I said:

For more than two years now I have sat regularly for days and for nights in conference with leaders of organized labor. These have been devoted to the purpose of making sure that the frontal attack on organized crime should never be of injury to the labor movement. And so it is that I have become your candidate. The workers need no longer accept the crumbs which drop from the table of vote-seeking politicians.

There can be no advance in our industrial society without collective bargaining. There are still businessmen who regard a picket line as a signal for a criminal investigation. The gangster had been the second obstacle to industrial progress. The racketeer is in no sense part of the labor movement. He is no more a labor racketeer than a business racketeer. Never again must the criminal underworld be permitted to sit between the employer and the worker, extorting from one and beating down the wages of the other.

On October 4, I said:

I have entered politics because there is too much politics in the administration of criminal justice. No one has yet discovered a Republican, or a Democratic, or a Labor, or a Socialist method for the prosecution of crime. There is certainly no political system for the administration of criminal justice, the protection and reformation of the youthful criminal, the social study of his environment, background, and possibilities of rehabilitation, or the proper administration of his parole. . . .

In mid-September there was a dramatic interruption when we captured Max Silverman, the associate of Lepke and Gurrah who had been on the scene during the murder of the union leader Billy Snyder in 1934. Our assistant chief investigator, John F. O'Connell, traced Silverman to a rented Hollywood, California, apartment, where he was living with his wife under the name of Green. Silverman was arrested, held on $25,000 bail, and flown back. A second dramatic interruption came when Pompez, the fugitive numbers banker, returned voluntarily from Mexico and gave himself up. The third dramatic interruption was, of course, the attempted murder of our witness in the Lepke-Gurrah investigation, Max Rubin, who was gunned down on a street in New York City.

I told a group of Armenian-Americans:

Our city is in the movies now. We've become a scandal so bad it's in the movies. Every day you go and see a gangster movie. You see the victim witness, the waitress, the shopkeeper, the decent citizen, who says, 'I'm afraid to testify. I'm afraid I will be murdered if I tell the truth!' This—in an American court, and it's peddled coast to coast.

On October 24, in one of a series of radio addresses, I turned the spotlight on a very important Tammany Hall leader, Albert Marinelli, the county clerk of New York County. He was a politician, a political ally of thieves, pickpockets, thugs, dope peddlers, and big-shot racketeers. I thought that Marinelli's story told much about the alliance between crime and politics in New York.

Marinelli was, in fact, one of the most powerful men in town. He was leader of the Second Assembly District downtown. He had been elected county clerk in 1933 in the teeth of the LaGuardia landslide. In 1935 he had put up a hand-picked candidate named Joseph Greenfield and had unseated David Mahoney as leader of half of the First Assembly District. In this election Mahoney charged that two notorious racketeers, Joseph "Socks" Lanza and John Torrio, had been active in Marinelli's career. Lanza was the gorilla who dominated the Fulton Fish Market. Marinelli's office building had also been home for the racketeers Doyle and Dio of the garment trucking wars.

Marinelli could be found routinely standing in the basement of the

Criminal Courts Building in Manhattan, quietly chatting with bonds-men, lawyers, and hangers-on. He lived on a comfortable estate, sur-rounded by an iron fence, on Lake Ronkonkoma on Long Island. From his several motorcars, he chose to drive back and forth in a Lincoln. His Japanese butler, Togo, served him well.

In 1932, when Marinelli went to Chicago to attend the Democratic National Convention, there was with him a well-dressed, pasty-faced, sinister-looking man with a drooping right eye. Together, they turned up in Chicago and played host in a suite at the Drake Hotel. They were constant companions at the race track in the afternoons. Mari-nelli's friend was Lucky Luciano.

In January 1935 the Marinelli Beefsteak Dinner in New York was a colorful affair. Benny Spiller, the loan shark in the Luciano hier-archy, bought tickets and attended in person. So did Jesse Jacobs, the Luciano bail bondsman. So did some of the Luciano bookers and other personalities of the prostitution racket. They all knew they had to buy tickets for the Marinelli Beefsteak Dinner because Little Davie Betillo was selling them.

The United States Government conducted an investigation of election frauds in Marinelli's Second Assembly District in the election of 1933. The records showed that Marinelli's people had added 4,534 votes to their own set of candidates and stolen 3,535 votes from the opposition.

In the 28th Election District of the Second Assembly District the chairman of the election board was George Cingola. He was re-sponsible for making sure there was an honest count. Cingola had been imported into the district for the election, and he registered from the home there of his sister.

Back in 1927, Cingola had been arrested for an election offense, and he had beaten the rap. Later he had been arrested three times, twice for assault and once for bootlegging, and he served a sentence for one of the assault raps in the county jail in Mineola, Long Island.

Cingola had also been found by three detectives of the Police Department narcotics squad sleeping with two loaded revolvers under his pillow. For this he was convicted in the Court of Special Sessions for a double violation of the Sullivan law but was somehow let off with a $25 fine.

For the 1933 election, Al Marinelli made Cingola the public official in charge of the polling place and graced him with the title of chairman of the local board of elections. After the irregularities were uncovered, the federal government indicted Cingola, but he was not heard from again, and the indictment was dismissed.

I thought the people of New York County were entitled to know who some of Marinelli's county committeemen were. I produced the official criminal records. The first one was of a man who had eight arrests to his credit, including charges of robbery, felonious assault, disorderly conduct, malicious mischief, grand larceny, and the selling of dope. The only charge that had stuck was the dope peddling charge, which had been brought in a federal court. On all the others, he had gone free.

The second county committeeman had been in the federal penitentiary at Atlanta for counterfeiting. He had since been arrested for extortion, carrying a gun, and homicide with a gun—and none of these charges had been made to stick.

The third county committeeman had started out in Hoboken, New Jersey, with an arrest as a horse thief. He got out of that rap, and also out of another for felonious assault. He was then convicted on an assault charge. This man kept his name off the police books for fifteen years but was again arrested for assault and robbery, and again let go. About a year after that, he was caught peddling drugs and sent to the penitentiary. When he got out he was appointed to the county committee but was rearrested and sent back to prison.

A fourth county committeeman was also sentenced to Atlanta for dope peddling and, after graduation there, he qualified as one of Marinelli's committeemen.

A fifth county committeeman beat a homicide charge in 1923, as well as subsequent arrests for robbery and manslaughter. When a narcotics charge did stick, he was fined $25. Later the man was arrested and charged with possession of a large amount of opium, but the case was thrown out.

A sixth county committeeman had a record of two convictions, first for impersonating a police officer, and second for narcotics violation.

A seventh county committeeman had started thirty years before as a discharged pickpocket, and he spent five years in a New Jersey prison for assault and robbery. He was released from a charge of homicide with a knife.

Of the newest recruits to Al Marinelli's unbelievable county committee, one had been discharged on complaints of automobile theft, robbery with a gun, and vagrancy. Another had beaten an attempted robbery charge, and a third a grand larceny charge. Yet another had beaten an automobile theft and felonious assault charge, and yet another had been released on charges of carrying a gun, and coercion. Finally, one of Marinelli's men and been charged as a fence, a receiver of stolen goods.

Adding up the county committeemen and the election inspectors in Marinelli's Second Assembly District, I found that thirty-two men had police records, and twenty had been convicted of various offenses at least once. Their attainments as citizens included seventy-six arrests on charges ranging from robbery to sex crimes, with dope peddling heading the list.

In a state-wide radio address, I said:

No wonder they are desperately fighting to keep the office of District Attorney in the same hands it has been in for twenty years!

No wonder Marinelli is joining with his pals, running the fight of his life!

The people of the Second Assembly District are entitled to know the facts about those who have been misrepresenting them in the political councils of New York. For years they have been terrorized at the polls and forced to submit to the domination of the gunmen who paraded their streets. And don't for one moment believe these are the only cases.

The office of District Attorney of New York County is the most cherished prize of the political leaders who want to continue their control of criminal justice.

These are the sinister forces who are fighting to keep the right to select assistants for the office of District Attorney of New York County.

These are the living obstacles to everything that's decent and clean in the conduct of our city!

This is not a political issue. There can be no difference of opinion on the questions involved. Gorillas, thieves, pickpockets, and dope peddlers in the political structure are not the subject of argument. There is nothing political about human decency!

On October 26, I dared Marinelli to have his whole committee fingerprinted:

I am still waiting, still waiting to get the rest of his county committee to submit to being fingerprinted, so that we can find out how many more of them are ex-convicts and dope peddlers.

I told the story of how Assistant Attorney General Charles Schneider of New York State had been the lawyer for Wolfie and Morris Goldis in the Avenue A murder.

I attended a dinner in honor of Benny Gottesman, the heroic leader of Local 1 of the waiters' union, who had defied the mob at the peak of its power.

On one of my campaign swings, which averaged ten to fifteen appearances a day, I said:

These are the districts that Charlie Schneider and Uncle Albert Marinelli said they owned—body and soul. They always said at Tammany Headquarters on Fourteenth Street that they could hand out a chicken at Christmas and kid them the rest of the year. They could hand them a chicken on Christmas Day and let them live in cold-water flats the rest of the year, and like it. But what is called for today, in our great cities, and particularly in New York, is to drain social and economic swamps and in the main to attack the twin problems of congestion and underprivilege in the same straight-forward manner.

On Election Eve, November 1, I summed up:

Why is it that in the last twenty years our people developed a terrible cynicism about the administration of criminal justice? Why did they decide it was safer to pay up and keep quiet? Why did they decide that it was not safe to testify in a criminal case for fear of re-venge?

It is because the big-shot criminal has operated with such complete immunity that victims have feared to go to their District Attorney or, when a brave man did complain, the complaint was fruitless.

You may tell your children every day that the way to live is to work hard, to save, and to obey the law. But our children are practical people. They are realists. If you tell your children one thing and they see another on the streets, they say, 'My father is an old fogy, my mother is just old-fashioned.' They soon learn what is happening. Realities speak louder than the things we can tell them in the home, the church, or in the synagogue.

The younger generation finds things out for itself. It knows all about the immunity of the gangster. It has come to believe that the underworld is more powerful than the law.

These have been some of the results of political control and political dictatorship.

With your help, we will restore criminal justice in the county of New York.

That was my final election speech.

On Election Eve, James J. Hines said: "Well, there is a vibration in the air that seems to say LaGuardia and Dewey. If it's a true guide, it's a sweep. When a sweep comes along, there's nothing you can do about it. Dewey is a very nice young fellow."

LaGuardia was re-elected Mayor of New York, swamping Mahoney, polling nearly a million and a half votes in the entire city and 328,995 in New York County alone.

I was elected District Attorney of New York County, defeating Hastings by 326,351 to 217,332.

Law and Order

Lucky Luciano, as a teen-age narcotics offender, defined his personal philosophy: "If I had to be a crumb, I'd rather be dead." After his rise to the leadership of the Mafia in New York—and after his sentencing to thirty to fifty years' imprisonment—he redefined his philosophy. Luciano said, "I was never a crumb. A crumb is a guy who works for a living."

In case anybody ever wondered what a Special Prosecutor thought about when he finally went home at night, I must admit I found myself constantly asking questions to which I had no ready answers. These were not generally questions about how crimes were committed and about how they were to be investigated. These were the business of the office. Instead I found myself asking what had brought offenders to the bar of justice, what could best be done to prevent recurrences among others. Also I found myself pondering some of the larger questions of the impact of crime upon the nature of our government and our society.

As lawyers, my associates and I had trained for many years for our profession. In return, the state had granted us a special license, and this might even have been termed a special privilege. Certainly this was an exclusive right to give advice to our fellow citizens and to represent them in controversy. As legislators, too, we lawyers were involved in formulating most of the laws and, as judges, some of us interpreted them.

In a larger sense our role was also one of appraisal of the problems of the world into which we were moving. We had always had an important role in shaping changes in society, as these had come about. If we were sufficiently alert and open-minded, that condition of leadership ought to continue into the future.

In fact, throughout modern history, lawyers had been in the forefront of the movements of their times. Without immodesty, we could also claim that lawyers had been a principal factor in seeing to it that the changes which constantly occurred were brought about with a minimum of shock and injury to individual liberties and to property rights.

Since the foundation of Anglo-Saxon jurisprudence, it even seemed to me, the freedom of individuals had largely been cherished in the hands of the Bar. Lawyers had prosecuted, defended, and judged. Lawyers had helped to smooth the adjustments between individual rights and property rights.

Of course we as lawyers also had the private right to sit comfortably in our offices and devote our entire lives to making money. But we had not, and we did not. If we had, then the Bar would have lost its vitality and its influence in the country, and we would all have long since become moribund and comparatively useless appendages to society.

So the Bar as a whole had accepted the broad duties of lawyers to participate in the problems of society and to work for their solutions. And if we were to perform these duties constructively and realistically, it followed that we should pause occasionally and view the scene on which we were moving and the times through which we were passing.

In the 1930s and in the years that followed it seemed to me that organized crime, linked with corruption in government, was the greatest single threat to our freedoms in America.

I considered the effect of crime on democracy.

Society was at the mercy of organized crime unless crime was checked.

Organized crime was an efficient, effective system to which society was paying bountiful tribute. Its criminal empires stood outside the law and aside from formal instruments of government, answering to no writ other than their own. The leaders of organized crime were despots who were able to force society to do their bidding.

Wherever organized crime flourished, unchallenged even by competent law enforcement, the public respect for law and order broke down. The people lost confidence in their government and in the meaning of democracy. Criminal justice languished from indifference. The way was opened not only to the lawlessness of crime but to frustrated, violent, dictatorial moves to stamp out crime, and the consequent spread of lawless vigilantism.

I considered the effect of municipal corruption on democracy.

Society was at the mercy of corrupt political machines, at all levels of government, no matter how elevated, unless the corrupt machines were checked.

The corrupt political machines appeared to the casual viewers to be efficient and effective, controlling key positions, dispensing benevolence to the general mass of followers, and awarding large favors to the privileged few. In the end, all recipients of favors paid bountiful tributes and forfeited personal liberties by accepting their obligations to the corrupt political machines.

The corrupt political machines, along with organized crime, also stood outside the law, aside from formal instruments of government, and were posing as super- or supragovernmental forces. Wherever corrupt political machines flourished democracy failed. The political dynasties claimed they were friends of the people but actually usurped the functions of government without accepting responsibility for helping shape the future of society.

The corrupt political leaders at all levels of government also tended to become despotic. Increasingly, they tended to require those who looked to them for benevolence to do their bidding in all things. Inevitably civil liberties were given up or infringed upon. In the absence of real leadership against the corrupt political machines the people were being led toward dictatorial systems almost by default.

I considered the solution to be an aggressive insistence on law enforcement against organized crime and corrupt political machines, leading toward a revival of our traditional concepts of justice. This concept would hopefully bring about a revival of our faith in democratic government.

This would require effective crime prevention measures, modernization of law enforcement processes, the appointment of competent law enforcement officials, and an awakening of the public consciousness to the destructive power of crime and the need to eradicate it. This would in turn require the leadership of civic groups, the contribution of the free press, and increasing participation by the people in the machinery of law enforcement. It would also require a recognition of the danger posed by theorists who were misled into "liberal" solutions that tended to obstruct justice, e.g. proposals, even in the 1930s, to outlaw court-ordered wiretapping by law enforcement authorities.

Smashing municipal corruption would require a similar awakening of the public consciousness against those public officials who were betraying their trust and for the need to eradicate them. The effectiveness of honest, competent public officials wherever they could be found would set a good example. Democracy would be strengthened when the public, which had to foot the bill, insisted absolutely that its officials be responsible to society, not to themselves, and certainly not to criminal bosses.

I also believed there should be a militant insistence on the part of the people against any change in our democratic system. Those who advised a recourse to Fascism or Communism were showing weakness, in my opinion. The solution was to strengthen instead the machinery of free government by throwing out the leaders who betrayed democracy and by putting in their places new leaders who would serve the people honestly and capably. There should be no substitute for integrity in government.

I believed the public would gain greater confidence in democratic processes as these were seen to be increasingly effective. I knew from my knowledge of my own generation that there was a large number of men and women of ability who would be available for public service. I felt that graduating classes of colleges and schools would furnish us new material for our fight against crime, appreciating the great fields open in public service, welcoming opportunities greater even than those open to our fathers when our country was still groping its way.

American youth, with its zeal and enthusiasm, could be counted on to help improve conditions and furnish bulwarks against any inroads of dictatorial methods. America needed to give its youth reason to be confident in democracy.

So, when I thought about these and related things late at night, I knew there was an enormous job to be done. The city was in bad shape. The country was. Organized crime was no myth—it really was so powerful that people in the highest places—judges, industrialists, editors and others—had reached the conclusion that we could never eliminate underworld influence in our lives by legal processes. When people of that stature reached that conclusion, then our basic forms of government were in serious trouble.

I thought the job could be done, that it was certainly a possibility, and that it could be done by the application of hard work and brains. I certainly was not sure it could be done, but I thought it ought to be tried. I also thought it was the most challenging situation the country had ever faced internally. It was certainly the most challenging situation that law enforcement and the administration of criminal justice had ever faced.

That kind of challenge I responded to by nature, so that I really had not done a lot of thinking about whether I would take on the job. This was just the chance to do the biggest job that any lawyer could do.

I had come to believe that those who said the mobs ruled America were not far wrong. The law had abdicated, failing to offer protection to the citizens and failing to defend our free society.

After all, our laws were supposed to reflect our ideals as a free people. And they had not been enforced. They were not being enforced. I believed it was possible to enforce the laws and, in that way, to make a contribution.

Over and over, during the Luciano trial and at other times, men and women would come up to me and say, "Oh, it's all right while you're carrying on this investigation, but when it's over things will go back to where they were."

I learned that the work of wiping out the fear, and smashing the criminal structure, and demanding integrity in government, could only be done on a long-term basis. Otherwise I was just running a cleanup, with all the old conditions of tribute, fear, and complacent prosecution due to return before long, allowing crime to rule again.

The question, then and since, was whether our people really

wanted law and order. Did our people understand that law and order were the guarantors of all our freedoms?

On the other side of the same problem, it was apparent to me—and to all other thinking people during the Depression—that law enforcement alone was a negative blessing. I was obviously not one to minimize the significance of destroying the arrogant structure of criminal-political power. The restoration of public confidence in the law and in its officers was of first importance in the Depression as in any other time. So, too, were the restoration of a sense of public morality and the redefinition of an example to be set to our children. The era of cynical contempt for the law had indeed to be put to an end.

But all law officers could do, in the immediate sense, was to cause penalties to be imposed and a deterrent to be invoked. Whether that penalty was probation and a helping hand, or whether it was dire imprisonment for hardened criminals, law enforcement alone could not solve the problems. Crime was of course the product of remoter causes, social pressures, and political cynicism. No less important than crime prevention was the need to get at the causes. We needed to create a healthier environment in our political, economic, and social life, and in the Depression we could get a consensus on that.

There were economic, social, and political crimes as well as legal crimes.

I never doubted that it was the function of the state to protect its people not only from terrorism, greed, avarice, and exploitation but also from the economic disasters which were sweeping away their means of livelihood, through no fault of their own. The state must, within the context of law enforcement, seek to encourage industry so that every worker would have a better chance of getting a job. So long as there were not enough jobs for our people, I also thought it was the first duty of the state to provide relief.

Generations raised in an atmosphere of despair would produce a shocking percentage of human wreckage, which would tend to undermine the community.

The criminal problem, in fact, was going to the roots of this kind of social life. It began with the children. For nineteen years or more Lucky Luciano and his ilk had been swaggering on their daily rounds. During that time their example had been thrust daily into the faces of the children we wanted to grow up to be happy and decent.

The influence of the home, the school, the church, the synagogue was being forced to compete with the reality of the protected gorillas on the streets.

The racket leaders were living in the best hotels, the best apartments, polluting our places of amusement. Squandering money with brazen impudence, they were demonstrating to millions of boys and girls that there was a safe and easy way to live during the Depression —the racket way. Sad to say, the motion picture presentation of the power and wealth of the criminal underworld was the truth.

The racket leaders moreover had influence and friends, and visibly so. They were the degradation of anything we ever attempted to teach our children about the meaning of freedom and the importance of democratic government.

As far as racketeering was concerned, the traditional objective even of catching and punishing lesser-level offenders who committed overt criminal acts was becoming almost futile. Its only justification was to eliminate or reform minor criminals, or to compel them to give testimony against their masters on the next upper level of the hierarchies. As we had seen in the Luciano case, the real organizers and operators of the rackets rarely appeared. Their work was done by hirelings whose apprehension seldom served even as an interruption of the work of the combines.

The minor agents of the rackets seemed to me to be symptoms of the malignant disease. And diseases were not cured by the removal of mere symptoms.

Actually some progress was being made toward understanding these lesser-level offenders. People were beginning to understand that these offenders might be injured, more than helped, by being segregated in a reformatory or prison cell. Probation was resulting even then in the saving of thousands of lives. Our objective at this level of law enforcement had definitely become the rehabilitation of offenders, and not punishment.

The days were passing when public prosecutors could regard the thousands of minor criminals being ground through the courts as assets in their prosecutorial records. The days were coming when criminal cases would be viewed in terms of people, their social background, their individual opportunities for rehabilitation to useful places in the community.

But this rendered all the more urgent the desperate need to apprehend and remove from our midst the racket leaders and their political friends and allies. It was in terms of their political influence that their threat to society was most insidious.

The racket leaders had operated behind the screen of politics in America for many years. Many of them had gotten their start in the lean days by supplying petty thugs to politicians to help carry elections. They obtained some pickings as their reward, but what they most appreciated was a kind word in the ears of the politicians' pet magistrates. Once these criminals were able to establish a reputation for being able to make "a fix" by using the "right contacts," then their importance began to increase rapidly.

The racket leaders were now ready to take over their industrial and labor union systems with brass knuckles and guns. They had political protection. They even stood well for a while with District Attorneys whom the politicians had put into office. They were able to build empires in an amazingly brief period of time.

We have seen how Lucky Luciano was able to take over the burgeoning prostitution racket by telling the bookers, "You guys are through. I'm giving the business to Little Davie." It was as simple as that.

So in the 1930s even the word "politics" came into disrepute, as crime began to affect the national identity. That politics should have fallen into disrepute in this, the greatest of all democratic countries, was a crime against the people. The science of representative government should always be our most honored and honorable profession. Politics is the lifeblood of democracy.

The history of all government, or so I reasoned, was a search for competence, honesty, wisdom, and temperance in the use of power. To that end, people sought for their leaders men and women with the ability and capacity to do the job for which they had been selected. But everything rested upon individual integrity.

So long as municipal government was being mishandled we had no reasonable right to expect the counterpart in Washington to be much different, or much better. If its roots were poisoned, so must be the tree. So, regardless of which party happened to be in power, the people would first have to clean up their own governmental back yards.

To attain this good government, sacrifices would have to be made. Local party objectives would have to be subordinated to the ultimate goals. Personal friendships or financial relationships would have to be placed second and freedom first. Traditional ties would have to give way to principle. The establishment of an honorable administration in municipal affairs would have to be placed ahead of party politics or economic and social beliefs.

For the country then, and I suspect since, was waiting for unity. It was waiting for internal peace and for co-operation among all the elements. Well-meaning people could make promises, but it would take character to keep the promises. We would have to have public servants who carried out their pledges. We would have to have administrations with the will to do what they said they would do.

It followed on logically that, in Washington, we would have to have administrations that respected the free institutions of this Republic. The Constitution of the United States provided for three coordinate branches of the government—legislative, executive, and judicial—each independent of the other. The courts were to determine whether any legislative or executive act was a usurpation of power. This system of checks and balances was the bulwark of American institutions. It was the guarantor of our liberties, and we would never surrender it.

The people would have to choose administrations which would respect their oaths of office. These administrations would have to place in its high offices men and women of proven competence and known integrity. The administrations would have to remember that they were the servants of the people, and not the masters. Above all, they would have to govern according to the dictates of common honesty.

My own power at the time was limited to dealing with various aspects of criminal justice. But within the limits of that power I determined that criminal justice should not be handed out in the back room of any political clubhouse. The defense of liberty was going to become, once again, as honorable as the defense of property.

Living as we did in the Depression, most of us were thinking largely in terms of the future. It was a time when men posed questions and sought to find answers to many of the problems affecting human society. In such a time there was inevitably a tendency on the part of some to believe that reaction or a preservation of an untouchable status quo was the ultimate aim. There were others who believed that only a radical transformation of human institutions could be a solution.

The Man who Gets Things Done

DEWEY

In early political career, Dewey was first non-Tammany Hall nominee to win election as New York County district attorney since 1915, came within 70,000 votes of defeating Herbert H. Lehman for governor in 1938. His electoral successes as a Republican reflected admiration for his fight against crime even though the mood of the New Deal days was overwhelmingly Democratic.

Dewey's hat on desk was not a hat thrown into the ring of presidential politics until the 1940s. His first runs for office were almost a by-product of his day and night hounding of the rackets.

All together now for New York City parade were former Governor Al Smith, at *left,* Mayor Fiorello LaGuardia, with raised hand, and at *right* of unnamed chairman, Democratic National Chairman James A. Farley, and at *far right,* Dewey. In 1930s battles, LaGuardia was pivotal; although running with Dewey in 1937, he paid key tribute to Dewey's opponent Lehman in 1938. Dewey said of LaGuardia: "He had a little green monster in him."

Dewey's political philosophy helped lay the foundation of "modern Republicanism." An advocate of state action to relieve social distress, he wanted to retain the "sound" elements of the New Deal at a time when Republican conservatives could only denounce FDR as "that man."

Dewey's religious training led him to admire the Mormons, and the "Jack Mormons" who could take a drink every now and then. Himself an Episcopalian, he attends church here with his wife and mother.

Dewey's advocacy of national preparedness did not conceal a lack of experience in foreign affairs which later hurt his career severely.

Dewey received honorary degrees, including one from Dartmouth which cited him for reviving ancient concepts of justice as "a flaming sword."

Dewey was much more than an amateur farmer and he built on his Owosso experience to keep his farm at Pawling, New York, "decently" in the black while enjoying his Holsteins.

Dewey at Gridiron dinner heard skit, "I see the White House just at three, I see a large-sized company, I see them shaking hands with me, why do I dream those dreams?"

Dewey, a keen yachtsman, abandoned one weekend cruise when a prostitute scratched Luciano's initials on her abdomen.

George Zerdin Medalie was a classics scholar who used to exchange notes with his wife in ancient Greek. A brilliant barrister, he set the styles and the rules as United States Attorney that Dewey's men worked and lived by, reaching for "the ruby nose" or the decisive point of any given case. Later he became Dewey's principal political as well as legal adviser.

Dewey and Lehman, seen here smiling together, annoyed one another intensely. Dewey thought Lehman claimed a monopoly on human welfare but was really a barroom fighter who waved the bloody shirt of anti-Semitism. Lehman thought Dewey was a prosecutor, not much more.

Grand prize of the Dewey versus Lehman duel was this archaic Governor's Mansion at Albany. This is a later picture, taken during Dewey's three-term tenure, after the Lehman finger-shaking, lecturing years, and before Nelson A. Rockefeller loaded the old building with modern art.

He killed himself in mid-trial. George Weinberg, while testifying as a
state's witness in the Hines trial, shot and killed himself in White Plains.
But his previous testimony was simply read out loud in court just the
same.

He changed clothes in Hope Dare's apartment. J. Richard "Dixie" Davis, another State's witness against Hines, was permitted this concession even though under arrest. Davis had been Dutch Schultz's counsel and was one of the ablest of the bad guys—perhaps *the* ablest—of the 1930s.

Defense counsel Lloyd Paul Stryker, a great orator, was able to blow himself up like a frog and proclaim a thought that had just occurred to him. He urged Hines jury to let the church bells ring in tempo—"Not guilty, not guilty."

Rodeo rider Hope Dare, raided with Davis in a Philadelphia apartment, came to New York to get help from Jimmy Hines. Meanwhile, Davis' wife went to Philadelphia to stand by Davis.

Judge Ferdinand Pecora declared first Hines trial to be a mistrial on a very tenuous point of law that outraged lawyers who
did not write New Deal treatises for the law review. He was
succeeded for the second Hines trial by Judge Nott.

James J. Hines, *center*, the Tammany leader of New York City, took $1,000 a week from the Dutch Schultz gang while going about his genial, straw-hatted way. His influence was extraordinary because his district attorney would not investigate the rackets or provide protection for injured citizens, because his Police Department puppets got rid of honest cops, because his controlled magistrates actually dismissed most of the charges brought against members of the mob. Hines was sometimes called the chairman of the board.

Thomas E. Dewey, the morning after Hines's conviction, at age thirty-seven.

In such a time, the very existence of our own freedoms called for an extraordinary amount of understanding and leadership by lawyers everywhere. Every institution, whether economic or social, lay in a sense within the province of the lawyer. For the law, broadly speaking, not only shaped such institutions but affected their working.

In the face of demands for rapid change veering sharply to the left or sharply to the right, the lawyer was expected to select the soundest solutions. It was his function as a lawyer not to be reactionary to the right, where he could not see the movements of a changing world. Nor was it his function to be radical to the point that he failed to prevent the destruction of institution, and concepts, of human rights.

All of our institutions were undergoing a period of re-examination and re-evaluation. Every aspect of the manner by which we had organized our lives was under critical scrutiny. Our whole economic system was under attack. Certainly only the institutions which broadly and effectively served the community were sure to survive.

In such a period, the point of view of the Bar needed to be one of unselfish and open-minded leadership. Our point of view in approaching this period would determine our usefulness and the relationship of the profession to the world we would live in.

But how should we arrive at a point of view?

Lawyers were very much like scientists. We had an innate yearning for the absolute. We should have liked to be able to go to the lawbooks and come back with positive answers to the questions which arose in the course of practice. Of course we knew that these absolute answers rarely existed. The law constantly moved, and the answers which were absolute yesterday might be doubtful today, and the reverse tomorrow.

It was a curious thing that laymen often viewed the law as a field where certainty was obtainable. The layman usually believed even more strongly than the lawyer in the absolute validity of the doctrine of *stare decisis*. Yet in his own profession or business the layman would readily recognize that conditions constantly changed from decade to decade, and often from year to year.

It followed inevitably that the great issues of tomorrow would continue to be solved in terms of a synthesis of conflicting trends. Amidst the internal struggles of society, if we, as lawyers, recognized that solutions would come from compromises and from mergers of ideas, the Bar could continue to serve in leading the way. It could serve as what you might call a catalytic agent for the forces of change.

This, it seemed to me, was the essential of our point of view. How, then, should it be carried into action? After all, law and order are matters of action.

Of course, the lawyer occupied a dual role. Professionally, he was an advocate for his clients. Personally, he was a leader of public opinion. For example, a lawyer might make a practice of defending burglars at the Bar. In doing so, he could perform the highest function of the lawyer, that of defending human liberty. But in his personal capacity that same lawyer was an expert in the field of criminal law, and he owed an obligation to the community to see that the criminal law was strengthened and the process of justice made speedier and more efficient. Accordingly, though it might be against the interest of prospective clients, I submitted that it was the duty of that same lawyer to help in the passage of legislation which would make more certain the punishment of the guilty.

In broader fields, the modern problem was more complex. The Bar tended inevitably to be linked in interest, as well as to some extent in philosophy of conduct, with its clients. Thus a man who represented financial interests tended to become in his capacity as a citizen an advocate of the viewpoint of his clients. A lawyer who exclusively represented labor unions tended to think in terms of the objectives of labor. A lawyer who represented real estate clients tended to become identified with their special point of view in the fields, for example, of property assessment and municipal taxation.

In such special representation, a lawyer often became a leading authority in his field, and, therefore, one of the most useful citizens for the public generally.

Now to whom did that lawyer's special knowledge or skill belong? Did it belong to the client who retained him? I believed it belonged to the client only in the particular matter for which the lawyer had been hired.

Did this special skill belong even to the lawyer? I believed it could not belong wholly to the lawyer, because he was specially licensed by the state to exercise the privilege of practicing law.

Then did it belong to the state? It did not belong to the state, except in totalitarian nations.

This special knowledge which we were acquiring as members of the Bar would have to be, inevitably, an asset of the community and of our fellow citizens as a whole. It followed, then, that except when under a specific retainer the expert knowledge we acquired in special fields must be contributed to the community. Moreover, it would have to be contributed solely in accordance with our own convictions as to the best interests of the community.

Clients might often disagree with a lawyer's independent judgments as a citizen. But in the long run the lawyer's independent judgment would usually be of greater good to the clients he served than if he followed only their views of the moment.

In short, we lawyers would have to be philosophers as well as craftsmen. We would have to think in terms more broad than the exigencies of the moment. We would have to be students of social changes. We would have to be prepared to lead public thought and to take our parts in molding it. If we lawyers were absent from such leadership we would fail to preserve the essentials of our system. If we were active in it we would progress and we would progress soundly.

I deeply believed that democracy was greater than cynicism. Decency would prevail over trickery. We would return to the way of common honesty. A people of integrity would insist upon a government of integrity.

As lawyers, we would have to think of laws and administration in such terms of large-scale perspective. We would view the future with open minds and participate in shaping it. This was not only the right of lawyers, it was our duty. And, if history was the guide to the future, then lawyers should be its keen interpreters.

Part III | DISTRICT ATTORNEY

CHAPTER XVII

The Secret Staff Meeting

Governor Herbert Lehman of New York State received a nineteen-page denial from County Clerk Al Marinelli of the charges brought against him during the campaign. "They are trying to crucify me," Marinelli said. "If it's a crime to help the underdog, then I'm guilty. Many East Side mothers came to me, asking me to intercede for sons who had fallen into minor troubles. If I had helped spring any big-shot racketeers, my tin box would show it. I have no bank accounts, no tin boxes. My limousine is a six-year-old car which has been the laugh of the community."

Governor Lehman sent the Marinelli denial to our office and invited us to submit proof of the accusations. Within a few hours our process servers, with police escort, went out with subpoenas for three hundred of Marinelli's people. Within another week I wrote Lehman:

> In my address of October 24th, I stated that Albert Marinelli was a political ally of thieves, pickpockets, thugs, dope peddlers and big-shot racketeers. I repeat this statement and I set forth the relevant matters to which I referred in this connection. . . .
>
> I am prepared to prove each of the statements herein by

documentary evidence, and the testimony of witnesses. Since you suggested that my charges be under oath, I am annexing my affidavit hereto so that in the event you desire to treat these statements of fact as formal charges, there will be no delay.

Lehman called on Marinelli to reply, but after a week Marinelli resigned as county clerk with its $15,000 salary and privileges. Subsequently Marinelli was tried in Brooklyn on charges of harboring a fugitive and was acquitted.

Assistant Attorney General Charles Schneider, whom we had also named in the campaign, resigned the day after the election. He said, "I would rather be Charlie Schneider, maligned, stigmatized, libeled and tossed about than be Mr. Dewey going to bed with this on his conscience, if he has a conscience."

District Attorney William C. Dodge, who had chosen not to run to succeed himself, left office with the statement: "Someday I may describe in detail how certain people not only sought to hide from the public the accomplishments of my administration, but actually interfered with the orderly administration of the criminal law in order that they might enjoy publicity.

"We are passing through a cycle of hysteria. It requires courage and a sense of humor to hold public office. The only true solution to the crime problem will be found in better living conditions, better parental care, and more attention to God."

Dixie Davis, in hiding, had heard me mention his name during the campaign. At a later date he wrote: "Dewey's sentences slashed me to the marrow. What made it worse was that he talked of me sympathetically, as if I were some misguided kid." George Weinberg, the other fugitive Schultz leader, had thought I would never be elected because James J. Hines was "the most powerful, individual political leader in New York."

On my return from a brief vacation in Bermuda, asked about whether I would run for the presidency of the United States in 1940, I replied: "That's a pipe dream."

On our own side of the election aftermath, Kenneth Simpson, the county chairman, came down on me with a list of proposed new appointees exceeding the number of jobs. I had had a bad time with Simpson the weekend before the election. He got hold of me and said, "Now, I want to tell you that the polls won't open Tuesday morning unless you get me $50,000. You've sopped up all the money that was available."

Instead of making political contributions to the organization, a lot of people had given directly to my own campaign. He said, "You've sopped up all the money, and, if I can't get that money for the district captains, and if they don't have $10 apiece for the captain and the co-captain, there'll be nobody at the polls on Tuesday."

There were three thousand or so election districts in New York, as I remembered it, and that was $60,000, and it was customary to give a district captain ten dollars to buy a box of candy for the election board, to buy him lunch and dinner, and to pay for taxis to bring people out to the polls, or maybe to keep. Some of them just showed up and looked at the polls, then went home, and kept all of it. It was a tradition. In Albany, they were given $200 per election district.

I told Simpson, "We haven't got the money, and I don't have any right to do that. I'm not in charge of the finances." He replied, "I can't get anywhere with these fellows, but I'm telling you. You're the candidate. If I don't get $50,000 by Monday, the polls won't open on Tuesday."

Well, he made some kind of settlement. I think the campaign committee did have some funds, and they did contribute.

Leadership has to deliver results and demonstrate its effectiveness, but Simpson was never happy with the patronage he got out of our office afterward. He did not get a quarter of what he thought he ought to have as a minimum. He just did not produce good enough people. He had twenty-three assembly districts, and they all had half a dozen young lawyers in them, all of whom wanted to get on our staff either for glamor, or glory, or principally for a job—it being 1937. I took some, but not too many.

Frank Hogan, incidentally, recalled a story about my return from the trip to Bermuda: "Dewey was returning by airplane. The office was greatly disturbed by the news that his plane was five hours overdue. According to the reports, it was battling strong head winds. A group of assistants and a few newspapermen were waiting for the latest information. There was little talk. Nerves were on edge. Finally Mike Claffey, a brick-colored Irishman who worked for the New York *Journal*, broke the tension by remarking, 'I know what you're all thinking. Wouldn't it be terrible if the plane fell into the ocean. Don't worry. Dewey will have something to say about that.'

"A few minutes later Dewey's secretary announced to the great relief of all that the plane had landed in Baltimore, which was where seaplanes landed in those days. 'Mr. Dewey just telephoned,' she announced. 'He says he is thoroughly rested and is ready to dig in and work. There will be a staff meeting tomorrow night.'"

Out of this press attention, one query prompted me to write to my mother:

> Mrs. George M. Dewey
> 421 West Oliver Street
> Owosso, Michigan
> Dear Mater:
> I am sorry to have been negligent about writing, but I am expecting to see you any minute now. When are you coming, and will you bring me Wilma Demuth's address? She sent me a wire, and I don't know her address.
>
> At what hour in the morning was I born? A number of horoscope magazines are hard up for copy. I told one of them that you would give them the hour. You can answer the letter, or ignore it, if you like, and Miss Rosse will take care of it.
>
> I am working long hours these days but am making some progress all the time.
>
> We will be seeing you very soon.
>
> > With much love,
> > s/Tom

Meanwhile we had secured the help of the WPA in remodeling the District Attorney's office as 137 Centre Street, plus the eighth and ninth floors of the adjoining Health Building, into a secure headquarters. This emphasis on the protection of witnesses, the prevention of leaks, the privacy of investigations had been proven out in our Special Prosecutor's office in the Woolworth Building. This time Frank Hogan worked out five separate entrances and a long corrdor lined with soundproof reception rooms. The New York *Herald Tribune* called the whole setup "a labyrinth of soundproof walls, solid doors and opaque glass."

Rupert Hughes called the new offices "a depository of secrets and a laboratory of investigation instead of, as before, a cave of the winds where politics and gossip ruled."

Meanwhile, also, we had prepared the new District Attorney's office budget. In 1936, Dodge's operations had cost $1,056,320. This included the appropriation of $229,795 for our own rackets investigation, which ought to have been conducted by Dodge's office. Dodge had also received two appropriations of $50,000 each to conduct outside investigations into the bond and mortgage and accident fraud situations. This brought Dodge's total to $1,156,320.

Our own budget submission was for $810,631. As it turned out, we were able through 1938 to do the District Attorney's work, and this included the rackets investigation, for $768,046. This was a saving of $388,274 from the previous year.

On December 31, 1937, I was sworn in by General Sessions Judge Charles C. Nott, Jr., at his chambers in the Criminal Courts Building, with my wife and mother present at the ceremony. On January 1, 1938, I swore in the first thirty-three of my assistants. One was missing. Former Chief Assistant William B. Herlands of the rackets investigation had now been chosen by Mayor LaGuardia to become the Commissioner of Investigations for the New York City government. I named Paul Lockwood to be the executive assistant of the new office. I named Frank Hogan to be the administrative assistant.

There were five regular District Attorneys all told in the city, with its five counties, with a total of 132 Assistant District Attorneys and a total appropriation of $1,560,275. There were also the Racket Bureau of the Attorney General of the state of New York, the Racket Bureau of the Attorney General of the United States operating in New York County, the United States Attorney for the Southern District of New York, including Manhattan and the Bronx, and the United States Attorney for the Eastern District of New York, embracing Brooklyn, Queens, and Staten Island.

There were, thus, five county prosecuting offices, the state prosecuting offices, and three federal prosecuting offices, whose total budgets were greatly in excess of $2 million. All these operated separately. Some are elected and some appointed.

In addition to prosecuting agencies, there were approximately 18,000 city policemen and the numerous agents and investigators of the eighteen federal investigating services. These last included the Department of Justice, the Post Office inspectors, the Secret Service, the Intelligence Unit of the Treasury Department, the narcotics agents, the Alcohol Tax Unit, and others.

Certainly this indicated an adequate number of law enforcement officials with substantial operating budgets. But here was also a labyrinth of procedure and overlapping and conflicting jurisdictions which would seem almost to have been designed especially for the comfort of criminals.

The business of the District Attorney of New York County was far greater than that of most of the states in the Union, and it would require far more of a departmental, administrative breakdown than had been the case in the Special Prosecutor's office. For example, our staff there had been 76, including 20 lawyers. In the District Attorney's office we would have a total of approximately 225 people, with Dodge's total of 64 lawyers increased to approximately 80.

Out of Dodge's 64 men, we kept 3, one because he was very close to becoming eligible for a pension, a second, Felix Benvenga, who went on to become one of the most eminent jurists in the state, and John McDonnell, who had won the Distinguished Service Cross in France, still carried a steel plate in his head, and was a thoroughly competent lawyer.

A brand-new Rackets Bureau was set up as the first order of business. This embraced our former rackets investigation, which was moved into the District Attorney's office in toto. Murray Gurfein took charge of the Rackets Bureau.

A brand-new Frauds Bureau was set up, reflecting my concern that complex stock and other swindles had never received adequate attention. Barent Ten Eyck, assisted by no fewer than seven Assistant District Attorneys, took over the Frauds Bureau. He would later be succeeded by Frank A. F. Severance.

The General Sessions Bureau was placed under Sewell T. Tyng. This was a workhorse bureau that, in an average year, would handle more than three thousand felony cases such as assault, concealment of dangerous weapons, burglary, grand larceny, forgery, and the receipt of stolen property.

The Homicide Bureau, which was open at all hours of day and night, was entrusted to Jacob J. Rosenblum.

The Special Sessions Bureau, handling some fourteen thousand misdemeanor cases in an average year, was put in charge of Sol Gelb and Eunice Carter.

The Indictment Bureau, under Stanley Fuld, presented evidence to the grand juries and drew up indictments.

The Complaint Bureau was headed by Thomas B. Gilchrist, Jr., and Edward Joseph; the Appeals Bureau by Felix Benvenga; the Bail Bureau by Ernest Lappano; the Abandonment Bureau, by Florence Kelley. This last bureau took care of one of the chores of the District Attorney's office, collecting money from husbands obligated to send money to their families living apart.

Goody Goodrich brought his whole accountant investigator apparatus over to the District Attorney's office. Goody also found work for twenty WPA accountants.

John F. O'Connell, the man who had located the fugitive Max Silverman in California, was made chief investigator.

Captain Bernard Dowd and Sergeant, now Lieutenant, William Grafenecker took charge of the detectives and police specially assigned to the District Attorney's office.

Harold Keller was secretary, assisted by LeMoyne "Lem" Jones, and Lilian Rosse, as always, was my personal secretary.

Michael Monz carried right on being the man at the door, the chief receptionist.

Among the new lawyers brought on board at this time were many who would make distinguished contributions to the law and much else. They included the future eminent lawyers William P. Rogers and Lawrence E. Walsh.

Early in 1938, I needed a chauffeur in a hurry, because my usual driver had been taken ill. Among the applicants was a dependable-looking, middle-aged man who came highly recommended by a New York State Supreme Court judge for whom he had driven for many months. The usual preliminary investigation was waived in this case, and he was put to work. In giving his background, he stated that he had spent two years at West Point. But a routine check brought us word from the Military Academy that his name did not appear on their rolls. Other facts could not be verified.

The detective assigned to the check now talked with the chauffeur at length. Explanations were given which, on further investigation, did not stand up. He was called to the office of the grand jury and was told that all members of our staff had to be fingerprinted. He reluctantly submitted but next day he did not show up for work. His record, as developed, showed two felony convictions and an imposing number of arrests.

The New York *Times* described my own office area:

> The place seems empty, particularly on the sixth floor, where
> Mr. Dewey has his office. There are no witnesses or lawyers, or
> politicians casually strolling about the corridors. The only sign
> of life is seen when a witness comes out of an office door and
> goes to the elevator, or when some busy man moves from one
> office to another and disappears. To observe this movement is
> like watching one of the old pantomimes, in which people
> popped in and out of openings with disconcerting abruptness.
>
> The office in which he sits is the same one used by his pred-
> ecessor but it is the quietest District Attorney's office this city
> has seen. A big desk is in one corner, and on it are very few
> things. A bottle of water and a glass, a desk set with a fountain
> pen, and a few papers.
>
> There is no telephone. Mr. Dewey answers only two or
> three phone calls a day and then goes into another room to do
> so. His calls are received and answered by his secretaries, or
> one of his assistants.
>
> Delegations wanting the help of the District Attorney, and
> all the visitors who used to take up much of a District Attor-
> ney's time, are received by Mr. Dewey's executive assistant.
> Mr. Dewey in turn has taken over the task of running the office,
> which used to be the function of the executive assistant.

I had said that my first job as District Attorney would be to reduce
the large population imprisoned in the Tombs in New York City,
awaiting indictment or trial. There were four times as many in the
Tombs as in the previous year. Out of 382 prisoners, 224 were awaiting
trial, and 158 were awaiting a grand jury hearing. Within six months
we had reduced this total to the lowest on record.

In addition to the two grand juries sitting with regard to the former
rackets investigation, two more grand juries were sworn in. At this
time the state legislature was considering a recommendation that
they pass a bill calling for the elimination of what was called "blue
ribbon" grand juries, which we had used extensively.

I argued that the blue ribbon jury was simply the selection from
the rolls of regular jurors of people who had sat through one or more
criminal cases. The idea behind a blue ribbon jury was that in any
society as large and cosmopolitan as that of New York there would

inevitably be a number of people who might be constitutionally opposed to the death penalty, for example, or people who might be opposed to law enforcement in any form, or people who might, if they were kept in a courtroom for several weeks, become hysterical.

A blue ribbon grand jury in a so-called "important" case would mean quite often that the people would be taken from the courtroom to lunch under guard, and back to the courtroom under guard, and to their hotels under guard. I did not think we could do that with a group picked helter-skelter off the street. The purpose was not to get bankers or businessmen on the panel. There were as many laborers and clerks on blue ribbon panels as on any other panels.

One schizophrenic on a grand jury—and this happened many times—could defeat justice. Or a juror who could not stand close confinement and really became mentally ill would also do a very serious injury to the administration of justice.

I argued that one of the best methods was simply to put on the grand jury panel people who had previously served through a long criminal trial.

At this time I was also becoming increasingly concerned about the cumbersome and verbose legal forms still in use. Stanley Fuld revised the formats and simplified the language, and copies of new, so-called "Dewey indictments" were sent to all the District Attorneys of the state. The *Harvard Law Review* later praised Fuld's work: "Although less spectacular than its successful drives against organized crime, the recent revision and simplification of its indictments by the District Attorney's Office in New York County promises to be a significant step toward a more rational criminal procedure."

The District Attorney, unlike the Special Prosecutor, also had a quasi-judicial function. His duty was not exclusively that of prosecution. His duty, as laid down by the courts, and by the various canons of ethics of the Bar, was to prosecute with vigor the guilty, and equally to protect the innocent.

Accordingly, whenever we prosecuted a gangster, we had to remember that we not only had to prosecute him. If, by any chance, we found out that he was innocent, we would have to see to it that he went free. In ninety-five per cent of the cases our first concern was to satisfy ourselves that the men charged with the crimes were in fact guilty of them. Our second concern was to ensure that they received fair trials. That involved the most difficult problem of seeing that defendants were adequately defended. The problem was difficult because a large percentage of lawyers had little individual interest in the administration of criminal justice, particularly in the trial of cases for defendants.

We made a steady effort to improve that condition and to get the Bar generally more interested in criminal justice. And we still had the responsibility, in bringing cases to trial, of making sure that the defendants' lawyers were competent and were properly representing their clients.

One month we encountered a young defense lawyer who seemed to want to try a case more than anything else in the world. He represented one of two co-defendants. An experienced practitioner represented the other. After the People's evidence was put in, it was apparent that both defendants were going to be convicted of assault in the first degree. It was also apparent that, after conviction, the defendants would receive a sentence necessary under the law, which was grossly out of line with the character and nature of the offense, and a substantial injustice would result.

My assistant offered to permit the defendants to plead guilty to assault in the third degree. The lawyer who was eager for a trial would not accept. My assistant then consulted with the other defendant's lawyer, who said, "Of course I'll plead my client to assault in the third degree, but I can't do that unless the other defendant does." The other lawyer again refused, even though it was clear that his client would go to jail for half of the rest of his life. And they could not change him.

My assistant finally had to go to the General Sessions judge presiding and say, "I don't want it on my conscience that this man is going to be convicted of assault in the first degree. He is certainly going to be convicted and if we let it go to the jury a great injustice is going to be done, just because a lawyer is a fool."

And the judge had to bring the lawyer to the bench, saying that he would publicly denounce the latter if he did not explain to his client that a plea of guilty to assault in the third degree would save him from certain conviction for assault in the first degree. That worked.

So one of the major problems was defending the guilty as well as prosecuting them. On another occasion a defendant's lawyer pleaded a young man guilty to a second-offense charge of grand larceny in the first degree. The young man's first offense had been the theft of an old typewriter worth about eight dollars. The guilty plea made it mandatory for the judge to sentence him to from ten to twenty years' imprisonment.

My assistant on the case was expressing his regret for such a cruelty and I interrupted the Court with a personal protest:

"The plea of guilty and mandatory sentence are an outrage, and I suggest that the plea of guilty be withdrawn. This young man has had an unfortunate and hopeless family life, but has always worked when he could get work. He and a friend, both unemployed and without funds, held up a man, but had no weapon, and committed no assault.

"The sentence would be a gross miscarriage of justice. I suggest that the defendant's counsel make an application to allow his defendant to withdraw his plea and plead guilty to grand larceny in the second degree. The District Attorney will join in the motion."

Judge Morris Koenig consented with the comment, "The Court commends the fine attitude of the District Attorney in his effort to attain the humane administration of justice."

Judge Koenig had also been uneasy about the conviction, on December 21, 1937, before I took office, of a friendless young black named Tim Smith, nineteen years old. Smith had been arrested by Patrolman Theodore Steinblinck and charged with felonious assault in the first degree and for illegal possession of a gun.

The judge had been particularly uneasy about the testimony of the patrolman that he had seen the defendant, along with two other blacks, in 127th Street between Lenox and Seventh avenues at 12:40 A.M., that he was walking east on 127th Street when he saw a knife in the defendant's hand, that he took the knife from the defendant, whereupon the defendant had drawn a revolver, which he had struck down with his truncheon, and that a mounted patrolman across the street had picked up the revolver and given it to Steinblinck. Two white men corroborated Steinblinck's testimony.

Defendant Tim Smith testified that the incident occurred on 128th Street between Lenox and Seventh avenues, that he never had possession of a gun, that the gun was lying at the curb, that Steinblinck had assaulted him and was trying to frame him.

The jury had believed the patrolman, and conviction followed. However, as a result of an investigation conducted by one of my assistants, Aaron Benenson, it was established that there were irregularities. The mounted patrolman, for example, who had not been brought forward at Smith's trial, said he would not have supported Steinblinck's account of the incident. The mounted patrolman said he could not state whether the gun found at the scene of arrest had been in the possession of Smith or of Steinblinck. Then it was established that the two corroborating witnesses were friends of Steinblinck's.

The two friends said they had joined Steinblinck, who had left his post, and they had all been drinking beer together. They said it was Steinblinck who had started the altercation with the defendant. They said that neither of them had seen the gun in Smith's possession. Finally, they said their evidence at the trial had been perjury, suborned by Steinblinck.

On the basis of this new evidence, my office motioned to set aside the conviction of Tim Smith on the ground that he had been convicted on perjured testimony. This was granted and Smith was set free.

On March 24, 1938, a grand jury authorized the filing of an information against Patrolman Steinblinck, for the crime of perjury in the second degree. On April 27, 1938, after a trial conducted by Benenson, he was sentenced to an indeterminate term in the penitentiary.

The District Attorney's business was, however, primarily prosecutorial, and after the murder of one policeman on duty and the severe wounding of another I told a meeting of city police: "I want to serve notice on the underworld that any man who points a gun at a cop will be prosecuted to the limit, and any man who kills a cop will go to the electric chair if the combined power of police and prosecutor can send him there."

Sometimes, in fact, our men would get to the scene of the crimes within minutes of the police. One of my assistants, Louis Pagnucco, was called out some time later on an emergency. A landlady, sick in bed with the flu, had been aroused about midnight by some screams in her kitchen, which adjoined the room where she was sleeping. The kitchen adjoined a room on the other side where her tenants, a man and wife, also lived. She arrived in the kitchen just in time to see the woman put an icepick through the heart of her husband. He died immediately.

The police arrived, arrested the wife and took her away. Pagnucco arrived and there was only one witness, the lady with the flu. So, contrary to the usual practice, which was to take witnesses in for questioning, Pagnucco decided he would question her there. He thought he would rather have a live witness than take her to the station and have her suffer a relapse. The police and Pagnucco all told the woman to go back to bed.

The police left the body lying in the kitchen. The medical examiner was not there yet. Pagnucco and a detective questioned the woman, who described what had happened. But the longer she talked about it the more she seemed to be building up a case of self-defense for the lady tenant.

Pagnucco recalled that, after half an hour's questioning, the landlady's memory was getting better and better. There had been a fight, and the man had beaten his wife, she said. Pagnucco knew she was lying. He told her that if she did not tell the truth she would be obstructing justice, and that was a serious thing.

Just at that moment there came a long, low moan from the corpse lying in the kitchen. Pagnucco said his hair stood on end, the detective froze, the stenographer taking testimony froze, and the lady in bed with the flu turned white.

Then Pagnucco, without batting an eye, turned to the landlady and said, "You see! You see! That dead man will haunt you the rest of your days if you don't tell me the truth."

Immediately the woman said, "You're right, you're right, I'll tell you the whole story." And she poured out the original version without a single pause for questions.

Pagnucco did not tell her, until she had finished, the real story about the moaning from the kitchen. In most corpses, about an hour or two after death, the lungs collapse, rigor mortis begins to set in, and the air from the lungs is forced out through the vocal cords. If the corpse was on its back, like the one in the kitchen, and if its mouth was open, it was likely to sound just like that.

On May 13, 1938 with staff, functions, and organization all set, with four months of work in hand, I spoke to a staff meeting at which these minutes were taken:

Dewey: Every place I go, people tell me about what they hear of my office. Of course, one man tells me that I have a wonderful staff, and the next man tells me I have a bunch of Boy Scouts. And I say both things are true. I give thanks for the Boy Scouts because they are the only kind of people who will work hard enough to enforce the law.

I tell the grand juries every month that my staff is young, and designedly so. That's the only way you can get the kind of enthusiasm you need to run a law office. With the exception of a few mature men, the way to run a prosecuting office is to have men whose futures are ahead of them and not behind them.

With regard to cops: they felt we were Boy Scouts beginning with the month of January; by the month of February and March, they discovered we knew our business and they developed a wholesome respect for our office. There are some specific matters about time off, and there are also some matters about the way you treat them.

A middle-aged policeman does not like to be told to come down here and be told curtly by a fresh young lawyer to sit down and he will see him when he is ready. It may be that he is just a cop to you or to other people. On the other hand, he get $3,000 a year from the city of New York, he has for many years seen ambitious assistant district attorneys come and go, and he is still on the job. He frankly isn't flattered by not being treated like a gentleman of senior years and experience. Don't keep them waiting unless you have to. When you do, apologize and your relations with them will be very much happier and more profitable.

The same applies to other members of the public. I think it is well to impress upon you generally that you are a bunch of kids. You're assistant district attorneys in the county of New York with the greatest prosecuting job in the United States. Nevertheless, your average age has been commented on widely, and unfavorably. Some people think it's wise, others do not. I think it is very urgent that you remember that you have been thrust into a position of power at a very early age, practically everybody in this room, and even the men here who are not the youngsters to whom I speak, have been in public office since they were youngsters, and they did learn it then.

You have got to get along with the New York Bar. You have got to get along with businessmen. You have got to get along with your witnesses. And you have got to remember that they are coming in here and seeing the youngsters, they are getting a shock, most of them, and therefore you have to treat them with more courtesy, unless they are the kind of witnesses you have got to shake down in order to get the truth out of them.

The first of the year I spoke of the treatment of judges: I think it was all too common practice for our predecessors to treat the judges as though they were boys from the same clubhouse. Many of the judges have told me of the insulting manner in which assistant district attorneys treated them. I see Benvenga back there shaking his head—

Benvenga: Just a little nervous. (*Laughter.*)

Dewey: That is one nice way out, but you, I think, are one of those people of whom nobody said that. It is a fact that many of the judges felt very keenly on that subject.

Every assistant must have a clean desk when he leaves. It is a rule of the office, and, if it is not observed, we will have to take means of picking up the papers off desks every night and deposit them in a central room and let the assistants call for them in the morning. It is not advisable to leave your papers for cleaning women and their friends to read, or such people as wish to bribe cleaning women to inspect them. Most of our business is absolutely confidential and it is a rigid rule of the office that your desks must be absolutely clean and the office closed up when you leave for the night. I hope there will be no violations of that rule.

Lockwood is the executive assistant of the office. He has got the dirtiest job in the office. If anybody else wants to sit up in that room and receive the abuse of magistrates, members of the public, my friends whom I won't talk to, and he has to meet my acquaintances, receive delegations, pastors, *shochtim,* religious organizations, and politicians, and then spend all night until 2:00 or 3:00 A.M. answering executive office mail, he can apply for the job. Lockwood is the boss of the office. That means when he wants to see anybody in this office they have got to come, and come then if he says so. You have got to recognize that, and I don't want any quibbling or quarreling with him. When he wants you to do something, I want it done.

Now, as to General Sessions, you are entitled to know that conditions in General Sessions are swell. We have tried more cases in that court than were ever tried in the same period, as far as I know. We have had a percentage of convictions of approximately seventy per cent, which so far as I know is the highest the office has ever run in history.

In regard to that, there is a certain sensitiveness about writing

DORs.* I appreciate that and endorse it. On the other hand, I see no reason for trying a case that is obviously no damn good, and never will be any damn good. There is no possible use in trying cases where you have a reasonable doubt yourself as to the defendant's guilt, or in the alternative where you believe that the proof is inadequate to warrant or to procure a verdict.

The only thing I would like to see is that you learn to write DORs. I believe I have received the worst collection of literature published in the English language in the form of DORs. They are simply unspeakable. I never saw such bad documents. I have to turn down about one out of two to Sewell Tyng, and he has to send down three out of four that come to him. You are all lazy. I hate to say it, but, in heaven's name, learn how to write English and to write it so that it makes sense.

The trial work of the office, I think, is finer than it has ever been in the history of the office, and I wouldn't swap the trial men of this office for the cream of all the offices there have ever been in the county of New York. I feel that very definitely. At the same time, I think we need a very much more definite sense of organization in the Court of General Sessions.

Judge Collins turned down a motion yesterday for a special panel. He wisely turned it down. I agree with him. He did it on the ground that we were exhausting the special panels. We were overworking them. And in the second place, it was wise to demonstrate that the judiciary did not always follow the orders of the District Attorney since special panels are under such very intense fire, and a number of people are convinced that they are an enemy of society, a number of blatherskite liberals are denouncing us for using them, and a number of the conservatives believe that we conspire with the Commission of Jurors in order to pick out for the special panel only jurors who take a great joy in hanging the defendant. I may have one fight of my life in connection with that problem, and I am starting to worry about that with the other D.A.s of this city. Stanley, will you try to go to that meeting, the County Lawyers? I can't go. Will you go and extend my apologies?

Fuld: Yes.

Dewey: The Complaint Bureau is handling thirty per cent more

* DOR is short for Discharged on Own Recognizance—the best news defendants can get.

work than in the past. Their trials, I believe, are fifty per cent greater than in the past. It is one of the most important and difficult jobs in the office. The men in the Complaint Bureau are probably handling a greater volume of business, and learning to make decisions and develop more rapidly, than any other single branch of work in the office, except possibly the Indictment Bureau.

We may make some shifts in the fall from one type of work to another. You can't make a trial lawyer overnight, you can't make a racket investigator overnight, you can't make a Complaint Bureau man overnight. When and if you are dissatisfied with your assignments, come to me and I will certainly not hold it against you because you are dissatisfied, and I will try to work it out.

I don't believe there is any branch of the office at the present time where, if the men will devote the necessary intensity to it, they won't advance two years at the Bar for every year they are at it. Nowhere in the city of New York can you get the kind of experience you are getting in any one of the bureaus of this office.

Bear in mind that we have too few stenographers in the office. We have a shortage of stenographic help. The result is, both for the benefit of yourself and the other men in the office, you have to be very sparing of the stenographers' time. In dictation, it is almost imperative that, when you send for a stenographer, you use the stenographer, and send him or her away. Don't send for a stenographer and then get launched on a Rosenblum telephone call, even the new Rosenblum telephone call, which is only half an hour. The use of stenographers when you get on the telephone is very bad. It wastes their time and is a serious obstruction to the work of the office. Simply tell the operator you cannot take any calls for an hour.

I have heard some comment around town that our office is highhat. I suppose there are some people in New York who regard anybody who is honest as high-hat. I think there are enough dirty fingernails around the office, from my observation, to clear us of that charge. On the other hand, I think it is well to remember in connection with my opening remarks that we can avoid that statement by being particularly nice to people. We have had more letters than I have ever seen in any public office, saying that our assistants were extremely courteous. People expect courtesy in a public office. They never get any in most public officials, but they always expect it and, therefore, when we get comments on it with regard to assistant after assistant in the Complaint Bureau and elsewhere, it is a mighty nice indication.

I think there has been some tendency to ignore the rule of the office, which is a very important rule, that the receptionists on your floor should know where you are all the time. I have wanted assistants from time to time, and they were not on the floor. It is imperative that we know where we can reach everybody in this office every minute of every day, except when you are out of the office on racket work. That is a different matter.

As for night work, that depends on the exigencies of the office. Some of you think night work is hard work. Most of you do work three nights and more in the week. I asked Colonel Stimson if he had ever known a New York lawyer who amounted to anything who had not worked ten and more hours a day, and he said, "No." And he said, "Well, I have been coming to class reunions now for a good many years and I see some old guy doddering around, and every time I find that fellow is a small-town lawyer who has not worked very hard, or is retired from the profession. And then I see somebody else, about seventy-five years old, walking with a spritely step, and I find he is a New York lawyer who has worked twelve hours a day for forty years."

If you want to amount to something at the New York Bar—and you would not be here unless you did—all I can tell you, I do not know anybody at the New York Bar who amounts to anything who has not worked hard. And, curiously enough, clients feel the same way. Perhaps it is more important that clients feel that way.

So, when ennui or spring fever or the desire to spend more time at social pursuits comes, I advise you that whatever your decision may be, or your own appraisal of your prospects, it is a fact that the only men who stay on top are the men who do not allow their spring fever to become a habit. This does not mean I am asking you to work any more than is required by your job.

On the subject of mail. As you remember, we launched a policy of the invasion of the civil rights and constitutional privileges of certain members of the staff by ordering that all mail should be opened in the mail room, and a great and overwhelming cry went up from the men about the violation of their rights. We suspended the rule out of deference to their great grief.

All my mail is opened downstairs, and it does not make any difference to me whether Joe Stone reads my love letters or not. He can also read my bank statements if he can get any comfort out of them.

On the other hand, it is my feeling that if anybody is going to get any love letters, or mash notes, or bank statements that he does not care to have examined in the mail room by Joe Stone, who has no interest in your affairs, I suggest you have your mail directed to your homes.

After all, you all have homes. Your homes are all, I think, by now, in New York County, even honestly in New York County.

A warning on photographs. Most of you would know it anyway as a matter of good taste. Don't let yourselves be photographed with a defendant. You must all remember the sheriff who had his pictures taken with his arm around Dillinger. It creates a terrific public reaction, so do not allow it to happen to you.

The press relations are very satisfactory. I think everybody understands the rule that Assistants are not to talk to newspapermen about their cases except in the presence of Harold Keller in his room. The newspapermen wander around the building. Mr. Claffey has a genius for wandering around the building from floor to floor. We frequently catch up with him on various floors. I do not want to call this fellow names and say, "You have to quit it." We can stop it if, whenever you see a newspaperman around, and he asks you one question, you say, "Listen, you know where to get information. I'll be glad to talk to you upstairs." Refer them to Keller.

On questions of law, I assume you all know they are to be cleared through Stanley Fuld. He has some swell research work available for the assistants on questions of law. It is well to remember before you start to look up a question that there may be a very complete memorandum on that question in his files. We have volumes of legal memoranda. They are very good and very useful. If you find he has nothing on the question and you want to look the matter up yourself, for goodness' sakes write a memorandum on it and let him have it. On all legal research, clear through Stanley Fuld, and you will save yourselves time and trouble.

Everybody here knows that private practice is not permitted by members of the staff, and that nobody here is to have a private office. I understand the question came up about private telephone listings, and that some people had not remembered to have their listings taken out of the telephone book. Anybody who has a telephone listed in his name for a law office should make a note right now, and see that he writes a letter to the telephone company before it is too late to have it taken out of the next issue.

I do not suppose this is necessary, but bear in mind that every public official is sold out by the guy he spoke to on the street corner. Therefore, when you want to associate in public with anybody, be very careful who it is. Bear in mind that there are people who would give a few years off of the end of their lives to be able to get something on any assistant attached to this office. Nothing would please many people quite so much as to catch somebody in this office in a mistake.

There are a number of people who would give their shirts to frame anybody in this office, and I have even heard a definite number of dollars named if anybody would do that job on anybody in this office.

Benvenga: What do you feel about assistants going to the race tracks?

Dewey: I have no strong views on it. Largely, it is who you go with and who manages to couple up with you that matters. I do not happen to go to the races.

Benvenga: Neither do I. I just asked because some former district attorneys prohibited assistants from going to race tracks.

Dewey: Well, if they had been as successful in prohibiting their assistants from doing other things, it would have been swell.

I do not think disaster will hit you, provided you are wise enough to recognize the pitfalls. I would not want to prohibit it.

I would like to prohibit night clubs and I think the race track is probably not a very good place to be, but if you have an overwhelming yen for the races I suppose it is all right. About prize fights, I am going to the one on the twenty-second of June when Joe Louis and Schmeling are going to fight it out. I don't think that is bad, and if anybody wants to go to a conspicuous fight, it is all right. But I warn you to watch where you go and with whom.

I have nothing else on here to mention.

Nobody has any cards calling himself an Assistant District Attorney? If you have, tear them up. We don't need those cards. We have shields.

Has anybody anything he wants to take up now? Sewell?

Tyng: I have nothing except what I can take up with individuals.

Dewey: Frank Hogan?

Hogan: I spoke to Paul last night.

Dewey: Murray?

Gurfein: Nothing.

Dewey: Stanley?

Fuld: Nothing.

Dewey: Sol?

Gelb: Nothing.

Lichtenstein (the office psychiatrist): I believe that it would be to the best interests of the District Attorney's office if we had a legislative body which would recommend certain laws which would be to the interests of justice.

Dewey: We have such a body now.

"Mistrial! Mistrial!"

Executive Assistant Paul Lockwood was sitting in his office one afternoon when a man we had very much wanted to see, and waited to see, dropped by. Lockwood's secretary told him that a stranger wanted to see him and had asked for him by name. The secretary added that the man was clean, with his hair combed and his shoes shined. She said he seemed sane and was claiming to have valuable information. Lockwood recalled:

"Middle aged, dark-haired, with dark piercing eyes and heavy set, he was very business-like when he sat down. He asked, 'Is that $5,000 reward for Davis the real thing?' When I said it was, he rejoined, 'I'll put the address on this paper, but I want the five grand in my hand right now—in twenty dollar bills.' Though I was somewhat startled, I managed to look unconcerned and said, 'My friend I don't know who you are, what your name or address is and I don't want to know.' After some talk about the chances of his being killed, I said, 'I can't pay you $5,000 of the city's money and have you walk out of here with it before Davis is captured or I'll be in jail too.' He answered, of course, that he did not want to be killed.

"After much discussion about leaks of his identity, I said, 'Well, let's look at the box we're in. You say you have the information and I've got the reward. You want to give me the information and in all good faith I want to give you the money. Now, let's sit here like two reasonable business men and work out some basis for the deal.' 'I took a great chance coming in here, Mr. Lockwood,' he replied, 'and when I go out of here you probably will have me followed by detectives for days until you find out who I am. I don't want to do business on that basis and get myself killed by the mob.' By the same token I pointed out, I could not ask the prosecutor to countersign a voucher, also signed by me, to pay out $5,000 of the people's money to an unknown individual for some unproved information.

"The argument went on most of the afternoon. For hours I tried to break him down by pointing out that the reputation of the Dewey racket prosecution for good faith and for protecting its witnesses was flawless. We could never do anything, I argued, to impair that underworld reputation without losing our main stock in trade. I would guarantee, if my word was acceptable to him, I said, that no detective would follow him, or, to use mob language, put a tail on him when he left our office.

"I hammered at him that none of us wanted to know his name, so we could never be accused of 'leaking.' In this way, I urged, we could not help but protect him. I could see finally that he was playing around with that idea. Then I summed up. 'Well, it's a question of good faith and it is past dinner time. You have something to sell and we have our reputation for good faith. The way for you to get your money is to give me the address right now. We will pick up Davis immediately if your information is right and you will get your money as soon as the banks open.' After a moment's reflection, he said 'All right; it's a deal.'

"I added: 'Now let me state the deal clearly so we have no misunderstanding. Without giving me any identification, you will give me the present whereabouts of Davis. I will immediately see to it Davis is arrested wherever he is as quickly as possible. You can go home, if Davis is some distance from New York City, and you can call me the first thing in the morning even if it doesn't make the papers. That is, if the bird has not flown the coop.

"'As soon as the Comptroller of the City of New York opens his office in the morning,' I told him, 'we will apply for the reward money, cash the check, and pay you as early tomorrow morning as you and I can get together somewhere away from this office.' Again he said, 'All right; it's a deal,' and we shook hands.

"He told me, but would not write, that Davis was living in a ground floor apartment at Forty-eighth and Osage Street in Philadelphia. Previously I had alerted Charlie Grimes, the Assistant District Attorney working on the Hines-Schultz case and also Mr. Dewey. Grimes got quite heated up and said, 'I think I had better talk to the guy.' I demurred, saying 'I don't think anything would be gained by that. The man doesn't want to talk to anyone else. He has given me the information. Let's act in good faith. Why not just get the cops and pick up Davis?'

"There was considerable work in getting detectives and investigators to Philadelphia with the necessary warrants, etc., without creating a disturbance or paving the way for a 'leak.' We could not arouse the newspapers or other persons we believed to be watching our office. Consideration to some sort of minimum liaison with the Philadelphia Police Department, not noted for its tight security, had to be given.

"About ten detectives and investigators left for Philadelphia in three unmarked cars leaving at different times with instructions to rendezvous at a given address. Mr. Dewey had to persuade the Comptroller of the City of New York, a somewhat nervous individual, to get $5,000 in small bills the next morning as soon as the banks opened. Now, it must be borne in mind, the Comptroller's Office of the City of New York is a very fine agency and Joe McGoldrick, then the Comptroller, was a college classmate of mine. However, the office is up to its ears in red tape. Ordinarily, the city's money is paid out only after everything has been scrutinized, rescrutinized, done in triplicate, and gone over by lawyers and auditors. To avoid this morass required tact, pressure, and diplomacy.

"I might add parenthetically, that we scrupulously lived up to our agreement with the informer that we would not trail him when he left our office in an effort to learn his identity. However, we did have a number of knowledgeable detectives inconspicuously posted around the building so that when he left he at least was scrutinized. Later the detectives all stated that none of them recognized him and that he was not a known figure in the New York underworld or along Broadway.

"Finally, Charlie Grimes and his force left for Philly and we at our end had nothing to do but wait it out. At a late hour that night, Grimes phoned me to say 'Well, we got him. We got not only Dixie but Hope Dare and George Weinberg.'

"Hope Dare was a very attractive young woman who had been a rodeo rider and a Ziegfeld Girl before she became Davis' mistress. George Weinberg was a killer, a prominent member of the Schultz gang, and brother of the notorious Bo Weinberg.

"According to Grimes, the apartment was a real 'fleabag.' Grimes related that our force, accompanied by a lone Philadelphia detective who, to make the arrest legal, had been brought along without any true realization of the importance of the pinch, just pounced in the windows and doors of the ground-floor apartment. Davis and Hope came out of the bedroom rubbing sleep from their eyes, but the killer Weinberg, who had been asleep on the hall couch, plaintively asked, 'Can I put my pants on?'

"Our chief clerk in the meantime had obtained a $5,000 check, and cashed it. At 10:00 A.M. he presented me with a fat envelope containing $5,000 in $20 bills—but he said "My friend, you've got to get me a signed receipt of some kind that can be given the Comptroller." A new headache!

"Shortly after 8:00 A.M. my informer phoned, saying 'Well, my word was good.' I replied that our word was good also. After congratulating him, I suggested we meet in a private room in the Yale Club at Forty-fourth Street and Vanderbilt Avenue. This really startled him. I pointed out that the Yale Club was certainly the last place that anyone would expect an underworld transaction to take place, and he agreed. Somebody on our staff suggested that for my own financial protection, I ought to have a witness to the fact that I paid over the money. Otherwise, I would be in the position of saying that I paid $5,000 of the city's money, entrusted to me as a lawyer, to some person I did not know and could not identify.

"Accordingly, we selected John F. O'Connell, then Chief Investigator of the District Attorney's Office. John was a former FBI agent with a long distinguished record and had done a real bang-up job in the racket prosecution, and he agreed to go along. The two of us went to the Yale Club and to the designated room. In a few minutes, there was a knock on the door. There stood my "unknown" man. He was somewhat taken aback by the presence of a third party but I reassured him that I had the money and that O'Connell was merely there as a witness to protect me. I then asked him to sign a receipt with his name and address. He snapped 'We agreed I didn't have to do that!' I just said 'I didn't ask you for your real name or address. I want a signed receipt with an address.' He smiled rather grimly and then affixed a name and address. If I remember correctly, the address was in Ocean City, New Jersey. The name I have forgotten. I counted out the $5,000 and in doing so, told him to pass the word among his friends that the Dewey office kept its word. We shook hands and he walked out."

That was the last Paul Lockwood ever saw or heard of our very important informant.

Dixie Davis offered to waive extradition from Philadelphia if Hope Dare was released. But there were no charges against Hope Dare, and she was released anyway. The former rodeo rider headed straight to New York, and she went to see James J. Hines himself. She asked Hines to use his influence to help Davis, but Hines put up no money, offered no helping hand. Dixie Davis' wife headed to Philadelphia and offered to stand by and help him. But Davis said he would be true to Hope Dare.

He was extradited, along with Weinberg, and he was lodged in the Raymond Street jail in Brooklyn on $75,000 bail. "This man Dewey alone inspired the vicious attacks," he said. "The reason I became a fugitive was because I knew I was to become a political football. Sure, I represented Dutch Schultz in the policy game. But I only acted as an attorney."

George Weinberg was the first to break. He wrote to Grimes asking for an interview. Grimes went to see him, accompanied by our trial strategist Sol Gelb. Weinberg said he might be induced to turn state's evidence. Later he promised to plead guilty and tell everything he knew about the Schultz racket and the high-level protection provided by Hines. Then Big Harry Schoenhaus, also a fugitive, surrendered and said he would plead guilty and testify.

Grimes and Gelb talked with Davis. I asked Gelb how Davis was getting along. Gelb said, "Fine." Davis said about Grimes's interrogations: "It wasn't torture, but it was psychology."

Gelb recalled: "Dewey is so orderly in his thinking that he wanted Dixie Davis to be as orderly, but I knew the kind of mind Dixie had. I gave him his head, you know, let him go on and on, let him roam. I'd make order out of it, but he didn't have to be orderly. I could make order out of this desk very easily, but it doesn't have to be orderly so that you say it's orderly.

"Dewey, I suppose, didn't prepare that way. He prepared Weinberg, and he was very precise. Now, if I had prepared Weinberg, I would not have been that precise. I have a different method of preparing a witness. I let the witness tell me everything he knows, and then I put it in order.

"Dewey wanted the witnesses to put everything in order the way he would put it in order. He was worried that Davis wouldn't be a good witness because he thought Davis was all mixed up. I said that Davis wasn't mixed up, but was very clear.

"At the beginning Dewey had told me, 'We'll have to try Davis, Weinberg and Schoenhaus, and you'll have to try this case. I want you to get it ready for trial, but if you can possibly do it, you know what I'm interested in. See whether Davis and the others can give testimony involving Hines.'

"Davis had been in jail awaiting trial, and he got disgusted because he figured that Hines was abandoning him. We arranged a meeting. Dewey knew all about it. Dewey told me to meet Davis. We arranged a meeting in a parking place up in Central Park, way up around Eighty-fifth Street, and some detectives brought Davis out of prison, and up there. The detectives sat on a bench, and I sat with Davis opposite them on another bench, and we began to talk about the situation. Davis said he wanted to know what I was interested in. I said, 'I want to know what you know.'

"We talked awhile, and he wanted to know whether he would be given any consideration, and I said, 'Anybody who testifies for the People, if they can use it, is entitled to consideration. I'm sure anyone will do better if he joins the side of the People than if he stays on the other side.' He said he'd think it over.

"After he had talked with Weinberg, Davis sent word to me that he wanted to meet me again, and we met down at Battery Park, and he agreed. He was going to co-operate with the People—so were Weinberg and Schoenhaus.

"Then of course Dewey wanted to know what evidence I could get from these people. During the next week or so, I suppose I had a number of conferences with Davis, who told me what these people knew, because he talked with them in jail. Also, Davis opened up avenues of investigation, told us of a number of things which required looking into and which, undoubtedly, would yield fruitful evidence against Hines.

"After about another week I said to Dewey. 'We got a case against Hines.'

"We went over it. Dewey said, 'He's a very difficult kind of man to prosecute. He's a very powerful man, politically.'

"I said, 'I don't give a goddam how powerful he is. We've been in this business now for several years, and we have never been afraid to proceed. What's more, once you present evidence against Hines, and get an indictment, the public knows by now that you're not a sloppy worker, that you mean what you do, that you don't issue reckless statements, nor obtain silly indictments that are unsupported by evidence.'

"That was a very ticklish point with Dewey. Indictments were not to be obtained for publicity. They had to be backed up with proof.

"I worked with Dewey very closely, and I've never worked with anybody and found it so easy as with Dewey because you never had to labor a point. You'd get three or four words out of your mouth, just starting to express a thought, and he would answer. He'd already gotten your thought. You'd discuss evidence, the law of evidence, and substantive law, all applying to a particular case, and it was so easy to discuss these things with him because his mind was freer from rubbish than any mind I think I've ever met."

Then Justice Ferdinand Pecora granted permission for Davis to visit an outside doctor, under guard, for repeated treatment of a throat illness. After each of these treatments Davis was perspiring so much it was thought he might catch pneumonia if he went back to his cell in his wet clothes. Davis kept his extra clothes in Hope Dare's apartment and, under guard, he went there to change.

Our office had the problem of how to handle a defendant who was turning state's evidence and who was an utterly invaluable witness. He was from the very center of the whole criminal organization, and he knew everything. We had to keep him reasonably contented.

On March 10, 1938, Richard Whitney, a governor and former president of the New York Stock Exchange, was accused of grand larceny. "I fully realize the gravity of what has been done, and that a penalty must be paid," he said.

Richard Whitney, no relative of "Jock" and "Sonny" Whitney of the

Long Island family, was the son of a Boston banker and a graduate of Groton and Harvard. After an apprenticeship with a Boston banking house he bought his own seat on the New York Stock Exchange at the age of twenty-three, and, seven years later, was the head of his own firm, Richard Whitney and Company. His older brother, George Whitney, was a partner in J. P. Morgan and Company. Thirteen years after that, he was said to have attempted to check the stock market crash when he bid several points above the market for several thousand shares of U. S. Steel. From 1930 to 1935, Whitney was president of the Stock Exchange, until he was succeeded by Charles Richard Gay. Whitney was an opponent of government regulation of the securities industry.

For some time, the Stock Exchange had required firms conducting a margin business with the public to answer a questionnaire on their financial status. When this rule was extended to firms such as Richard Whitney and Company, whose business was largely with brokers, Whitney's responses to the questionnaire brought about an investigation by the auditors of the exchange.

On March 7 the business conduct committee of the Exchange went before the Board of Governors to prefer charges of "conduct apparently contrary to just and equitable principles of trade." The governors voted to suspend Richard Whitney and Company. The firm notified the Exchange that it was insolvent.

The District Attorney's office of New York County indicted Whitney, specifically, for pledging against a personal loan $105,000 in securities from a trust set up by his late father-in-law. He was arrested and released in $10,000 bail. The Attorney General of the state of New York, John J. Bennett, had Whitney rearrested on the following day. Whitney was charged with moving $103,000 in negotiable bonds from the deposit box of the New York Yacht Club, of which he was treasurer, and pledging these with other collateral for a bank loan. He was released on $25,000 bail, making a total of $35,000 bail.

There were reports that as much as $800,000 had been used up, that Whitney had suffered serious financial reverses while speculating in applejack distilling investments, that his company had in effect suffered a private failure as long as five years before.

Sewell Tyng took charge of the case and, with little delay, Whitney pleaded guilty. I urged in a memorandum to General Sessions

Judge Owen W. Bohan that Whitney be given "a substantial and punitive sentence."

The investigation led to the conclusion that the entry by the defendant into ventures outside the field of his brokerage business, requiring the continuous addition of large amounts of capital, was the ultimate cause of the failure of his firm.

The defendant had no means with which to finance such ventures and therefore resorted to the misappropriation of the property of his customers and his friends.

With full knowledge of the consequences, he embarked upon a deliberate course of criminal conduct, covering a period of six years, involving larcenies, frauds, and misrepresentations, and the falsification of books and financial statements.

Furthermore, by reason of the position held by the defendant, his conduct amounted to a betrayal of a public trust.

The defendant handled the affairs of Richard Whitney and Company as his personal business, which he managed in his own way for his own purposes, and for which he considered himself under no obligation to account to anyone.

As late as March 5, Whitney had sought the aid of Francis D. Bartow, a partner in J. P. Morgan and Company. At this interview the defendant made a truthful statement concerning his own conduct. He told Bartow he had misappropriated customers' securities, using them as collateral to secure personal loans and loans of his firm, that grave charges were about to be preferred against him by the Stock Exchange, and that he needed $200,000, the amount of the unpaid balance of his loan at Public National Bank and Trust Company.

He needed the money in order to release the securities he had taken and to make restitution before the charges were brought against him. Bartow said, "This is serious." Whitney replied, "It's criminal." Bartow conferred that night with John W. Davis, counsel to J. P. Morgan and Company, who advised that any loan to Whitney under the circumstances would be improper and would raise the question of the solvency of Whitney and Company.

Bartow then met Charles Gay, the president of the Stock Exchange, at the Metropolitan Club and requested at least twenty-four hours' delay in the presentation of the charges. Gay flatly refused any postponement. Bartow returned to the Links Club and told the defendant there was nothing further he could do.

On the next day, a Sunday, Bartow drove out to Long Island where he presented the situation to his senior partner, J. P. Morgan.

Morgan made no suggestion.

Richard Whitney, who had pleaded guilty to the two indictments charging grand larceny, was sentenced by Judge Bohan to from five to ten years' imprisonment. He was sent to Sing Sing.

On May 25, 1938, James J. Hines, the most powerful Democratic politician in the state, was arrested on a complaint sworn by Assistant District Attorney Grimes. Hines said: "They'd better not try me at this time. I don't like this kind of publicity."

Hines was born in 1877, the son of a blacksmith who worked in the Tammany Hall organization. After a spell as a district captain, Hines had been chosen leader of the Eleventh Assembly District on the Upper West Side of New York City. He got this position in 1912 and still held it at the time of his arrest. Hines had made an important decision in the Democratic National Convention of 1932, when he stepped aside from the Tammany favorite, Al Smith, and supported Franklin D. Roosevelt. Hines became the principal dispenser of patronage for President Roosevelt in New York City. In the early New Deal days many people owed their jobs to Jimmy Hines. In 1937, however, the LaGuardia-Dewey landslide was such that Hines was unable even to hold his own Eleventh District. That year, there were no free Thanksgiving turkeys.

According to the deposition of Assistant District Attorney Grimes:

> On or about the 19th day of February, 1934, in the City and County of New York, James J. Hines did commit the crime of contriving, proposing and drawing a lottery in violation of Section 1372 of the Penal Law of the State of New York, in that he, the said James J. Hines, did knowingly and wilfully contrive, propose and draw a lottery, being a scheme for the distribution of property by chance, among persons who have paid, or agreed to pay a valuable consideration for the chance, and did aid and assist in contriving, proposing and drawing said lottery.
>
> Among other things, his participation involved agreeing to influence and intimidate judicial officers and others charged with the duty of enforcing and administering the laws of the State of New York, to refrain from properly performing their duties, and thereby obstructing justice, to the end that those en-

gaged in this criminal enterprise would be permitted to continue the criminal acts they performed of contriving, drawing
and proposing lotteries, unmolested, and without being sub-
jected to the punishment and penalties provided by law. . . .

It also appears that the said James J. Hines received large
sums of money for his aid and participation in said criminal enterprise.

Justice McCook issued a warrant for Hines's arrest, and Hines
came in voluntarily with his attorney, Joseph Shalleck, and submitted
to arrest in Grimes's office. Grafenecker, who executed the arrest, and
Sol Gelb were also on hand. The group moved over to the Supreme
Court Building, where Hines was arraigned before Justice Ferdinand
Pecora. After about five minutes of going over the documents, I said:

This is the result of a three-year investigation which began in
1935 into the numbers racket in New York. Raids instigated in my office in January of 1937 resulted in the first indictments. The other defendants in this case are J. Richard Davis, George and Bo Weinberg,
and other members of the Dutch Schultz mob.

This defendant was a co-conspirator and part of the Dutch
Schultz mob. He conspired to the perfection of lotteries in numbers
in this city. In indictments to be handed up, he will be charged with
approximately the same number of felonies as is charged in the indictment of the other defendants.

At the opening of this conspiracy, he, Schultz, Bo and George
Weinberg conspired to force all independent numbers operators under
one domination by force, violence, beatings, and other means until
they were all brought into line.

The function of this defendant was to control judges and other
public officers to see that they did not perform their legal duties and
to see that they provided protection to the whole numbers racket.

There were, in fact, kidnapings, violence, and other acts in this
conspiracy. This defendant received a number of payments from this
conspiracy, beginning with $1,000 a week, and thenceforth from $500
to $1,000 a week . . .

Shalleck then said: "Mr. Dewey has consistently brought forth
Hines's name through all his trials. Hines was not a member of any
of those conspiracies, and the name of a citizen has been dragged
into cases in which he was not interested. He imputed to Hines the

terrible reputation of the defendants in those cases. This is un-American, and it smacks of the actions of police departments in certain foreign countries.

"I venture to predict that no judge or judges will be named in the indictments. Mr. Hines, for the past two or three years, has deliberately remained in New York for fear that the forces trying to drag him in would say that he had been away and was a fugitive.

"He is an influential politician, and a character well known in this city. Bail of $1 million would not be too much, for thousands of decent citizens of this community would come forward to add their share to raising it. This man Hines has been for years a dominant factor in the Democratic Party, and people respect him, because they know his strong influence in politics.

"Why, a few years ago, the President of the United States praised Mr. Hines for his humanitarian activities. Even today, people crowd into his office in such droves that he can't take care of them.

"Never in his life a blemish, and he'll come forth in this case without a blemish, as he did in the Seabury and other investigations.

"His name is legion. He has been a father to thousands. He's an angel. He never took money for a favor in his life."

I said, and for the record: "I've listened to a lot of drivel in my experience as a lawyer, but never any like this."

Hines was released on $20,000 bond. A professional bondsman was on hand with surety for $15,000. Judge Pecora said he would accept that amount for the time being, and an additional $5,000 would have to be posted the next day.

Hines went from the Supreme Court Building to the Elizabeth Street police station to be booked. While he was waiting to be booked, with Grafenecker at his side, Hines was asked what he thought about it all. He said, "Well, I guess I got to watch my step. I think it's a lot of baloney."

Before the trial, both sides were intensely active. Our staff handling the Hines case had been reinforced. Administrative Assistant Frank Hogan was added to the Hines staff, as was one of the principal trial assistants of the Homicide Bureau, Herman McCarthy. Always on the job were Grimes and Gelb, assisted by Livingston Goddard, who had started out in the rackets investigation as a dollar-a-year man in 1935.

Hines engaged as his trial attorney the eminent Lloyd Paul Stryker, one of the most famous courtroom orators in the country.

On June 6, before Pecora, a New Deal Democrat, Stryker asked for a change of venue so that Hines could have a "fair trial." Stryker said: "Dewey wants to stage a Ringling Brothers circus with Hines as the gorilla, solely for the purpose of advancing his political ambitions. He has started a reign of terror in which every Democratic judge is left under a cloud of suspicion." But Pecora denied the plea for a change in venue.

On July 11, after Hines had been brought before him and had pleaded not guilty, Judge Pecora then sustained an important Stryker petition. Stryker had asked for a bill of particulars to be presented showing which judges Hines had attempted "to influence, intimidate or bribe." Our trial pattern had always been to define the general framework of rackets before describing the roles played by specific defendants. We moved for a reargument, and secured a modification in the ruling, but we were compelled to comply.

So we named former District Attorney Dodge, City Magistrate Hulon Capshaw, and another magistrate who had just died, Francis J. Erwin. At once Dodge denounced these charges as "an outrageous and malicious assault upon my office. During my term as District Attorney, more than seven thousand prosecutions were conducted by my office." The Chief Magistrate relieved Hulon Capshaw of all duties.

Judge Pecora then reacted angrily to newspaper photographs said to have been taken of Dixie Davis visiting Hope Dare's apartment. Davis, in all, had been permitted to change clothes at Hope Dare's apartment eight times in three months. Judge Pecora now refused to sign any more permits for Davis to leave the Tombs for his throat treatments.

Meanwhile Davis had been told in prison that, if he talked, he would be killed. He told Grimes, "Nobody will believe me whatever I do. I might as well go all the way. I'll testify in court."

Judge Pecora accepted Davis' guilty plea and once again rebuked us for letting Davis visit Hope Dare. But he dropped Davis' bail of $75,000 and paroled our star witness in my custody. For the duration of the trial we moved Davis and Weinberg around from one hiding place to another so we could keep them alive.

Stryker was getting rougher. He said: "Dewey must get Hines to get the nomination for Governor. Let Mr. Dewey say that if the nomination is offered him he will not serve. Then this case will cease to be a political football and a springboard from which he hopes to reach high office."

The trial opened at 10:00 A.M., August 15, 1938, in an atmosphere remininiscent of the trial of Lucky Luciano. The Supreme Court Building was the same, and the courtroom was the same, and there was a crowd of thousands milling about outside. Seventy detectives and policemen were on guard. NEA News Service reported:

> Pecora is sunburned to a dark hue. A wide streak of gray spreads over the crest of his bushy hair. His mouth is drawn into a frowning, curving line. Stryker's close-cropped ears lie flat against his head, his small blue eyes are close set. His brows slant downward so that he forever looks as if he is peering. He struts with his hands on his hips and when he scores a point against Dewey, he glances at the other as though he were saying, "There, how do you like that?"
>
> And then there's James J. Hines himself. He's very polite to reporters. As he talks to them during recess, his little blue eyes roam over everyone and everything. When court resumes again, he looks up and cries, "There it goes," and he bounds away eagerly as if it was someone else's trial he was going to. He sits in the well of the court and listens closely. And he looks like a paternal father who is watching his kids cut up. His tiny mouth is drawn into a line, his button of a nose supports his spectacles. Sometimes he bites his lips.
>
> When things get hot, Hines rubs his big, thick fingers across his thumb. During a lull, he looks around at gray-haired, patient, well-preserved Mrs. Hines. "Tired?" he asks, and he comes over.

Within two days the jury was selected, and I began my opening address. I described how the numbers racket worked. I told the story of Dutch Schultz's life and the growth of his criminal empire. I explained Hines's importance as "the man who made this huge lottery enterprise possible, by providing protection." I described the role of Dodge, Hines's man, as District Attorney, and spelled out Hines's control of elements of the police and certain magistrates. I detailed the key role of Dixie Davis as Schultz's lawyer while the Dutchman was alive, and as one of the principal successors after Schultz's death.

I said I would introduce, out of 5,000 people involved in the numbers racket, just 55 witnesses. I led off with Wilfred Brunder, the numbers banker whom we had convicted for income tax evasion in the early 1930s. But then Stryker was on his feet attacking our whole plan of procedure. He insisted that we must prove the existence of a conspiracy in which Hines had been involved before we could bring in any general testimony, in fact any other testimony, about the numbers racket.

Long afterward I reflected that we could not present an entire conspiracy through one witness. There was no order in which you could devise the giving of testimony so that everything a man said would be relevant. So we had to tell the judge, in effect, "we will connect this with evidence," and he had to take our word for it.

If we misrepresented our intentions we ran the risk of having the case dismissed for lack of connection with evidence. If we put in prejudicial material and the case was dismissed, the defendant acquired immunity from further prosecution. So the judge in all probability would accept the word of a prosecutor, because the penalties were so enormous if the prosecutor was inaccurate. Nobody with the slightest grain of common sense would either be inaccurate or deliberately mislead a judge.

In the courtroom, Pecora did not heed our arguments, and he demanded that we introduce at once our evidence supporting the existence of a conspiracy.

So we called George Weinberg to the stand. Weinberg told how he had met Hines at a conference in Schultz's apartment. There Schultz had told Hines he had to have protection. This meant no police drives against the numbers operation and satisfactory solutions in magistrates' courts. Weinberg testified that Hines replied he did not control the whole Police Department but could take care of the Sixth Division in Harlem where the numbers game was played the most. Weinberg testified that Hines said he could also take care of the magistrates' courts.

Weinberg testified that Schultz then paid Hines $1,000 and instructed him, Weinberg, to pay Hines $500 a week, and "any other reasonable amounts up to $1,000." Weinberg said he did this until

June 1935, when the salary was cut in half by mutual consent because of hard times.

But Stryker countered that all the other witnesses of the meeting in Schultz's apartment were dead. Then Stryker forced Weinberg to admit that he had previously committed perjury on more than one occasion.

For the next ten days we provided a detailed description of the operation of the numbers racket. Our witnesses included Brunder and the other bankers, Pompez and Ison. Yet another banker, named Flores, confirmed the existence of the racket. One of our witnesses, a district captain for Hines, testified that he had been coerced by the prosecution, but we had the statement he had signed voluntarily and also his voluntary testimony before a grand jury. There were frequent debates with Pecora.

Weinberg, back on the stand, said he heard Hines ask Magistrate Capshaw to dismiss charges against Weinberg and fourteen other men arrested in a raid on the Pompez bank. He said Capshaw told Hines, "I will take care of it." Weinberg said he paid Hines the weekly fee at Hines's home at 444 Central Park West. The defense countered that Hines did not live at that address at that time. Hines broke his silence and said to Weinberg, "You know you lie."

Gelb commented: "Weinberg made a mistake as to where he delivered money to Hines. Stryker got a good break. Dewey was quite disturbed about it, you know. How the hell did he make that mistake? I said, 'It's not so important. It would be important if this was a one-week trial, but he's a first witness, and you've got close to sixty witnesses. A week from now, nobody will remember what Weinberg testified to about 444 Central Park West, but they will remember in substance that he paid Hines money in different places.'

"About ten days later, the case was going well, and the proof was piling up, and during a recess Dewey turned to the people from the press whom he knew, and he said, 'Do any of you remember what Weinberg testified to concerning 444 Central Park West?' Well, they didn't even react to the question. It was forgotten."

On August 24, the prosecution introduced a succession of respectable witnesses, lawyers, businessmen, and others, and former District Attorney Dodge's campaign manager testified that he had been sent to Hines for campaign money. At least $11,000 cash had been passed at various times, always in large bills, he said. Weinberg had previously testified that Dutch Schultz contributed $30,000 to help assure the election of Dodge.

Then there was the basic question of whether Hines and Schultz actually knew one another. The prosecution introduced a convincing witness, the owner of a riding academy in Connecticut, who testified that Hines, who had a taste for horses, had met Dutch Schultz there while the Dutchman was a fugitive.

A former Tammany leader, John F. Curry, a rival of Hines's, testified that Hines had often asked for and obtained transfer of policemen from one district to another in the city. There could have been a reason why, and I asked, "Being transferred is commonly known as being broken, isn't it?" Stryker was on his feet: "Mistrial! I demand a mistrial!" But he did not get it.

Dixie Davis now told the intricate, inside story of the Dutch Schultz racket, much as described in previous chapters of this book. He testified that thousands of dollars had in fact been paid to Hines for top-level protection in the District Attorney's office, with the Harlem police, and in the magistrate's court. Davis told how Dodge had tried to detour the 1935 grand jury away from the significant rackets. This tactic had been defeated when the grand jury "ran away." Davis testified that he had personally warned Hines to make sure that Dodge did not appoint me as Special Prosecutor.

Davis added an important new fact. He said that Hines, at his advice, had sought the help of the lawyer Max D. Steuer to help Dutch Schultz with income tax problems. Davis was corroborated by Steuer, who took the stand and said everything had happened just the way Davis had described it.

Then a lawyer of unimpeachable reputation, James D. C. Murray, took the stand to corroborate some more of Davis' testimony. Murray said that Davis had taken him to see Hines to warn Hines about my becoming Special Prosecutor.

Dixie Davis' sister testified that she had delivered a $500 check to Hines, and this had been endorsed J. Hines on the back. The signature was not in Hines's handwriting but had been appended by one of Hines's representatives. Next, the prosecution introduced testimony from United States Treasury agents and detectives based upon the evidence obtained four years before. We had been using wiretaps in our attempt to locate Schultz, then a fugitive. The taps had picked up Hines when he had called Dixie Davis with reference to his weekly payments. Big Harry Schoenhaus, one of the Schultz treasurers, testified that Hines had been on the payroll for three years.

Finally, a fire chief from Troy, New York, a Democratic county leader, testified that Hines had telephoned him repeatedly and asked him to stop the local police from "pushing Dutch Schultz around."

Rupert Hughes commented:

> As defense counsel does, Stryker moved for a dismissal of all charges as not proved. Normally, this formality ends in the Judge's prompt denial, and the defense moves up its witnesses. But in this instance, Judge Pecora's attitude was so encouraging to the defense that Stryker was stimulated to make a hard fight for his motion. . . .
>
> Judge Pecora stated that he also found weaknesses in Dewey's case as to the nature of the conspiracy, and whether it had been outlawed or not. Dewey rebelled at this so hotly, that Pecora said "You must not assume that I am playing devil's advocate."
>
> Pecora questioned his own jurisdiction, since the policy banks had been moved out to New Jersey in 1935. Dewey answered this by pointing out that the bets had been collected in New York and paid in New York.

At this point I insisted that "the testimony in the record is uncontroverted and unscratched in its fundamentals." I reminded the court that fifty witnesses or more had given testimony, and thirty had given direct corroboration.

On September 8, Judge Pecora said the case would go on, and it was now the turn of the defense.

Stryker produced one witness for the defense, a slim young attorney named Lyon Boston, who had been Dodge's newest and youngest Deputy Assistant District Attorney in 1934 and 1935. Boston said Dodge had entrusted him with an investigation of the numbers racket and had also picked him to work with the grand jury in 1935. Stryker, in a very significantly worded invitation, told Boston to tell "the entire story" of his work with this grand jury.

Under cross-examination, Boston conceded that he had been

placed in charge of a most difficult investigation when he had had almost no experience with criminals "except as a child detective during the war." Judge Pecora then asked if we were trying to prove Boston incompetent, whereupon I said, "I want to show that this man was assigned to do the utterly impossible, all alone, and was deliberately so assigned by his superior." Even while we proved that Boston was the lowest-paid and least experienced man on Dodge's staff, Stryker kept on raising objections, most of which were sustained by Judge Pecora.

Of course we knew that the runaway grand jury had heard from such witnesses as Police Commissioner Valentine and Commissioner of Markets Morgan that Hines was the high-level official who was protecting other rackets such as poultry and slot machines. Of course we also knew that a defendant on trial for one crime could not be confronted in a courtroom with evidence showing that he had committed other crimes.

But Stryker had "opened the door" with his invitation to Boston to tell "the entire story" of his experience with the grand jury. Whenever a defense counsel chooses to open the door to a matter by bringing out testimony about a part of it, then the prosecution has the right to develop the entire matter so that the jury does not gain a false impression. This is so even if the development of this line of questioning shows that the defendant has committed other crimes.

When I mentioned that Commissioner Morgan had testified before the grand jury in 1935, Boston said, "I don't recall that."

Then I asked the next question:

"Don't you remember any testimony about Hines and the poultry racket there by him?"

Stryker's assistant whispered something, and Stryker was on his feet with a loud shout:

"I demand a mistrial! Your honor! Your honor! I demand a mistrial!"

I said, "The subject was opened by the defense," and I made reference to Stryker's opening the door by inviting Boston to tell "the entire story."

Amid a general uproar in the courtroom Judge Pecora said, "There was no such subject opened up, and I think you should not refer to it in any way, shape, or form." I said, "I shall be glad to discuss it at the bench." But Stryker declined to confer and Judge Pecora adjourned the court, took the matter under advisement, and said he would rule after the weekend, on the Monday.

It was then 2:20 P.M. on the Saturday, and on the following day we had a 20-page brief delivered to Judge Pecora's home in support of our view that the question was legitimate. Stryker had his brief ready on the Monday morning.

Once again, on the Monday morning, Judge Pecora adjourned the court, until 2:00 P.M. For a couple of hours Stryker and I argued questions of law in his chambers. At worst, it seemed to us, the judge could have ruled that the question on its own was improper, and he could have instructed the jury to disregard it.

Judge Pecora reopened the court and gave a two-hour lecture about law and justice. At its conclusion he granted the defense motion for the mistrial.

After the jury foreman had left the box, the clerk of the court asked, "Do you wish to concur in the mistrial, Mr. Dewey?"

I replied, "I certainly do not. I am of the firm opinion that the question asked was correct and proper, as are the two chiefs of my Appeals Bureau and my Indictment Bureau, Felix Benvenga and Stanley Fuld. Unfortunately, however, the People of the State of New York have no appeal from this or any other of the decisions in this case."

Hines was still held on bail and was subject to a second trial, but for a while he was a free man. He was cheered outside the courthouse by his supporters and was carried on their shoulders for a hundred yards. When we walked down the steps a few of the spectators booed. With Sol Gelb and some of the others, I returned to the office. I said there, "Don't worry, boys. There'll be another trial, and we'll win it."

That evening, after a meeting with Medalie and some others, I put out a formal statement:

"Make no mistake about it, Hines will be brought to justice."

Gelb recalled: "I am a realistic person. Pecora declared a mistrial. I knew there was no escaping another trial. How could Hines escape conviction in so strong a case? It had to be brought to trial. Every way you looked at it, there was evidence which in some way or another involved Hines and the protection of this numbers combine."

Many years later I concluded that it was a very bad time. We had a memorandum in hand on the question before I asked it, and we were supported by the law. But we knew so much about Hines that they did not know which way to turn without running into more truth.

The day after the mistrial, I received a wire from my mother:

AM PROUDER THAN EVER AFTER READING THE MORNING PAPER. YOU ARE SURE TO WIN EVEN THOUGH THE JUDGE THROWS OUT THE CASE.
    MATER

I responded:

HOPE YOU ARE RIGHT. MUCH APPRECIATE YOUR WIRE. LOVE
    TOM

CHAPTER XIX

Law Enforcement and Public Opinion

During these years as Special Prosecutor and as District Attorney of New York County, I delivered a few speeches and statements to professional and other organizations on the roles of lawyers in the community.

To the District Attorneys Association of New York State, January 25, 1936:

Together with reform of the criminal law, there must go a far more effective co-ordination between the work of criminal investigation and criminal prosecution, and a strengthening of both. It still seems to me that effective investigation and enforcement is of even greater importance than reform of the criminal law, and that we should direct our attention to the law in action, as well as to the law on the books.

Both the reform and the enforcement of the law are ultimately controlled by the will of the community, but I am convinced that public demands today are far ahead of the realities of both the criminal law and of its administration.

I should confess immediately that I am not familiar with law enforcement conditions in many of the smaller communities of New York State. Where organized crime has not yet laid its heavy hand, the problem is radically different from that of New York City and many other large cities of the state. The problem created by the vast body of men who, from childhood to the grave, live by crime does not exist in these communities, at least, not as yet. There the prosecutor and the judge are close to the people and faithfully reflect their sentiment. By and large, when a criminal is apprehended, prosecution is swift and punishment appropriate.

Throughout the state, however, I have heard with surprising frequency from Bench, Bar, legislators, and even prosecutors an expressed devotion to outworn theories and technical obstructions of the criminal law. They still blindly worship at shrines long since devoid of meaning or usefulness.

The unsatisfactory condition of the criminal law is a logical result of this philosophy. So, also, in the larger cities, are the incredible frequency of the suspended and inadequate sentence for convicted criminals, and the acceptance of pleas to misdemeanors from habitual felons charged with serious crimes.

Why do we so often find among public officials, members of the Bar, and others, a definite apathy toward criminal law enforcement in the face of the criminal conditions with which we are all too familiar? Why does the legislature year after year fail to pass bills, so obviously in the public interest, for the correction of the most glaring flaws in the criminal law?

Why is it that, in order to bring about even the most obviously necessary reforms in the criminal law, it was necessary for the Governor of the state to convene a great conference on the subject?

In my opinion, the reason is that the lay public generally has had little or no conception of the uncertainties in the enforcement of the criminal law, the great preponderance of the odds in favor of the professional criminal, the long delays which inevitably accompany criminal prosecution, the widespread intimidation of witnesses, the rarity of conviction as compared with commission of crime, and the great disparity which exists between the degree of crimes committed and the sentences finally imposed.

The results of these conditions are, however, gradually but with increasing force becoming a part of the public consciousness. The ever recurrent gangster killing, usually committed with impunity, causes the community to wonder what conditions exist to make criminal operations so profitable that men will kill each other in a struggle for control of the basic rackets.

The question is constantly looming larger as to why these rackets can exist, and the public is becoming increasingly aware of the basic reasons why rackets continue to flourish.

I am convinced that the public expects and has always expected vigorous and efficient law enforcement. It has submitted to outworn legal technicalities and pampering of professional criminals only because it was unaware of the cumulative social effects of these conditions, which are now becoming evident.

In their defense of useless and outworn legal obstructions, the Bar and leaders of public opinion are sowing a whirlwind, and unless they join wholeheartedly in the movement initiated by the Governor to overhaul the entire structure of the criminal law and its enforcement, I predict that there will be a reaction of incalculable force.

The truth is that we are living in an age of oxcart criminal law enforcement. It has not yet risen even to the efficiency of the horse and buggy days. We are still submitting, in criminal law enforcement, to the strait jackets imposed centuries ago upon royal tyrants by revolt of an oppressed people. The privilege against self-incrimination now embedded in our Constitution is an appropriate example.

This privilege was established for the purpose of protecting innocent commoners from torture by arrogant jailers to compel confession of crimes they had not committed. Today, this privilege has been built up over a long period by judicial decision, founded upon misguided legislation, into a serious obstacle to the effective enforcement and prosecution of certain types of crimes. It has hedged criminal law enforcement about with obstacles such as were never contemplated by those who conceived of the privilege as a bulwark of liberty.

I daresay most of you have reached the conclusion that today the privilege against self-incrimination goes hand in hand with the third degree, the final descendant of the very practice which the privilege sought to abolish.

What possible objection could any fair-minded person urge to the prompt examination, under proper safeguards, of an individual charged with a crime as to his alleged complicity?

As practical prosecutors, we all know that if this were possible the third degree would rapidly disappear and the rights of no innocent person would be impaired as a result.

Again, I do not believe the public has yet the slightest conception of the delays and technicalities incident to the prosecution of crime. Every time the average member of the community has any contact with the prosecution of criminal offenses, he expresses bewilderment and disgust that he should be forced to attend at a magistrate's court while delay after delay is granted to the defendant, and then, after months of further delay, he should be brought to court again and again upon repeated adjournments before the case comes to trial.

Likewise is it incredible to most reasonable men that, far in advance of a trial, the prosecution should be compelled to publish to the world the names of its witnesses, written on the back of the indictment. So also it is that a District Attorney, where a witness has been intimidated or bought, may not show when he has called a witness to the stand that the witness has previously testified under oath in support of the prosecution.

Equally unfortunate is it that neither court nor District Attorney may comment to the jury upon the fact that the defendant stands mute in the face of charges of serious crime.

In the same category with these and many other outworn relics of a primitive condition of law enforcement is the requirement of a unanimous jury verdict. In its early days, the unanimous jury verdict offered no such obstacle to law enforcement as it does today, when one bribed or partisan juror may, and often does, cause either an acquittal or a mistrial.

You will perhaps recall that, in the biography *Carson the Advocate*, it is recorded that only in the last century Lord Carson, as a young Irish barrister riding the circuit with the county judge, was not infrequently accompanied by an oxcart full of jurors who were being jolted from place to place until they reached not only a unanimous verdict but one in accordance with the judge's view of the facts.

Today we quite properly have no oxcarts, but we still have the legal technicalities erected in their day. Present criminal conditions render intolerable legal concepts framed to meet conditions no longer existing.

The great danger no longer is that innocent men may be found guilty, but rather that guilty men who engage in organized criminal pursuits consistently go free.

To the District Attorneys Association of New York State, June 11, 1938:

Together, the elected District Attorneys of this state represent all of the people of the state of New York in the protection of their lives, their liberties, and their property.

You represent the solid opinion of the people that the law shall be enforced, that the people shall be made safe against organized crime, and that there shall be no trifling with the law enforcement structure.

I am here to discuss certain proposals which in theory would enlarge the rights of the people, but in practice would subject them to the depredations of organized crime. The proposals of which I speak relate to search and seizure and wiretapping. The time has come to place on the record the facts about both.

It has been said that we have no provision protecting the people of this state against the unlawful search and seizure of their property. Now, the fact is that Section 8 of the Civil Rights Law has been on the books of this state for a hundred and ten years in language identical with that of the Constitution of the United States. Both read as follows:

"The right of the people to be secure in their persons, houses, papers and effects against unreasonable searches and seizures shall not be violated."

Not only is this the law, but there are also statutes which provide the most complete protection for innocent citizens whose rights are invaded. Thus, in a recent case where it appeared that an unreasonable search had been made, our Court of Appeals said:

"The officer might have been resisted, or sued for damages, or even prosecuted for oppression."

I think it is safe to say that nowhere in the whole United States are the rights of the people more tenderly guarded by law or, I may add, by the practice of public officials, than in this state.

Under our law, as it is and I hope always will be, the guilt of every man accused of crime must be proved by proper and competent evidence beyond a reasonable doubt. Criminal convictions cannot and should not be procured upon improper evidence.

But now it is proposed that legal evidence, however incriminating, may not be used, and must be given back by the People to the criminal before trial unless it is procured upon a search warrant or subpoena. In other words, if a policeman makes a misstep in picking up evidence, then the guilty will go free.

This attempt to handicap the protection of the people is serious and fundamental. Let me illustrate. Some years ago, the Dutch Schultz and Vincent Coll mobs were fighting it out with guns for control of the beer racket. In the course of one of the fights, several men were killed. Two members of the Coll gang were suspected. One of them claimed that he had been upstate at the time of the crime, but when the police questioned Coll, they found the stub of a railway car dining check on his person. This led them to the dining car employees, through whom it was found that four people had been in the car together, that they had come to New York City before the crime. Several members of the train crew identified as one of the party the man who claimed he had been upstate, and his alibi was completely destroyed.

If a search warrant had been necessary, that stub would never have been discovered in the gangster's pocket, witnesses to the murderer's presence in New York City might never have been found, and a vicious killer would have escaped punishment.

District Attorney Foley of the Bronx tells me of a case in the Bronx in which the owner of an apartment house disappeared. No crime was even suspected. His wife reported him to the police as missing. It seemed just the same as the hundreds of other cases which occur regularly, in which a husband has deserted his wife.

During a routine investigation, a police officer spoke to the superintendent of the building, who told him that he had not seen the owner for several days. The superintendent's helper who lived in the basement was then questioned.

During the interview, the officer noticed a stove. He opened the door and found a torn express receipt. He picked out the torn pieces of paper, patiently put them together, and then went to the express company's office. There he discovered that the receipt called for delivery of a trunk to Richmond, Virginia. The express company identified the helper as the person who had shipped the trunk.

Word was sent to Richmond, and the trunk was found to contain the murdered body of the missing man. Confronted with these facts, the helper confessed the murder, and implicated another man as well.

If the provision now advocated had been in effect, two murderers would have escaped conviction.

Supreme Court Justice Love of Rochester, New York, told me recently of a conspicuous murder case in Monroe County where the sheriff actually walked in while the suspected murderer was in the process of grinding away the identifying numbers of the gun used in the murder. Now, that sheriff did not have time to go and look for a judge. He did not have time to find a stenographer and dictate a long affidavit, as you have to do for a search warrant.

He did his duty and seized the gun before its value as evidence could be destroyed. He preserved the evidence for the murder trial.

Let me cite to you the words of one of the greatest liberal judges who ever graced the courts of this state, Justice Benjamin N. Cardozo. This whole question was before our Court of Appeals back in 1923 in a case where a criminal was seeking to force the prosecutor to give back to him some very incriminating letters upon which he would clearly be convicted if they were left in the hands of the state. The criminal demanded their return before his trial because of a so-called unlawful search and seizure.

In denying this demand, Judge Cardozo declared that the protection of the people against crime is of paramount public importance. Otherwise, he said, "Letters to or from accomplices found on the person of the conspirator and evidencing the plan of the execution of the conspiracy will be returned to the prisoner for concealment or destruction." The same result would follow, he added, in the case of "a murderer's garments, stained with blood in the course of the affray. Garments thus bespattered are typical examples," he wrote, "of the things that precedent and practice permit the government to keep."

There is another and even more dangerous aspect of this proposal. Let me quote to you again the words of Justice Cardozo in another case, dealing with the very argument. Speaking for the unanimous Court of Appeals of our state, he said:

"The pettiest police officer would have it in his power through over-zeal or indiscretion to confer immunity upon an offender for crimes the most flagitious. A room is searched against the law, and the body of a murdered man is found. If the place of discovery may not be proved, the other circumstances may be insufficient to connect the defendant with the crime. The privacy of the home has been infringed, and the murderer goes free.

"Another search, once more against the law, discloses counterfeit money or the implements of forgery. The absence of a warrant means the freedom of the forger. Like instances can be multiplied."

So it is with the so-called wiretapping proposal. Capitalizing on our natural hatred of the snooper, the proponents wish to abolish one of the best methods available for uprooting certain types of crime, and again their arguments are misleading.

The fact is that under the law of this state it is now a felony to tap the wire of any person. Out of their wide experience, the New York courts have held, however, that evidence of crime obtained by police officers by intercepting telephone messages may be used in a criminal trial. With due regard for the personal rights of our people, the courts have refused to shackle the public officers of the state in the apprehension of criminals and the detection of crime.

During the years in which I have been a public prosecutor in New York, I have never known of a single case in which wiretaps were used, without the overwhelming corroboration of other evidence. Nor have I seen a single instance where the police, in the tapping of criminals' telephones, have exceeded proper limits. I believe the people of this state are willing to trust the elected District Attorneys and the police to use their powers properly. Any other theory asserts that democracy is a failure. And I do not believe that democracy is a failure.

Who are the people who would be protected by these proposals? Call the roll: Al Capone, Lucky Luciano, Waxey Gordon, Dutch Schultz, Tootsie Herbert, and all the others.

In every one of these cases, proof of guilt was strengthened by seized evidence and by information obtained by tapping the wires of criminals.

Modern methods of the racketeer require modern methods of law enforcement. The people of this state want criminals punished, and will soundly rebuke those who wish to make their public officials helpless against an organized underworld.

We are coming, I hope, to the end of the time when the press, the motion picture, and the radio can portray as realities the sway of the mob, the intimidated witness, and the gangster killing. Our people have the courage to deal with these problems, and our government has the method of handling them. This is not the time for reactionary and dangerous limitations on the power of the State to protect its people. It is not time to sabotage the progress we have made.

Address in Station WNYC series on "The Jury System," April 20, 1938:

Last week the distinguished presiding justice of the Appellate Division of the Supreme Court spoke to you on this program about grand juries. He told of the important work accomplished by grand juries in protecting wrongfully accused persons from prosecution for crime, and of the honor and importance of grand juries.

But when the work of the grand jury is finished, the wheels of justice have only started to turn. The persons accused of crime must be brought to trial in open court. The true administration of criminal justice depends in part upon the learning, and industry, of the judge, and in part upon the energy and initiative of the prosecutor, but above all it depends upon the integrity of the trial jury. The safety of the city and of every citizen is in the hands of those juries of twelve whose decision is the last word in every prosecution.

Jury service is not just a responsibility. It is a rare opportunity to see at first hand many of the major problems of your community. As you sit in the jury box in the criminal courtroom, there is unfolded before you the living drama of crime. You learn the causes of crime and the handicaps of the underprivileged. You witness the tragic effect of crime on its victims, the unbelievable viciousness of the underworld, the hardships under which the police and other law enforcement agencies labor, and the schemes and tricks to which criminals resort to get around the law.

There are eight courtrooms in the ancient and almost collapsing General Sessions Court Building down on Centre Street, where my assistants are presenting evidence every day to eight trial juries. The men and women on these juries listen daily to proof of murder, assault, robbery, dope selling, extortion, larceny, kidnaping, sex crimes, bribery, and many others. Woven into those trials is evidence concerning the illegal sale and distribution of guns, the all-important channels for disposing of stolen goods, the tricks by which men attempt to obstruct justice.

Too often do lies fly thick and fast in the courtroom, and appeals to passion, prejudice, or sympathy are present in the defense of every case. But the veteran juror cannot be hoodwinked. He becomes the most efficient lie detector in the world, and his work in the jury box makes him an expert judge of human behavior.

Here too, more quickly than by reading a thousand books, or listening to countless speeches, you will learn the true nature of the evil effect of broken homes, bad housing, and economic distress upon our people. You will see their effects in the making of wayward young men and juvenile delinquents, and how, after conviction, they are carefully studied for possibilities of help and reformation by probation and guidance.

You will see the seamy and tragic side of life, but you will learn how to help to make it better, and what great things remain to be done.

There are a hundred thousand trial jurors in the county of New York and during one month in each two years these men and women will sit in a jury box and work for you. They work well and hard. Yet you hear every day the grumbling citizen who condemns the jury system. From my experience I can tell you that the jury system works well, but I must also tell you that it does not work well enough.

Let me give you one instance. A few years ago in Brooklyn, an unsavory professional criminal was on trial for his liberty. He had a long criminal record and, when the government had presented all its witnesses, the defendant did not take the witness stand. It is, of course, the right of every man to refuse to answer or testify concerning criminal charges against him. However, our law also prevents either the prosecutor or the judge from making the slightest reference to the fact that a man accused of crime has failed to explain, or even offer to explain, his acts.

When the case was submitted to the jury, one juror was so uninformed on the fundamentals of criminal trials that he argued that the District Attorney was unfair because he did not call the defendant to the witness stand. In that jury there was not one man who knew enough to point out that the District Attorney could not call the defendant to the witness stand and that, if he made the slightest reference to the subject, the judge would be forced to declare a mistrial.

The jury thereupon marched into court and acquitted the defendant. Thus a criminal was again turned loose on the community because twelve jurors had ignored the facts as well as the judge's charge on the law.

With millions of intelligent citizens in New York who are available for jury duty, how could such a thing happen? The explanation is unfortunately simple. For years there has been a growing feeling that private business affairs are more important than public service, that jury duty is a burden to be passed on to someone else, and that the administration of justice is a nuisance, to be left in the hands of those who do not have the influence to avoid their duty.

Some years ago there was a judge in the criminal courts of New York who used to get on the bench every Monday morning with what used to be known as the "Monday morning blues." His disposition, normally, was not too good. On Monday morning it was uniformly bad. On the first Monday of a court term, with a new panel of jurors in the courtroom, his honor suddenly declared: "All jurors who want to be excused, stand up!" Almost everybody in the room rose. "Sit down," the judge directed. "Now," he proceeded, "all jurors who want to serve, stand up!" A meager handful rose. "Get out!" said the judge. "If you are anxious to serve, I don't want you. All the others will stay and serve."

I remember a case where a woman shot a man in cold blood. She or her lawyer cooked up an ingenious defense. She admitted the killing and, amid tears and dramatics, explained her act to a sympathetic jury, which promptly acquitted her.

Shortly afterward a man I know wrote a long and solemn article condemning such juries which acquitted women who shot their husbands and lovers, and the lawyers who got them off. I saw the man not long afterward and said I quite agreed with some of his ideas. But when, I asked, had he last done his bit on a jury? Perhaps it was a little unkind to ask that embarrassing question, but the man admitted that he had never served on a jury and did not intend to.

Every critic of our judicial system, of our courts, and even of our democracy, admits that the jury system is fine in theory but bad in practice. Yet these very people, when charged with crime, call quickest for a jury trial. Those who shirk the worst clamor for their rights the loudest.

The citizen who evades jury duty deserves a badge of dishonor. The man who begs off every time he is called is as false to his fellow citizens as a slacker in time of war.

And yet it is true today that a vast number of responsible citizens are undermining the jury system by dodging jury service and leaving it to those who cannot dodge it or are too honest to do so. They criticize its results, shun its labors, and then refuse to help improve it.

There is, however, a more hopeful side. Within the past year women have been given the right to serve on juries for the first time in New York. Thousands of them in this county alone have seized the opportunity. They have approached this duty seriously. Many women's organizations have conducted lecture courses for new jurors, with instruction from experts. Individual women look forward to their service and have arranged their household or personal affairs so they can answer the call of the Court. After a short experience in the criminal courts they quickly learn to distinguish between sham defenses and real ones, to judge lying witnesses, and to see that justice is done.

A large share of the success in the fight against the rackets in the past three years must be credited to juries which proved that the law can protect the public. It has been shown conclusively that both the law and the jury system are bigger than the criminal underworld. Today there is not a racketeer of first importance left in New York. Every one of the ten chief public enemies listed by the Police Commissioner three years ago has been removed. Some are dead of gangster bullets, some have left New York for good, and the rest are in jail.

So far this year, 1938, the juries in New York County have convicted eight men for murder in the first degree, seven of them cop killers. This is by contrast with last year, when there were only two first-degree murder convictions in the entire year.

To the Association of the Bar of the City of New York and the New York County Lawyers Association, May 11, 1938:

I have reached the firm conclusion that a major aspect of the administration of criminal justice requires a complete and urgent overhauling. Every layman knows that everyone is entitled to his day in court. He also knows the theory that rich and poor stand equal at the bar of justice. These are basic principles. These are the foundation of our liberty.

But for many years there has been a growing body of opinion that justice is not really blind, and that criminal justice in particular takes notice of the size of the defendant's purse. Only too commonly, it is said that only the wealthy defendant receives his day in court.

On the other hand, it is too often said of that small section of the

Bar known as criminal lawyers that what is actually meant is lawyer criminals. The occasional conviction of the lawyer who has allied himself with the criminal underworld lends force and substance to that charge.

The exact degree to which these observations are true is not so important as the fact that a large part of the population believes they are true. The public has come to believe that crime is in part due to lawyers, and that the Bar leaves the administration of criminal justice to its least desirable element.

To some extent, lawyers themselves share this belief. The Bar draws its clean skirts aside as it passes the Criminal Courts Building and its ablest members are rarely, if ever, seen there from one year's end to the next. The vast majority of New York lawyers have never stood in a criminal courtroom.

For this, there are two reasons. Most criminal practice is not lucrative. Much of it involves fees which are not a proper compensation for the time involved and it is natural that, with office expenses, and the grocer to pay, lawyers simply cannot specialize in a type of work which does not even pay the overhead.

Furthermore, the demands of some defendants in connection with their defense disgust decent members of the Bar, who decline to represent them simply on ethical grounds. The defect lies, of course, in the fact that other counsel will conform to the improper suggestions.

Whatever the causes, we are compelled to face the result. The defense of human liberty has been abandoned to a handful of the profession.

The racketeer, the swindler, the bucket-shop operator, and the fence have counsel almost before they reach the Tombs. These general counsel of the criminal underworld are in a different and very small class indeed. But let us consider the plight of that vast army of defendants who are accused of crime and have no funds with which to retain counsel. More than fifty per cent of the defendants indicted for felonies in New York County last year had no money for a lawyer. They usually had few if any friends, and no means to procure their witnesses. This is the crucial point at which our system breaks down and needs your urgent attention.

Out of the funds largely contributed by members of the Bar, the Legal Aid Society maintains a small group of lawyers known as Voluntary Defenders to handle criminal cases for impoverished defendants. These men defended more than 2,400 cases in the criminal courts in 1937. Of this number, 1,520 were in the Court of General Sessions but only 389 were by assignment of the court. This is the maximum number of cases the judges have ever assigned to the Voluntary Defenders and, as a matter of fact, it is all they are able to handle as they are now financed.

More than 1,200 other felony cases were assigned to a collection of lawyers who sit more or less regularly on the benches. The result is a tragedy and a farce. These bench warmers, most of whose offices are in their hats, represent our profession. You are entitled to know how our profession is represented there.

Not long ago, one of these lawyers was assigned to a case. In violation of his oath as a member of the Bar, he squeezed $25 in fees out of the defendant. Difficulties arose between them, and the Voluntary Defenders took over the case. They soon learned of the fee and reported it to the court, which ordered the attorney to return the fee. A week passed and he returned $12.50, stating that he had spent the balance on expenses. These expenses, it developed, amounted to carfares for two visits to the Tombs. Again, the court was advised, and finally, after protracted delay, the lawyer gave up the other $12.50.

Only last month a lawyer who regularly makes his office in the magistrate's court came out of the courtroom at the end of the morning session well satisfied. He confided to a friend that it had been a good day. He was assigned by the magistrate to defend a woman on charges of vagrancy, and at the end of the case she was convicted. But she so aroused the magistrate's sympathy that he suspended sentence and gave her $5 out of his own pocket. Said the lawyer to his friend, "This was just enough to complete my fee, and when we got downstairs, I made her turn it over to me."

One of these lawyers was assigned to represent a sixteen-year-old defendant under indictment. Immediately, he began writing letters to the boy's family in another state, demanding $250 for his services, and threatening that, unless he was paid, the defendant would be sentenced to thirty years in prison. While every lawyer and social worker would know that no such thing was, as a practical matter, either likely or possible, this lawyer delayed the trial for weeks until he completed his efforts unethically to extort a fee.

Last month a defendant had all his money on deposit with the cashier at the city prison, a total of twenty-five cents. A member of the New York Bar was assigned to defend the case and his first act was to procure an assignment of the twenty-five cents from the defendant, and collect it from the prison cashier.

Now, add to these the effect of cases like this: a lawyer was assigned six weeks ago to defend a young man charged with robbery in the first degree. The defendant was twenty-three years old, and his criminal record consisted of stealing two watches and a mirror in Florida, for which he had served six months in jail. This time he had stolen $32 and an overcoat.

Technically, the circumstances made this robbery in the first degree. In the magistrate's court he had confessed his guilt and offered to plead guilty. He was, in fact, clearly guilty. Yet equally clearly he was not the kind of person who should go to jail for ten to thirty years. There was a real chance that a moderate sentence with a long probation was the sound solution of his problem.

But the lawyer for the defendant was both ignorant and arrogant, and, furthermore, he wanted trial experience. He refused even to consider a plea of guilty or to recommend it to his client. He went to trial and, after exactly seven minutes of deliberation, the jury rendered the only possible verdict, robbery in the first degree.

Here was the essence of tragic incompetence and the frustration of justice, tempered only by the fortunate availability of provisions for reformatory sentence because of the youth of the prisoner.

These conditions place a challenge squarely before the whole Bar. As lawyers, we enjoy privileges before the courts of justice. We also have obligations. Only a duly admitted member of the Bar has the right to defend a man accused of crime—and with that right goes the duty to do so.

I could appeal to you tonight to make even more generous contributions of your money to the Legal Aid Society to add more lawyers to carry this burden. I will not make such an appeal. I do not believe that the primary duty of the Bar to defend human liberty can be discharged with money. No amount of money, it seems to me, can discharge a personal, professional obligation, an obligation both to the community and to the Bar itself.

To point for a moment to another learned profession: you are all familiar with the clinic and ward services performed by doctors generally throughout the city. Rare indeed is the reputable doctor who does not devote three, four, or even five half days a week to the

wholly charitable work of attending to the ills of impoverished
patients. So well established is this practice that you accept it without
a thought.

Yet, with an equally great social problem, and an equal professional obligation, where in the Bar can we find that regular, almost
daily clinical work of the lawyer?

To speak perfectly plainly, it does not exist, except in the office
cases which lawyers so frequently take without compensation. It
scarcely exists at all on the criminal side.

To some extent, the Bar is discharging its obligation to the public
by the contribution of necessary money to the Legal Aid Society. I
propose that it should also contribute a part of its time.

The Bar will again become an integrated unit. That unsavory
stigma attaching to criminal work will in time be definitely removed.
By the incomparable experience of criminal court work given to rising
members of the Bar, our sadly depleted trial Bar will have many additions to its too few members. The courts of criminal justice will again
be places where all lawyers are not only willing but proud to attend in
the performance of their privilege and their duty.

In People Are Honest, 1938:

I am sometimes asked whether my experiences as a public prosecutor have not prompted me to lose faith in human nature. My
answer is an emphatic no. I am just as firmly convinced today that
people are honest as I was the first day I reached New York. And that
day I had reason to be thankful to an honest man.

Twenty-one years old, fresh from Michigan, I had come to study
law at Columbia. Right in the middle of my first look at the big city,
I realized the old dog-eared wallet containing my savings was gone: I
had left it behind on the train.

The clerk at the "Lost and Found" counter in Grand Central
Station seemed amused when I told him my story. "Thomas E. Dewey,
Owosso, Michigan," he repeated. Then he reached into a drawer behind him. "Here y'are, Owosso," he said, and there was the wallet,
not a dollar missing.

The black porter who found it had turned it in immediately.
Thanks to his honesty, I got back my money, all I had saved to start
life in the overwhelming, magnificent city. I went away convinced

that most people are honest, even in New York, just as they were in Owosso.

Take taxicab drivers, for example. New York's drivers are as cosmopolitan a lot as you could find in the world. They come from all over, quarrel noisily at every opportunity, and occasionally, when on strike, they tip one another's cabs over and perform other violent acts. They are rowdy, noisy, and not too well paid. But the record shows that they are overwhelmingly for law and order. If you leave something in a cab, the odds are 99 to 1 that it will be turned in at headquarters when the driver ends his run.

Taxicab drivers figure in many holdups, but usually they are forced at the point of a gun. Often, when one hackie is driving as badly as possible to save his life, another is driving as well as possible in hot pursuit with a policeman on the running board.

In solving mysterious crimes, taxicab drivers are often the first source of information. No other body of civilians gives such prompt and intelligent aid to the police. It goes without saying that they give information when asked. But, in certain important murder cases, taxicab men have distinguished themselves by volunteering leads which could only have been arrived at by a combination of close observation and wishful thinking.

I wish I felt free to name the cases and the drivers who helped to solve them. Criminals who use taxis for a getaway are not smart. The chances are that they are riding with a good citizen who is firmly on the side of the law.

What is true of taxicab drivers is also true of most people. They uphold the law and want to see it enforced. Only in extreme adversity do they seek favors from government.

One of the unforgettable scenes that I shall carry with me all my days is the picture of five thousand poor women in line, and actually rioting, for jobs as charwomen. This happened in New York City, where I suppose public relief is more easily obtained than anywhere else in the United States. Those women did not want relief. They wanted jobs, the chance to earn honest dollars by honest toil.

Those of us who strive to protect the public against crime can count on the support of wage earners nearly one hundred per cent. And, ultimately, most businessmen respond to the appeal of law and order against the racketeer. Of course some of them move more slowly than their employees, but their delay is undoubtedly due more to fright than to the temporary economic advantages offered by the racketeers. In some cities there are real grounds for thinking that the police might not protect the victims of a business racket who sought their help. But once the vicious circle of fear has been broken by public authority, victims come in with their testimony, showing great courage and patriotism.

Even in the worst of our racketeering cases I discovered anew that the average citizen backs honest officials whenever the issue between clean and dirty government is continuously drawn by aggressive leadership.

The political bosses I have had to fight are as fully aware of this as I am. They know that the public is ninety-nine per cent honest and asks nothing more than a square deal. These bosses get power and money by dominating the one per cent and organizing them to prey on the public.

But any able and courageous public official who proves that there are rats in the corncrib can count on the great majority of the people rallying to his side to help drive them out.

That is the ultimate strength, the unbeatable element, in our democracy—this response, once the issue is drawn, between right and wrong. America will be that way as long as the nation endures.

Why does it seem necessary to emphasize this basic honesty we all used to take for granted?

My reason is this: a subtle change has been wrought by all the accusations and suspicions flung about during the past six and a half years. Once, when a responsible person made accusations, he was required to give precise details, answering the questions who, where, what, when, how. But today our leading accusers seldom go into helpful detail. Instead, they bring blanket accusations against whole classes of unidentified persons, omnibus indictments of unnamed economic royalists and other imaginary groups. In this atmosphere of distrust, thick with the poison gas of suspicion, can constructive business enterprise flourish?

Indeed, in this respect, we seem to have reached a position exactly opposite to that on which the Republic was founded. Then, the responsible citizenship and honesty of the common people were taken for granted, and extreme care was taken to keep private affairs from government interference.

Now it seems that the government must have its hand in, and its eye on, all activities. Government acts on the false assumption that the people are not to be trusted in their ordinary concerns, and that businessmen must be watched over in the same spirit that a jailer watches a prison road gang.

Government has been trying to reform the people. Now it is time for the people to start reforming the government, which has grown too unwieldy, extravagant, and interfering to please an honest people, traditionally devoted to simple procedures. Toward that wholesome national ideal, based on mutual confidence in our common honesty, America must now turn for a revival of its old vigor.

Running for Governor

On September 29, 1938, I accepted a draft for the Republican nomination for the governorship. It was seventeen days after the Hines mistrial, and six weeks before Election Day. Instrumental in the draft movement were Medalie, Speaker of the Assembly Oswald Heck, Simpson, Newbold Morris, Bruce Barton, the congressman and advertising executive, and Edwin F. Jaeckle, the energetic leader of the Republican organization in Erie County, which includes the city of Buffalo.

The dominating factor on the other side was whether the popular Governor Herbert H. Lehman would run for re-election on the Democratic ticket. After the death of United States Senator Royal S. Copeland, Lehman had announced for the Senate. The other United States senator was the famous Robert Wagner, who wanted nothing more than to succeed himself in office.

At the Republican State Convention at Saratoga Springs on September 29, the placing of my name in nomination set off an enthusiastic demonstration. After seconding speeches, Speaker Heck declared me to be the unanimous choice of the convention as its candidate for Governor. Our candidate for Lieutenant Governor was state Senator Frederick H. Bontecou.

At 7:30 P.M., in my acceptance speech, I said:

My decision to accept your nomination has not been made lightly. It would have been easier to say no. I have been urged by many friends, some of them Republicans, to refuse this nomination. This advice boiled down to two things.

One was addressed to selfish, personal considerations. I was urged to stay in a job where my only enemies were criminals and their friends. There are big cases developing in my office, and I was reminded that from them I could safely advance my personal reputation. I was told that it was risky to venture among the complex issues in the battlefield of state affairs. I was urged to play it safe.

Had I taken that advice, I should have been shirking the bigger job, the harder fight. I shall not shirk that fight.

The second form of the advice was more to be considered. It was urged that I *ought* to stay in my present job as District Attorney of New York County. That was based on the flattering but false assumption that I was the only man in New York who could run a large law office, investigate rackets, and prosecute crime. Well, the trouble with that is it just isn't true.

For nearly eight years now I have been a public prosecutor in New York City. During all of those years, slow but steady progress has been made in removing the grip of organized crime and its political protectors from New York.

Last year I ran for office and was elected District Attorney. The objective was to rescue that office from the domination of the political allies of the criminal underworld.

That objective has been achieved. In my campaign I made a single promise. It was that the People would be represented by an office of competent, hard-working lawyers, and I specifically promised that my assistants would not be chosen by Al Marinelli, Charlie Schneider, or any of the other district leaders now choosing my opponent at the Democratic State Convention.

That promise has been kept, and the record shows what its results have been. In that office, there now is a staff of seventy-two able, energetic, high-principled lawyers who know how to prosecute crime, how to investigate rackets, how to uncover facts, and how to prove them.

They can and will keep on doing that job whether I am there in the District Attorney's office or not. I intend to stay in the District Attorney's office until the end of the year. As Governor, on January 1, I shall appoint an able and outstanding successor to that office.

That office in New York County is only one small sector of the battle front in the war against crime. In the years in which I have been a public prosecutor, it has become increasingly clear to me that the powers and implements of any one District Attorney in any one county are inadequate to the task. Organized crime, with all its complex structure of corruption and political connections, is not confined within county lines. Nor is the criminal structure limited to any one level of society. Its power is greater than the mere physical terrorism of the gangster. Its influence reaches to high places. Moral responsibility for the criminal structure reaches far beyond the little criminals who pour through the courts, beyond even the big shots who sometimes can be called before the bar of justice. It reaches to those who have never committed a punishable breach of the law but whose acquiescence makes them moral co-conspirators.

The only weapon of a District Attorney is the Penal Code as applied to the illegal acts of those individuals within his own county against whom evidence can be obtained.

Fighting against the underworld, with all its sprawling tentacles, a single District Attorney of one county is not unlike the deep-sea diver who encounters an octopus and tries to fight one of its arms at a time. As he fights that arm, he is likely to find himself attacked by the other tentacles, while the rest of the creature goes on placidly about its predatory business.

The Governor has wider powers. He can, if he will, command the faithful enforcement of the laws in all of the sixty-two counties. He can, if he will, strengthen the District Attorneys who are doing the job. He can, if he will, command effective and honest police cooperation. He can carry the fight beyond the mere skirmish lines of law enforcement.

The next Governor of the state will face many problems which still demand solution. The problem of housing for more than a million of our people under decent, safe, sanitary conditions, both in New York City and in the other great cities of the state, has been grossly neglected by succeeding state administrations. For thirty years the ownership and use of the natural resources of the state for the production of electric power have been the subject of sterile political controversy. Elements of our own party have opposed the inevitable and perpetual ownership of our natural resources by the people of the state. On the other hand, the Democratic Party has exploited water power as a political issue for many years, accomplishing no substantial result except the election of its candidates for public office.

Repeated, fumbling attempts to improve the lot of the dairyman and the farmer generally in the state of New York have resulted in an accumulation of statutes on the lawbooks, and privation for the farmer.

Much has been accomplished in the good fight for the rights of labor and for better standards. We must protect those rights and make those standards effective. During the course of this campaign I shall speak specifically and in detail concerning these and other problems.

Whatever New York's Democratic governors have been able to accomplish has been subject to the limitations placed upon them by the old crowd of New York City's Tammany district leaders. Without meaning to be so, any Democratic governor is, perforce, the good-will advertising, the front man, the window dressing for a thoroughly corrupt machine. The objectives of responsible governors have been dangled as bait before the people by a political organization whose sole basic purpose was politics for profit.

Speaking now to you who have nominated me, it is fitting that I should talk about the Republican Party. Let us consider the party, as realistic men and women, facing facts.

Since the great, progressive days under the leadership of Theodore Roosevelt and Charles Evans Hughes, the power and influence of our party in New York has steadily declined. For this, there were obvious reasons, which should be honestly stated.

As recently as eight years ago, through causes for which no individual or group was immediately responsible, the two-party system of government had ceased to operate in New York on a state-wide basis. We had one-party rule by Republicans upstate, and one-party rule by Democrats in New York City.

At stated intervals, the emissaries of the two groups met at Albany for a quiet session of horse trading. To the people of the state outside of New York City, their Republican legislators gave honest, competent representation in this situation. But nobody ever yet heard of a

Tammany Hall district leader who ever represented anybody but the district leader.

The people of the greatest city in America were, in fact, not represented at all in the legislative halls. Tammany Hall and its city allies were in full control of their people's destinies. It was the fact that the people of the city had fallen to the mercies of a mob of political racketeers.

That situation no longer exists. The people of the city have been aroused and in two great elections they have written the doom of political racketeering. In New York City today the Republican Party stands alive, strong, and ready to assume the responsibility of a majority party.

Tonight we go forward to restore representative government to the state as a whole. It is the job of the majority party to build, not to tear down, to go forward, not to obstruct. It is not the function of a political party to die fighting for obsolete slogans. It is not the function of political leadership to bark at the heels of political success.

It is the function of a political party, and it is the job of a political leader, to seek positively to represent the whole people in the solution of their daily problems. It is in this spirit that I approach the campaign.

There will be, among us, many shades of opinion. Let us compose those differences among ourselves and mold our party into a progressive vehicle for democratic government—in which sectionalism, factionalism, and the drag of special interests shall disappear before the needs of the whole people . . .

On September 30, 1938, the Democratic national and state chairman, Postmaster General James A. Farley, told the Democratic State Convention: "The governor will run again." Then President Roosevelt sent Lehman a telegram pledging his support to the whole ticket as "insuring the continuation of liberal government in my own state."

Governor Lehman said in his acceptance speech: "I did not believe that Mr. Dewey would abandon, almost before it started, that important work for which he was chosen by the people less than a year ago, and for the consummation of which he accepted an obligation to the people. Every man and woman knows of my deep interest in clean, honest government, and in law enforcement, of which the designation by me of Mr. Dewey as Special Prosecutor to act against racketeering and corruption in New York City was only a part."

Governor Lehman termed his new opponent "entirely inexperienced in either administrative or legislative activities. There is no indication that he is familiar with either the fiscal or socal problems of the government of a great state of thirteen million people."

The Republican Party campaign was now confronted with several realities that were conjoining less than six weeks before Election Day. The first was that President Roosevelt himself was so popular that he had carried the state by 1,100,000 votes less than two years before. The second was that no Republican had been elected governor in the state since 1920, and that such Democratic governors as Al Smith, Franklin D. Roosevelt, and Herbert Lehman constituted a tradition of leadership that had little relationship in the public mind, statewide, with Tammany Hall. The third was that Mayor LaGuardia, our ally against Tammany Hall, was also an ally of the New Deal, and he would probably support Lehman for re-election. The fourth was that the American Labor Party, which had supported the LaGuardia-Dewey ticket in 1937, was for Lehman in 1938. The A.F.L. and the C.I.O. endorsed Lehman, and so did the International Longshoremen's Association.

Governor Lehman, the dominating factor, was pretty shifty, and skillful, but he was experienced. He had been through a lot of state campaigns. He had been on the management side, back in the 1920s, of the Lehman Brothers group, and he was a wealthy man who did not need and did not seek dirty political money. He was a tough, rough barroom fighter with a good deal of skill. He always yanked out the good old "bloody shirt" of anti-Semitism on the Saturday nights before elections.

But people forgave Lehman for doing things that a man should not do in campaigns. They thought that his heart was in the right place, that he was faithful and a hard worker. Lehman was a very hard-working public official.

He took everything very seriously, lived with his problems. He had an absolute conviction that everything he had ever said or done was of necessity the best that any man could ever do. He had a rather unique confidence in his own superior purposes and judgment.

As Jim Farley put it, Lehman had announced for the Senate almost before the late Senator Copeland "had a chance to lie down." But Farley and some others had talked him into running for Governor again. On the eve of the convention, Albany County Democratic boss

Dan O'Connell had reportedly sat on Lehman's bed, making his last-minute appeal.

It was undoubtedly true, on the other hand, that Democratic governors had a sense of being surrounded and had a limitation on their freedom of action which Republican governors did not have. That resulted from the fact that the Democrats had a better organization. They controlled the city of New York, delivering a large margin to start with, while the Republican margin upstate was not controlled by any single organization, or any five organizations.

But when a Republican did get in, he would feel that he was pretty independent. The Democrat felt that he owed his life to the organization and that, of course, was a basic difference between the parties in operational terms.

Interestingly, the freest of all the Democrats was a man who owed the most, and that was Al Smith. Al had come up the hard way. He met every political obstacle. He knew them all by their first names, and had known them for a generation. He could tell them to go climb a tree. But you bring in these outside people who have a slight feeling that they are slumming when they deal with political managers, county chairmen, or district leaders, and these men make far greater concessions to the demands of a machine than did Al Smith.

Al was the machine's product and its boss. Lehman and Roosevelt were men who came in from the outside and served from the top, but never came up from the bottom, never were of it, were not the same flesh and blood as the machine. They were outsiders who had money and name which the machine wished to use.

During the 1938 campaign the national interest as defined by the Democratic Party was only a key to the fact that the Democratic Party plays politics hard all the time. The Democrats pay attention to little things like governorships coming along when they are in Washington. They miss no bets. They work at it all the time.

Regrettably, the Republicans either do not have the skill or many times do not have the desire for that kind of politics. They are either too busy for it or maybe not smart enough. But the Democrats play politics all the time, and 1938 for the Democrats was just another one.

They did not want *any* Republicans elected, so Roosevelt came all the way to New York to make a speech against me on the Friday night before election.

On our side of the 1938 campaign, I decided to take a fairly independent approach, and I mean by that independent of the record of my party in the Congress, and not closely allied to the record of the party in the state. This was because the Democrats had succeeded in convincing the people, rightly or wrongly, that the Republican Party's record in both places was not very good.

It was not my job to try to sell the people on a conviction that the Republican Party had done a good job. My job was to get elected and then to do a better job if need be, and at least to do a good job.

Therefore I was taking first things first. So it is a fact that I ran a comparatively independent campaign as far as the speeches, points of view, and voting records of the Republicans in the House and Senate and in Albany were concerned. And I did not encourage the Republicans to send any people into New York from outside to help, because New York is a very complicated state. People from other sections of the country often do not grasp the point of view of New York very easily. I always had trouble when they wanted to send somebody from, say, Indiana, Iowa, or California.

Organizationally, Medalie was a chief adviser, and I relied heavily on Jaeckle, and also upon a vice-president of the American Smelting and Refining Company, Roger W. Straus. He was the son of Theodore Roosevelt's Secretary of Commerce and Labor. Dulles, Brownell, Seabury, and our close personal friend Carl T. "Pat" Hogan were on board as they had been so often in the past. So was a fellow lawyer, Arthur Ballantine, who would be one of my partners later in life.

On October 11, James O. Moore, a Buffalo lawyer, became campaign manager. Speaker Heck was upstate manager and Straus the manager for New York City. Millard Ellison, our campaign manager of 1937, was put in charge of headquarters, with Ballantine in charge of fund raising.

On campaign financing, Harold Keller recalled: "TED's view of favoring the financing of political campaigns through public treasuries was expressed on a train ride after the Albany Legislative Correspondents Dinner in March 1938. He maintained that the political spoils system could never be abolished as long as candidates had to depend on private campaign contributions.

"TED suggested a plan whereby city, state, or federal government, depending on the offices affected, allotted money for each candidate's expenses and limited, or prohibited, private contributions. Kenneth F. Simpson, New York County Republican chairman, one of the group on the train, insisted this would destroy the party system and make political party organizations ineffective."

Paul Lockwood, my executive assistant and a veteran Young Republican, was my personal representative throughout the campaign. Harold Keller, Hickman Powell, and Lem Jones worked on campaign material, as usual, and Bernie Yarrow put together another foreign-language operation, this time assisted by Barrie Ten Eyck.

On October 10, before the campaign organization was completed, I spoke about the gigantic failure of the State Unemployment Insurance Act, under which more than 122,000 claims were unpaid, 20,000 in arrears, and 48,000 in dispute. I said:

Unemployment insurance has become a sound and necessary part of social service and of the self-confidence of our people. With financially sound operation and efficiency of administration it can be made a broader base for human security and happiness. Badly administered, it is an obstacle to social progress and a deception of the people.

On October 17, I concentrated on housing:

Let us recall the story of Elizabeth Horan and her brother Joe, who lived in four, tiny, airless rooms on the fourth floor of an old tenement house near New York City's Harlem. The Horans paid $25 a month for the rooms, and for the privilege of breathing their neighbor's cooking, instead of fresh air.

Joe Horan was a retired printer, sixty-four years old, and his younger sister, Elizabeth, kept house for him. One night last June as they slept in their beds the call of fire rang through the halls. The Horans heard it, but too late. There was ample evidence of that when firemen found their bodies. Joe was dressed only in his trousers and had collapsed as he fought his way through smoke to a front window. His sister, too, still dressed only in her nightgown, was struck down before she even got out of her room.

Joe and Elizabeth Horan, who died in a firetrap this year, were not the only people who have paid with their lives for the neglect of the state. Fire after fire has occurred in tenements of our state and, worse than that, more fires are going to occur and more people are going to die.

In New York City alone, there are nearly 2,000,000 people living in 58,000 outmoded, decrepit buildings which were unwholesome the day they were put up. Death by fire is in reality the least of the threats under which almost a third of the population of New York

City must live. In such houses, the tuberculosis death rate has been 129 per cent higher than elsewhere in the city, death from spinal meningitis has been 119 per cent higher. The general death rate is 93 per cent higher.

We should adopt a housing amendment immediately, providing $300 million of state loans and modest subsidies for low-cost housing throughout the state. With the aid of the cities, we may reasonably expect that $500 million will be put to work in New York State for low-cost housing on a sound financial basis.

On October 19, in Rochester, I concentrated on the Democratic machines:

Fellow Republicans, once more the drums of victory are beating along the Mohawk.* The Republican Party stands ready to reassert its leadership in New York State. The choice is between a fresh administration, against one cluttered with the by-products of Tammany, Brooklyn, and Albany headquarters. There can only be one decision on the issues: corrupt political machines must go.

My opponent in this election is an honorable and conscientious gentleman. I have the highest admiration for his personal integrity and devotion to public service. But this is not enough. Let's look at the facts. After six years of the present state administration, the corrupt machines of the Democratic Party are still doing business at the same old stand.

The Democratic Convention was a strange assortment of human beings. High-minded and honorable men and women were there. Many of them, I am sure, have struggled against odds within their party. Also there were Al Marinelli, Charlie Schneider, Ed Flynn, the Brooklyn machine, the Albany machine, and others whose names I am sure will come to your mind.† They were there for a purpose. Let's pause and reflect. Were they there to promote the cause of good government?

Al Marinelli, the political ally of thieves, pickpockets, dope peddlers, and big-shot racketeers. Imagine his grin as he voted for the law enforcement plank.

* Rochester is not on the Mohawk. In Utica, which is on the Mohawk, I said the next night: "Last night in Rochester, I told a vast crowd that once more the drums of victory are beating along the Mohawk. We could hear them away over in Rochester."

† James J. Hines was also at the Democratic State Convention.

Ed Flynn, boss of the Bronx machine. Imagine his grin as he voted for the civil service plank.

Charlie Schneider who, at a time when he was Assistant Attorney General of this state, helped turn loose the man who murdered a labor leader. Imagine his grin as he voted for the labor plank.

The worst political organization in America pretending to represent the people of New York in the cause of good government? In meeting the hopes and aspirations of the people of our state?

No, my friends.

On October 20, in Utica, I concentrated on political monopolies:

Monopolies were supposed to have been abolished in this country a generation ago, but we still have them. We have the beginnings of a serious monopoly in the national, political scene. The branches of that monopoly are like chain stores that owe their living to the continuance of that monopoly nationally. The individuality of the states is threatened. One of our great newspapers has repeatedly said every year that the governorship of New York is now a mere bookkeeping job. The Governor should be more than a branch manager in a chain-store system of national politics. Who runs the Democratic Party? Is it my opponent? If it were, why isn't he running for the United States Senate, where he said he wanted to go?

On October 23, in Suffolk County, I concentrated on state finances:

During my eight years as a public prosecutor I have found many things in books of account. The indictment of Dutch Schultz, the convictions of Waxey Gordon and the restaurant racketeers, and Tootsie Herbert and many others, have been based on the work of skilled accountants who worked with me. Let us look at some facts about the books of the state of New York. The Governor's greatest boast in this campaign is that he has balanced the state budget, that last July the state had a surplus.

A nice bookkeeping job—taking credit for receipts that did not come in! Advancing tax dates to get them in a fiscal year! Delaying payments to put them in the next fiscal year!

On October 24, in a radio address, I concentrated on a major exposure that turned out to be one of the sensations of the whole campaign:

Who are the bosses of Albany? First, lawyer Ed O'Connell is the front man. Then there's Dan O'Connell, a sporting man, who boasts of some of the best fighting cocks in the state. Twice convicted, Dan is the actual boss of Albany. He is high in the councils of the ruling political machines of the state of New York.

His convictions have been no secret. The first was in 1927, for the crooked $4-million-a-year baseball pool which cheated the people who trusted it with their money. Dan was safe in Albany where he rules with immunity from the law. But the federal government finally caught up with him in Boston, and he pleaded guilty to the crime of conspiracy. Again, in 1930, under another investigation by the federal government, he said under oath that it would tend to incriminate him if he told the truth about this crooked racket. No wonder it would, since henchmen of his had sworn in federal courts to his sharing in the profits of the pool to the extent of tens of thousands of dollars. He was convicted of contempt, sentenced to three months, and served his time in jail.

The third O'Connell is Solly—a shadowy figure. The less said about Solly the better. Solly has a son named John. A few years ago John was the victim in the famous O'Connell kidnaping case, about which many things still remain unexplained. At the moment young John is the general manager for the Albany machine in one of its local monopolies, the Hedrick Brewery of the city of Albany. Ed O'Connell is the president of Hedrick's and Dan is vice-president. It is one of the family enterprises.

Now, let's have a look at the Hedrick Brewery. It is typical of the things that go on in Albany County. It is the kind of political racket we are fighting in this election.

The beer salesmen in Prohibition days were muscle men—gangsters with guns. The racketeer took over a territory, and every speakeasy in the area had to buy beer from the big shots or else. Well, beer is legal now, and Albany is the O'Connells' territory.

Other breweries in the O'Connell territory have from eighteen to thirty-four licensed salesmen. But the Hedrick Brewery gets the business. And it needs no licensed salesmen at all. In Albany the barrooms sell Hedrick's beer or else.

It is Hedrick's beer only on draft at the city's two largest hotels. Hedrick's is the only beer on draft in 200 out of the 259 grills and taverns in the city of Albany. It's Hedrick's or else.

When a tavern keeper puts in Hedrick's, 100 per cent, the sky's the limit. He gets his license renewed without a hitch. He can have slot machines, hostesses, music, dancing. He can forget every technical regulation. He can stay open all night and throw away the key.

I have in my hand the affidavits of tavern keepers who put in another brand because their customers would not drink Hedrick's. Here is one. He dropped Hedrick's and put in another beer. The first week he sold four times as much. But his troubles also increased four times as much.

City police and Alcoholic Beverage Commission inspectors swarmed over his tavern day and night. They poked into his icebox to see that he had food on hand. They inspected closets and lockers. They pored over his books. They rushed about slamming doors and snooping in corners. They announced in loud tones that he would have to close sharply at 1:00 A.M., even though the Hedrick's places stayed open all night.

When it came time for the tavern keeper to renew his license the application was denied. There was an illegal door. It had been there for several years and no one had objected. He had to board up the door. Still they held up his license. His old license had expired. He was paying rent, but he could not sell beer. His customers found new places.

In desperation he turned to the approved channel in Albany. He saw his Democratic ward leader. He also saw former Sheriff Joe Henchy, now the state's building superintendent. They promised to help. A meeting was arranged with liquor inspectors in a downtown store. It looked at last as though he would get his license. But again it did not come through, and again he was met with the old refrain, "Sell nothing but Hedrick's, and everything will be smoothed out."

At last the politicians gave him the okay. He squared himself and he finally got the renewal six weeks late, six weeks during which he sold no beer, saw his customers go elsewhere, saw his business shattered.

Another man sold Hedrick's in his little restaurant, but his customers did not like it. He put in another beer. And the boys cracked down, the same old troubles. The climax came when a Hedrick henchman said: "You may lose money with Hedrick's beer, but put in the slot machines, and you can make it up."

One tavern keeper in nearby Cohoes stood up and fought. Right in the files of the State Liquor Authority is his affidavit. He swears that the Hedrick agent said: "They have the courts, they have the board, and everything their way, and they are going through with it. Those who don't take Hedrick's 100 per cent will have to take the consequences."

A political machine filled with racketeers by the admission of the men who run that machine, the men who stand high in the councils of the Democratic Party of the state of New York! These are the shocking conditions we are fighting.

No wonder my opponent is sick of being Governor of New York. He was tired of it two years ago. This year he was tired of it again. He wanted to go to the United States Senate—to get away from it all. But they would not let him go.

At the convention they induced the Governor to run again for an office he did not want. The newspapers report that the Democratic national chairman told a touching story about a politician who sat on a bed in a hotel room. He was begging the Governor to run again— to make the sacrifice. That politician was the twice-convicted Dan O'Connell.

Now, the Governor of this state is an honorable and conscientious man. I respect his integrity and devotion to duty. I don't know whether he knows about these conditions. But it does not make any difference. The Democratic machine is too much for any man. It is a system, a habit, a political way of life. No Democratic governor can cope with it.

I know the people in the Democratic Party do not like these corrupt and reactionary machines. I know the candidates for state office on the Democratic ticket do not like these machines. That is why you, the voters, Democrats and Republicans alike, must crush them at the polls on November 8.

Only the people can bring their power to an end . . .

On October 25, in Albany, I repeated the charges against the O'Connell machine and added new charges of vote fraud and voter persecution by the machine. I said:

Tax oppression is one of the most vicious methods of destroying human liberty, It is one of the worst methods of political monopoly. Let's look at what goes on right here in the city of Albany.

There are three breweries in Albany, the Beverwyck plant, the Dobler plant, and Hedrick's, which is owned by the O'Connells.

The Beverwyck plant is more modern than Hedrick's. It was assessed at $429,000 in 1937, and the Dobler plant at $410,000. But look at the Hedrick. The assessment was $250,000, only a little more than half of the others. This year, they adjusted the tax rolls. They cut the Dobler $9,000, or two per cent. They raised the Beverwyck plant $3,000, just under one per cent.

Now, let's look at the Hedrick plant. We can assume they were not cheating themselves when they put their own plant on the rolls at $250,000 last year. What happened this year? They cut the assessment $125,000—exactly half.

I have here photographs of homes in Albany. They tell the story of injustice and oppression. Take just the value the assessors put on the houses. Look at this one. A handsome two-and-one-half-story dwelling, gabled, and with a three-car garage at 50 Rensselaer Avenue. The owner's brother is an officeholder in Albany. So therefore the assessment is only $1,800.

On the other hand, look at this little shingled house, up close to the street on a tiny lot. Its owner is Elmer Ludlum, who made the mistake of registering as a Republican, and his assessment is $7,500, almost four times as much.

Look at this palatial, ivy-covered brick residence of the Rosch family with its expansive lawn at 236 Loudonville Road. It is assessed at $2,500. The Rosches registered right. Now look at this one. Ernest Hendricks is a Republican. He has a little stucco home set back a few feet, on Quail Street. It is assessed at $8,500, again almost four times as much. Its owner registered wrong. The power to tax is the power to destroy, and well the O'Connells know it. It is low taxes for favorites, and high taxes to destroy all opposition.

The new 1938 City Directory of the city of Albany lists a total of 95,269 men and women over twenty-one years of age, of whom 2,000 died before the book came out. Of the remaining 93,000 names, almost 14,000 live in suburban towns and are ineligible to vote in the city. That leaves 79,000 adults listed in the City Directory, which is supposed to contain as nearly as possible all the permanent residents of the city.

Now, let's just suppose that every man and woman in Albany is a citizen, well, healthy, and interested in voting. Just imagine that, if you can. Why, they would have 79,000 voters. This year, they registered 82,000 voters. In the city of Albany—3,000 more than the City Directory can find.

The Tammany braves are pikers by comparison with this machine when it comes to vote frauds.

Let me tell you about some of the people in this machine. First, Sammy Magliocca, alias Sammy Shoemaker. Sammy is a self-confessed gun toter and a confessed burglar, seven times arrested, four times convicted.

When Sammy was a young man up in Albany they used to send him to jail when they caught him. But now he is one of the boys. Four times in the last four years they had to lock Sammy up in Albany. Three times he pleaded guilty, and three times he walked out with a suspended sentence.

For years Sammy had a place on Dongan Avenue—a low dive known as the Blue Moon Tavern. It was not a big place, but crowded in the two upper floors he had twenty-two cots. Sammy was usually pretty tough with his customers but toward Election Day he became civic-minded. Sammy believed in democracy and the election franchise. He believed that if it was good to vote once, it was good to vote a dozen times.

In 1935 there were 78 persons registered as voters from Sammy's tavern. Sammy had an explanation. There were only twenty-two beds in the place, but his flock of voters slept in three eight-hour shifts.

Sammy actually got himself arrested that year for election frauds. But that was all right. Nobody wanted to prosecute him. Since he was arrested last spring for having untaxed liquor, Sammy's Blue Moon Tavern is no more. He has a soft job in the Administrative Department of the WPA. One of my friends called up the WPA office the other day and asked for Sammy. Sammy wasn't in. He was said to be out taking voters to the polls.

Here is another enthusiastic machine supporter. She is a woman, so I will not mention her name. In the autumn of 1936 she was eager for Election Day to come around, and an acquaintance asked her why. The affidavit I have quotes her as answering: "I need some new clothes." Said she, "I made $287 voting last year."

How much money she made voting in 1935 we do not know. Rough estimates are that she voted thirty-odd times. She admitted voting half a dozen times. But that is nothing in Albany. She pleaded guilty, and went back happily to her husband.

Now, who was he? Her husband is known as "Frog." Back in 1936 he had a public job as chauffeur to the general manager of the

Albany Port Commission. Now, I do not know how many times Frog voted that year, but they had to indict him for voting twice. Did they prosecute him? Certainly not. He was one of the boys. They promoted him. Now he is foreman of maintenance of the port of Albany.

And so it goes. Now and then the machine has to make a horrible example. They have to make believe the law is enforced. Take the case of Charlie Crawford. Charlie did not have any friends. He had to live in an almshouse. Somebody had him register three times in 1935. He was arrested. He pleaded guilty. But nobody went to the front for poor Charlie. He was not part of the machine. He was not on the public payroll. He went to prison for a term of two to five years.

Let's take the case of a young woman who had a clerk's job in a state office. Just before Christmas of 1936 she was called in by her boss and told she was to be fired because she had voted the Republican ticket. She insisted it was her sister who voted Republican. But they said she had been watched by one of the henchmen as she voted. There was no appeal from that. She was dismissed from her job in the public service.

But that was not all. The tax boys went to work on her mother. The next year, without a single change in the house itself, they jumped the assessment on her mother's home from $2,400 to $4,000.

Things got so bad in 1935, there was actually a grand jury investigation of election frauds. So let me tell you about the Albany grand jury. A grand jury is supposed to be representative of the community. Its members are supposed to be chosen by chance from a drum in which their names are placed. Out of the 120 or so grand jurors who served in Albany County between September 12, 1935, and November 19, 1936, 104 were enrolled Democrats, and only 7 were enrolled Republicans. Nine were not enrolled.

The grand jury which was supposed to investigate the election frauds of 1935 had 19 registered Democrats out of its 23 members. The foreman of that grand jury was a man whose company had in one year done $36,000 worth of coal business with the city of Albany. The secretary was a former Democratic supervisor. On that jury were a deputy superintendent of public buildings, a Democratic ward leader, an inspector of the county Alcoholic Beverage Commission Board, a deputy in the State Tax Department, a former county clerk, and the county sealer of weights and measures.

No wonder the Albany machine rules with such an iron hand. No wonder the lid has never come off before. I do not know whether the Governor of the state knows these conditions. But his political advisers could have told him.

I recognize the high-mindedness and personal integrity of my opponent in this election. I recognize the sincerity of his purpose, but say in all solemnity that no Democratic governor in the state of New York can crush the machines from which the votes come for his election.

The days passed, and Governor Lehman made no denial of the charges. The corrupt machine issue was dynamite because we were seemingly able to prove that the alliance between organized politics and organized crime was, in fact, statewide. Finally Jim Farley himself denied only that O'Connell had sat on Lehman's bed while persuading him to run. I referred to Farley's denial.

Well, I was wrong about that. We have it on the word of Mr. Farley, the chairman of the Democratic National Committee, that Dan O'Connell did not sit on a bed. He sat in a chair, a nice, big easy chair. Pardon me, ladies and gentlemen, I stand corrected. I said he was sitting on a bed. He was really sitting on an easy chair.

And that was the only answer we have had to the exposure of political corruption in the very shadow of the state Capitol. There has been no explanation of the Albany machine, no repudiation of the Albany machine, no apology for the Albany machine.

I am sure the Governor did not know the iniquities of that machine. But his political advisers could have told him.

Defeat by 64,000 Votes

On October 27, 1938, in Elmira, New York, I made a campaign speech about the civil service:

Less than fifty per cent of the regular employees of the New York State public payroll are in the competitive civil service. More than half of all the state employees are subject to removal at the whim of a politician.

On October 28, in Binghamton, I concentrated on agriculture:

Today the net income of most of New York's great farming population does not pay the cost of the hired man. These are things you know too well. You also know that the problem of our farm income did not begin with the Depression, but had been serious to all of us for more than sixteen years. I was born and raised in a farm community, and I worked on a farm as a boy. It never occurred to me then, and it does not occur to me now, that necessity for a decent farm income is a matter of political debate.

At the end of the month, in White Plains, I concentrated on welfare and unemployment insurance:

The welfare of its less fortunate people is a primary concern of the state. According to the latest figures, there are 104,000 inmates in our state hospitals and institutions. There are blind people and crippled children dependent on the state. There are 101,000 persons receiving old-age assistance.

There are more than 225,000 persons in this state with their families who are dependent on WPA jobs for their support. More than 2,000,000 people in this state are today directly or indirectly dependent upon public funds for their existence.

Last year the Governor's budget failed to provide sufficient appropriations for their relief. It was the Republican Assembly which forced an additional appropriation of $24 million. That money was needed. Without it, the relief funds would have run short. I pledge to you that the Republican Party will continue to see that these obligations are met. The no man's land between unemployment insurance and relief must be wiped out.

Good government unhindered by the barnacles of political corruption is the birthright of every American. Let us this year prove that democracy can maintain itself, that we can feed the hungry, house the homeless, and provide work for the idle, that these things can be done without the help of corrupt political machines.

On October 31, in Syracuse, I concentrated once again on farm land issues:

Conservation of the soil is a problem that government must face. The farm and pasture lands of the state are among its most treasured assets. The impoverishing loss through erosion can and must be stopped. The state can and must encourage practices that will conserve the soil.

Eighty thousand farms, more than forty-seven per cent of the farms in this state, have never yet had the benefit of electricity. Rural electrification can and must be encouraged by the state. The state must also expand its program of farm-to-market roads. It must at the same time protect its vast investment in highway repair. An orderly program to restore the 3,000 miles of highway now verging on decay will be a boon to the farmer in reaching his market.

On October 31, in a state-wide radio broadcast, I returned to the crime situation in New York City, with special reference to the Drukman murder case in Brooklyn. I explained that this was an outrageous matter because a Democratic District Attorney in Kings County had dropped the case and let three killers walk out on the streets as free men. But the local police would not let the matter rest and, finally, the Governor appointed a Special Prosecutor in Brooklyn. This Special Prosecutor obtained convictions and life sentences for the murderers.

But the Governor did not remove the District Attorney. So a special grand jury brought charges against the District Attorney for neglect of duty and asked the Governor to remove the man from office. The Governor held a hearing which lasted fourteen days. Afterward, the Governor said he thought the District Attorney was an honest man and dismissed the charges.

On November 1, in Buffalo, I spoke about issues of concern to organized labor:

On Election Day the people of New York State will ratify Amendment No. 6, approved by the Constitutional Convention by the vote of Republicans and Democrats alike. That amendment will become the basic law of this state. It will write into the constitution fundamental rights of labor, among them the right to collective bargaining through representatives of their own choosing, the clear statement that labor is not a commodity, and the requirement that workers on public contracts shall be paid the prevailing rate of wages with the eight-hour day.

I strongly urge every voter in the state to vote for this amendment and to make certain that these guarantees of the rights of labor become part of our fundamental law.

I believe in these fundamental rights of labor. I believe in the gains that labor has made through years of struggle. For these gains, I will continue to fight.

On November 2, in the Bronx, I concentrated on Governor Lehman's claim that there was in New York State more effective regulation of utility rates than at any time in our history:

Well, the Governor may be happy with our utility rates. I am not. I have had some experience in the past eight years in digging out facts for the people of New York. Utility facts are just like any other facts.

Right here in New York City, for 40 kilowatt-hours, a family pays $2.41. That is not very much electricity over a month. It is just enough to light a few rooms and to make the morning toast. It will not include an electric refrigerator or many other appliances.

Even in the notoriously ill-governed Chicago, the rate is only $1.94—47 cents less every month. The people of Cleveland pay only

$1.60 and that is 81 cents less every month. In Washington they pay 85 cents less, and in Cincinnati 96 cents a month less.

In upstate New York, what do our people pay? In Rochester, the average family pays $2.26 a month. But in Louisville, Kentucky, they pay 56 cents less. In Syracuse, New York, a family pays $2.00 a month, but in Akron, Ohio, they pay 39 cents less.

On November 2, in Queens, in New York City, I replied to a telling point Governor Lehman had made on the crime and politics issue. Lehman had revealed that a former sheriff of Cayuga County in upstate New York, a Republican, had made Dutch Schultz a deputy sheriff some six years before. I said:

The important thing is what happened to that Republican sheriff after it came out that he had appointed Dutch Schultz. His term had expired before that fact came to light. But when the Republicans in Cayuga County found out about it, that sheriff's political career was ended so far as the Republican Party was concerned. He was expelled from the party councils in that county.

I do not claim my party has a monopoly on virtue any more than I admit the claim that my opponent has a monopoly on human welfare. But I do want to re-emphasize that when a Republican officer betrays his trust he is dealt with speedily and according to law. He is not promoted in the party council. He is expelled.

On November 3, at the Manhattan Opera House in New York City, I commented that this was a victory meeting, that I sensed the panic and confusion on the other side, and that the forces arrayed against us were becoming disorganized. I noted that President Roosevelt himself had come into the state to help Governor Lehman's campaign. Then I talked about my over-all social philosophy:

Let us discuss the rights of the individual and the duties of government. You will note that I put the rights of the individual ahead of the duties of government. Man lived on this planet first, and government grew after his arrival. It grew in response to his need. The duty of government to respond to man's need continues, and shall always continue.

Sometimes government forgets how it came into being. Sometimes governments—or, rather, the small group of men in control for the moment—fail in their duty. When any small group of men selfishly use their power toward self-perpetuation, then the integrity of government is at stake.

Freedom itself is threatened. That is bad government.

Sometimes a government, with the best intention in the world, fails in its duty through clumsy administration. The need of man which it represents is not satisfied. The rights of man are not preserved. That too is bad government.

Both kinds of government are bad for the people. Both should be speedily removed. These are fundamental things.

Now, we must never forget the most important function of government, to preserve by orderly, well-considered processes the rights and the dignity of the individual. There are many such rights, but first among them is the right to freedom—freedom to enjoy a full life, freedom of opportunity to win the good things of life, freedom to achieve a proportionate share of the modern luxuries which make life happier and more complete.

Under the broad heading of the right to freedom are many rights. Economic security, security from disaster for which no individual is responsible, has become a right of the people. It includes the right to a job at fair wages. It includes the right of a farmer to decent prices for his crops. It includes the right of labor to bargain collectively through representatives of its own choosing. It includes the right of the small businessman to protection against unfair competition. It includes the right of the very young, and the old, the sick and the infirm, to shelter from the winds of chance to which their youth, or age, or infirmity exposes them. Many of these rights are still denied to our people. For many of these, we still must fight.

There are other rights—basic rights of the free man: the right to worship as he sees fit, the right to think clearly and honestly, and act on such thoughts, the right to freedom of speech, freedom of the press, freedom of assembly. These rights must not be violated.

When anyone for political purposes appeals to racial or religious passion or prejudice, he betrays everything for which this government was founded. He betrays the very principles upon which this great and free country was founded. We must never forget for political purposes, or otherwise, the principles of freedom and religious tolerance upon which our country was built. We must never permit prejudices to grow in our midst against any human being or group of human beings because of their racial origin. When it creeps into government, the seeds everywhere find fertile soil. Where such prejudice sprouts, we must root it out.

Another important right of the people is freedom of expression in government itself. The people must always have a voice in their government—that is the philosophy of the democracy under which we live. The people must always hold the reins of government in order to preserve democracy. At regular intervals, under our Constitution, the government is referred again to the people in order that they may express a new choice if they feel that those in control have not made the best uses of their power.

These rights are fundamental, but we must be ever vigilant in their preservation. We are armed with a most potent weapon in any war for the preservation of human rights—the ballot. We must use that ballot with care—that is our duty to ourselves . . .

On November 4, with the polls now indicating a close race, President Roosevelt delivered a fireside chat from his house at Hyde Park, New York. Although Lehman had not supported Roosevelt's attempt to pack the Supreme Court, Roosevelt considered a Lehman victory in 1938 very important. Now Roosevelt belittled me as "one who has yet to win his spurs," and he contrasted our prosecution of the underworld with the Democratic Party's nation-wide struggle against "the lords of the overworld." Referring to our campaign, he said: "By their promoters ye shall know them."

Roosevelt added: "Governing the state of New York is more than being an Assistant Secretary of the Navy or a local District Attorney. The Governor of the state is called upon to administer eighteen great departments of government, and supervise state institutions that house over one hundred thousand wards of the state.

"As a resident and voter of the state of New York, I urge my fellow citizens and voters to vote for Herbert H. Lehman."

On November 5, in our final campaign rally, I replied to Roosevelt at the Academy of Music in Brooklyn:

Another generation has passed on to us a sick world. It is sick economically with 11,000,000 of our people still unemployed. It is sick spiritually, poisoned by hatreds. It is sick politically when a candidate for Governor of the great state of New York does not dare repudiate corrupt elements of the party which support him.

It was well said by the President last night, and I quote his words: "By their promoters ye shall know them." In this campaign, I am promoted by no man. No man or group of men told me what office I could not run for. No man or group of men, on an easy chair, or a bed, or otherwise, told me what office I could run for.

By their promoters ye shall know them. Our opponents still rely on the discredited and repudiated forces of old and reactionary political power in Albany, Buffalo, and here in New York City. I have pointed out name after name of men convicted, either in the courts or before the people, as betrayers of the public trust. After exposure, they have maintained their political power.

To this there has been no answer, no word of explanation, no word of apology.

My opponent suggests that I should have known that Dutch Schultz had once been a deputy sheriff of Cayuga County. Since his address, I have investigated the activities of Dutch Schultz as a law enforcement agent.

On July 31, 1925, Arthur Flegenheimer, alias Dutch Schultz, was appointed deputy sheriff of Bronx County, in New York City. At that time he was already in the Rogues' Gallery of the Police Department, and already was an ex-convict. Now, let's look at the copy of his warrant of appointment. I have it here. Let's see who was sheriff of the Bronx in 1925. Who appointed the man who at that time was a trigger man for Legs Diamond and Owney Madden and was preparing to build up his own vast racket empire?

Let's see the name at the bottom of this certificate—the name of the sheriff who made the appointment, administered the oath, and gave the badge of a law enforcement officer to this notorious Dutch Schultz. Let's see the name. Here it is. Edward J. Flynn.

Boss of the Bronx, Democratic chairman of the county committee, chairman of the executive committee of the Democratic Party in the Bronx.

Now, was this Ed Flynn thrown out of the councils of his party? No. He was promoted. Six months later he was appointed chamberlain of the city of New York under the old regime. And in that office he had the custody of trust funds belonging to widows and orphans.

You all know the record of the city chamberlain's office under Boss Flynn's administration. You all know about the notorious State Title and Mortgage Company, many of whose officers have since been convicted of crimes. You all remember how $6.5 million of these trust funds were invested in so-called guaranteed mortgages and certificates, how more than one third of that amount, over $2 million, was invested in the certificates of the State Title and Mortgage Company. It is this man to whom the widows and orphans whose funds he held in trust look in vain for payment on the investment of their funds.

Now, the damage caused by Flynn's reckless investment of other people's money was not really known until the crash came some time later. And when the crash came, where was Ed Flynn? Again, he had been promoted. He had arrived at the exalted office he now holds.

Secretary of State of the state of New York, at $12,000 a year, by appointment of the Governor of the state of New York. As Secretary of State, he has custody of the great seal of the state. He has official custody of the laws of the state. He administers the oath of office to the governors of this state, to other state officials, and to members of the legislature.

He is still Democratic boss of the Bronx. He is still one of the most important leaders in the councils of his party. And only recently, he was again promoted. Today, he is the Democratic national committeeman from the state of New York.

My opponent raised this subject. Investigation brings out the devastating facts on the record.

Because I am devoted to representative government, I have stressed the necessity of ridding it in New York State of those who betray it. This must be done to make sure that our form of government will not go the way of those ancient, as well as modern, democracies which have decayed and rotted away under the domination of political overlords. This must not happen here.

My opponent, with all of his honorable intentions, is helpless after six years. I believe I will accomplish what he has failed to do . . .

On November 6, almost on the eve of the election, Governor Lehman accused the Republicans of waging a campaign of racial and religious intolerance. Lehman did that every election. He seized on some tiny, irrelevant incident and blew it up into a whole campaign. Everybody who was against him was anti-Semitic. Years later he used this tactic against Foster Dulles when he was running against Dulles for the United States Senate. Nobody on earth was less susceptible to that kind of stuff than Dulles, so Lehman dug up an old representation Sullivan and Cromwell had had for Germany, and claimed that they were representing the Nazis.

The Democrats always played race or religion in New York, and the habit sometimes became so strong that they hurled it against each other. Their former Lieutenant Governor, William Bray, was a Catholic, and he was dropped so that Lehman could put a liberal non-Catholic named Charles Poletti on the ticket instead. A Children's Court judge named Herbert A. O'Brien urged Catholics to break away from their Democratic regularity. He said that Catholics were a majority south of Westchester County, but that they were represented in part by thirteen Jewish assemblymen. It was a shocking thing for a judge to do to inject himself into politics like that. He had no business doing it.

There had been violent objection from many quarters to the dropping of Bray from the Lehman ticket. It was felt that Poletti was a lefty, as well as not a Catholic. It was said that the Democrats dropped a conservative Catholic from their ticket and put on a left-wing fellow of no religion, I guess, or he might have been a Protestant, a Baptist.

The next suggestion of racial and religious intolerance in the 1938 campaign surrounded President Roosevelt's arrival at Hyde Park. A story was put out that the President had been told that an anti-Semitic whispering campaign was under way in upstate New York. Which *he* put out. *He* invented it. Roosevelt played that game too. Shortly after that incident I issued a statement to the effect that I would rather be defeated than be elected on votes of race and religion.

But one of those rabble rousers from the Middle West arrived in New York and said that he was going to support me. I always thought that he was paid by the Democrats to do it. He was an anti-Semitic rabble rouser, a no-good fellow. He was of the Ku Klux Klan stripe. I think he arrived in Brooklyn, though I do not remember exactly where he arrived, but I always thought he was paid by the Democrats to come in. I repudiated him very strongly.

Our company manager in New York City, Roger Straus, commented that copies of a statement supposedly made by Benjamin Franklin in the Constitutional Convention with respect to Semitic peoples had been printed and sent out in our envelopes to Brooklyn and Manhattan addresses. These envelopes were either forgeries or were stolen from our envelope supply in headquarters.

Fred Bontecou, our candidate for Lieutenant Governor, prepared large posters upstate with a slogan on them, "Vote American." The Democrats seized these posters as evidence that we were running an anti-Semitic campaign. This happened so late that by the time head-quarters learned about it there was no time to set things right.

Early in the evening of Election Night, November 8, 1938, the race was tight and even. The *Daily Mirror,* in one edition, announced my election. The New York *Times* telephoned and said they were putting out an extra stating that I had won. But I told the caller that I had my chief accountant, Goody Goodrich, on the other line telling me that I had lost. Goody had a man-made system all set up to analyze and project early returns from key election districts. Before midnight, I sent a telegram to Lehman: "Heartiest congratulations on your re-election. I wish you every success and happiness. With best personal regards."

Governor Lehman said: "My opponent, Mr. Dewey, can rejoice in having waged a vigorous and strong fight. To him, I extend the as-surance of my wholehearted support in the exacting task that lies be-fore him as the District Attorney of New York."

Lehman was re-elected, as we learned when all the figures were in, by a plurality of just 64,394 votes. His running mate, Senator Wagner, was re-elected by a plurality of 438,414 votes.

Of a total of 4,821,631 votes cast, Lehman polled 1,971,307 Demo-cratic votes and 419,979 from American Labor. I polled 2,302,505 Republican votes and 24,387 Independent Progressive votes.* Lehman received a plurality of 681,369 in New York City, overcoming my lead of 616,975 elsewhere in the state.

The Los Angeles *Times* summed up: "A shift of thirty thousand votes out of nearly five million would have made Dewey Governor against the combined efforts of the country's most powerful City, State and Federal machine, plus the utmost influence of the President, on behalf of an incumbent candidate as nearly invincible as candi-dates get."

I did not contemplate any national possibilities. I just went back to work. I had jobs to do, important things to do. I was, as always, just buffeted by too many things to do. Things arose from the office that required more hours in a day than I had. They arose from the fact that I had become a national political figure. For example, I was asked to make the speech for the Republican Party at the next Grid-

---

* Because there were more Republican votes than Democratic, the Republican Party in this election won placement on "the top line" on voting machines, an important advantage in the next election.

iron Dinner, when I was the fellow who did not get elected. There were many prominent Republicans who did get elected.

On December 17, 1938, after a brief vacation in Bermuda, I gave this speech at the Gridiron Dinner at which President Roosevelt was guest of honor:

I have gained a lot of experience in the last few months. First [at the Hines trial] I asked a question. Instead of getting an answer, I got thrown out of court. Then I was nominated for Governor. For a few hours they let me think I was going to run against a fellow named Elmer. Then somebody changed the Governor's mind.

Now, you gentlemen down here in Washington may never know what a fine senator Herbert Lehman would have made. Even I thought he would make a fine senator.

This dinner seems just like old times back in September and October, when I was in politics. There we were, up in New York, fighting a campaign against Governor Lehman, Charlie Poletti, Bob Wagner, and the other New Yorkers. And then the Washington invasion began. The Postmaster General, the Democratic state chairman, and the chairman of the Democratic National Committee all came up to New York at once and tried to get into the fight.

Immediately, I threw a hotel bed at him. Jim Farley tossed back an easy chair, but all he did was hit Governor Lehman. That was enough for Jim. Things weren't going too well. So Jim sent a hurry call for help. Up came a section of the Cabinet. And still it didn't go so well. Now, the President doesn't take part in local elections, so they brought up the titular head of the Democratic Party.

I never felt so much like a Democrat in my life as I did on the Friday before election, when the distinguished guest of honor this evening came to New York and made a speech against me. I thought for a moment I was the object of a Senate purge. But Election Night showed I was wrong—I lost.

Well, the head of the Democratic Party came through with a double play. He kept me out of Albany, and Governor Lehman out of Washington.

As I said before, I learned a good deal in this campaign. After all, it isn't everybody who received lessons at such good hands. I listened with deep interest to the President's speech and later read some of the interpretations you gentlemen placed on it. The underlying theme in support of my opponent was, "Once a Governor, always a Governor."

But I am still not clear as to whether it also meant, "Once a President, always a President."

Seriously, Mr. President, for your leadership in social progress in the nation, I salute you. For that leadership, I am sure I may say the whole people salute you.

Now, gentlemen, permit me to suggest that the elections of last month did *not* create a pause in the progress of liberal government in this country. Nor, in this election, did the people turn their backs upon the sound social progress which has been made. On the contrary, it seems to me that there was a mandate that the *sound* measures which have been adopted shall be perpetuated by the rapid elimination of the unsound, and by the more efficient administration of those which remain.

Furthermore, it seems to me that the people have declared democracy cannot be served by a one-party monopoly and, in the face of the purges, they have also declared that there is room in both parties for sincere men despite their differing opinions.

A resurgent Republican Party comes to Washington to encourage federal leadership but to resist government domination. It comes with instructions from the people to make every effort to achieve their dreams, but to do so with a little less sleepwalking.

Today, all can recognize that neither party has an exclusive agency to represent the people, and both parties contain within themselves differing views as to which side of the road to travel to the same goals.

In the face of attack from many quarters, the perpetuation of our political system requires that the leaders of both parties learn to respect the integrity and purpose of each other. Our political affairs can do with more sober debate and less name-calling and abuse.

For only if we respect each other can we preserve public respect and confidence in the institutions of democracy. These Gridiron Dinners typify the blessings of our system. Here, in complete freedom, and in the presence of our political opponents, we speak our minds. The good sportsmanship we see here is one of the fundamental characteristics of the American people.

Bitterness and intolerance have no place in the American scene. The flames of intolerance must not be fanned by bigots or soreheads.

From this election, let us go forward with no resentment in defeat and no arrogance in victory.

CHAPTER XXII

James J. Hines—and
Appeals Court Judge Manton

Things in the mail of a famous person—according to Harold Keller—in the District Attorney years of 1938 and 1939:

"Letters received at the District Attorney's office addressed, 'Racket Buster, New York' with no name and address, or 'T.E.D. Enemy of Corruption,' with no name and address, or Dewey pictures pasted on the envelopes, with no name and address. A front page of a Washington, D.C., newspaper with the pictures of Dewey and Hines and identifying captions reversed, on which somebody had scrawled, 'One look at him and I knew he was guilty—I hope you get him.'

"Love letters written on District Attorney stationery had been mailed without postage, were returned for the necessary stamps, and were traced to a WPA worker somewhere else in town. A beer license application complete with a $50 money order was mailed in a 'Dewey for Governor' envelope without postage, and was returned to the District Attorney's office long after the campaign. A letter from a doting father said that his ten-year-old daughter was disappointed because there was too much rain, and she was threatening to sue God. 'You can't win such a lawsuit,' I told her. And she said, 'I could if Dewey was my lawyer.'"

Big talk and random chitchat by a budding national figure, again according to Harold Keller:

"The big talk was due to be delivered to the American Newspaper Publishers Association in April 1938, and Dewey had worked hard in the preparation of what he regarded as an important and effective speech. But just before he rose, the toastmaster called upon another honor guest, Henry Ford, the automobile magnate, to say a few words. Ford said to the publishers in effect, 'Keep on giving the New Deal hell—we're behind you!' Ford stole the applause and the show, and the next morning's headlines, while Dewey's role was reported almost as 'also spoke.' "

Other glimpses provided by Harold Keller.

"During a conference in the office, Dewey remarked on an unshaven area above the mustache of one of his aides—Keller. 'Letting it grow bigger?' Dewey asked. 'No,' I replied, 'I've cut myself there several times recently.' 'How do you shave there—up or down?' 'Down.' 'Oh, I shave up,' said Dewey, 'and never cut myself.'

"While driving through Vermont en route to Dartmouth College to receive an honorary LL.D. degree, our car stopped for gas at a service station where the proprietor also sold homemade doughnuts. Munching on a doughnut, Dewey was asked by the proprietor if he wasn't Tom Dewey. When Dewey said yes, the Vermonter responded, 'Pleased to meet you, Mr. Dewey, and glad to have you as a customer. Tell your friends to drop by and buy some of my doughnuts.'

"Dewey on vacation in Augusta, Georgia, in the Forest Hills Hotel: to the accompaniment of the string trio at the hotel, with Paul Lockwood and William Lyon Phelps as his whole audience, Dewey gave a recital of songs including 'The Evening Star' from Tannhäuser, 'Ave Maria,' and 'Smoke Gets in Your Eyes.' "

Dewey letter from a Republican leader in Oklahoma, Henry O. Glasser, located and quoted by Harold Keller:

"Glasser referred to an influential Reverend Murphy who was concerned about the fact that Dewey took an occasional cocktail, and said there were two issues on which prejudice was great in the Middle West, liquor and religion. Dewey replied: 'I understand the Reverend Murphy's views concerning the religious and alcoholic practices of the country and, as far as liquor is concerned, I thoroughly understand them. It would be tragic indeed if a firm and uncompromising stand against religious intolerance should be a political handicap in this country. If it is, that handicap is mine.'"

Lighter moments around the District Attorney's office, as recalled by Sol Gelb:

"It was a lot of fun. I used to come in never on time. I would work late and never come on time. Dewey would send for me, and I wasn't there. He'd say, 'Why the hell can't you come in on time?' I said, 'Because I was trained in the federal courts.' Their courts open at 10:30 A.M. I would shave in the office, and he tried a few times to get me in on time, and to get me not to shave in the office, but he gave it up. One day he was in the office with a couple of assistants and they needed me. He said, 'Don't waste your time. Sol's not in yet.'

"He forgot about it. Hell, we'd leave at night. Sometimes Dewey would drop Harry Cole and me off, and we'd go into a bar and get a few drinks. Dewey always tried to stop us because he figured we wouldn't be in the next day. Well, we finally got him into a bar on some occasion, and we had a lot of fun.

"We had some very nice fellows there. When there was work to do, we worked hard. That's why I say that's a job for a young man. Today, I couldn't work like that. I wouldn't want to. That's the point. This man was an electrifying man. To work for him made men feel it was a privilege. Very seldom do you get a public official who makes the men feel that way."

Question put to former dollar-a-year man Manny Robbins: "Wasn't it you who commented that Dewey defined acceptable night clubs as Childs Restaurants?"

Robbins: "Virtually. There were a lot of stories about that. And did I tell you about the time I went to the race track with Judge Koenig?

"Well, we thought that going to a race track or even knowing about horses was tantamount to public corruption, and we were constantly warned that our attendance at a race track would be viewed with a great deal of suspicion.

"But there came a time when I was trying cases before Judge Koenig, whom I did not know until I was assigned to his courtroom for three months. I had a car in those days, and Judge Koenig quickly found that out and asked me what I was doing Saturdays. I, being single, had nothing much to do on Saturdays. I usually worked. He said, 'Well, come down to the office, and we'll go out to the track. I've got a pass and a box.' I said, 'I can't go to the track.' 'Why not?' 'Dewey doesn't want his assistants going out to the race track.'

"Judge Koenig said, 'If you go with me, it's all right.' I said, 'I don't know.' He said, 'Well, go ask Mr. Dewey.'

"I had to go and see Dewey and tell him my predicament. I was before Judge Koenig for three months. He was an elderly, kind gentleman. I was tempted not to brook his ill will at the start of my three months' stint. I asked Dewey, 'Should I make an exception in his case?'

"Dewey said, 'In this case, it will be all right if you go with the Judge, but mind your P's and Q's with whom you consort out there.'

"I had to have that clearance, and, par for the course, the District Attorney had about eleven detectives stationed out at the track waching for various suspicious characters, who was talking to whom. I drove Judge Koenig out to the race track. His eyesight was failing at that time. I personally had to shepherd him everywhere. We sat in somebody's box. I never was quite sure whose it was, but I think it belonged to Sam Koenig, the judge's brother.

"For a while, messenger boys came up to take our bets. There were no parimutuels there. The bookmakers had a ring at the track. The word 'bookmaker' itself struck terror in my heart. I did not even know enough to know that the bookmakers' ring was legal then. That was the place to make bets. The law allowed that, but I did not know anything about it. I remember something about it in Special Sessions, but I never got the details down because the whole subject was taboo.

"In any event, for the first few races, some messenger took our money, went down to the bookmaker's ring, and placed our bets. Our bets were all of two dollars, and in most bets the two dollars was split up between Judge Koenig and myself.

"People were coming up and giving the judge information. If they were talking to Judge Koenig, I avoided even looking in their faces. I winced every time someone leaned into the box and told him something. I thought surely this was some minion of the underworld.

"Finally there came a time when no messenger came to take our bet, and Judge Koenig asked me to go down and place a two-dollar bet with a bookmaker named Max Caillik who was then known as 'Kid Rags.' This man had actually testified as a character witness for

Lucky Luciano! The last person I wanted to go up to with Judge Koenig's two dollars was Max Caillik, and I refused the judge's request point-blank. He asked me why I would not go, and I told him, 'I can't go up to Kid Rags with all his background with your two dollars. God knows what will happen.'

"Judge Koenig said, 'Why can't you do it? He's a bookmaker, and he's standing where the bookmakers are supposed to stand.' I said, 'I can't do it.' He said, 'If that's the case, if the assistant district attorney won't go, the judge will go.' So he took the two dollars back from me and, in his blind, faltering way, he went all by himself to place the two-dollar bet with Max Caillik. That was an example of my apprehensions and cautions of the time.

"Judge Koenig never forgot that story. The next day—that is, the next court day—I had to see him at the noon-hour recess, and Judge Wallace came into Judge Koenig's chambers. Judge Koenig told Wallace the story. I did not see anything funny about it then, but all the court attendants laughed, and I just bit my lip.

"I had done what I thought was right, but thereafter for a while I went to the track every Saturday with Judge Koenig. I would never go down and see Kid Rags. I think we lost thirty-two races in a row."

More reminiscences from Manny Robbins:

"There was less of a tension in the District Attorney's office than in days of the special prosecution. We were no less dedicated, but the pressures were not as great, and we had more time to relax, and Dewey relaxed with us. He never was a great relaxer. He did not luxuriate around the office, chinning or passing the time of day, but we all had time to chat personally. I played squash with him a couple of times.

"When I got married, Frank Hogan invited my fiancée and me up to his home just for a social evening. There were Mary and Frank Hogan and a few of my friends—Livy Goddard, Sol Gelb, Bill Rogers. That was the crowd I went with in those days. So Frank and Mary invited us up and did not tell us—my fiancée had never seen Dewey—that Dewey and Lockwood were coming. Lockwood was always Dewey's shadow, you know, the buffer. That was one social evening with Dewey. In fact, we met Mrs. Dewey. We live right in the neighborhood, and see her from time to time."

Excerpts from letters to Owosso during these District Attorney years, as saved by Miss Rosse:

April 19, 1938

Dear Mater:

A little late with this one, but I have been quite loaded here. Yes, the Luciano [appeal] decision was a great relief, and removes the terrific burden of having to retry such portions of the case as could possibly be again presented to the court. . . . I am exceedingly happy with the result.

Things are boiling along here at the usual speed, with nothing out of the ordinary, but some racket cases which may reach trial soon, a nice murder conviction by Rosenblum, and the necessity of preparing two or three speeches.

We are now considering summer places. During the next two or three weekends, we are going to make quite a study of this subject, and I don't now expect that we will go back to Tuxedo. I would like to try the seashore, but I don't know whether we will be able to find the kind of place we want at a reasonable price. We might go to Connecticut.

Frances is definitely under par. Dr. Carter examined her last week, and is very much dissatisfied with every aspect of her condition. Accordingly, she is taking pills, has stopped smoking cigarettes, and may have to go on a strict regimen of diet, exercise, sleep, etc. He says her constitution is splendid, but her condition is rotten, and we are going to take vigorous steps.

We gave a very successful dinner party last Friday night with the McCooks, Simpsons, the Allen Dulleses and the Harpers, guests of the Simpsons, spending a holiday here from their permanent home in Paris, where he practices law. . . .

Frances thought I ought to enclose this picture for you from yesterday's *Herald Tribune*. Having gone to church in the morning, I took Tommy up to see the new flower gardens in Central Park. They are beautiful indeed.

That's all the news of the moment.

With much love.

May 3, 1938

Dear Mater:

Last week was a perfectly terrible week. I worked Monday night until two o'clock, Tuesday night until two o'clock and all

Wednesday night until seven in the morning on Thursday. I then slept until Thursday afternoon, came to the office briefly, and then went up and made the American Newspaper Publishers Association speech which you undoubtedly saw in the New York *Times*. Friday was almost as bad, because I got into the office late, as you might imagine, and then left at one o'clock for very special reasons. It was Tommy's first chance to go to a circus, and so Frances and I took him Friday afternoon. It was a magnificent performance, lasting from two-thirty until ten minutes to six, and he had a very good time indeed.

After the circus, I came back to the office and worked some more Friday night, and then got up at six-thirty the next morning to go to the country and look at houses. For two weekends now we have busily looked in Connecticut, and we have had difficulty finding something satisfactory, within our means. $1,000 would produce a satisfactory house, but I don't believe we can afford to pay that much since I must live within my salary. Finding a suitable place, though, for $500 or $600 is a very tough job. We were all over Connecticut weekend before last and then, on Saturday, we again covered Connecticut and part of upstate New York. We are still looking.

At the end of a long day on Saturday, we ended up at the Sulzbergers' home in White Plains at eight o'clock for an eight o'clock dinner. There were present Frank P. Noyes, recently retired after thirty-eight years from the Associated Press, Anne O'Hare McCormick, who is probably the most famous newspaper woman in the world, and her husband, the Sulzbergers and three or four of their friends. We stayed overnight and Sunday there was a lawn party of 45 or 50 of the leading newspaper publishers including, incidentally, Colonel Frank Knox, who was the Republican candidate for Vice-President in 1936, and I had a very long and pleasant chat with him. We stayed for supper, and then came on home, bringing Mr. Noyes back to his hotel. . . .

With much love.

August 10, 1938

Dear Mater:

I am greatly concerned about the reports of amoebic (I doubt the spelling) dysentery in Owosso. I gather from the reports that there have been six deaths and that it is quite wide-spread there. This is what the children had, you know, and it is a very serious thing to get in this country. I really think that you ought to be exceedingly careful.

Don't be disturbed about the press reports of conflict in the courtroom. It is highly necessary to cool off my noisy opponent once in a while, and both interchanges have been highly profit-able. I don't believe I can educate him into conducting himself like a lawyer, but I do think I can teach him that some things will do him more harm than good. If I can do that, the [Hines] trial will move more rapidly.

I am glad the car is so fine, and hope it continues to be as satisfactory as it now is. . . .

I spent a nice long weekend in the country last week, and hope to do it again this weekend, before the trial [formally be-gins]. I think we are in good shape. The trial will be long and difficult, but very much in the public interest and worth while.

With much love.

On January 26, 1939, the second trial of James J. Hines on charges of high-level protection of the Dutch Schultz numbers racket got under way.

After Judge Pecora had declared the first Hines trial, in 1938, to have been a mistrial, I had said: "Make no mistake about it. Hines will be brought to justice." And I had also said, "I will move for a new trial at the earliest possible date. It will be the same identical indictment." The date for the second trial was set back to November 14, just one week after the gubernatorial campaign was due for decision. It was subsequently moved back into January 1939.

I exercised my right for the second trial of requesting the assignment of a different judge. I took the matter straight to Pecora, and I asked him to yield jurisdiction, and also to let the General Sessions Court take over the sentencing of the three witnesses who had turned state's evidence, Dixie Davis, George Weinberg, and Big Harry Schoenhaus. Pecora himself signed the order for the transfer of the trial out of his authority but retained the power to sentence Davis, Weinberg, and Schoenhaus. The second trial was assigned to Judge Charles C. Nott, Jr., a sixty-nine-year-old jurist who, before his election to the bench in 1913, had had a distinguished career as an assistant district attorney.

Judge Nott's father, incidentally, had been appointed to the United States Court of Claims by President Lincoln a short time before the assassination. President Cleveland had promoted him to Chief Justice of the United States Court of Claims.

During our pre-second-trial preparations, the District Attorney's office was also summing up the first year's work over all. In General Sessions Court, our office had disposed of 3,253 cases. We obtained convictions in 79 per cent of these, as compared to 65 per cent for my predecessor Dodge and 61 per cent for his predecessor, Crain. In major cases we obtained a record of 65 per cent convictions, compared to 48 per cent for Dodge. When we took office we had found 382 prisoners in the Tombs, with 158 awaiting grand jury action. By January 1, 1939, there were 167 fewer in the Tombs, and only 30 awaited grand jury action.

The statistics of all our bureaus reflected intense activity: more than 160,000 persons had actually called in person at our offices, 34,127 letters had come in, and 35,094 gone out, and there had been 188,089 outgoing telephone calls. Our process servers had served 110,531 subpoenas. Our accounting staff, under Goody Goodrich, had prepared complete reports in no fewer than 345 cases after minute auditing and inspection of voluminous account books and records returned to our office under 2,620 "forthwith" subpoenas. The Volunteer Defender program, which I had urged before the Bar Association, was showing encouraging gains.

The Rackets Bureau, under Murray Gurfein, made a brilliant probe of the New York taxicab industry. This industry had not previously been organized. Various attempts to form taxi drivers' unions had always failed, but the Mafia had moved in. The head of the racket was a gangster named John Andosca, nicknamed "Papa," who was allegedly a henchman of Mafia leader "Three Finger" Brown. Others were Joseph Biondo, an associate of former Democratic County Clerk Al Marinelli, and Lorenzio Brescia, the Luciano bodyguard who had testified at the Luciano trial.

The thrust of the racket was familiar: the mob would win control of a taxi chauffeurs' union, then it would warn the taxicab companies that their cabs would be turned over in the streets and their drivers beaten up unless they paid off the mob. We indicted Biondo and seven others for extortion. Brescia fled. Andosca was captured later, but he had a serious heart condition and upon medical advice his trial was postponed. Papa Andosca died without being tried.

Gurfein followed two fruitful lines from the taxicab rackets investigation. Goodrich found there were unexplained, large disbursements in the books of one taxicab company, and its president was called in. We found that large sums of money had been paid out to Charles A. Harnett, the state Motor Vehicle Commissioner. The taxicab company had wanted permission to be a "self-insurer," rather than insure its taxicabs for public liability with regular insurance companies.

The case against Harnett was completed before the grand jury while I was still running for Governor, but I asked that no indictment be handed up until after election. I did not believe in the use of the prosecuting office for the purposes of political advancement, so no indictment and no mention of it was made until the election was over.

Gurfein recalled: "The process of obtaining corroboration in these cases is a difficult one. New York law requires testimony of an accomplice or even any number of accomplices to be corroborated by such evidence as tends to connect the defendant with the commission of a crime. Mere association between the accomplice and the defendant is not enough. Finally, however, sufficient corroboration was obtained to procure the indictment of Commissioner Harnett.

"He was an unstable man, and the shock and the disgrace of the indictment put him over the threshold. He became mentally incompetent and was sent to a mental hospital."*

Gurfein's second line of inquiry into the taxicab racket, once again initiated by Goodrich's findings, led to a second taxicab company and further unexplained, substantial disbursements. The state legislature had created a joint legislative committee to investigate taxicab regulations and fares, and the chairman was a prominent state assemblyman from Brooklyn named Edward S. Moran, Jr. After a careful investigation it was determined that the disbursements had been paid as bribes to Moran, and Moran was indicted on six counts, two for accept-

---

* The Louisville *Courier-Journal* commented: "American politics never presented a more astonishing example of self-denying courtesy than Dewey's suppression, during his campaign for Governor, of an indictment already returned against the state Commissioner for Motor Vehicles. The disclosure would have fitted snugly into his issue of Democratic machine politics. . . . Self-respect, which maintains one's intellectual integrity at all costs, is scarce in public or private life, and that is not the first demonstration of it by Mr. Dewey."

ing bribes, two for accepting fees as a public officer in connection with legislative duties, and two for official extortion. During Moran's trial, one of the joint legislative committee counsel testified there had been so little work to do that he had protested to his boss. But Moran said, "Don't bother me. If you want to work, lick postage stamps." Moran was sentenced to two and a half to five years' imprisonment, and Judge Wallace complimented Gurfein on "brilliant trial work."

Meanwhile, the Indictment Bureau was looking into allegations of crooked dealing on the part of state Senator Julius S. Berg in connection with the granting of concessions at the New York's World Fair and also with regard to liquor licenses. When Berg was asked to come in to tell his side of the story he went to the hospital for a rest, returned to his office, obtained a revolver, and shot himself.

In the electrical industry, ten wealthy contractors were brought to trial, and nine pleaded guilty of conspiracy in restraint of trade. In the fruit industry, a union official was indicted for extortion of money from thirty-four fruit merchants.

Our office launched a long and complex investigation into the affairs of the McKesson and Robbins Corporation, and of three brothers named Musica who had taken over the corporation under assumed names and gone into gun-running and bootlegging on the side. Sewell Tyng was in charge of our investigation. Goodrich even sent one or two of his men to Canada where the firm supposedly had a large operation. They found a dummy office with a girl sitting in it, not far from the office of their accounting firm, Price Waterhouse & Company.

Other investigations into the Musica brothers were being conducted by the federal government and by the state District Attorney. One of the brothers, under the name of F. Donald Coster, shot himself at his home in Connecticut. We indicted the other brothers for grand larceny, but the federal government tried and convicted them for defrauding McKesson and Robbins of more than $11 million. One brother served almost 2½ years, the other more than three years, at the Federal Penitentiary at Lewisburg.

We investigated and indicted a group of thirty-six employees of the city-owned Independent Subway System for the purloining of 25 million nickels from the turnstiles. That added up to $1,250,000. It turned out that the maintenance men who worked on the turnstile mechanisms had arrangements with station agents, so they could say something like, "I'll set this back so that it will show four hundred less fares than the machine took in." Twenty-nine pleaded guilty and were sent to prison.

Barent Ten Eyck obtained conspiracy indictments against twenty-four lawyers and runners for ambulance chasing. Jack Rosenblum, in his tenth successive conviction in a homicide case, obtained the first death sentence ever carried out on a client of the renowned criminal lawyer Samuel S. Leibowitz.

One afternoon, Rosenblum was interrogating a murder suspect, who seemed restless and troubled. Jack asked what was wrong. The man said it was the anniversary of his father's death and he had to get to a synagogue to say a Kaddish for his father. Kaddish is a Jewish prayer recited on the anniversary of the death of a close member of the family and it requires a minimum of ten men, a *minyan*. Jack promptly said he would get a minyan together. Goody Goodrich assembled ten of our staff of the Jewish faith and Jack led the service in person. After the man had recited the Kaddish for his father, he returned to Jack's office to complete the examination.

On January 26, after two postponements and a three-day process of jury selection, the second trial of James J. Hines got under way. Inevitably, there was less publicity and less public interest because the cases for the People and for the defense had been thoroughly aired during the first trial. The attorneys were also the same: I led off for the prosecution, and was assisted by Grimes, Gelb, Hogan, and McCarthy, and Lloyd Paul Stryker opened for Hines. Judge Nott permitted the general description of the numbers racket before the documentation of the conspiracy, and said: "I do not consider myself bound by every ruling that Judge Pecora made."

On the Sunday after the beginning of the second Hines trial, word came that George Weinberg, one of the key prosecution witnesses, had shot and killed himself. Weinberg had been moved around under our protection along with Dixie Davis, but he brooded over the fear of a gangland killing in retribution for having turned state's evidence. According to Davis, he kept asking, "Who will protect us when Dewey goes out of office?" When Weinberg read that two of Lepke's and Gurrah's men, Danny Fields and Louis Cohen, had been killed on the street, his fear was greatly increased. In a rented house in White Plains, he grabbed a gun that a guard had left in a closet, went into a bathroom, and shot himself.

Keller recalled: "One group of Dewey assistants was working with him in the office preparing for the ensuing week of the Hines trial, and another was consulting with him in drafting impeachment charges to be presented to the Judiciary Committee of the House of Representatives against Presiding Judge Martin T. Manton of the United States Court of Appeals, Second Circuit. Then word came that George Weinberg, one of the two key witnesses against Hines, had killed himself."

Gelb recalled: "I remember that several of the assistants who were connected with the Hines case were very alarmed. Weinberg was a very important witness who had testified at length about his dealings with Hines, about paying Hines money from Dutch Schultz—so much per week. He was dead."

Only one senior man in that room was not a lawyer, Goody Goodrich. And it was Goodrich who said that Weinberg's testimony in the first trial could simply be read out loud at the second trial. Goodrich was right.

Gelb recalled: "Under the law, when a man has been examined and cross-examined, his evidence may be read at a new trial. Dewey took the information and the whole thing very calmly, saying, 'Hmmm. He's dead. We'll have to use his testimony for trial.' That was all he said at that time."

Keller recalled: "The strategy for completing the Hines case without a living Weinberg was perfected in the rest of that day, and the document against Manton was completed, rushed to Washington, and released to the newspapers. Just after the last reporters left my office, Frances Dewey came in to keep a dinner date with her husband. 'What's doing, Harold?' she asked. 'Nothing ever happens around here,' I said, and then I told her. That kidding remark became a private saying between us on many another occasion thereafter when the dramatic tensions were particularly thick."

The first trial day after that, the news of the suicide was kept from the jury and the first of twelve new witnesses was brought in by the People. He was Edward Severi, a bartender at the Embassy Club. He testified that Hines and Dutch Schultz were "steady customers" who often used to eat and drink there together and he pointed to Hines in the courtroom when he made the identification.

Then followed a battle about the admissibility of reading the testimony of the late George Weinberg. Judge Nott sent the jury out of the courtroom. Stryker insisted that he should be allowed to tell the jury that Weinberg had committed suicide and to comment on what his motive might have been. Stryker thought Weinberg had preferred death to another courtroom ordeal. In the end, Judge Nott decided that Weinberg's former testimony was admissible and that he himself would inform the jury of the suicide.

So, for most of the next three days, Weinberg's testimony under direct and cross-examination at the first trial was read in court. McCarthy read Weinberg's words, and Hogan read mine.

Meanwhile, Governor Lehman took heed of speculation that Weinberg had been murdered, and sent a telegram to me and the press: "I assume you will investigate the circumstances surrounding the death of George Weinberg and make inquiry into the statements." I wired back: "Your assumption is correct. I did so last Sunday, the day he died. So did the District Attorney of Westchester County, the medical examiner, the police officials of White Plains, and the New York police. It is incontrovertibly established that George Weinberg committed suicide."

I had known from the time I was Chief Assistant United States Attorney that Appeals Court Judge Manton was corrupt, but I could not prove it. Then I had the incident with reference to Lepke and Gurrah, in which Manton had released them on $10,000 bail apiece after having assured me he would not. I launched an investigation even then, a very quiet one, into his activities. We brought down a good many witnesses, and we got testimony from a good many of them. Before we got through, it was clear that Martin T. Manton was a man who was taking bribes quite widely, actively soliciting bribes, when he was holding one of the highest judicial offices in the federal courts of the United States.

It was not until some time after the Lepke and Gurrah bail incident that we caught Dixie Davis. When Davis began to talk with us, he said that Lepke's and Gurrah's people had sent out $25,000 in cash to Manton the night before he let Lepke and Gurrah go on bail. But we never could corroborate this. We only had Dixie Davis' testimony and he was not a witness to the actual passage of money to Judge Manton. He just knew about the arrangement. We could never get a corroboration of this testimony, so we never used it.

Meanwhile, a brilliant job was being done on Manton's activities by the staff. I did not join it myself, though I did guide it. This was one investigation in which I took an intense, personal interest. We were convinced that Manton was a thief. And we had to be sure of the facts. Afterward Judge Learned Hand commented to Murray Gurfein: "We suspected that Manton did political favors from time to time, although we could not prove it, but that he took money, *money,* this we never suspected."

By January 1939, I felt that it would not be in the public interest to leave this situation without public exposure, and some form of action had to be taken. We considered the question of a prosecution for evasion of New York State income tax laws, but that would have been minor jurisdiction compared to charges of bribery of a federal judge.

By this time, of course, our subpoenaing of accounts books and interrogation of witnesses had brought matters to the attention of a number of people in addition to Judge Manton. Important friends of Manton even sent an emissary to see Murray Gurfein with a proposal that Manton would resign from the bench if the investigation was stopped.

We discussed this and of course we turned it down summarily.

The Manton matter was about to become public knowledge. The New York *World-Telegram,* in the person of reporter Bert Heath, had prepared a series on Manton which would eventually win a Pulitzer Prize. The *World-Telegram* said it would be willing to make its information and its informer available to us if, before the law took action, they were given the time to write and publish their articles. They were told they would get the first break on the story.

Victor Herwitz, one of the veterans of the special prosecution days, an Assistant District Attorney who had unraveled much of the Manton mystery, now spent days at the *World-Telegram* office in a room set aside by the editor, Lee Wood. It was tragic that Heath, after winning his Pulitzer Prize, later disappeared with a group of other correspondents in an airplane flight in World War II.

The Attorney General of the United States by this time had a number of FBI agents going around the banks seeking records which would justify a full-scale federal effort in the Manton matter. So I decided that, in view of the paramount importance of pursuing this case without any jurisdictional limitations, we should turn over our evidence to the federal authorities. I telephoned John Cahill, who was then the

United States Attorney, and he came over with his chief assistant
Mathias M. Correa. In conference, Gurfein and I explained to them
the nature of the case, and I instructed Gurfein to turn over all the
information in our possession.

So, on that Sunday afternoon, I was at the office concentrating on
getting out a letter to Hatton Summers, the chairman of the House
Judiciary Committee in Washington, charging various high crimes and
misdemeanors against Manton, each of which, of course, we were
documenting to the hilt. I was preparing to sign that letter as a private
citizen, with all the risks involved, when the word came in about
Weinberg's suicide. Having decided that we could read his testimony,
I went back to the Manton letter, finished it, and sent it down by an
assistant to Chairman Summers.

The Manton letter read, in part:

I deem it my duty to lay before you certain of the facts in my
possession. They are as follows:

The Schick Electric Razor Case: On November 10, 1936, a
decree was entered by the United States District Court for the
Eastern District of New York in the case of Schick Dry Shaver,
Inc., against Dictograph Products Corporation, Inc. The suit involved the basic pattern for electric razors. The Schick company
was suing the Dictograph Products company, which manu-
factured the Packard Razor, for alleged infringement of its
patent. The District Court decided in favor of Schick. An
appeal was taken to the Circuit Court of Appeals.

The late Archie M. Andrews, in 1936 and 1937, controlled
the Dictograph Products Corporation, Inc. Andrews also controlled a number of other corporations, including the Progress
Corporation, which marketed the razors, and the International
Ticket Scale Corporation. George M. Spector, an insurance
agent, was an associate and confidential agent of Archie M.
Andrews.

Shortly after the appeal was taken, and while it was pending
in the Circuit Court of Appeals, Spector received checks from
various Andrews corporations totalling $12,500, the proceeds of
which were deposited in his own bank account. There was also
withdrawn from various Andrews corporations cash in the sum
of $57,000 charged to sundry accounts for which no reasonable
explanation has been made. During the same period, Spector

deposited cash in his own bank account, $40,200, as to the source of which no reasonable explanation has been made. All of this occurred between December 19th, 1936, and January 28th, 1937.

During the same period of time, Spector gave or lent corporations wholly owned or controlled by Judge Manton a total of $52,000. No part of these monies has been repaid by Judge Manton's corporations to Spector except an alleged interest payment of $2,500 charged to Spector on the books, but, in fact, deposited by Judge Manton in his own bank account.

Following the payment of these sums to Judge Manton's corporations, the Circuit Court of Appeals of April 12th, 1937, announced its decision reversing the District Court in the case of Schick Dry Shaver, Inc., against Dictograph Products Corporation, Inc., the decision being in favor of the Andrews corporation by a divided court, Judge Manton voting for the reversal.

Beginning two days after the decision, and between April 14th and May 26th, 1937, Spector received $20,000 by direction of Andrews, and an additional $5,000, the source of which is not determinable, making a total of $25,000. During the same period, Spector paid over a total of $25,000 for Judge Manton's account as follows:

$3,000 to the Forest Hills Terrace Corporation.

$1,803.90 to a creditor of Judge Manton.

$20,196.10 to Marie D. Schmalz, Judge Manton's official secretary.

On September 1, 1938, Spector was prosecuted by my office for contempt of court for obstruction of this inquiry and was convicted. An appeal is now pending from this conviction.

The McGrath Transaction: John M. McGrath is a trustee of the Prudence Company, Inc., in reorganization under Section 77b of the Bankruptcy Act in the United States District Court for the Eastern District of New York within the Second Judicial Circuit. McGrath was appointed by the District Judge in charge of the bankruptcy proceeding on February 1, 1935, as one of three trustees. He has continuously served from that time to the present. Judge Manton had made a recommendation to the District Judge that McGrath was worthy of appointment as a trustee in important matters.

By May 28th, 1937, McGrath had received $32,000 in fees as a trustee in the Prudence matter. On May 28th, 1937, he gave Judge Manton $12,000 under the following circumstances. McGrath withdrew $12,000 from the Nydel Corporation, a corporation of which he was one of two stockholders. He cashed the check. With this cash, he purchased a bank cashier's check, which he turned over to Judge Manton. No part of the $12,000 has been repaid.

The Kings Brewery Transaction: In December 1934, the late James J. Sullivan, the business partner of Martin T. Manton, was one of two trustees of the Kings Brewery, then in reorganization in the Eastern District of New York under Section 77b of the Bankruptcy Act.

William J. Fallon, a close associate of Judge Manton, approached Charles A. Rogers, an insurance broker, and requested him to make a loan of $10,000 to Judge Manton, representing that if the loan were made, the Judge would see that Rogers received the insurance business on the Kings Brewery from Sullivan. Immediately thereafter, Fallon introduced Rogers to Judge Manton, who made the same representation.

Rogers thereupon made a loan of $10,000 to Judge Manton, receiving therefor a note signed by Sullivan and endorsed by Judge Manton. The proceeds of the loan went to the Forest Hills Terrace Corporation, a personal holding company of Judge Manton.

Rogers did not obtain the Kings Brewery insurance business and, over a period of time, the loan was repaid in installments of cash. Fallon was prosecuted by my office for commercial bribery and convicted in connection with another matter arising out of this investigation. On December 27th, 1938, Fallon was sentenced to an indeterminate term in the penitentiary.

The Lotsch Matter: John J. Lotsch was chairman of the Board of Directors of the Fort Greene National Bank of Brooklyn. On December 19th, 1935, he was indicted in the United States District Court for the Southern District for soliciting a bribe while acting as a special master. On January 6th, 1936, Judge Manton, knowing that Lotsch was under indictment in the District Court, obtained a loan from Lotsch's bank for the National Cellulose Corporation, a Manton company. This loan was obtained by Judge Manton through the intervention of Lotsch after other banks had refused to make the loan.

Thereafter, Lotsch was acquitted by a directed verdict in the District Court and was immediately reindicted on a charge of extortion. Lotsch sued out a writ of habeas corpus. The writ was dismissed in the lower court and he took an appeal to the Circuit Court of Appeals. At the time the appeal was heard, Judge Manton was personally indebted to the Fort Greene National Bank in the sum of $37,500. The defendant Lotsch was the controlling stockholder of the bank. Judge Manton did not disqualify himself from hearing Lotsch's appeal. He sat on the case and participated in the court's decision, which reversed the judgment below, and ordered the indictment dismissed.

The Warner Transaction: On May 5th and 6th, 1933, the appeal in the case of Cinema Company, Inc., versus Warner Brothers Pictures, Inc., was argued in the Circuit Court of Appeals for the Second Circuit, Judge Manton presiding. This appeal involved the validity of the Gaumont patents covering the machine processing of motion picture film. The decision of the court was announced on September 12th, 1933 (*66 Fed 2d 744*), in favor of Warner Brothers.

Between the time of the argument of the appeal and the time of the decision, Judge Manton borrowed a total of $50,000 from Harry M. Warner, an officer and substantial stockholder in Warner Brothers Pictures, Inc.

Twenty-five thousand dollars of the total sum borrowed was paid to Judge Manton on July 20th, 1933, out of the funds of the Colfax Trading Corporation, of which Harry M. Warner was president. The check was drawn to the order of Judge Manton and deposited by him the following day to the account of the Forest Hills Terrace Corporation, a personal holding company of Judge Manton. The remaining $25,000 was paid to Judge Manton in checks of $12,500 each, drawn on September 11th, 1933, the day before the decision of the court was announced. These checks were drawn out of the trust accounts of Doris Warner and Betty Warner, two daughters of Harry M. Warner. They were endorsed by Judge Manton to the Forest Hills Terrace Corporation and deposited to its bank account on October 11th, 1933, a month after the decision.

The $25,000 lent to Judge Manton by Warner under date of September 11th, 1933, was repaid on June 12th, 1934. Of the $25,000 lent to Judge Manton from the funds of the Colfax Corporation on July 20th, 1933, $15,000 has been repaid up to the time of this investigation, and $10,000, represented by a note of the Forest Hills Terrace Corporation, endorsed by Judge Manton, is still unpaid.

Lord and Thomas, Inc., Loan: On May 3rd and 4th, 1932, the case of Richard Rogers versus George W. Hill and the American Tobacco Company was argued in the Circuit Court of Appeals for the Second Circuit, Judge Manton presiding. Rogers, a stockholder, sued to recover for the corporation bonuses of more than $10,000,000 allegedly paid illegally by the American Tobacco Company to Hill and its officers.

Attorneys for the defendant Hill, president of the American Tobacco Company, and for the company, were the firm of Chadbourne, Stanchfield and Levy.

After the argument of the appeal and while the decision was pending, on May 11th, 1932, James J. Sullivan, Manton's business partner, received a loan of $250,000 from Lord and Thomas, Inc. Lord and Thomas, Inc., were the advertising agents for the American Tobacco Company. Sullivan gave Lord and Thomas, Inc., his demand note for $250,000, and pledged as collateral 15,604 shares of the National Cellulose Corporation.

The circumstances of the loan were as follows: Albert D. Lasker, president of Lord and Thomas, Inc., made the loan at the request of Paul Hahn, assistant to George W. Hill, president of the American Tobacco Company. Hahn arranged for the loan to Sullivan by Lord and Thomas, Inc., at the suggestion of Louis Levy of the firm of Chadbourne, Stanchfield and Levy, counsel for the American Tobacco Company, and for Hill.

Judge Manton has testified in a Surrogate's Court proceedings in the administration of the estate of James J. Sullivan, now deceased, that he sent Sullivan to Louis Levy for the purpose of arranging a loan for Sullivan from one of Levy's clients.

Out of the $250,000 loan, $232,981.44 was paid out by James J. Sullivan for and on behalf of Judge Manton personally or for corporations in which he had a controlling interest.

The withdrawals from the Sullivan account for the benefit
of the Manton corporations began on May 16th, 1932. On June
13th, 1932, the Circuit Court of Appeals, by a divided court,
decided in favor of the defendants Hill and the American
Tobacco Company. Judge Manton wrote the opinion for the
majority.

No part of the $250,000 advanced by Lord and Thomas,
Inc., has been repaid.

There are a number of other matters in character similar to
the foregoing which cannot be fully set forth at this stage of
the inquiry.

This investigation has been conducted under the direction
of Assistant District Attorney Murray I. Gurfein, who has from
time to time been assisted by Assistant District Attorneys Frank
S. Hogan, Victor J. Herwitz, Lawrence E. Walsh and Aaron
Benenson. A. J. Goodrich, chief accountant of the office of the
District Attorney, has been in charge of the accounting aspects
of the work. Each of these gentlemen is available for conference with you concerning these matters if you so desire.

If upon the foregoing facts, the House of Representatives
should assume jurisdiction, I am prepared to present evidence
before your committee in support thereof.

Respectfully yours,
        Thomas E. Dewey
        District Attorney

On January 30, 1939, the charges were published in the morning
newspapers, Chairman Summers having received the letter the night
before. That afternoon Judge Manton resigned. There was to be no
impeachment. President Roosevelt accepted his resignation.

Manton did not have anything to do except resign. He was
ultimately tried and convicted on the evidence we had given to the
United States Attorney, John Cahill, and he was sent to prison. He
was sentenced to two years' imprisonment and was fined $10,000.

We gave the federal authorities everything we had. It was a really
useful effort in our continuing struggle for a judiciary beyond reproach.

CHAPTER XXIII

Declare to the People
They Are Free

Suddenly, in the second Hines trial, the People introduced as a witness Mrs. Arthur Flegenheimer, the widow of Dutch Schultz. The defense was stupefied as she testified that her husband had indeed known James J. Hines. She said that her husband had introduced her to Hines and had told her afterward to forget she had ever met him. She also said she had met Hines often with Dixie Davis, and that Davis had funneled money through to her while her husband had been a fugitive from justice. This was one witness Stryker did not dare to question any more closely, and he let her step down fast.

After a repeat appearance by the Tammany leader John F. Curry, the rival of Hines who had sworn that recalcitrant policemen were transferred, the People produced another surprise witness. He was former Chief Inspector John O'Brien, who had come out of retirement in answer to a subpoena. O'Brien confirmed Curry's testimony that policemen who cracked down on the Schultz numbers banks were indeed transferred or reduced in rank.

Big Harry Schoenhaus and Dixie Davis retold the stories they had told in the first Hines trial. Attorney Max D. Steuer said again that Hines had asked him to help solve some of Dutch Schultz's income tax problems. Dixie Davis' sister, Mrs. Rose Wendroff, repeated that she had passed on a $500 check to Hines. Then we introduced another surprise witness, the bookmaker's cashier who had made the final endorsement on the $500 check. The witness said that Hines, on the exact day he deposited this $500 check, had received a credit on his account with the bookmaker.

Defense counsel Stryker produced new defense witnesses. The first, former Police Commissioner James S. Bolan, testified that he would only approve transfers of policemen for neglect and incompetence in handling police duties. But he did not look good when we showed him the excellent records of some of the men he had transferred.

Magistrate Hulon Capshaw, who had been named in the first Hines trial but not indicted, testified that he had never been influenced in his judicial duties by Hines. Capshaw insisted that he had dismissed so many defendants brought before him in numbers cases purely on the merits. Asked about a raid on a numbers or policy bank in Harlem, Capshaw said, "I didn't know what a policy bank was." This statement coming from a magistrate who had tried more than two thousand numbers cases was obviously untrue and it could have been no help for the defense. Then Capshaw was asked who all the people were who had been brought in after a numbers raid. He said they might have been "cooks and waiters working in the place."

Former District Attorney William Copeland Dodge now took the stand. His direct examination by Lloyd Paul Stryker went, in part, like this:

Q. Did Mr. Hines ever tell you to keep your mouth shut?

A. He never did.

Q. Did Mr. Hines ever say that Dixie Davis and Dutch Schultz were responsible for obtaining the money for your campaign, and that your investigation must stop?

A. He never did.

Q. Did you ever tell Davis that he would be called before the grand jury and it would be a perfunctory examination and that he would not be needed again?

A. I never did.

Q. When Dewey came into office, did you co-operate with him?

A. Yes.

Dewey: I must object as incompetent. We can't try everything this man did. We are trying James J. Hines.

The Court: . . . Overruled.

A. (continued) . . . We sent all the testimony taken before the March (runaway) grand jury and delivered a hundred of files to his office.

Dewey: Objected to, unless he can tell us what files, if any.

The Court: You can bring that out on cross-examination.

Q. Did you speak to Mr. Dewey on the phone?

A. I did.

Q. Did Mr. Dewey seek your advice?

A. I offered it many times.

Q. Did you ever conceal or withhold any documents in the files, whether relating to policy or not?

A. Of course not.

Q. How long have you known James J. Hines?

A. Twenty years.

Q. And is he a friend of yours?

A. I always have regarded him as such.

In my cross-examination, I ascertained at the start that Dodge, in 1927, when he was an Assistant District Attorney, had heard of a vacancy in magistrate's court. He had served as a magistrate before becoming District Attorney in 1933.

Q. And you wanted that vacancy [on magistrate's court]?

A. I did.

Q. You then consulted some political leaders in your effort to get it?

A. I did.

Dodge said he had gone to see George Olvany, then leader of Tammany Hall—"There is no political party known as Tammany Hall. It is an historical society." Dodge said that he also asked Mayor Walker to endorse him, and he served as a magistrate for six and a half years.

Q. And you knew Hines?

A. Yes.

Q. For twenty years?

A. I have said so.

Q. Knew him intimately some years before you became magistrate?

A. Yes.

Q. Was it a very warm, close, personal friendship?

A. Well, we used to meet frequently, and he has been to my home, and I have been to his home.

Q. You played golf together?

A. Yes.

Q. Would you characterize it as a relationship between mother and son?

A. I've never been a mother. I could not say. (*Laughter.*)

Q. When did you make that decision, to make a flippant remark in this courtroom? Didn't you, yourself, in the past, volunteer this mother and son relationship? . . .

Before answering, Dodge was asked to read the testimony he had given to a grand jury on July 22, 1938, in which he had characterized his relationship with Hines as akin to that of a mother and son.

A. Naturally, like a mother would be to a son, I was very fond of James J. Hines. . . . like a mother believes her son innocent, I believed in Hines' innocence. . . .

Before the campaign for District Attorney in 1933, Dodge said the party leaders had spoken to him and had said, "Well, Bill, it looks like you'll be D.A."

Q. Was it your understanding that you would do as you were told, and it was not necessary to ask you to run?

A. No.

Q. But you never told anyone you would accept?

A. No.

Q. You were nominated, and you accepted. Was it a surprise to the leaders?

A. I don't know what was in their minds. . . .

Q. You knew Schultz had not been convicted of a serious charge in New York?

A. Yes.

Q. You knew the Schultz mob had been free of police interference?

A. Oh no.

Q. You knew they had not been convicted in New York County?

A. Yes, I knew the higher-ups had not been.

Q. You knew there might be layers of gangsters between the numbers bankers and Schultz?

A. Yes, it was all a belief. I had no evidence.

Q. You knew that this was an arduous, backbreaking task to break the numbers combination?

A. Yes . . .

My cross-examination was leading up to the basic question of why, then, Dodge had entrusted his numbers investigation to Lyon Boston, the youngest, the least experienced member of his staff, operating alone. Dodge replied that Boston was a good man to co-operate with the police.

Q. You knew he had no experience?

A. Yes.

Q. You had experienced men on your staff?

A. Yes, but they were affiliated with the Democratic organization, and I pointed it out to the police.

Dodge seemed to be saying that his assistants affiliated with the Democratic organization were not so well qualified to co-operate with the police. And he admitted on the stand that he had been so concerned about the lack of campaign funds for the 1933 election that his manager had gone to see Hines. Dodge testified that, when the money started coming in, in big bills, he had never asked where the money came from.

Lyon Boston told his story again, and this time he was not asked the question about the poultry racket which had led Judge Pecora to declare the mistrial. Neither, in this second trial, had the defense opened the door to broader testimony of this nature.

Then came the climax of the whole proceedings: the time had come for Hines to take the stand in his own defense, if he would. We had had two Assistant District Attorneys working for six months, preparing the material for the cross-examination of James J. Hines. Gelb recalled the moment: "We rolled into court, on a little roller, a big file cabinet, a four-drawer file cabinet. Stryker leaned over to me and said, 'What's that? Material for the cross on Hines?' "

Gelb continued: "It *was* the material for the cross-examination of Hines if he took the stand. But Hines *couldn't* take the stand. There was so much damned material on him, stuff that we had dug up which would have shown him to be a corrupt man. Nobody could win that case for the defense."

Stryker, as no doubt had previously been decided, did not bring Hines to the witness stand to testify in his own defense.

Stryker now, with his case running out, delivered this oratorical summation to the jury:

"The last stand of liberty is here. I can imagine a prosecution in Berlin or Moscow. Now here, gentlemen: I see you. Stand fast there. Stand fast, this squad of justice, with your bayonets poised in your hand, ready to repel those lying rogues.

"Stand fast for justice and for the liberty of an American citizen. We know how hard won those things were, the right to a fair trial in an American court. Those Anglo-Saxon concepts of the presumption of innocence and the requirement that the state did not prove its case beyond a reasonable doubt. Those did not come easy. They were sweat for, and bled for, on a thousand battlefields. Down the ages those heritages come to us. It is yours now to preserve them.

"The men of old who gave us our liberties and our English law— our English law—God bless our Anglo-Saxon institutions. If we do not cherish them, you will live where public officials can do as they choose with the individual.

"Gentlemen of the jury, I have finished. This is the last time that I can talk to you. Forget my defects and my deficiencies. But remember that there is no one in this court more interested in justice than I am.

"And I ask you with my heart and my soul, go out into that jury room and come back, come back, so that the church bells may ring on Sunday morning, 'Not guilty! Not guilty!' and let Weinberg in his grave, his suicide's grave, and Davis in his hideout know—in Germany and Russia perhaps this kind of thing can be done, but not in the United States of America.

"God help you, God bless you and go with you in these councils.

"Not guilty!"

Trial continued February 24, 1939.

(Met pursuant to adjournment; appearances same as before.)

Dewey: Shall I proceed, sir?

The Court: Yes.

Dewey: May it please the Court, Mr. Foreman, and gentlemen of the jury. . . . It has been said that 'When an orator meets a fact, he makes a detour.' I do not intend making detours to Gettysburg, Williamsburg, the battle of Runnymede, Germany, Italy, Russia,

Switzerland, or South America. I shall not burden you with details about my wife, my children, or my family. . . .

One thing occurred yesterday which I must speak about with some firmness. There was an attempt, studied, willful, to create some kind of vague impression that a corrupt politician, sponsoring gangsters, allowing crime to breed freely, and interfering and preventing the law from protecting our citizens, there was an intimation that that kind of politician has something to do with the preservation of democracy, there was some kind of intimation that Hines and his counsel were symbols of a democracy, and there was some kind of intimation, vague, veiled, not daring to say it, that the public prosecutor or his assistants were importing foreign methods of prosecution. That I resent as a dirty business, and I suggest to you, with probably more feeling than I shall use at any other time today, that was a willful and a filthy attempt to arouse some kind of passion on behalf of a betrayer of the essence of democracy.

I did not intend to talk about things like that in summation. It is not my custom. Does anyone think that Herman McCarthy wants to bring to this country the principles of Germany? Does anybody think that Sol Gelb wants to bring the principles of Germany, or Frank Hogan, or Charles P. Grimes, or I?

When you haven't got a defense, try everything in the world and end up with an emotional plea, but don't discuss the facts. This is the last and the most despicable importation into the defense of a criminal. . . .

Gentlemen, to the law, there isn't any difference between a Democrat and a Republican, or a Socialist or a Communist if you will. There isn't any difference to me, I may say, and I will prosecute a Democratic district leader as quickly as I will prosecute a Republican Richard Whitney. That has always been true in the eight years of my life as a prosecutor. I hope it will continue to be. . . .

Now the charges in this case have not been referred to in a long time . . . it was a part of the conspiracy that they agreed among themselves to influence, bribe, and intimidate judicial officers and others charged with the duty of enforcing and administering the laws of the state of New York, that they should represent that they dominated and controlled judicial officers and others charged with the duty of enforcing and administering the criminal laws. . . .

We have the brazen establishment of a criminal enterprise, a whole criminal empire, by the most notorious gangster of New York, who was concededly the intimate and associate of the defendant Hines. We have him boasting brazenly that, "You can complain to the police from here to the Battery and it will do you no good." We have the testimony of witness after witness as to what happened. . . .

These are all conceded, undisputed, unarguable facts in the case. Who else but Hines could be responsible for these things, the pal, the associate of Dutch Schultz? How else in heaven's name could they have been brought about? . . . They have given you no explanation. There is no explanation. There is no way, in God's earth, except Hines, that those things could have happened, and you are driven to that by the established, unarguable facts in this record. . . .

If I were a cop, I do not know whether I would stay in the job if I could make a living any place else. I suppose I would if that is the only thing I knew. But if I were a cop and I got threatened by the Dutch Schultz mob, and forty-eight hours later I got transferred, I would think I would turn crooked. And I am amazed, utterly amazed at these men, that they don't. . . .

Now, let us go ahead. Weinberg testified, and incidentally so did Ison and Pompez and all the other witnesses without any cross-examination on the issue—there is not any controversy on this one—that during the entire years 1932, 1933, 1934, so long as they were in the combination and the others afterward—that there was not a single arrest at a numbers bank owned by any one of them, except those which the chief inspector's squad did, which had the whole city to cover. That is a fantastic charge to make. . . .

Counsel said yesterday I should have indicted Capshaw, and Bolan, and Dodge. Gentlemen, there is no evidence in my possession or anybody else's as far as I know that any of those men knew they were doing anything more than a favor for a politician to whom they were beholden. Now, a political contract was not invented by me. A political contract is something which was known, I suspect, a long time before I was born. A political contract is something you do for a politician.

Corrupt? Wrong? Yes. And where done for a politician who is protecting a mob which is preying on the people of a whole city, something which strikes at the very heart of organized society. But that does not mean and I do not contend that Capshaw knew he was doing this for the Dutch Schultz mob, or Bolan, or Erwin, or Dodge, or anybody else. All they knew is that the most powerful man to whom they were beholden said, "Do this for me," and they said, "Okay, boss. I have never let you down yet. I want to be reappointed to that magistrate's bench when my term expires, I want to stay, I want to be elected, I can't be without you." Obviously. . . .

Well, Frances Flegenheimer was here, and you noticed how gingerly she was cross-examined. I never saw such walking on eggs, and I would like to illustrate exactly how that cross-examination was conducted.

Q. It was a public restaurant?

A. Yes.

Q. Other people there?

A. Yes.

As I remember, that's all. They didn't try, they didn't try with Frances Flegenheimer. In the month of December, while all these things were going on, what else is going on? Schultz was dining alone, with Hines, in December, the first meeting. Hines walks into a restaurant, the Stable, the place where Schultz was all the time. You remember Weinberg's testimony. He met Schultz there all the time, and I think some other people so testified.

Schultz is in there, dining with his wife. In walks Hines. He walks up to the table, shakes hands, is presented to Mrs. Flegenheimer, and then he and Hines go back to the restaurant for a private conference, a half or three quarters of an hour.

What were they doing, gentlemen? Why was Hines coming to the Stable, seeking out Dutch Schultz for a conference, if it wasn't with reference to this, if Hines wasn't there on business connected with the game? What else could it be?

Hines was there visiting his co-executive in a huge criminal enterprise which he was perpetuating and making it possible for it to exist. . . . How they must have been gloating about the way the business was going, how the magistrates were throwing out the cases, how the cops were laying off, and how the business was prospering by leaps and bounds with immunity from the law. . . .

And then, in the summer, do you remember this little forgotten bit? Abadaba was in Dave's Blue Room, one of those hangouts on Broadway. Detective Canavan was in there looking for one of the Schultz mob, and Abadaba says, "I see you are still in uniform—I mean, in plain clothes. . . ." He said, "You got plenty to worry about." "Why?" "They are working on you to get you transferred, you know they can do it. . . ."

Salke—there's a whole saga in Salke. I would like to, oh, you could write a story about him that would take an hour to read, I will touch it very briefly. Salke was the fellow who was assigned by the New York police to work with the United States Government on Dutch Schultz. At that time, he was sitting on wiretaps, doing tail work, bothering the mob, harassing Bo Weinberg, sticking him up, searching him, searching the mob. Salke was undesirable to them in the doing of those things, that is recognized, as to which there is no argument in this case, no controversy, and there cannot be, because they are uncontradicted facts, even the un-cross-examined facts. . . .

Repeatedly, he was threatened by Bo Weinberg that if he did not quit he would be in a bag, you remember the words, in a bag, on Staten Island, the word "bag" being a policeman's uniform. Salke stuck to his job.

In the month of December of that year an order came down from Bolan to get rid of Salke. I am quoting the record. Lyons is Deputy Police Commissioner at the time he testified, and he said that he was sent for and was told, "The Commissioner says get rid of Salke." Lyons then went to see the United States Attorney and said, "This is awful"— I cannot tell you what he said, I am sorry, it is not in the record. He went back with a message from the United States Attorney, and that transfer did not go through. . . .

Gentlemen, you come to a point where things are irresistible . . . A couple of months later, or a month later, I don't know which, the chief inspector's squad is knocked to pieces. Hines said he would do it. How else could it be done? How else could this complete destruction be achieved? Terminelli, Fleming, Turner, Jones, and McCarthy, these five, they had been raiding Dutch Schultz's banks. Then Gray, Canavan, and Stilley. Then Salke. Then Kiley. Then Maher. Every one transferred, as it happened, directly under Bolan, every one of them. Tragic business, gentlemen.

. . . Now we come to the campaign. Well, is Dodge Hines's man or isn't he? You remember the relationship. You heard it described . . . you have heard from Davis and Weinberg how Schultz and Schoenhaus—how Schultz was vitally interested in that election, ordered all the help possible, and ordered the money to be raised for it.

And we know how it was raised: Pompez, Pompez again, the man who was utterly unimpeachable in this case. Ten thousand dollars was taken from the Pompez bank for that campaign. This is one of those facts in this case. It is one of those things that is brought solidly, and will stay there forever. Ison—$5,000 from his bank. I am only sorry we didn't have Maloney and the other bankers here. The total was $30,-000 and the total, by testimony, was turned over to Hines. . . . Sobel, the campaign manager, he got the money from Hines. Why was he sent to Hines in the first place? Why, when he went to Curry and said, "We need money for Dodge's campaign," why did Curry say, "Go see Jimmy," or "Go see Hines"?

. . . Hines, Hines. Why Hines out of thirty-five district leaders in New York County? Why Hines, unless the truth is as has been testified.

Hines picked Dodge. Hines financed his campaign. Hines asked for no other candidate that year on the county ticket. He was interested in only one on the city-wide ticket. No county office, no judicial office, just District Attorney. Why just District Attorney?

Why is the man like Hines interested only in the District Attorney? . . .

Well, if you were Dutch Schultz, trying to figure out how to keep your power, to be safe, what would you do?

Wouldn't you like to have the youngest and most inexperienced member of the District Attorney's staff, all alone, without help, set to prosecuting these cases, and have him get all excited about a contempt case against some lawyer, and get nothing bigger than a collector or employee in a bank, so that there is a pretense of activity while the mob is safe? That is the result. I hate that you could think in the same terms but, for a moment, let us attempt it—what would you like to see done? I suggest that is what you would like to see done. I certainly would, if I were Dutch Schultz. . . .

Remember James D. C. Murray, a member of the New York Bar for many years, a warm personal friend of the defendant? Davis had retained him to try a lawsuit for a civil client, and they were working on it on a Saturday afternoon. And then Davis and Weinberg, who was there with Hope Dare and Murray, drove Murray home, and on the way they stopped to have a talk with Hines.

Davis was greatly worried. Davis understood the worry, perhaps, better than Hines, who was still too confident. He said, "Jim, I brought Jim Murray to explain to you the dangers we are up against," and he explained the dangers of the appointment of a Special Prosecutor, and I want to read you one sentence. It is perhaps as revealing as anything.

. . . Hines says after it, "I will see what I can do," something like that. Davis said—this is Murray's testimony—Davis said, "He will destroy all of us." Hines says, "I will see what I can do."

That one phrase, used in the year 1935. Were they all in a bag, in a criminal conspiracy together like this, or weren't they? . . . I don't know whether Hines was the chairman of the board and Schultz the president, or Schultz the chairman of the board and Hines the president, but they certainly were jointly directing their criminal enterprises. . . .

There has been talk about the statute of limitations. My goodness, the thing continued to within eleven months of the day of indictment, to say nothing of the two-year statute of limitations. That is one of the questions his honor will have to present to you, like all the others, but I think it is so clear I shan't even argue it with you. . . .

Sentence in this case on the defendant is secondary. It is no concern of mine. The Court can suspend sentence, give one day, one year, whatever he pleases. That is up to the Court. It is none of your business and none of my business. I don't want it to be. The important thing is that you declare to the people of New York, the police of New York, that they are free, that they won't be betrayed any longer by a corrupt alliance between crime and politics, that that alliance is going to be smashed by this jury and branded as something we won't stand for, because we want to keep the kind of a system we have in this country, and we don't want it polluted by a betrayer and protection of gangsters by political leaders.

You are good New Yorkers and you love your city. You want your city to get better and better and to remain and become cleaner. You want to remove cancers that grow at the heart of your government, wreck the morale of your police force, wreck the morale of your courts, and wreck the morale of any public official who has to come within the contaminating influence of a politician operating with gangster money as his background, and, if you do not do that, gentlemen, what are the consequences? What notice are you serving on the police and on the public and on everybody else? You know, I don't even need to outline it.

Here is the very thing which makes organized crime possible. Without it, there couldn't be organized crime for five minutes in this country, if the paralyzing hand of a crooked politician weren't available to break an honest cop, or to tell a magistrate what to do, or to use gangster funds to elect a public prosecutor who is under his control.

Let us decide what we want for ourselves and our community. Do we want to remove that cancer? Do we want to see that in the future it shan't happen again? Do we want to keep the processes of our system clean, or do we want to say, "No, no, we will go back, and take the consequences," and then you will have the kind of things my friend was talking about. No, I don't think we want that. I think we want to see that the men who are ultimately responsible for these things are punished for their sins, that notice is served on the world that that shan't happen again, that for these things we know there is a certain retribution visited by the community, which is you.

We are helpless, gentlemen, unless that is visited. I know you will do your duty. I know you will not say, "Go back, prosecute the players and the collectors, prosecute the burglar who gets caught, prosecute the boy who steals from the stand on the corner, but don't get the man who sent him to steal, prosecute the cheap and the petty, and turn loose those who made it possible."

I thank you for your long attention. I know you will do your duty as citizens of New York.

On February 25, 1939, after seven hours of deliberation interrupted by two requests of the judge for more information on points of law, the second Hines jury filed back into the courtroom. The foreman, Leonard T. Hobert, a meat salesman, took his stand and awaited the question.

"On the first count, how do you find the defendant?"

Hobert replied: "Guilty!"

On the remaining twelve counts, Hobert said, "Guilty!"

Hines was standing to receive the verdict. Stryker reached over and patted him on the shoulder. Hines had said only four words during his first trial, and none in his second trial. Now, in the crush of the courtroom as the trial began to break up, he was asked how he felt. "How would you feel if you were kicked in the belly?" Hines said.

Asked for a statement, I said:

"The members of the jury are entitled to the thanks of the whole community. By their verdict, they have reasserted the ability of democracy to clean its own house and cast out those who betray it. I cannot praise too highly the work of the men who have been responsible for the investigation and presentation of the evidence in this case, Assistant District Attorneys Charles P. Grimes, Sol Gelb, Frank S. Hogan, and Herman McCarthy, as well as the police officers and investigators who have worked so hard on the case for many months."

Judge Nott, who continued Hines on his $20,000 bail, returned from a brief vacation to impose sentence. He denounced Hines, noting only that his age, sixty-three, justified leniency. The judge sentenced Hines to four to eight years in the state penitentiary, warning that if any attempt was made to interfere with any of the state's witnesses he would recommend that Hines serve out the maximum term.

Judge Pecora, meanwhile, imposed sentence on Dixie Davis, Big Harry Schoenhaus, and the two bankers Pompez and Ison. He gave Davis one year's imprisonment, and suspended sentences on the other former members of the Schultz mob who had turned state's evidence. Davis, after his release, married Hope Dare and moved to California. He died on December 31, 1969, of an apparent heart attack, after learning of an armed robbery at his home in Bel Air. His wife, maid and a grandson were tied up and his home ransacked. Davis came home, sat down in the living room, and lost consciousness.

On April 4, 1939, after Stryker had withdrawn from the case, Hines appointed Martin W. Littleton as his new counsel. Littleton won from Supreme Court Justice Peter J. Schmuck a certificate of reasonable doubt. Pending Hines's appeal, Hines was re-released on $35,000 bail and out he came again from prison, to be cheered again by his supporters from the Monongahela Club in Manhattan.

The Hines appeals raised and settled several important problems of the law. For the first time, an appellate court of New York State was called upon to consider the criminal status and responsibility of a "fixer." The Court of Appeals held, in *People* v. *Hines, 284 N.Y. 93,* that a person who fixed or attempted to fix arrests and prosecutions—who obtained for his confederates a freedom from arrest and a virtual immunity from conviction—was a principal in the crimes with which his associates had been charged, and that he could be prosecuted therefor. In so ruling, the Court of Appeals wrote:

"Defendant was charged and found guilty of the acts of affording protection from arrest and, if arrested, immunity from conviction. Hence, he was an indispensable cog in the inside running of this enterprise, or he was nothing. As the Appellate Division noted, the proof was to the effect that the numbers game 'could not have been carried on without such protection.' . . .

"The proof of the conscious participation by defendant in the criminal enterprise of the combination . . . conclusively establishes him as a principal in each of the substantive crimes committed in furtherance of the conspiracy."

Not until October 14, 1940, was the whole appeals process completed—and on that day Hines began to serve his time at Sing Sing. In August 1944, after serving almost four years, Hines was paroled. He returned to live in New York City. He died in 1957 at the age of eighty.

Only Lepke and Gurrah were now left of the major criminal figures of the 1930s, and they were fugitives from federal and state as well as New York County law enforcement officials. Gurrah, in ill-health, was the first of the two to give up, and he was worked through the several judicial processes. Finally, in 1943, Gurrah was brought to trial by my successor as District Attorney, Frank Hogan. At that point the chief of the Rackets Bureau was Aaron Benenson. Hogan reported:

"Jacob (Gurrah) Shapiro was brought to trial on an indictment charging him with thirty-two counts of extortion, involving a total of $514,000 in shakedowns from garment manufacturers. For three weeks, businessmen who had lived in terror of the Lepke-Gurrah mob testified to the threats to their person and property, and of the large sums of money they had paid for the privilege of doing business in New York City.

"At the conclusion of the People's case, Gurrah gave up the fight and pleaded guilty. His serious illness delayed imposition of sentence until May 1944 when, as a fourth felony offender, he was sentenced to serve fifteen years' to life imprisonment in the state prison. The once heartless overlord of terroristic rackets in a dozen industries blubbered convulsively as sentence was imposed. He died in prison."

In the summer of 1939, New York City was persuaded to increase its reward for Lepke from $5,000 to $25,000, and portraits and measurements of Lepke were displayed on motion picture screens throughout the country. Federal, state, and local law enforcement agencies were conducting the manhunt and Lepke began to negotiate a surrender. Because the federal charges against him were less than ours, he finally turned himself in to the FBI. It was a dramatic scene. First,

Lepke surrendered to the Broadway columnist Walter Winchell. The columnist took Lepke straight to FBI Director J. Edgar Hoover, who was waiting, in person, in New York City, to take custody of the criminal.

The federal government first tried and convicted Lepke on narcotics charges. Then he was tried and convicted on murder charges in connection with mob operations in Brooklyn. Then he was brought to trial and was convicted on bakery racket charges in our jurisdiction. On our charges, Lepke was sentenced to a term of thirty years' to life imprisonment, but the murder conviction was to take precedence.

As Governor, I found no merit in his appeals for clemency and, in March 1944, Lepke went to the electric chair. No man deserved it more.

AFTERWORD

AFTERWORD

On May 2, 1939, not three months after the Hines conviction, and almost seven months before he announced his candidacy for President of the United States, Dewey said on receiving the Newman Award* at the University of Illinois:

I accept the Newman Award with deep gratitude and humility. For any man must be humble as he contemplates another who lives on after death in the minds and hearts of mankind. There are many whose names are recorded in history for the things they have done, but their deeds have ceased to be living things. Like the pyramids, they are barren monuments to a dead past. There are others—a few—who live on because the thoughts they expressed and the ideals they lived have become part of the thinking and living of succeeding generations. Cardinal Newman was such a man.

He lives with us today because he was not content merely to theorize about the fundamental principles of right conduct. He fought to

* The Cardinal Newman Foundation at the University of Illinois voted Governor Dewey its annual award in 1939, citing him as a person who "has made an outstanding contribution to the enrichment of American life."

make those principles live, to make them work. With rectitude and profundity of mind, he combined courage and action. Today, again, we urgently need not merely faith in fundamentals but the will and courage to make them work in the face of difficulties. That is the spirit with which the people of America have always met their problems. It is the spirit with which they always respond when their problems are clearly brought into the light.

In your citation tonight, you call attention to the renewed confidence of our people in their institutions, and in the power of government under law to protect itself from enemies within. I should like to accept the Newman Award, not personally, but as a tribute to the thousands of citizens who made that renewed confidence possible by their faith and by their courage.

I refer to thousands of grand jurors, petit jurors, businessmen, and workers who dared to stand up and fight. They fought against deadlier enemies from within than our society had ever before known.

We long ago left behind us the day when the burglar or the highwayman was a serious problem in the lives of our people. We learned how to deal with the common criminal. But, as the progress of an orderly society brought mastery of that problem, a new and more serious threat developed. Crime became organized in a more subtle and far more dangerous form. Huge combinations came into being. They were under the control of small groups of powerful and dangerous men. They regarded every aspect of society, legal and illegal, as their legitimate prey. The racket became a supergovernment outside the law.

With the rise of large rackets in city after city, and state after state, crime itself became big business. Whole communities knew it, feared it, and kept silent. Too often, as racketeering grew and operated, the eye of the law itself seemed to be blind. Often people of influence were closely involved. No longer could crime take the ordinary business risk of the old-fashioned marauder. So crime went into politics. The racketeer became a power in America and with political power came immunity. Local overlords dictated the selection of men for public office. Unfit, even dangerous men who thus acquired high office carried with them into positions of public trust the morals of their sponsors and bosses.

Worse than this, there came into people's lives a distrust of their political system, a distrust of the law itself, a cynical disregard of the true function of politics. Whole communities felt helpless before a new and menacing power over which they seemed to have no control.

The relationship between crime and politics was winked at in high places. The support of such combinations of political power was accepted by those in high places and, in return, they gave to those combinations recognition, reward, and still more power.

Against these conditions, twenty-three grand jurors started a fight in New York more than four years ago. Courageous newspapers demanded action. Courageous grand jurors undertook to give it. They called in public officials who recognized the problem. But they had no solution. Witnesses were called from all walks of life, but they were silent and afraid.

It wasn't long before the foreman of that grand jury and some of its members began getting messages. They were told it wasn't good business to put their noses in other people's business. They were told it wasn't healthy. But they had the courage to carry on. After four months of effort, they were unable to penetrate the blank wall of silence and fear. They demanded the intervention of the state. After a long battle, they won a special investigation, and other grand jurors took up the work.

Finally, private citizens, too, acquired courage and faith. The racket victims themselves began to believe that the community, through its grand jurors, meant business.

Confidence came back again to people in all walks of life. For example, there was a chambermaid in a leading New York hotel. On trial was Lucky Luciano, probably the most vicious gangster who ever dominated the underworld. His co-defendants were eight gunmen and thugs. His defense was that he did not even know these men, his own henchmen, and that he had never seen any of them in his life. Into the tense atmosphere of that crowded courtroom came Marjorie Brown. That is the name we called her by, because it was not her name. Calmly, she told how she had seen one after another of the gang go into the room of the boss for long conferences day after day. She well knew the character of the men on trial. Yet she walked down from that witness stand and put her hand on the shoulder of each one of them. The whole defense collapsed. The courage of Marjorie Brown and others like her did the job.

And so it was with trial jurors. In every racket trial in my experience, there has been fear in the minds of jurors, and the courage to overcome it. Such was their fear that, in every trial, members of the jury have asked for bodyguards when they left the courthouse at the end of each case. But such was their courage that, by their verdict, they did their duty to themselves and their neighbors.

Thousands of men and women left their daily tasks to do their part and carry on the fight. It was their courage which won the fight. In so doing, they proved their faith in their own institutions. They proved that society's problem could be solved without new laws, without new powers, and in the best traditions of a free republic.

Today, the extermination of organized crime is gradually progressing from city to city. Its sponsors are being exposed and driven from power. The people have learned they need no longer tolerate the furtive alliance between the upper and the under world. In high places, it has been learned that clean government can also be good politics. It will take years to finish the job but the good news of today is this—America is cleaning its own house.

So, in your citation for the Newman Award, I see recognition not of an individual but of thousands of individuals who demonstrated confidence in their institutions and the will to make them work. As private citizens, those thousands of men and women earned your award. For they have shown again that when the American people see their problems they themselves, out of their own strength, demand and procure a solution.

My own experience has convinced me that in the long run the people get what they want from government. Corrupt power may delay the result. But it only serves finally to make the change more decisive.

I have not devoted eight years of my life to the administration of justice because I take pleasure in prosecuting and convicting. Rather I think of them as eight years spent in one of the laboratories which tests the qualities of government and its ability to make right those things that are wrong.

In that laboratory we learn that punishment is not a cure. It is only half of the job. It is vital that we have laws to prevent man from injuring his neighbor—and that we make these laws work. But no nation was ever made good or strong by laws alone. The pretended strength of government is never a substitute for the real strength of the individual. It has been shown in many countries that excessive reliance upon government has the effect of weakening the individual.

The tower of a high building is no firmer than the weakest part of its foundations. Similarly, society cannot endure if government is built on a mass of weakened individuals.

The real prevention for crimes against society is not to be found in legal devices but only in the gradual restoration of man's ideas of what is really worth while.

Last week a seven-year-old boy was called by one of my assistants as a witness for the People in a criminal case. When the judge asked him whether he knew what an oath meant, he said, "No." Then the judge asked, "Do you know what it means to tell the truth?" And the child's eyes lit up and he said, "Yes, sir." "What would happen if you didn't tell the truth?" the judge asked, and the boy answered, "Oh, God would punish me."

Instinctively, our people turn to the teachings of religion as the source of fundamental truths. In childhood the conception of such truths is clear and untarnished by worldly cynicism.

Many men, particularly as they become older, grow cynical and skeptical of any values except those they can see and enjoy. They come to believe that their own life is an end in itself. Consequently, they strive to pack within it the maximum of material gains.

Out of such worldliness are born the worst crimes—the betrayals of trust, the reckless striving for money and for power. And toward such crimes we find indifference—an indifference which always prevails among those who share the same motives and hold the same estimate of life.

We live today in a changing world, in many parts of which is reached a new, but really age-old, paganism. Some would go back to the Dark Ages. They exalt the state as the supreme source of all authority. Duty to the state is taught as a substitute for duty to God. They would drown the voice of conscience with the rattle of drums, and would substitute for moral law the dictates of expediency. False prophets teach that the individual and his freedom must be suppressed for the glory of the state. They display that same blunted moral sense toward crimes against whole peoples that some men display toward individual wrongdoing.

"If the Church falls sick," said Cardinal Newman, "the world shall utter a wail for its own sake." The danger is never to religion. The danger is to those who abandon religion. For where material values are set above spiritual values religion ceases to be vital. And where religion is no longer vital pagan philosophies move in. The need of the world today is for vigorous spiritual strength, flowing from divine guidance.

The day is at hand when all men must unite and fight invasion by pagan ideals. Fortunately, in all faiths, leaders are stepping forward to carry on this fight. Naturally there are differences of creed. In the right of expression of these and other differences between free men lies the very essence of their freedom.

A real unity of purpose will emphasize the importance of man as an individual, obedient to the God he worships in his own way, and not as a cog in a materialistic society. Our common belief is that there are values other than material ones, and objectives more noble than any that can be fashioned by men. These beliefs need more general acceptance in modern life. They need to become a more practical influence on the conduct of men. Thereby, as I see it, we can wage successfully the other half of our battle for a clean and healthful society.

The world today is not too militant. It is militant in the wrong way and for the wrong purposes. We need—and desperately need—a spiritual militancy.

In bronze letters at the entrance of the Newman Foundation are these words from George Washington's Farewell Address: "Reason and experience both forbid us to expect that national morality can prevail in exclusion of religious principles." In those words we may well find the beacon of wisdom for the America of today. We shall reject false gods of materialistic philosophies.

With unity of purpose we shall carry forward the religious ideals without which no country can remain free. Adhering to our own traditions, we shall preserve them. When we have cleaned our own house, we shall keep it clean.

Index

PHOTO CREDITS

United Press International - 2, 13, 24, 27, 52, 55, 59, 60, 61, 62, 63
Dewey Family Picture - 7, 10, 11, 12, 14, 15, 16, 17, 18, 19, 20, 21, 22, 23, 25, 32, 33, 34, 50
Wide World Photos - 9, 43, 58
New York *Post* Photograph by Stein, Reprinted by Permission of New York *Post* - 26
Underwood & Underwood - 31
Thomas E. Dewey Papers, Property of the University of Rochester Archives, Rush Rhees Library - 35, 45, 46, 47, 49, 51, 53, 56
Greystone & Stoller Corp. - 36
Harris & Ewing - 37
Photo by Lee Doran - 48
Greystone Studios - 51